Global University for Sustainability Book Series

Series Editors

The book series aims to publish books and monographs drawing on the expertise of the Global U Founding Members by offering a succinct analysis of global crises affecting the ecological, social, political, and economic aspects, as well as to explore transformative visions and praxis for sustainability. Some books may be translated from their original language into English.

Rémy Herrera

Money

From the Power of Finance to the Sovereignty of the Peoples

palgrave
macmillan

Rémy Herrera
CNRS—National Center of the Scientific
Research
Paris, France

ISSN 2752-7379 ISSN 2752-7387 (electronic)
Global University for Sustainability Book Series
ISBN 978-981-19-2847-5 ISBN 978-981-19-2848-2 (eBook)
https://doi.org/10.1007/978-981-19-2848-2

Cover illustration: Alex Linch shutterstock.com

This Palgrave Macmillan imprint is published by the registered company Springer Nature Singapore Pte Ltd.
The registered company address is: 152 Beach Road, #21-01/04 Gateway East, Singapore 189721, Singapore

"May the CETIM (Centre Europe—Tiers Monde/Center Europe—Third World) and its team be sincerely and warmly thanked for having been at the origin of the order for this book and for having published it in its initial version in French (La Monnaie—Du Pouvoir de la Finance à la Souveraineté des Peuples) in January 2022 at the Editions du CETIM in Geneva".

Introduction

«Новац не представља толику вриједност какву је поставио човјек према њему. Сав новац ја сам улагао у изуме са којима сам омогућио нове проналаске омогућујући човјечанству лакши живот

(Novac ne predstavlja toliku vrijednost kakvu je postavio čovjek prema njemu. Sav novac ja sam ulagao u izume sa kojima sam omogućio nove pronalaske omogućujući čovječanstvu lakši život)».

"Money does not represent the value that men have placed on it. All my money has been invested in experiments with which I have made new discoveries that made life a little easier for mankind."

Nikola Tesla ("A Visit to Nikola Tesla", D. Petković, Politika, April 27, 1927, Belgrade)

In our contemporary societies, monetary issues, especially those related to the determination of the nature of money, are probably among the most difficult to address. They pose such numerous and profound problems to economists, both in theory and in practice, that it is not exaggerated to maintain that economics has not really succeeded in providing a unifying interpretation of what money is, nor even completely satisfactory definitions. This is unfortunate for a discipline that claims to be the science of quantifying wealth and its allocation—and that, in addition, captures only exchanges that have a monetary expression, i.e., that give rise to money transactions. Beyond a more or less artificial and ambiguous facade of agreement about the functions of money, the various currents of economic thought, and within them the authors, are opposed to the precise meaning given to it. Thus, and probably more than in other fields, the theme of money sometimes inspires extravagant ideas, which compete in inconsistency and irresponsibility.

Part of the explanation for this state of affairs lies in the fact that money is full of paradoxes. It locks individuals into a hierarchy of inequalities and ties them to sordid interests, but it can liberate many initiatives and energies. It is visibly available only in counted quantities, but seems to be able to be created in an unlimited way—by the Central Banks—and moreover ex nihilo. It is closely related to debt, to the point that confusion may arise between State money and credit money, the former being commonly used by the general public and the latter being put into circulation by almost universally private banking and financial institutions. Furthermore, it can take very different forms, material for the best known, but also more and more frequently, and for a long time, dematerialized. With the recent rise of crypto-currencies, or crypto-assets, it is the object of all fantasies, as in the old days of alchemists and coin founders or, much later, of the invention of paper money.

Another reason for this situation lies in the fact that money is a phenomenon whose analysis, to be serious, must go beyond the strict perimeter of economics in order to be enriched by the results of research carried out in other fields of scientific thought—without projecting onto them concepts or methods that are not their own. This is true for many other fields of knowledge: archaeology, anthropology, history, law, sociology, geopolitics, of course philosophy, but also, particularly since the appearance and multiplication of innumerable digital or electronic currencies, the new computer technologies.

This suggests that money is not simply a neutral tool or a transparent veil, as most mainstream economists assert (and as implied by common expressions such as "making money work" or "making money grow," which forget that only human beings are at work and that there is nothing natural about money). Money is, on the contrary, a complex, contradictory social reality—just as inflation reflects, in its own way, the intensity of power relations and social conflicts within a country. Thus, the problem we are dealing with here is eminently political, because money represents a major attribute of power, of national sovereignty. Based on the confidence of a community, it also has a psychological, or rather imaginary, dimension, as well as an identity character, which can be seen, for example, in the symbols affixed to banknotes or metal coins.

However, the fact that the problems of money and monetary policies are unfolding on a difficult, malarial and murky terrain does not justify abandoning these subjects to the "elites" and their "experts" who, under the guise of technicality, come to confiscate them, generally for the sole benefit of the big shareholders of high finance, and consequently to the detriment of the peoples. This book will therefore not approach these themes from an academic angle, but will adopt an applied approach, insisting on concrete cases and seeking to make the developments as accessible, illustrated and useful as possible.

This does not mean, however, that in what follows, conceptual presuppositions will be ignored and theoretical underpinnings neglected. On the contrary, let us warn readers that the proposed arguments are against the neoliberal tide and in a spirit of critique of the dominant economy. Thus, our final analyses will attempt to identify alternative, coherent and credible conditions that would make it possible to wrest money from the grip of high finance and to place monetary policy, thanks to powerful public mechanisms, at the service of the peoples.

The present book contains eight chapters of roughly equal size. After having first discussed in Chapter 1 the conceptual, historical and institutional elements necessary to understand the subject, the next six chapters deal with its manifestations and implications by major region of the world, namely successively the United States, Europe, Africa, Oceania, Latin America and the Caribbean, and Asia. The last chapter synthetizes the transformations of the world system in order to identify the risks posed to our societies by economic crises, currency wars and changes in the very forms of money, but also to formulate the broad outlines of solutions to current problems.

In the body of the text, here and there, short boxes shed light on points of particular interest. Two appendices complete the text with a chronology of the history of the facts and a selective presentation of the main thoughts on monetary matters. A glossary of particularly important terms, indicated by an asterisk in the eight chapters, is finally provided to the readers. An indicative bibliography will guide those who wish to deepen and broaden the reflection—a reflection that we wish to be as demystifying and emancipating as possible. For the common appropriation of money by the peoples will be a sine qua non condition for the mastery of their collective future.

Contents

1 **Rationale for the Existence of Money: *Conceptual, Historical and Institutional Elements*** 1
From Belief to Confidence… and to Measurement 3
From the Earliest Days to Modern Times 7
The Metamorphoses (and Contradictions) of Money 11
Changes in the International Monetary System and National Policies 20
The Current Systemic Crisis 25
Anti-crisis Monetary Policy Measures 30
References 33

2 **The Monetary Hegemony of the United States: *The Power of High Finance, the Reign of the Dollar and Global Chaos*** 35
High Finance, from Its Controversial Origins to Its Current Contested Hegemony 37
The Return of the Domination of High Finance in the Era of Neoliberalism 40

From Another Currency Crisis (1997–1998) to the Global and Systemic Crisis (2007–2008) 46
After the Shock (2008), the Monetary Policy Counter-Shocks (Since 2009) 48
The Dollar as a Deterrent Weapon 51
The United States Focused on Maintaining the Global Supremacy of the Dollar 55
The Dollar Again, Still a Global Problem 58
References 61

3 **Europe, Between Aporias and Dead Ends:** ***From the Straitjacket of the Euro to the Logic of Every Man for Himself*** 63
Monetary and Financial Aspects of French "Socialism" (1981–1986) 64
The Mechanisms of Regulation (of the State by the Financial Markets) 67
From the "Strong Franc" to Frankfurt 69
The Euro, a Monetary Straitjacket 73
Every Man for Himself as a Collective Operating Mode 77
The ECB, an Atypical and Ultra-Rigorous Institution 81
Single Currency… or Common Currency? 83
European Countries Whose Currency Is Not the Euro… 87
… or Which Are Not Members of the European Union 90
References 92

4 **Africa Under Influence, but in Struggle:** ***Persistent Neocolonialism, Perpetual Debt and Neoliberalized Pan-Africanism*** 95
Exchange Rates and the Vulnerability of African Economies 97
A Variety of Monetary Policies Among the Countries with Flexible Regimes… 101
… but (Almost) All Subject to IMF Dictates 104
The CFA Franc, a French-Style Anachronism? 106

Effective Functioning and Alleged Advantages of the CFA Franc 111
Limits and Criticisms… 114
… Limits and Criticisms Again 117
The Eco… but Which One? 119
References 123

5 **Oceania, Often Forgotten, but So Revealing: *Archaism of Peripheral Traditional Societies… or of the Forms of Central Monetary Domination?*** 125
An "Irrational" Attitude Towards Money? 126
A Special Space: Scattered but Hierarchical and Placed Under the Thumb of the Dollar 130
Papua New Guinea, or the Direct Passage from Colonialism to Neoliberalism 132
Mechanisms of Monetary and Financial Dependence on Australia 134
Monetary Compensations 138
The CFP Franc: "Financial Community" or… "French Colonies" in the Pacific? 140
References 143

6 **Latin and Caribbean America on the Way to Its Second Independence: *Monetary Lessons from a Region in Rebellion*** 145
The Other America of the Dollar: From Caribbean Tax Havens to Mexican Turmoil 146
Argentina of the "*Kirchnerismo*" 151
"*Petista*" Brazil 153
Monetary Aspects of Three Revolutionary Advances: Ecuador, Bolivia, Venezuela 158
The Cuban Experience 164
From Dollarization to De-dollarization, the Challenge of Cuban Monetary Sovereignty 167
References 170

7 **Asia in Search of a Better Future for It (and for the World):** ***From the "Asian Crisis" to Controlling Monetary Policy*** 173
An "Asian" Crisis… Which Does Not Really Have Its Origin in Asia 175
South Korea, or Neoliberal Relentlessness 178
Resistances in 1998: From Malaysia to Vietnam 181
The Domination of the U.S. Dollar, Again 186
China (I): Facing the Power of the Financial Markets 191
China (II): Building a Great Monetary Wall 194
China (III): Placing Money at the Service of Development 198
References 200

8 **The March Towards Currencies at the Service of the Peoples:** ***Systemic Crisis and Currency Wars or Alternatives of Sovereignty in a Multipolar World?*** 203
Systemic Crisis and Currency War 205
Some Nice Solutions, but Limited (or False) 212
Recent Changes in Money and the Responses to Them 216
Crypto-Currencies*: New Forms of Fictitious Money… and of Power Relations 218
Towards a Multipolar World of Currencies… and of Crypto-Currencies 222
The Chinese Yuan, Finally a Major Opponent to Face the Dollar 226
Cooperate Between Southern and Eastern Countries to Loosen the Hold of the Dollar 230
The Money Is Ours: Alternatives to Democratize Monetary Policy 235
References 240

Conclusion 243

Appendices 247

Glossary 309

Index 331

About the Author

Rémy Herrera is a French economist and researcher at the CNRS (Centre National de la Recherche Sientifique, or National Center of the Scientific Research). He graduated from a Business School (École supérieure de Commerce [1988]), from the Institute of Politival Studies (Institut d'Études politiques de Paris [1990]) and the University of Paris 1 Panthéon-Sorbonne (Master of Philosophy [1994], and PhD in Economics [1996]). He is currently directing doctoral theses at the Centre d'Économie de la Sorbonne. He has worked in financial auditing (1988), at the OECD (1992–1997) and for the World Bank (1999–2000). He was a member of the National Committee of the CNRS (2000–2005) and of the Scientific Council of Paris 1 (2001–2006). He has taught at various universities, including Paris 1 (for more than 25 years), Aleppo (1998), Cairo (1999–2000), Vitoria in Brazil (2005), Complutense in Madrid (2009–2013) and Lingnan in Hong Kong (2018). He has received the title of "Distinguished Economist" from the *Asociación Nacional de Economistas de Cuba* (Havana) and has been an advisor to research programs at Chubu University (Nagoya). He is or has been associated with the Union of Radical Political Economics (New

York), the International Initiative for Promoting Political Economics (London), the *Sociedad de Economía Política Latinoamericana* (São Paulo) and the Third World Forum (Dakar). He was the Executive Secretary of the World Forum of Alternatives (WFA). He is a member of the International Crisis Observatory and of the Global University for Sustainability. He also works regularly with the CETIM (Centre Europe Tiers-Monde, or Center Europe Third World), supporting it in its advisory role to the UN Human Rights Council.

Personal website: http://remyherrera.com.

List of Boxes

Box 1.1 From the suppression of money (in the Soviet Union) to demonetization (in Russia) 18
Box 1.2 High finance, the ultra-rich, and dominant market forces 28
Box 2.1 Cuba, 1898: A step in the march of U.S. high finance towards global hegemony 39
Box 2.2 Israel, 1985: An economy saved from monetary collapse by the United States 53
Box 3.1 Germany haunted by its past: Hyperinflation, Deflation, Ordoliberalism and the Bundesbank 71
Box 3.2 Switzerland, that island of (monetary and banking) happiness 85
Box 4.1 Sanctions against South African apartheid and their circumvention by Western banks 100
Box 4.2 Rwandan genocidaires and their generous Western financiers 109
Box 5.1 An example of "primitive money" in Oceania: The rai or fei of Yap Island 128
Box 5.2 "Commodity currencies" in the shadow of transnational corporations 136

Box 6.1	Colombia trapped in mortgage loans, ten years before the subprime crisis	149
Box 6.2	Haiti, debt vs. development	163
Box 7.1	Lebanon, prisoner of the rapacity of its bourgeoisie… and of the U.S. dollar	184
Box 7.2	The unpleasant surprises of microcredit	189
Box 8.1	The tottering monetary and military pillars of U.S. hegemony	209
Box 8.2	Dollar and yuan in the currency war	228

1

Rationale for the Existence of Money: *Conceptual, Historical and Institutional Elements*

> *Non è facile parlare di denaro. Diceva Basilio di Cesarea, Padre della Chiesa, ripreso poi da san Francescod'Assisi, che "il denaro è lo sterco del diavolo". Lo ripete ora anche il Papa: "il denaro è lo sterco del diavolo". Quando il denaro diventa un idolo, comanda le scelte dell'uomo. E allora rovina l'uomo e lo condanna.*
>
> It is not easy to talk about money. Basil of Caesarea, Father of the Church, echoed by St. Francis of Assisi, said: 'money is the devil's excrement.' The Pope repeats it again today: 'money is the devil's excrement.' When money becomes an idol, it controls man's choices. And then it destroys man and condemns him.
>
> Pope Francis, Speech of February 28, 2015

Nowadays, money has invaded all areas of life, or very nearly so. With the exception of a privileged few, the existence of every adult, and even that of hundreds of millions of working children, is shot through with the oppressive anxiety of earning it. It is the most invisible and effective constraint that forces some to work in an attempt to survive; for others, the enslaving obsession that pushes them to accumulate more and more wealth, when the thirst for gold devours their spirit; for some still, an

R. Herrera, *Money*, Global University for Sustainability Book Series,
https://doi.org/10.1007/978-981-19-2848-2_1

opportunity to be seized to finance the choice of activities or projects. Not being able to read and write is a terrible handicap, but not being able to speak the language of money, even if it is only basic, is a mortal danger, because, apart from Robinson Crusoe, no one can provide for himself or herself without being able to count it.

If a majority of people still cannot get enough to live in dignity and freedom, while a tiny minority has an inordinate amount, money would be as "natural" to everyone as air and water. Like them, it would be translucent and self-evident, so much so that most mainstream economists feel exempt from the need to elaborate a theory of it, or even just to integrate it into their arguments, most often conducted in a universe they describe as "real," that is to say, paradoxically, devoid of money. In real life, however, money is omnipresent, omnipotent. Everywhere it is king, reigning over human beings. Worse, it is deified. Printed on the famous U.S. currency, the phrase "in God we trust" should not be translated literally into foreign languages, but rather as "we believe in the dollar"; just as the "*God zij met ons*" that adorns the current Dutch banknotes should be read as: "May the euro be with us"!

The ambivalence of money is summed up in the myth of Ploutos, god of wealth, told in a comedy by Aristophanes, who presents him as a miserable old man. Jealous of the power of Ploutos, Zeus had made him blind in order to prevent him from distinguishing between human beings and to be able to distribute fortunes by rewarding the most virtuous. Ploutos could not pass the door of the home either of the prodigal, who squandered it (by throwing it out of the window), or of the miser, who buried it at once (by hoarding*). So, when it comes to money, since you have to know how to save well, but also how to spend well, it is all a question of measure. As well as of confidence. Only then could wealth "be aggregated" to (i.e., to enter) a house or *oikos*; hence the words "economy," "econometrics"…

From Belief to Confidence... and to Measurement

As a matter of fact, for a very long time now, money has taken on the appearance of a divinity—ambiguous, enigmatic. For the path of this identification (or rather of this resemblance) was sinuous, serpentine. A hieroglyphic text dating from about 2600 BC tells us that in Old Kingdom Egypt, the *shât* was used as a standard of value; it was later replaced, after the reign of Ramses II (from −1279 to −1213 BC), by the *deben*, worth twelve *shâts*. We do not know what such a unit of account* looked like materially, or whether it even had an existence other than an abstract one, but what we do know is that it was based on an arithmetic equivalence in gold. Nevertheless, since the latter, which symbolized for the Egyptians the flesh of the gods, had a very marked sacred significance, the close connection between religion and this precious metal, however, forbade its use as money for some time. The silver metal was preferred for this purpose, which certainly also represented a part of the body of the deities (in this case, their bones), but was relatively less venerated. Unlike gold, silver was scarce in the Nile Valley and had to be imported from the Middle East—where it was abundant and already circulating as money. It thus seems that these cashless currencies or scriptural* money, which existed in writing sets (e.g., on scribal tablets), preceded those consisting of metal coins, which made it possible to settle a debt and whose value was based on the trust of the users.

Then, a little later, the Gospel of St. Matthew commands: "You shall worship either money or God." It is, moreover, sometimes by the word of Aramaic origin *māmōn* (or *matmon* in Hebrew) that the term "money" is designated. It would be, in these religious texts, the devil, the god of the underworld whose "gold that [he] offers to his followers turns into excrement as soon as it leaves." And we remember that it was this same money that made Jesus of Nazareth himself explode in anger when, in a (unique) fit of violence, he lost his temper and chased away merchants and money changers from the Temple of Jerusalem.

Coins and bills, whether in the pocket or the wallet, are what we call fiduciary money*, an adjective whose Latin root *fides* is the same as that of the noun "faith." Ditto for the word "credit," which comes from the

Latin *credere*. Cousin of the Spanish *dinero*, of the Portuguese *dinheiro* and of the Italian *denaro* designating money, the term "dinar"—the name of the currency* of several countries, from Algeria to Iraq, via Libya and, on the other side of the Mediterranean, via Serbia or Northern Macedonia (with its *denar*), which were formerly Ottoman—certainly derives from *denarius*, the Roman "denier" based on decimal calculation. However, this dinar is also close to the Arabic word *dîn*, which means "religion" this time (like the Turkish *din* or the Wolof *diine*), while its suffix is a neighbor of *nar*, which in Arabic means "fire"—in this case, that of the underworld. Religion and money are intertwined.

Among the Aztecs, following the Mayans, cocoa beans were used to make a special beverage called *xocoatl*, prepared in honor of Quetzalcoatl, the highest deity of this pre-Columbian American civilization, but also to function as a "means of payment*." As to it, the root of the word "money," taken from the Latin *moneta*, still leads to the doors of a place of worship, located on the Capitoline Hill in Rome: the temple of the goddess Juno Moneta (the equivalent of Hera for the Greeks, sister and wife of Zeus), in charge, among other things, of protecting wealth. It is near this temple that the very first Roman coins are said to have been minted in the Third Century BC.

Like the primitive currencies that preceded them, the first coins had a less economic than religious function. In other words, as soon as we deal with money, the notion of "belief" or, in secularized language, "trust" is absolutely fundamental. For money is a social connection, which "links" all individuals to each other and to a community within which it enables the population concerned to identify and to be identified. In this respect, we speak of a "bonding currency," with a marked symbolism, which helps to structure social relations by stabilizing hierarchical or alliance relations, by conferring a prestigious status on those who possess it and by associating spiritual (or totemic) connotations with it. This means that money is a power, a socio-political institution. It will later require the legal guarantee of the prince, then of the State, for its issue and its circulation in society.

But let us not forget that the god Ploutos had for parents Demeter, the goddess of agriculture, and Iasion, the sower of fertility who steals and violates the divine power over the natural order of things. Here we are finally on the field of economics. The etymology of the vocabulary relating to money is indeed and generally much more down to earth; it thrives on the fields of agriculture and animal husbandry. In connection with the latter, the Latin *pecus* ("cattle," having given the English "pecuniary"), bringing back to Greece (to *pékos*, "wool" or "fleece"), like the Greek *boûs* (which gave "bovine") and, upstream, *rūpya* in Sanskrit, all refer to a livestock (or "*cheptel*" in French, from which "*capital*" derives, that is counted in heads of domesticated animals), that is, to a movable wealth. Money at that time took the form of horned animals. This, before the portrait of the sovereign came to replace the face of the animal. The first heavy silver coin minted in France in 1514 by Louis XII, known as "the father of the people," was called the "teston," from the Italian *testone*, or "head." But aren't there still many places today, between Kenya and Madagascar, where the zebu is considered as capital money? And others, from Estremadura to Texas, where the number of cows is used as a basis for calculating bank credits or mortgage loans?

Very ancient references, especially in several places in Mesopotamia, link the first "modes of payment" to measures of cereal grains (in particular, barley in Sumer, in the south of present-day Iraq). In all these situations, which are very prosaic, it is the accuracy of the measurement of the weight that was to lead to the confidence of both parties in the exchange. By the way, some names of currencies have retained those of old physical units of measurement. This is the case of the pound (Carolingian, Byzantine or more recently sterling, Syrian...) or the lira (Italian or Maltese, just a few years ago), as well as the mark (German or even Bosnian), which comes from an archaic unit of mass, the "marc," or half-pound. But this is also the case with the name of money in Chinese, which is called *qián* and represents a unit of mass measurement (corresponding to 3.7 grams, tenfold of the *fēn* and tenth of the *liǎng*).

A similar approximation is found in various examples from the Indian world; among others, in Sanskrit: *paṇa*, decomposable into units of shells (denoted *kaurī* in modern Hindi) and having their equivalence in quantities of seeds; or *kārṣāpaṇa*, which corresponded to the physical weight of a peasant (*kārṣā*) and signified "wealth," "reward," or "contract," but was also a weight of copper used as currency and exchangeable for grain.

The drachma, the monetary unit of Greece before the adoption of the euro, was an ancient Greek and Roman measure of mass, which found an extension in the Anglo-Saxon system of weight (with the avoirdupois ounce) and volume (we say "to drink a dram" to have a drink, for example a glass of scotch). From the word "drachma" derives the word "dirham," the currency of the old Alawite dynasty and the Kingdom of Morocco now, or that of the United Arab Emirates, as well as the subdivision of the Qatari riyal, the Jordanian dinar or the Libyan pound. The ruble, as to it, was originally a "fraction" (in Russian, the verb *roubit* means "to cut") of the *grivna*, which designated a silver ingot as well as an ancient mass unit. And the *hryvnia* is the name of the current Ukrainian currency.

In Spanish, "weight" is called *peso*. Today, it is the common denomination of the currencies of nearly ten countries: Chile, Uruguay, Colombia, Dominican Republic, but also the Philippines... In the past, from 1497 and for more than three centuries, a *de plata* currency circulated (*plata* meaning money and silver, in both the monetary and metallic senses), the *peso fuerte* or *duro* ("strong" or "hard"), known as the *real de a ocho* ("royal" of eight), throughout the Empire of Hispanic America, as well as in the United States, where it was legal tender until the eve of the Civil War (1857). As the first truly international currency, it was accepted throughout the world—in many parts of Africa, throughout Asia and even in Australia.

This currency was originally known as the Spanish thaler, which soon became known as the Spanish dollar, by deformation of the word. The base-eight method of calculation inherited from this Spanish *real de a ocho* explains why in the United States, until recently, stock exchange quotations were made in eighths of a dollar (each part being worth 0.125)—and particularly on Wall Street, until 1997, when the switch to decimal accounting was made. The origin of the symbol of the U.S. currency ($) goes back to the Spanish eight-real coin, sometimes called *dollar pilar*, on which, like the coat of arms and flag of Spain, we can see ribbons wrapped around the columns (or pilars) of Hercules and drawing "S" crossed by two lines. And more modestly, the name of the Haitian currency, the gourde, comes from the same peso, known as *columnario* ("columnar"), minted in the Eighteenth Century in Mexico City, Lima or Potosi, and also known as *peso gordo* ("big"), or "strong piaster." It should also be added that, following the peso, the Sahrawi peseta is issued (unofficially) by the Polisario Front—which currently claims a territory that used to be the Spanish *Rio de Oro*.

From the Earliest Days to Modern Times

Thus, from this link between measurement and trust, we understand that the primary functions of money, of all the most decisive, albeit very abstract, are those of unit of account and measure of value*, but also of price standard*—as soon as the exchange values* of the different products of labor arriving on the market and becoming merchandises are converted into prices, that is to say, into monetary denominations or wealth imagined through money. From then on, what is designated as money in fact reveals a complex social relationship, based on trust and assimilated to the belief in a liberating power* attached to a particular object. The latter can take on extremely diverse aspects. The multiplicity of its expressions is illustrated by that of "primitive currencies," known as proto-currencies or paleo-currencies, which appeared several thousand years before our era, in one form or another, in all human societies, during the processes of establishing social relationships, and in a manner distinct from the market system itself.

Salt, for example, whose symbolism is mobilized in many religions (including pagan ones) and which motivated in ancient times the opening of trade routes and/or military conflicts—mainly because of its food-preserving qualities—served as a means of exchange for a lot of peoples, from Senegal to Eritrea (via the Sahara), from India to China (via Tibet). In the Roman Empire, the salt ration—or *salarium*, which is the origin of the word "salary"—was used, in addition to coins, to pay for the services of soldiers. In the past, bean seeds in Kabylia, tea bricks from Siberia to Mongolia or Burma, rice grains in the Japan of the shogunate, cocoa beans among the Maya of Guatemala or Belize, the braids of tobacco leaves in pre-Columbian North America (found again in the form of sticks or chopsticks used by European settlers in

Virginia in the Seventeenth Century or in New Zealand in the Eighteenth Century) also constituted primitive currencies with consumable or agricultural goods as their medium.

Among the innumerable proto-currencies that have existed, we can also mention animal teeth (of pigs in New Guinea, of bats in the Solomon Islands, of sperm whales in Fiji, of walruses in Alaska, of elk among the Amerindians of the Pacific coast), bird feathers (in Melanesia), woven mats or loincloths (in Samoa or in the ancient Congo), bracelets or rings (shackles in Ghana or Nigeria), silk fabrics (in China), dried fish (in Iceland)… or a whole range of utensils, tools or weapons (tripods, pestles, mortars, choppers, kettles, wires, shovels, hoes, spades, nails, knives, spearheads…), musical instruments (drums, gongs …), boat anchors, canoes (*oumiaks* of the Inuits of the Great North in particular), etc. Axe-coins are also found from Central Africa to New Caledonia (*bwa vaik*), North America (*zappozats*) or Brittany (Armorican socket axes). One of the best-known proto-currencies was the *wampum*, a shell necklace used by some tribes in Northeast America and adopted as a medium of exchange by European settlers in the Seventeenth Century if metal coins were lacking—along with other alternative currencies: guns, alcohol, cigarettes or… the bundle of animal skins (which is called buck in English and popularly nicknamed the U.S. dollar). As with modern money, inflation in the price of a commodity was reflected in an increase in the number of beads in the necklace exchanged… and forgeries were discovered by the use of lower quality shells.

These proto-currencies were most frequently made up of elements present in nature (stones, jade, quartz, amber, ivory, pearls…), used as are or more or less transformed. In the latter case, the objects selected as moneys generally had a "value" proportional to the time it had taken to collect them or to make them. One of the most widely used primitive currencies was the cowrie. This shell was used in China more than two millennia before our era. During the First Century AD, its range of dissemination extended to the Indian Peninsula and its surroundings, and as far as the Pacific islands. In the Maldives, in the Indian Ocean, this type of shellfish farming was quite advanced in the Fifteenth Century. It was through Arab traders that cowries were introduced to the eastern coasts of Africa, where they circulated, particularly in parts of Tanzania and Ethiopia, until well into the Twentieth Century. In the meantime, they had reached the western part of the continent, first through Sudan, then through Guinea, Mauritania, and Morocco.

This enumeration of proto-currencies covers very different periods and locations. However, it was a laborious maturation, common to the whole of humanity, which began, in all likelihood, with robbery, well before consensual exchange (do not forget that Mercury is the god of trade as well as of thieves). Then came the gift* and the counter-gift (like the *potlatch** of the Chinook Amerindians of Oregon) and, little by little, the barter*, in a more or less "pure" form of relations slowly freed from direct violence, apparently pacified, but restrictive. Exchange, rather than being innate to human beings, is above all a social construction, historically and geographically determined, and not devoid of relationships of domination and exploitation, far from it. It is only very gradually that money became an intermediary facilitating exchanges—its function as a means of circulation*—so that it could serve not only as a means of invoicing commercial activities, but also as a means of dissociating the acts of selling and buying goods in time and space. Relating to interpersonal relationships, the trust placed in it was strengthened by the establishment of a set of guarantees and institutions, gradually controlled under the supervision of the State over a national territory, which consolidated its property of being immediately accepted (and free of charge) by all individuals in the transactions they carry out among themselves.

In the early days of humanity, the agricultural or pastoral surplus produced in excess of needs was the exception and in fact limited exchanges between clans, tribes or peoples to a minimum. The production of surplus for commercial exchange developed slowly, stretching over millennia and requiring mutations towards evolved forms of social relations where the trade of merchandises could become predominant. Such a process was neither continuous nor homogeneous, with considerable disparities between populations, and even within them. Throughout the Mediterranean, trade relations took a quantum leap under the Roman Empire, before its collapse plunged entire regions into autarky in the Middle Ages, and supplies were limited to luxury goods destined for the palaces. Expeditions and wars propelled exchanges again, whose network became denser and the roads crossed in fairs and squares that formed urban agglomerations where monetization penetrated much faster than in the countryside.

Merchant exchange and the currencies themselves, as well as the initial forms of what would later be called "capital," commercial or banking, developed historically long before the rise of the capitalist system, and well beyond Western Europe. Nevertheless, with the transition from feudalism to capitalism, economic flows intensified thanks to long-distance trade and the multiplication of transoceanic voyages. From the end of the Fifteenth Century onwards, the "discovery" of the New World and the exploitation of its mines, which led to an influx of precious metals into Europe, as well as to a surge in prices, sharp fluctuations in interest and exchange rates, and a transformation of markets (for goods, but also for currencies and financial securities), changed the course of things. But it was only with capitalism, which was imposed at the time, that a mode of production was propelled that was entirely enclosed in the logic of money for money. The desire to replace commodities with money grew among capitalists. Money, intermediary or "medium," became an end in itself, and was adopted as the dominant form of capital*. It acquired the property of functioning as capital, whose movement was now aimed solely at profit.

It is fundamental to understand that a multitude of objects can be used to fulfill the functions of money, as shown by the numerous primitive tangible supports that we have previously mentioned. Thus, to ensure the very important function of a reserve of value*, i.e., the capacity to guarantee the conservation of purchasing power and its transfer into the future, stored goods (agricultural products, raw materials, various merchandises) can do the trick. The same is true of movable assets or financial securities, but to become means of payment*, these different goods must most often first be transformed into money—in the full or modern sense of the term, and at the cost of a more or less onerous conversion—because it is liquidity* *par excellence*. In other words, of all commodities, it is the most trusted and credible.

Although money has now conquered almost all the circuits of exchange in modern societies, the process of monetization has taken a long time and remains very heterogeneous at present. There have been dazzling "advances" in this area, often followed by long-lasting setbacks.

Among these, let us mention the invention of paper money—representing a debt payable at sight in coins or in kind—probably in China during the Tang dynasty in the Eighth Century. Paper money, similar to banknotes or promissory bills*, circulated in the Tenth Century under the name of *jiaozi* from the city of Chengdu in Sichuan. Their use spread under the Northern and Southern Song dynasties, then under the Ming dynasty who tried to control their dissemination, before suppressing them completely in the Fifteenth Century. Modernized banknotes reappeared in this country some 350 years later, after having developed in Europe. The modification of the characteristics of money has endowed it throughout history with new functions which, as they were acquired, came to transform it in return. All in all, money was able to free itself from its materiality and even from the need to be physically present during exchanges.

The Metamorphoses (and Contradictions) of Money

The difficulties specifically linked to the conversion of the products of human labor into values and to their comparison were overcome in the relations between sellers and buyers by the selection of singular goods, likely to be accepted by the greatest number of people and having the ability to measure in monetary form the value of all the other goods available on the market. This choice was itself made in the course of a historical process that made it possible to identify those very special commodities that, thanks to their material qualities (solidity and durability, divisibility and reversibility, uniformity and similarity of parts, handiness and transportability, ease of identification or even concealment), proved to be the most suitable for this function of "general equivalent," both in space and in time. Beyond the symbols, they then became money and were recognized as such socially.

The noble metals, which met the criteria required to acquire the properties of money, stood out. They proved to be a very practical means of exchange in the circulation of large quantities of goods, as well as an ideal store of value*, since they had the capacity to concentrate and preserve in small volumes of material important working times. Ancient rulers, from China to Greece, at the head of State outlines, seized the privilege of coining money—and of owning the mines from which these precious metals were extracted and which determined the rate of issuance. Initially, the standards that were structured were those of silver, in the first instance, and gold, in the second, with one subsequently predominating over the other or with both operating jointly. In practical terms, their monetary use did not risk compromising production or consumption—money intervened directly in neither of them, although it did have an indirect influence on them by making circulation easier, and the specialization of activities more thorough. The minting of divisional coins was done in less noble metals (copper, iron, brass alloys…). Thus, for centuries, in Europe, any owner of gold or silver ingots could bring them to the workshop of a goldsmith and minter in order to have them transformed into an equivalent quantity of coins, after payment of the seigniorage fee*—which continues to be levied today by the modern States.

Nevertheless, to evaluate and calibrate prices, the quantity of precious metal associated with a coin must remain strictly constant in its monetary unit as well as in its subdivisions, independently of variations in the value of the metal—which are reflected in prices—in order to be considered an invariable measure of values. This has not always been the case, however, and in fact the quantitative equality between the value of money and that of commodities is not systematically maintained. Throughout history, the quantities of precious metals contained in coins have not remained the same and the weights of coins have often been reduced due to (intentional) fraud or (natural) wear. These monetary "devaluations" can be interpreted as an intrinsic contradiction of the currency, between its functions as a measure of value and as a price standard.

A solution to this problem was found thanks to the substitution of gold (or silver) money by an abstract and symbolic representation of values, which took the form of paper money. More than the coins, the paper bills, as they were "fiduciary" money, but objects of little value, had to rely on a reinforced confidence in their facial values. This movement of dematerialization of the money did not take place without resistances nor clashes so much the monetary crises were numerous, and the distrusts of the populations anchored. In order to be accomplished, it required authoritarian intervention by the States, in particular through the use of paper money at forced tender*. But the difficulties were only displaced, not overcome, and they did not fail to manifest themselves on the occasion of crises where agents fled from paper money to take refuge in gold, foreign currencies or even merchandises, accelerating the devaluation of the national currency through inflationary pressures.

Furthermore, the basic contradiction of money, linked to the possibility for a producer to sell without necessarily being obliged to buy immediately, persisted and constantly contained within it the risk of a crisis, since money can always be hoarded and, consequently, commodities produced can find themselves without a buyer, and therefore, sellers can be without a revenue. Through its function as a means of payment*, money functions as a dream mode of settlement by transforming the seller into a creditor and the buyer into a debtor. In effect, one of the exchangers sells merchandises that exist in the present, while the other buys them with money to come. The function of means of payment, at the origin of credit money, has become more idealized as the system of financing economies has become more sophisticated, as a global matching of the expenditures and incomes of the different agents; on the one hand, those with a need for financing (most often, governments and businesses), and on the other, those with a capacity for financing (very generally, households and the "rest of the world"). Thus, and this is an essential point, money has moved even further away from the materiality of gold (or silver) to be replaced by credit, that is to say, by debt securities that come to function as if they were in fact money. The autonomous creation of these securities by the credit system allowed them to substitute for money itself in several of its functions, notably as means of circulation, payment and hoarding.

Within the financing system, the key intermediation role played by the banks gradually gained in importance. They thus specialized in centralizing producers' reserves and transforming them into bank credit, a decisive lever for the expansion of capital. In the heart of the European Middle Ages, merchants had turned to the business of money trading, carrying out exchange operations between the various coins that existed, but also towards more diversified activities (including the recording and clearing of transactions, etc.). One of their tasks was also to keep in safe custody the precious metals of depositors or other merchants, who in return received receipts representing the same value and which, once accepted as a means of circulation, replaced the metallic wealth in the monetary circuit. In this way, these money merchants became bankers. The latter lent money more and more often to European sovereigns (such as the great Florentine financial families of the *Quattrocento*), in exchange for obtaining commercial monopolies which allowed them to acquire considerable power in the exchanges of these countries.

With the rise of the Western economies and the impetus of the influx of precious metals, deposits grew faster than conversions into gold (or silver), so that these early banking institutions were able to increase their credit, first in gold, then on the basis of the issuance of certificates of deposit—the ancestors of banknotes—convertible into gold and lent at interest on the money market against a promise of repayment. Another form of credit was the circulation of commercial papers* (bills of exchange* or promissory notes* resulting from forward sales), i.e., acknowledgments* of debts (or I.O.U.s, "I owe you," that is, written promises to pay back debts) signed by a buyer and used by the seller to repay his or her own loans or to discount them with a bank. Through a multiplier effect, the total means of payment increasingly exceeded the monetary base*. Credit money took off.

In Western Europe, from the industrial revolutions and especially from the beginning of the Nineteenth Century, the creation of money became less and less the counterpart of gold or silver stocks and more and more linked to credit issues by banks. Frequent crises of illiquidity complicated the strengthening of confidence between private contractors, creditors and debtors. However, the changes in money also led the States to resort to repression so that the populations would eventually accept the replacement of metal coins by debt securities when a risk of devaluation was associated with the unconvertible forced exchange paper money, without remuneration or maturity date, since the agents had no protection or recourse against such evolutions—except, when they had the means, those of converting their savings into loans by feeding into interest-bearing accounts, just as banks convert their clients' deposits into interest-bearing capital. The more complex the financial securities became, with varying degrees of liquidity and credibility, the more confusion spread between the nature of real money and that of credit.

In the context of a monetary system that remained private, deregulated and exposed to crises, the capitalist State progressively extended its control by assuming on behalf of society, in the supposedly general interest, the so-called "primary" creation of money—the "secondary" being carried out through bank credit, which was entirely private (or almost). The State authorities took charge of the minting of coins, the hoarding of gold and silver stocks, but above all their replacement by paper money. To this end, they enacted rules for hedging and declared banknotes to be legal tender*, which allowed them to be widely used, including in interbank transactions.

For a long time, the keystone of the device was the convertibility* of paper money into gold, which could be exchanged at the request of its owner with national Treasuries or Central Banks. These latter entities, born from one (or several) ordinary commercial bank(s) called "second-tier," but having quite privileged links with the State, most often nationalized (or remaining partially private, like those of the United States and Japan today), emerged to monopolize the primary creation of money and structure the whole system. During periods of crisis or war, the State sometimes decided to suspend gold convertibility and impose forced and legal tender. Nevertheless, in normal times, gold convertibility has gradually given way to convertibility in Central Bank notes. The bills issued by commercial banks then became inconvertible in gold, since they were convertible into Central Bank money, before the State finally withdrew from these institutions the authorization to print them. Later came bank checks, then myriads of writing instruments or scriptural money, counterparts of claims and acknowledgements of debts that disappeared as the indebted agents repaid their credits.

With the diffusion of paper money, according to the historical path we have briefly described, we understand that "money" has been transformed almost entirely into credit money—whether bank or State money. In reality, money is indeed an acknowledgement* of debts that circulates as a means of payment. But this reality appears to us to be inverted: in the case of banknotes, for example, it is the State that is in debt, while it seems to be the "owner" of the money it creates, while the economic agents, although creditors, appear as if they were its debtors. And what we can observe is that on the basis of the State's paper money, a pyramid of deposits, private or public debts, negotiable securities and the most diverse financial investments has been built up.

Nowadays, money circulates in extremely different forms—including the new electronic, virtual or digital currencies which, despite their dematerialized and decentralized aspect, are now the object of struggles for their control and issues of sovereignty. At present, the money supply* is essentially composed of scriptural money, that is to say, accounts and credits granted to companies or households by banks, within the framework of a system in which money is largely commoditized and its supply privatized. The means of payment that makes this scriptural money circulate are cheques and bank cards—in addition to coins and notes. Over the past half-century, the proportion of coins and banknotes in the money supply has declined sharply, while the share of demand deposits (or current accounts) has become predominant. In other words, only a very small part of transactions is carried out using fiat* money or Central Bank money, and the vast majority of transactions being performed via accounting balances within and between banks. This is the case for payments by check or credit card, which are generally accepted after verification of the issuer's identity for the former and after a commission for the latter. This makes them slightly less liquid means of payment than coins and notes, but they are included in the money supply in the form of current accounts used to carry out their operations. The credit system has increased the number of payment methods beyond the traditional tools (checks, etc.), through credit or debit cards and revolving credits, among others, eliminating the need to use paper money in most commercial transactions. Other bank accounts, such as savings books, correspond to "potential" means of payment, as they can be converted into Central Bank money under certain conditions only.

With the rise of credit, primary money creation gradually became detached from the circulation of paper money, and secondary creation took off by adopting new forms. For a long time, the State had to have gold mined in order to use it. Then, its money issues were made by direct recourse to paper money in settlement of its purchases or debts. Today, the current Central Banks can issue money by making transfers to the reserve accounts of second-tier banks, or deposits on individual accounts of companies or households for the payment of purchases or salaries, but also by lending money to private banking institutions through purchases of debts on the financial markets, or even by buying currencies on the foreign exchange market.

Logically, the amount of money needed in the economy should be determined by the volume of commodities in circulation—multiplying this by their respective prices, and dividing it by the number of circuits made by the money (called "velocity of circulation"). However, hoarding acts as a "leakage," and the emergence of ownership of means of payment and then the accelerated growth of the credit system have changed and complicated the way in which the necessary quantity of money in circulation in the economy is determined. Not only the speed of circulation of money, but also the innumerable payment schedules (at maturity or pending), as well as the duplication of functions of money (as a means of circulation or payment, for example) will have to be taken into account.

The difficulties go up another notch, especially for monetary policymakers, when we remember that money, the expression of a social relationship, is not a good like any other, governed by the laws of supply and demand, by examining the mechanisms of its "production." On the one hand, money appears as a by-product of activity. Households go into debt to consume or acquire housing, companies seek credit to invest and innovate... The creation of money follows, in a way, the growth of the economy. On the other hand, the banking system, with the Central Bank (in principle) at the top, can influence economic activity, either to slow it down or to stimulate it, thanks to modifying the quantity of money in circulation, among other things by granting loans and setting interest rates.

Nevertheless, we have insisted on the fact that, for the realization of the circulation of goods, real money has been replaced by credit money and, increasingly, thanks to computer networks, by automated compensations between debit and credit operations of the bank accounts of the various agents. And within today's giant transnational firms—whose balance sheets or profit and loss accounts exceed the GDPs of many countries—not even the function of means of payment is now necessary for transactions integrated into value chains and carried out through accounting records of transfers between subsidiaries and parent companies. Money would just tend to become a unit of account again, as in the days of the Egyptian scribes' tablets or the steles of the Babylonian Code of Hammurabi. From then on, would we be moving, not only towards a dematerialization of money, but even towards the possibility of its… suppression?

Box 1.1 From the suppression of money (in the Soviet Union) to demonetization (in Russia)

The alienating and oppressive monetary constraint imposed by the capitalist system on the lives of workers has led Marxist-inspired political leaders to propose the abolition of money. In Soviet Russia, the Bolsheviks decided as early as 1918 an experiment to abolish money—insofar as the latter was identified with monetary capital—before being interrupted at the time of the New Economic Policy (NEP) in 1921. Then, with the introduction of planning, money was maintained in the Soviet system, but with a subordinate role. In the USSR, as in the European countries of the Soviet bloc that depended on it, money fulfilled three functions: (*1*) that of a measure of value, which concerned the formation of product prices, as well as the determination of income, both of which were very different from capitalism; (*2*) that of a means of exchange, for both the consumption of individuals and the production of producers; and (*3*) that linked to savings and accumulation in the State economy.

At the beginning of planning, inter-firm relations were carried out in physical balances without direct monetary exchanges between production units. Nevertheless, from the end of the 1950s, under the influence of the economist L. Kantorovich in particular, market mechanisms were reintroduced for price formation, with the emphasis on productivity, especially in the productive goods sector. The debate on money had echoes in other socialist countries, especially in the German Democratic Republic (GDR), Czechoslovakia, Hungary and even Yugoslavia (in quite different ways), but also in China, Vietnam and Cuba. In the latter country, under the impetus of Ernesto *Che* Guevara, who was for a time president of the Central Bank, there was a desire to revive the

Bolshevik attempts at a non-monetary economy. The system of "budgetary financing," opposed to that of "economic calculation," aimed to limit the role of money to the properties of measurement of value and means of circulation, blocking as much as possible that of means of payment.

The logical outcome of *perestroika*, Russia's return to capitalism in 1991 resulted in the collapse of the economy and the State, accompanied by partial demonetization (quite extensive in some regions) and a reappearance of barter—in addition to a demographic cataclysm due to the increase in mortality, itself caused by the violence of the measures implemented by the IMF from late 1991.

Before the collapse of the USSR, the Soviet republics formed a monetary union around the ruble, which remained inconvertible internally and externally. After the dissolution, the member countries of the Commonwealth of Independent States (CIS) continued to operate within a system supported by the ruble (except for the Baltic States), which was still circulating. The new Central Banks, created on the basis of the former branches of the Soviet Gosbank (Central Bank of the USSR), retained the right to issue credit in rubles, although the notes were still printed in Moscow. Each government could issue bonds to cover its financing needs and transfer part of the inflation to its neighbors. Therefore, the liberalization of prices and the uncontrolled monetization of budget deficits within the CIS led to a sharp rise in inflation (and even hyperinflation, as in Georgia, Armenia and Ukraine) in 1992, revealing the weakness of the currency. Restoring monetary order required discipline and coordination among the 12 Central Banks that remained pegged to the ruble or the substitution of national currencies for the ruble. The first option proved impossible in the midst of political and economic chaos, and sometimes military chaos (Caucasus or Moldova). The rules of the ruble zone were thus abandoned, and in 1992, the Azerbaijani manat was created, followed in 1993 by the Kyrgyz som, the Turkmen manat, the Kazakh tenge, the Armenian dram and the Moldovan leu, then in 1994 the Uzbek sum and finally, in 1995 the Tajik ruble.

The Baltic countries were the first to want to leave the ruble sphere. As early as 1992, they had introduced their national currencies, pegged to the deutschmark (Estonia), the IMF's special drawing rights (Latvia) or the U.S. dollar (Lithuania), based on a currency board* regime, entirely (Estonia and Lithuania) or virtually (Latvia). Subsequently, they became increasingly market-oriented and pioneers in the transition to capitalism, then members of the European Union in 2004 and of the euro zone between 2010 and 2015. All of these States, including Russia, experienced in 1992–1995 years of economic instability, marked by declines in production, budget deficits financed by money creation, inflation and sharp depreciations of the new currencies.

Changes in the International Monetary System and National Policies

While currencies within national territories were evolving towards credit, the currency accepted at the international level to settle balance of payments imbalances remained gold for a long time. Nevertheless, as the link between precious metal and paper money loosened, a similar process took place on a global scale, whereby certain powerful countries at the center, struggling for hegemony over the world system, succeeded in having all other economies—starting with those of the peripheries—adopt their own central currencies as international reserves. Since the end of the Twentieth Century and the era of high finance, States, especially those in the South and East, have been forced to build up exorbitant foreign exchange reserves in the form of foreign currencies held by their Central Banks in order to defend their national currencies against speculative attacks. Henceforth, such accumulation is no longer carried out in gold, but mainly in U.S. dollars held as a store of value and interest-bearing capital invested in loans to the U.S. Treasury or in various other financial securities.

The exchange rate regimes* have evolved over the course of modern history; they have combined to overlap, become embedded and applied in specific configurations, differentiated according to the tools of the external components of the monetary policies of each national space. Even if, in practice, we are dealing with a range of standards and convertibility systems, we can identify a succession of major international monetary systems. Beyond their technical aspects, these systems are part of a set of power relations between States, just as the measures adopted by the latter with regard to the internal components of monetary policies—and their attitude towards inflation and the monetary illusion it conveys, especially with regard to wage distribution and public debt management—are interwoven into the framework of conflicts between social groups over the distribution of the wealth produced. Money is power, let us insist, and the degree of control that a State chooses to have over it reflects the extent of a people's sovereignty.

Great Britain, having achieved world hegemony from 1815 onwards, because of its undisputed industrial and technological, military and financial superiority, found itself in a position to be able to impose the gold standard system on other countries. Implemented in principle soon afterwards on its soil and making gold the universal monetary standard, it turned out in practice to function on an international scale as a pound sterling standard, which relied on the gold supply provided by the Australian and South African colonies. During the latter part of the Nineteenth Century, this system was adopted by most economies in place of the previous silver standard or bimetallic (gold and silver) regimes. The various currencies were then exchanged at fixed parities corresponding to their respective weights of gold. The convertibility of banknotes into gold coins was guaranteed, including for individuals, as well as the transferability of funds abroad. Debt payments arising from trade deficits were made in gold. However, external equilibrium by stabilizing the exchange rate often led to risks of inflation and recession. The First World War forced the belligerents to issue paper money in quantities far in excess of their gold stocks—except for the United States, which entered the conflict very late and became the creditor of the rest of the world, holding considerable gold reserves. This led to the suspension of gold convertibility—so that Central Banks could protect their reserves and create the volume of money required by the war effort—and finally to the end of this regime.

The interwar period ushered in the period of the gold exchange standard and the transition from British to U.S. hegemony. These countries maintained the external convertibility of their currency into gold, while the free minting of gold coins (that is to say, internal convertibility) was abandoned. As metallism weakened, dematerialization has taken longer on a global scale. Each country continued to define the value of its currency by a certain fixed weight of gold, but Central Banks were no longer obliged to convert banknotes—for the reason that most simply did not have sufficient gold stocks. Countries that were well endowed with gold—foremost among which was the United States, which had a good third of the total at the time—or that were committed to gold, could restore convertibility at will, after any measures to contain prices. Three countries ensured this gold convertibility: the United States (as soon as 1919), Great Britain (from 1925) and France (in 1928), which became "gold centers," while their currencies were key currencies* enjoying the privilege of being used by all States to settle international trade, or kept as reserve currencies by their Central Banks. But the economic crisis of 1929 and the Second World War once again disarticulated the international monetary system.

The Bretton Woods conference in 1944 re-established a system, but to the exclusive benefit of the United States, the new post-war world hegemony. The edifice rested on three pillars: (*1*) all currencies were freely convertible into dollar, which in turn was itself convertible into gold, but only at the request of the Central Banks; (*2*) the conversion of currencies among themselves was carried out on the basis of fixed exchange rates; and (*3*) revisions of exchange rates (in reality, devaluations) required the prior agreement of the IMF, which played the role of "mutual fund." Each country deposited liquidity (called "quotas") in the Fund in order to help members facing difficulties, if necessary.

The United States, with its dominant position, was making large investments in Europe at the time. Dollars were thus circulating in abundance in European economies, but also in Asian and oil-producing countries, and constituted money that, like the reserves of the Central Banks (or dollar balances), was supposed to remain pledged to the U.S. gold stock. Nevertheless, the expansion required more gold than was in circulation or held by the Treasury in its reserves, effectively pushing the State to issue more notes than its gold stocks. Beginning in the 1960s, the total amount of dollars circulating in the world began to exceed the value of gold at Fort Knox. Some countries, including Charles de Gaulle's

France, demanded that the dollars they held be converted into gold. This led to speculative rushes and a dollar crisis. Unable to ensure the repayment of the paper money in gold, Washington was going to strike the ultimate blow at the Bretton Woods system with a decision that sounded like a thunderclap: that of canceling the gold convertibility of the dollar. This took place on August 15, 1971, and had cataclysmic implications at the global level, two of the most fundamental and closely related of which were, as we shall see (Chapter 2), the extension of the monetary hegemony of the United States and the imposition by high finance of so-called "neoliberal" policies.

From then on, all currencies remained defined in relation to the dollar (the standard dollar system), but there were no rules for converting currencies between them. The value of currencies could vary against the dollar according to the supply and demand for them on a daily basis. The world switched to a flexible or floating exchange rate regime. However, these floats remained contained, by agreement between the main countries of the North, within certain limits (±2.25%, i.e., a fluctuation margin of 4.50%) in relation to the U.S. dollar. It should be noted that the Canadian dollar fluctuated the least against the U.S. dollar over the long term. A new international monetary system was outlined in 1976 at the Kingston (Jamaica) conference. A world monetary standard, or joint international reserve, was represented by the Special Drawing Rights (SDRs*), a fictitious currency whose management was entrusted to the IMF and whose value was determined by a weighted average of the prices of five key currencies.

In 1944, the gold dollar had been imposed as the world's reference currency, replacing the British pound sterling, but in the early 1970s, the crisis that had been brewing in the previous decade broke out, and in 1971, the dollar was no longer pegged to gold. It was at this historical point that the petrodollar was introduced, following a special agreement between the U.S. administration and the Royal House of Saudi Arabia. The petrodollar was the currency that expressed the interests of U.S. transnational firms, which had already extended their hold on Western Europe and Japan. It was also these same companies that dominated the production, international trade and global consumption of hydrocarbon-based energy. They therefore had the power to make such a pact and to impose the new world reference currency, the petrodollar, as a tool of extortion forcing all the countries of the world system to exchange real product and work for a currency without counterpart and supported by promises to pay, that is to say, by a pure process of indebtedness.

Today, there are more than 160 different official currencies in the world for 195 countries recognized by the United Nations. Some of them circulate in several economies at the same time, such as the U.S. dollar or the euro, while other countries tolerate the simultaneous circulation of various currencies. In the first case, we can mention the dollarized economies or those of the euro zone and the CFA franc—noting here that the term "dollarization"* does not refer only to national spaces where the dollar circulates (it can apply to other currencies), and that the expression "eurocurrency"* is not exclusively reserved for Europe. For the second case, let us cite, for example, Zimbabwe, where are (or have been) legal tender, among other currencies, the U.S. dollar, the pound sterling, the South African rand, the Indian rupee and, although its issue is irregular, the Zimbabwean dollar itself—a paper note of which, worth about five U.S. dollars, could reach the face value of 100 billion dollars…

In these conditions, managing a fixed exchange rate, defended in case of an attack on the currency, is a possible form of monetary organization. The issue is made entirely in local currency and it is the exchange rate that is to be kept fixed. This pivot ensures the currency's credibility on the external scene—as long as it is not carried away by speculation. Such a choice may allow "small countries" to fight inflation and join a regional currency bloc in order to avoid the disadvantages of exchange market uncertainty. However, a regime of fixity is far from having only advantages in a global system that remains monetarily flexible. For floating capital flows can destabilize economies, especially if they have "opened" (i.e., liberalized) their capital accounts*. We will, of course, come back to this in what follows.

The Current Systemic Crisis

For nearly half a century, the capitalist world system has been going through a very deep crisis, which is much more serious than a contamination of the "real sphere" of the economy by disturbances on the financial markets. It is, in fact, the aggravation of the same structural crisis of the expansion of capital, of which one of the most visible and mediatized manifestations has been revealed in the "financial sphere" due to the extreme financialization of contemporary capitalism. We are dealing with a systemic, multidimensional crisis, now affecting the center of power of finance, which has controlled accumulation for over four decades. This translates into an excess of saleable production, not because of a lack of people who want to consume more, but rather because of a polarization of wealth so disproportionate that it excludes growing proportions of the population from the possibility of buying goods they need.

Nevertheless, instead of observing a standard overproduction of merchandises, what we see is rather a boom in credit and financial markets that now allows capital to accumulate in ever more abstract and "fictitious" forms of money. It is important not to confuse money with financial operations on debt securities, which are no longer really money, but already "money-capital." The concept of "fictitious capital"—the principle of which is the capitalization of an income derived from a future surplus-value—can help to better understand the current crisis. Its place of formation is at the intersection between corporations and capitalist States, namely: bank credits, stock market securities, hedge funds, but also public debts, among others. At present, some of the privileged vectors of this fictitious capital are securitization*, i.e., the transformation of relatively illiquid assets into financial securities that can be easily resold on the capital market, and derivatives*, which are contracts that support transactions and fix future financial flows according to variations in the price of underlying assets. Among the most commonly used derivatives are swaps* (of exchange rates or interest rates) and options*. These products are often combined (this can lead, for example, to "swaptions," or options traded on swaps); this leads to the activation of several levels of fictitious capital, since the supports are themselves derivatives. The complexity of the composition of many hybrid instruments is such that it is sometimes no longer even possible to accurately calculate the risk associated with them.

In a context where money is changing form to become ever more "immaterial," this concept makes it possible to grasp the "fictitious" movements of capital, which include the credit system and monetary capital. The analysis of the expanded reproduction of the capitalist economy must be carried out in connection with the exorbitant rise of increasingly unreal forms of capital, to be understood as sources of valorization autonomized from so-called "real" production, seemingly appropriated without any human labor, as if by magic. This fictitious capital is complex in nature, because it is both unreal and real: while it is largely parasitic, it benefits from a distribution of surplus-value, because its liquidity gives its owners the power to convert it, without loss of capital, into money—liquidity *par excellence*. It demands to be remunerated and obtains its remuneration through the transfer of surpluses of productive capital and a pressure to increase the exploitation of labor power. And, in so doing, it feeds an accumulation of additional fictitious capital as a means of its own remuneration. This is the logic of the accumulation of money for money's sake in modern times.

The crisis that broke out in 2007 in the subprime segment of the U.S. housing market had been prepared by decades of overaccumulation of fictitious capital. It must therefore be interpreted in a long-term perspective: that of the worsening of the dysfunctions of the regulatory mechanisms of the capitalist world system since the 1960s and the excess of money-capital linked to U.S. deficits, to tensions on the dollar and to the multiplication of eurodollars, and then petrodollars, on the interbank markets. Certain events had a decisive impact on this process, first and foremost the decision by the United States to demonetize gold and make the exchange rate flexible from 1971 onwards, as we have said, but also, shortly afterwards, the decision to deregulate financial markets with the liberalization of exchange rates and interest rates at the end of the 1970s. At the roots of the crisis, there are, at work, these waves of deregulation and integration of monetary and financial markets within globalized networks, shifting the center of gravity of planetary power to high finance and allowing the latter to impose its diktats on economies.

However, it is also necessary to understand the present crisis at the articulation of the financial and productive domains: many of its factors are of a real nature, due to the austerity measures adopted. Thus, the subprime crisis, through which many modest families found themselves in default of payment, can also be explained by the neoliberal policies that had been pursued for nearly 40 years, pushing for a rigor that dismantles public services, breaks down wages, makes employment more flexible, massively increases unemployment and degrades the living conditions of the greatest number of people; policies that have broken demand and activated engines that make it artificial and unsustainable in the long term. Economic growth has only been maintained by drawing on credit lines to the maximum and by doping private consumption. But this extraordinary dilation of credit eventually revealed the modern version of the crisis of overaccumulation.

In the era of neoliberalism—which remains an empty word if it is not linked to the power of the giant oligopolies of high finance—markets have become more sophisticated, notably through the introduction of risk hedging instruments. Derivatives are among these insurance tools, which have become indispensable as a result of the flexibilization of exchange rates and interest rates, but which are in fact most frequently used for speculative strategies, by playing on the "leverage effect"*, by taking a high risk from a limited stake—especially when they give rise to "short" sales, i.e., forward cessions of an asset (e.g., a currency) which is not held at the time of the negotiation, but which will have to be held on delivery. As a result, the sums corresponding to this creation of fictitious capital—among other things, the contracts traded over the counter* and recorded off-balance sheet, with few or no prudential rules—quickly and largely exceeded those intended for the reproduction of productive capital.

The amounts of derivatives exchanged, measured daily in trillions of dollars and estimated in high and increasing multiples of real production, are traded by a core of financial oligopolies, especially the primary dealers (which the Fed calls the "G15": Morgan Stanley, Goldman Sachs and 13 other private Leviathans). Recently, it is mainly credit derivatives that have posed, and continue to pose, a problem, with synthetic, extremely complex, opaque and therefore perilous arrangements, such as collateralized debt obligations* (CDOs), as well as credit default swaps* (CDSs). These new instruments have transformed the conception of credit, activating in a speculative delirium several "powers" of fictitious capital (such as CDO^2, or CDO of CDOs, and even CDO^3, or CDO of CDOs of CDOs, etc.). Under these conditions, the collapse of these pyramids of uncontrolled financial securities was inevitable.

In a society where ever more people are excluded and disenfranchised, the expansion of opportunities for the owners of capital could perhaps delay the devalorization of the surplus capital in the financial markets for a while, but certainly not prevent it. Therefore, one of the spectacular manifestations of the 2008 crisis was the enormous destruction of fictitious capital as the capitalizations of the world's major stock markets fell by half during the year. The downward spiral in asset values, to be expressed in trillions of dollars, was accompanied by a serious loss of confidence and a situation of illiquidity in the interbank market—in a world that is apparently over-liquid, however—with the most likely hypothesis being that of the insolvency of many banks. Thus, knowing that the prices of composite securities and their respective risks are poorly assessed (in fact, not assessable) by the rating agencies*, the problems moved from the subprime segment to that of real estate loans, then to that of creditworthy loans themselves, before the implosion of the bubble of instruments backed by real estate mortgages contaminated all the other segments of the financial markets and, from there, the (interbank) money market as such. As a consequence, the entire system of financing the U.S. economy, first, and then the world economy, froze and came to a standstill. In other words, the major banks no longer trusted each other and refused to lend money to each other.

Box 1.2 High finance, the ultra-rich, and dominant market forces

High finance is composed of a dense network of giant banking and financial oligopolies that own most of the transnational corporations operating at the worldwide scale in all sectors of activity. The ultra-rich are the largest shareholders in these oligopolies, as well as in the companies they own. This is not the "1 per cent" decried by the Occupy Wall Street movement, but the 0.00001% of the population, so hyper-concentrated is the ownership structure of capital today. They are the ones who dominate the polarized and hierarchical capitalist world system, which functions in each national perimeter by building pyramids of indebtedness, forcing agents and States to strive to remain productive and competitive in order to be able to repay their huge debts—even if it means that many individuals, societies and the environment are damaged. The constraints imposed on States (e.g., the constraint prohibiting the European Central Bank [ECB] from lending to the Treasuries of the member countries of the euro zone) make them dependent on the owners of high finance, self-proclaimed subjects of history under the name of "financial markets." The latter have managed to "privatize" money in order to place it almost exclusively at the service of their own interests, leading to a situation where more than 95% of monetary creation is destined, not for social spending, consumption, investment, production or ecological transition, but rather for the accumulation of wealth through the purchase of securities that are to increase in value ("shareholder value") on the stock market.

An idea of how the global network of high finance is structured was proposed by Vitali, Glattfelder and Battison (2009) at the Swiss Federal Institute of Technology in Zurich: at the end of the 2000s, 737 companies controlled some 80% of transnational firms, and one "super entity" alone composed of 147 companies controlled more than 40%, half of which were located in the United States (with the United Kingdom, Japan, France and Switzerland far behind). Of the 25 companies with the densest connections, 12 belong to finance: J.P.Morgan Chase, Morgan Stanley, Goldman Sachs, Bank of America, Bank of New York Mellon, Merrill Lynch, Barclays, UBS, Deutsche Bank, Crédit Suisse, Société Générale and Mitsubishi Financial, that is, some of the most powerful institutions on Wall Street and in the City.

These oligopolies are the determining actors in the world's chains of values, powers and hierarchies, holding, in intertwined portfolios, the essential part of the ownership of the capital of transnationals through majority control, minority holdings ensuring a decisive influence within groups of shareholders or via entities on which a cascade of indebted institutions depends. It is also these oligopolies that set, according to their will, the interest rates on the segments of the financial markets that they dominate, or create, through the credit system over which they have the upper hand, the quantity of money that they judge appropriate. And it is they who have jeopardized public finances and social budgets by demanding that States nationalize their private debts and, when they deem it absolutely necessary for their survival, their banks in difficulty—while transferring the cost of these operations to the peoples. A large part of the wealth produced in the world is captured by these financial networks, in a concerted or more conflicting way (notably between the main dominant fractions of high finance in the United States). It is the strategy of unbridled speculation, of undivided enrichment and of dictatorial domination of this tiny minority of owners of capital, with colossal fortunes hidden by offshore companies in tax havens where they rub shoulders with those of criminal finance that has recently led the economies of the planet to catastrophe.

Anti-crisis Monetary Policy Measures

In 1929, when the stock market crash* was caused (already) by compulsive financial speculation, the U.S. Central Bank reacted belatedly and inappropriately by raising interest rates, which contributed to the contraction of activity and the plunge of the country's economy, and then that of the world, into the great depression of the 1930s. But clearly, in 2007–2008, the lesson was only half learned, since the monetary authorities were slow to assess the concrete consequences of the collapse of the financial markets, and in particular the nature and extent of the risk of systemic destabilization. The real turning point in anti-crisis policies was the sudden realization of the public authorities that followed their failure to intervene at the time of the collapse of the investment bank Lehman Brothers on September 15, 2008. From that date on, a change of course was decided by the Fed and the U.S. Treasury. In the meantime, it must be realized that the entire oligopolies and institutions of high finance have tottered and were on the verge of collapse at the very center of the capitalist world system. No more and no less. This is not a matter of imagination; it is a statement of fact—unfortunately too little known to the general public.

The anti-crisis monetary policy measures taken by the governments of the Northern countries consisted, first of all, of coordinating the actions of their Central Banks in order to inject gigantic amounts of liquidity into the interbank market, to offer special credit lines to the largest commercial banks and to reduce interest rates to almost zero. The purpose of this abundant creation of "primary" money was to bail out the endangered banking and financial oligopolies and to accompany their hyper-concentration movement, by trying to slow down the vertiginous fall of asset prices on the markets, so that derivatives could be paid for as close as possible to their face value and the devalorization of fictitious capital remained as limited as possible. But, beyond that, it is no exaggeration to say that the essential objective of these State interventions, without any precedent in history, has been to save the system of financing capitalism. To save it, at least for a while.

And to do this, under the influence of the largest shareholders in finance, the public authorities no longer hesitated for a single moment before resorting to methods that neoliberal ideologists vilify when progressives call for their implementation in order to transform society, but which suddenly became recommendable—and even indispensable—when it came to rescuing a failing capitalist system. This was the case for two key measures. (*1*) Speculation through short selling was temporarily suspended in order to avoid contagion effects, until the financial markets showed some signs of stabilization. (*2*) Where State recapitalization funds, public loans or hive-off vehicles* (to mop up toxic securities*) had not been sufficient to keep a collapsing banking-finance-insurance sector afloat, outright nationalizations of failed private institutions were decided upon: AIG in the United States, Royal Bank of Scotland in Great Britain, Hypo Real Estate in Germany, etc. This, like in a "vulgar" socialist country—but with the difference that neoliberalism continued to be imposed and the State was careful not to point to the big financiers as being the real culprits of the disaster, or even to try to steer the nationalized entities in the direction of support for the productive economy and a real satisfaction of the social needs of the population. By the authoritarianism of its interventions, which accentuated social injustice and the monopolization of power, the State, flying to the aid of the shareholders of high finance, gave proof of its submission to the interests of a minority of the ultra-rich.

After the recapitalization of the Fed that is itself running out of steam, the most decisive step taken by this institution to plug the gap in an international monetary system that was threatening to collapse was, in October 2008, the "unlimited" extension of "swap lines" (used for the first time in the aftermath of the terrorist attacks of September 11, 2001) to the Central Banks of the North and strategic allies of the South, so as to ensure them access to the U.S. dollar and to guarantee liquidity and solvency, and thus relative stability. At the domestic level, monetary policy became "unconventional," with the introduction of Quantitative Easing*.

This mechanism, which consists of a Central Bank buying up debt securities (private or public) on a massive scale from commercial banks and transnational companies in order to provide cash, was initiated in 2001 by the Bank of Japan in an attempt to pull that country out of recession. It was taken up by the U.S. Federal Reserve from 2008 (and until 2014), then by the Bank of England and finally, in 2015, by the European Central Bank. In 2020, the depressive episode marking the COVID-19 pandemic saw the return on a very large scale of measures combining asset buyback programs, interest rate decreases, special credit lines and massive aid to private companies. As we can see, the nature of contemporary money, freed from any attachment to a materially based monetary standard, gives Central Banks, in the present era, the possibility of creating money (apparently) without limit; just as private banks can also push credit to the maximum. In reality, however, there are limits to the creation of money: those posed by the problems of convertibility of these credits into Central Bank money (for the second-tier banks) and (for the State) of convertibility of the national currency into foreign currencies. But also the problems linked to the credibility of the monetary authorities and the confidence of agents in such institutions…

References

Aglietta, M. and A. Orléan (1982), *La Violence de la monnaie*, Paris: Presses universitaires de France.

Amin, S. (1977), *La Loi de la valeur et le matérialisme historique*, Paris: Éditions de Minuit.

Braudel, F. (1979), *Civilisation matérielle, économie et capitalisme*, 3 Volumes, Paris: Librairie Armand Colin.

Carcanholo, R. (2001), "O Capital especulativo e a desmaterialização do dinheiro," *Revista da Sociedade Brasileira de Economia Política*, n° 6, p. 26–45.

Cartelier, J. (1996), *La Monnaie*, Paris: Flammarion.

De Brunhoff, S. (1976), *La Monnaie chez Marx*, Paris: Éditions Sociales.

Herrera, R. (2013), "La Domination de la haute finance étasunienne," *Marché & Organisations*, n° 19, p. 127–146, Paris.

——— (2015), *La Maladie dégénérative de l'économie: le néo-classicisme*, Paris: Éditions Delga.

Herrera, R. and P. Nakatani (2010), "Keynes (et Marx), la monnaie et la crise," *La Pensée*, n° 364, p. 57–68, Paris.

Lavigne, M. (1970), *Les Économies socialistes soviétiques et européennes*, Paris: Librairie Armand Colin.

Marx, K. (1977) [1867], *Le Capital. Critique de l'économie politique*, 3 Volumes, Paris: Éditions sociales.

Maucourant, J. (1991), "La Question de la monnaie en Égypte ancienne," *Revue du MAUSS*, n° 13, p. 155–164.

Morin, F. (2015), *L'Hydre mondiale: l'oligarchie bancaire*, Montreal: Lux Éditeur.

Nakatani, P. and H. Gomes (2010), "Dinheiro: natureza e funções," *mimeo*, Vitoria (Brasil): Federal University of Espirito Santo.

Tutin, C. (ed.) (2010), *La Pensée monétaire de l'âge classique à nos jours*, Paris: Le Monde - Flammarion.

Vilar, P. (1974), *Or et monnaie dans l'histoire*, Paris: Flammarion.

Wallerstein, I. (1980), *The Modern World System*, 2 Volumes, New York: Academic Press.

2

The Monetary Hegemony of the United States: *The Power of High Finance, the Reign of the Dollar and Global Chaos*

The Americans have no idea how to make these institutions into operating international concerns, and in almost every direction their ideas are bad. Yet they plainly intend to force their conception through regardless of the rest of us. [They] think to have the right to call the tune on practically every point. If they knew the music, that would not matter so much, but unfortunatedly they don't.

John Maynard Keynes, *Letter to Richard Kahn* (March 13, 1946)

The period of time since 1945 has been characterized by a multidimensional hegemony of the United States, which has imposed itself above all on the economic, political, ideological and military levels, and which today intends to assert itself more than ever. However, this hegemony is now in crisis, threatened by the recent evolution of global power relations. Neither Europe, which still does not exist as a unified political power, nor Japan, which has had to lower its ambitions to the regional level, is willing to challenge this hegemony, both of them mired in stagnation. Since 1968–1975, the foundations on which the boom of the previous decades was built have crumbled. What has taken its place seems less like a new world order than a severe instability unknown since

R. Herrera, *Money*, Global University for Sustainability Book Series,
https://doi.org/10.1007/978-981-19-2848-2_2

the interwar period, a chaos far from being overcome. What these two sub-periods (1945–1975 and since then) have in common is the domination of the U.S. dollar, in spite of everything (except in the USSR and the Soviet bloc, even if these countries, plus those of the South in socialist transition, remained in certain aspects dependent on the capitalist world system). And the inflection point, which can be seen in the 1970s, is the return to power of high finance.

The power of the dollar, which has become the key international currency and a unit of account on the external credit market, has been built on the power of U.S. finance, the owner of financial capital, which itself controls the transnational companies that dominate the world today in all sectors: from agribusiness and mass distribution to the automobile industry, from energy to the new information and communication technologies. Even though globalization tends to erase borders and value chains are becoming more complex as they closely interlock the productive and commercial structures of different economies, many of these firms are U.S. ones. This is especially the case in the most strategic sectors, such as the military-industrial complex (with Lockheed Martin, Boeing, General Dynamics, among others), "Big Tech" (former "GAFAM," now "GAMAM," for Google, Apple, Meta [Facebook]), Amazon, Microsoft) and "Big Pharma" (Pfizer, Johnson & Johnson, Moderna, etc.). The same is true for a large majority of the banking and financial oligopolies (such as J.P.Morgan Chase, Morgan Stanley, Goldman Sachs, Bank of America, Bank of New York Mellon, Merrill Lynch…) which currently and generally control or have ultimate ownership of the major transnationals on the worldwide scale.

The global credibility and demand for U.S. dollars are such that the most fundamental monetary policy measure during the subprime crisis of 2007–2008 to prevent the collapse of the financial system—let us repeat, as incredible as it may seem: the financial system did almost collapse—was the decision of the Federal Reserve to give the European Central Bank and the Swiss National Bank "unlimited" access to the U.S. dollar through a system of "swap lines" from mid-December 2007.

After the failure of Lehman Brothers, which shook the whole edifice of world finance in mid-September 2008, this scheme was extended to the other Central Banks of the North (England, Japan and Canada on

September 18, then Australia, Denmark, Sweden and Norway on the 24th of the same month, and finally New Zealand on October 28), before also being opened (on October 29, 2008) to certain selected countries of the South, which were considered to be decisive for the stability of the capitalist world system (such as Mexico, Singapore, South Korea and Brazil). These operations were fundamental to averting a systemic risk by avoiding the serious problems faced by many U.S. banks from spreading to their foreign counterparts awaiting transfers of funds and risking payment default due to widespread dollar illiquidity.

The various Central Banks of the countries with the most widely used international currencies (in addition to the dollar, the euro, the pound sterling, the yen and the Swiss franc in particular) found themselves in the worrying situation of not being able to respond on their own to a large and urgent demand for dollars—since they do not issue the U.S. currency themselves—and therefore of no longer being able to assume their essential role as lenders of last resort. Thanks to these swap lines, the commercial banks of the countries concerned were able to benefit from direct access to coordinated support in dollars issued by the Fed, but provided through the effective channels of their respective Central Banks. Presenting themselves as the global lender of last resort and preserving the continuity of international payments, the U.S. monetary authorities, on this occasion, reminded their foreign partners of the strict hierarchy of national currencies that must always be respected within the capitalist world system in crisis.

High Finance, from Its Controversial Origins to Its Current Contested Hegemony

To identify the links between the strength of the U.S. dollar and high finance, let us examine the origins of the latter for a moment. The beginnings of finance capital go back to the history of the United States in the late Nineteenth Century. The widely disseminated myth that the great bankers made their fortunes through hard work and savings turns its back on reality. The authentic story is that of the "robber barons," the new lords and their dynasties who came to "control the people with the people's money," in the words of Howard Zinn (2002). Let us take the examples of John Pierpont Morgan and John Davison Rockefeller, at the origin of two of the world's most gigantic financial empires.

The first, born in 1837 and died in 1913, who managed to build up an industrial-financial group extending from banking to electricity, steel and transport, started with a rather special business: J.P. Morgan bought defective rifles intended for scrap from a military arsenal at a low price and sold them, despite their dangerousness, to soldiers (on his side) at ten times the price on the battlefield. Like so many young men from great families, such as Andrew Carnegie or James Mellon, two other financiers whose names have been engraved in golden letters in history, he had escaped his mobilization in the northern ranks during the Civil War by paying himself a substitute for a few dollars. Years later, he led a consortium of bankers who were asked by the federal government to issue in its place hundreds of millions of dollars of Treasury bonds for lucrative commissions, or who bailed out the official reserves by exchanging gold for State securities which were right away sold for huge capital gains. As for the second, J.D. Rockefeller (1839–1937), who, at the turn of the Twentieth Century, got his hands on 90% of the oil refined in the United States, he started out in this sector by buying up an extraction company, from which Standard Oil was born, and by paying henchmen to go and sabotage or blow up neighboring competing refineries. He thus became the first U.S. citizen to become a billionaire.

In the United States—as in England, which it has gradually caught up with—, the owners of the giant financial oligopolies placed the State under their guardianship, notably through the mechanism of public debt. The collusion between public and private affairs undermines the thesis of the opposition between law and force, leading mistakenly to believe in the neutrality of the capitalist State, which, situated above social conflicts, would embody political rationality, whereas in reality it subordinates supposedly "free and equal" individuals to the interests of those who have taken possession of it, in the logic of the generalization of private ownership of the means of production. Finance organized itself as a dominant power within the modern State, after the fusion of its activities of banking and industry. The State, whose repressive character became ever more pronounced in the face of intensifying popular revolts, thus managed money by ensuring its reproduction as a general equivalent in circulation, but under the control of an aristocracy of rentiers speculating on convertible public securities. Such control of State financing acted as a gas pedal of accumulation through the rise of financial markets, transforming unproductive money into reproducible capital. Held in this way, State debt served as an impetus to joint-stock companies, to the trade in negotiable securities and to various stock market games. As a matter of fact, it was under the leadership of high finance that the U.S. government set out to conquer the world in 1898, starting with the Cuban War (Box 2.1).

Box 2.1 Cuba, 1898: A step in the march of U.S. high finance towards global hegemony

A Spanish colony and the world's largest exporter of sugar from the early Nineteenth Century, Cuba became economically dependent on the United States at an early stage. In 1895, the island was its second largest foreign market for merchandise trade. The war of 1898, by which the United States was to take away Spain's supremacy over Cuba, certainly revealed its will to power, which had already sent its armies beyond its borders more than a hundred times since 1776 (to Argentina, China, Angola, etc.). The aim of this war was to get its hands on strategic places in its zone of influence, as declared since the Monroe Doctrine. Nevertheless, what distinguished it from the past was that it was the consequence of the push of the great oligopolies of financial capital and the very condition of their expansion. Lenin interpreted it as "the first imperialist war" in the history of the United States, where high finance had previously acquired its fabulous power and from where it was about to rush out to dominate the world.

Despite its small size, Cuba offered opportunities for capital exports, productive investments and even portfolio investments—including public debt, which combined illegal activities with the submission of the country's corrupt elites. The Platt Amendment, which authorized the United States to intervene militarily and ceded the Guantánamo base to the United States, was drafted by the lawyer of a friend of President Theodore Roosevelt, the banker Speyer, whose establishment financed, among other things, the disarmament of the Cuban liberation army and its replacement by a professional army commanded by the U.S. Army. The economy was then dollarized. In 1900, the first U.S.-owned company (Cuba Co.) was established, with the two future masters of the island, Morgan and Rockefeller, sitting on its board of directors. The ownership structure of capital concentrated plantations and sugar mills in holding companies operating in cartels. And in 1915, funds were raised directly on the U.S. stock market. Morgan also had control over mines, electricity, telephone, railroads...

The banking liquidation law of 1920 marked the bankruptcy of the local banks, which were quickly absorbed. In addition, finance managed the accounts of the Cuban Treasury, and the State itself was placed by the public debt in the orbit of a pool of creditors dominated by Morgan, assisted by the Rockefellers' Chase Manhattan. The path that allowed corporate finance to control the island is littered with economic scandals, military threats and political corruptions. In 1925, Cuba was the third largest recipient of capital exports from the United States. When the crisis of 1929 hit, the constraint of a one-peso to one-dollar exchange rate and the ban on devaluation amplified its dramatic impact on Cuban society. At the end of the great depression, the Rockefellers, taking over from Morgan, had acquired Cuba, so to speak. However, the misery of the people was massive. The Revolution was in the making.

The Return of the Domination of High Finance in the Era of Neoliberalism

The planetary expansion of high finance, driving a process of capital accumulation under the hegemony of the United States and supported by the dollar, experienced a parenthesis of nearly half a century between the crisis of the 1930s and that of the 1970s, which marks the advent of the era of neoliberalism. The latter can be interpreted as the return in force of the globalized strategy of domination of finance, composed as we have seen above of the owners of the most powerful banking and financial oligopolies, holding in their portfolios most of the transnational firms and, consequently, most of the globally dominant capital.

This high finance, whose axis of gravity is most often located at the heart of the hegemonic center of the capitalist world system, was re-imposed from the 1970s onwards, when the gold exchange standard that had been implemented at Bretton Woods at the end of the Second World War was dismantled in order to establish the reign of the U.S. dollar.

The decline in profit rates in the core countries from the late 1960s onwards deepened in the following decade into a generalized crisis. This return to the power of finance, which was born at the end of the Nineteenth Century and placed under the supervision of the States after the 1929 crisis (some neoliberal authors prefer to speak of "financial repression" on this subject), took place between August 1971, when the Nixon administration announced the end of the gold convertibility of the dollar and the beginning of floating exchange rates, and October 1979, when the U.S. Federal Reserve*, the world's lender of last resort*, decided to accelerate the increase in its key interest rate (overnight). This increase was an attempt to counteract the decline in the rate of profit recorded over the past decade and represented a "financial coup d'état" by which the most powerful U.S. owners were able to regain the leadership in capital accumulation, a leadership that they had lost since the great depression. The "Volcker shock" (named after the [Democratic] governor of the Fed at the time), or the "monetarist" reorientation of central capitalism, was soon to hit both the economies of the North, whose policies yielded to the external constraint that weighed on the components of their monetary policy—external component (defending the exchange rate) and internal component (controlling the money supply)—and those of the South, where the conditions for the outbreak of the coming debt crisis were being established.

Historically, the military interventions of the United States in the Korean and Vietnam wars caused—in addition to the human tragedies we know about—serious imbalances in the U.S. economy throughout the 1960s; imbalances that are found at the root of the structural crisis we are currently experiencing, which is simply a continuation of the crisis of the 1970s. These wars gradually caused the regulatory mechanisms of the capitalist world system under U.S. hegemony to malfunction, as the latter's internal and external deficits increased its foreign debt and spread Eurodollars*, then petrodollars*. The gold reserves of the U.S. Treasury represented less than half of the dollars that could be converted. The pressure on the dollar proved to be untenable; hence the suspension of the convertibility of the dollar, the demonetization of gold, the flexibilization of exchange rates and the deregulation of financial markets, tipping the world into monetary chaos. It was on this basis that, from the 1960s onwards, fictitious capital* had developed in the United States, of course, from Wall Street to Chicago, but also in the City of London.

This return to power of high finance took place on the ruins of the old international order, through the questioning of the type of regulation of capitalism in the North (during the "stagflation," i.e., the coexistence of inflation and unemployment, in the 1970s), the failure of the programs of the national bourgeoisies in the South (with the debt crisis of the 1980s) and the collapse of the Soviet bloc in the East (bringing about the end of the USSR and the Council for Mutual Economic Assistance [CMEA or COMECON] at the beginning of the 1990s). The historical conjunction of these three series of major events caused a profound modification of the capital-labor balance of power on a planetary scale. Concomitant with the retreat of the positions once conquered by socialist advances, by national liberation movements and by popular struggles, the neoliberal offensive has its dogmas, which we know only too well. At the global level, they aim to perpetuate the supremacy of the U.S. dollar, through flexible exchange rates, and to promote free trade, through the removal of protectionist barriers and the liberalization of capital transfers. At the national level, they attack the State, which, each in its own way, voluntarist development strategies had previously placed at the heart of their respective projects for transforming social formations, in an attempt to autonomize the conditions of their accumulation and reproduction in global relations: the "Keynesian compromise" in the North, planning in the East or in the other socialist countries, and "developmentalism" in the South. The aim was to deform the ownership structure of capital in favor of the private sector, through the privatization of public enterprises; to reduce budgetary expenditure, starting with social spending; and to impose wage rigor as the pivot of a disinflation that took precedence over all other considerations, with higher real interest rates and a sharing of added value favorable to capital.

Thus, we have been dealing with a strategy of both deregulation—that is, re-regulation of the markets by the forces of private power alone—and globalization—without a supra-State political entity to face the power of global high finance. The planetary standardization of this neoliberal strategy was the function of international organizations and local monetary institutions, first and foremost the Central Banks. These have had to become "independent" of States, and therefore of sovereign government decisions, in order to come directly under the yoke of financial oligopolies. For their part, the international financial institutions, after asserting in the 1980s that the debt of the South was an (internal) public finance problem and not an (external) balance of payments problem, a decade later made recommendations to their "client countries" on "good governance"—an inverted symmetry of what one would expect from a good government. Among the IMF's advice is, of course, along with the delegation of defense and the privatization of tax collection, the substitution of foreign currency for domestic currency. Hence the paradox of the international financial institutions calling on the countries of the South to internalize decisions to abandon crucial State functions, dictated from outside, at the very moment when foreign financial oligopolies penetrate the ownership structures of these economies and dispossess their people of the monetary tool of national sovereignty. Nevertheless, from the point of view of these oligopolies, managing the State apparatus of the South from the center of the system, while neutralizing their State power, would basically be the secret of "ideal" governance? In this context, the project of forging a sovereign development strategy—at the heart of which would be currency—is simply prohibited. The fact remains that, beyond the oscillations ordered by the Fed, with mixed success to say the least, the dollar is clearly overvalued over the long term with respect to the "real fundamentals" of the U.S. economy. Indeed, the United States consumes much more than it produces, and it has accumulated "twin deficits" in foreign trade and the government budget. However, it has the power—the privilege in fact—to close these gaps through the use of disproportionate debt. No other country is allowed to do this and to live so much at the expense of other peoples with impunity. Moreover, it is in Washington, D.C., between 19th Street and H. Street N.W., where the two international institutions (the World Bank and the IMF) are based, with the mission of overseeing the application of the strictest financial discipline to all the economies of the world. Everywhere, but the United States. Yet without such strong global demand for it at all times, the dollar would surely undergo a "correction" that would probably—in fact, inevitably—lead to the end of U.S. hegemony.

"The Dollar Is Our Currency, but It's Your Problem"

This statement, attributed to U.S. Treasury Secretary John Connally and addressed at the end of 1971 to his counterparts in the finance ministries of the ten richest countries in the North (including Switzerland), is still relevant today. The whole world has been suffering from this "problem" ever since the United States obtained for itself the "exorbitant privilege" of being able to issue a national currency which is at the same time the key currency for exchanges and reserves within the international monetary system. Is this acceptable? Especially since the dollar also allows to denominate the vast majority of raw materials and basic commodities listed on world markets or traded over the counter*, whether they are agricultural products (wheat, sugar, etc.), minerals (gold, copper, etc.), hydrocarbons (oil, gas, etc.), strategic metals (rare earths, etc.) or other elements (silicon, rubber, etc.). Established after the Second World War, U.S. monetary hegemony—from which the socialist countries had previously only partially escaped—did not come to an end, far from it, with the Jamaica agreements which, in January 1976, turned the page on the Bretton Woods agreements (see Chapter 1).

The management of the structural crisis of the capitalist system—the same one that started at the end of the 1960s and has been worsening ever since—had to deal with huge surpluses of floating capital generated by the submission of economies to the exclusive criterion of maximum profit. Thus, the liberalization of capital transfers, the adoption of flexible exchange rates, the rise in interest rates, the U.S. external balance deficit, the indebtedness of the Third World and the privatization of State-owned assets are all part of this policy, which offers hot money flows the outlet for a headlong rush into ever more speculative financial investments. The Fed tends to behave like a Central Bank operating on a global scale, but determines its monetary policy to serve the exclusive interest of the United States. It sets its interest rates and prints money as it sees fit—in fact, under pressure, or at the behest of high finance—for what suits the United States; or more precisely, the globalized financial oligopolies. And logically, the implication of these unilateral decisions is to destabilize foreign economies, even to sink them.

Thus, when the Fed decided to raise its interest rate to almost 20% in May 1981 (compared with 10% at the beginning of 1979, and 5% at the end of 1971), with the intention of halting the decline in the rate of profit and pulling the United States out of the stagflation into which it was sinking, what it did was create a monetary tsunami that got their European and Japanese allies into serious trouble and sent most of the economies of the South into a debt spiral (especially those with short-term, floating-rate loans)—and even put some of them in a position where they had to declare a debt moratorium, as Mexico did in 1982. With their foreign debts owed mainly in dollars and interest rates having risen sharply, developing economies found themselves bearing greatly increased debt service burdens. Continued repayment could only be ensured through new borrowing, which was undertaken under even more draconian conditions—under the rule of the IMF. In the second half of the 1980s, other countries experienced episodes of hyperinflation, fueled by a rush to the dollar and speculative movements against the exchange rate of their national currencies, with very painful effects for their peoples, as was the case in Peru (1983), Bolivia (1985) and Argentina (1988), among many others.

Almost all of Latin America was indeed going through the "lost decade" of the 1980s, during which production declined and poverty worsened as a direct consequence of brutal and selfish U.S. monetary policy decisions. In almost every corner of the continent, neo-fascist regimes—which Washington had helped to bring to power by force (from Chile to Argentina, from Brazil to Ecuador, from Colombia to Guatemala...)—judged that the moment was the right time for nationalizing part of the private debts owed by the local bourgeoisie in order to make their peoples bear them, according to the principle of socialization of losses, while national public enterprises, sources of foreign currency and tax revenue, were privatized—as were the profits from financial speculation. U.S. monetary policy then offered Latin America, in addition to misery and dictatorship, subjugation by perpetual debt.

From Another Currency Crisis (1997–1998) to the Global and Systemic Crisis (2007–2008)

A decade later, the 1997 crisis began with the collapse of the exchange rates of several Asian currencies pegged to the dollar, which earned it the name "Asian crisis"—even though the problem was rooted in the erratic fluctuations of the U.S. currency and their repercussions on economies whose dynamics obeyed distinct determinants. For the main trigger of this crisis was a Fed interest rate hike (a small one, barely a quarter of a point), intended to regulate the money supply, and more broadly economic activity, nowhere else but in the United States, but causing a sudden appreciation of the dollar on the foreign exchange market. Immediately after this—or even a little earlier for traders* who had anticipated these increases in interest rates and exchange rates in the United States—large masses of floating capital left Southeast Asia (Thailand, the Philippines, Indonesia, etc.) to come and invest in the more lucrative U.S. financial markets.

The continued appreciation of the dollar, which was at the root of the destabilization of Southeast Asian currencies and stock markets, amplified this contagion effect and, combined with the concomitant fall in oil prices, passed on the pressures of the financial markets to other economies. Thus, in mid-August 1998, Russia had to declare itself in default on its public debt bonds and immediately abandon the system of fluctuating margins for the ruble around the dollar. The devaluation of the Russian currency caused it to lose three-quarters of its value in a few months. But if this huge country was brought down, what about the much smaller and vulnerable countries linked to it? The panic that swept through the foreign exchange market at the time spread to Russia's Central Asian and Eastern European outskirts. Ukraine had to renegotiate its public bond debt and, like Kazakhstan and Kyrgyzstan, experienced a banking crisis. The economies of the region all saw their currencies plunge and their inflation rates soar between mid-1998 and mid-1999—except for Armenia and Azerbaijan, but these two countries were just emerging from war.

The chain of currency crises had even more distant consequences: in Brazil in 1999, where the intensification of capital flight forced a surge in interest rates (approaching 50%) and a devaluation of the real, followed by its abrupt fall after its undocking from the dollar; again in Asia, this time in Turkey, where, in a context of financial liberalization, the banking system froze up under the effect of a liquidity crisis and the Turkish lira lost almost half its value against the dollar between the end of 2000 and the beginning of 2001.

Each of these events is also part of national economic structures, singular social and institutional formations, and specific long-term historical perspectives; it is certainly not explained solely by the "exogenous shocks" caused by the supremacy of the dollar, but the fact is that the impact of such shocks is overdetermining, in the sense that it crushes, essentially through the exchange rate and external indebtedness essentially, the trajectories taken by all internal indicators, and especially the relationships between variables within what orthodox economists call the "real sphere" (such as industrial production), i.e., the economy supposedly freed from monetary and financial aspects.

Even structurally solid countries in the North that are performing well conjunctural results risk seeing their currencies used as a support for speculative games with no other aim than to maximize the profits of private operators on the markets. This is what happened in Japan between 2005 and 2007. During this period, large international speculators took positions of consisting in yen debt and converting it into dollars placed in the United States to take advantage of the spread between Japanese (low) and U.S. (higher) interest rates. This caused a strong demand for dollars and consequently the yen fell. When the loans matured, they had to be repaid by converting them in the opposite direction, i.e., by selling dollars and buying yen, at a more favorable bilateral exchange rate than initially, since the Japanese currency had weakened against the dollar. Speculators accumulated gains from the exchange rate and interest rate differentials, but the result of these transactions was a depreciation of the yen, even though the "fundamental" indicators of the Japanese economy were much better than those of the United States.

The upheavals that shook the capitalist economies in 2007–2008 illustrate this reasoning, even if it is more than a currency crisis, or the "financial" crisis to which it has often been reduced. It is a global, systemic crisis that we are facing. In many countries, the repercussions observed at the time in the foreign exchange market were devastating, especially because of the exacerbation of the pre-existing "currency war" and the aggressive change in the U.S. line. In short, what dominated was indeed the implication of the shock caused by the adoption of the so-called "Quantitative Easing* (QE)" strategy. The global liquidity crunch was solved from spring 2009 onwards by a policy of the Fed and, in turn, of other Northern Central Banks, to issue extraordinary amounts of money. This allowed the United States and the other economies at the center of the capitalist world system to avoid a collapse—but not a very deep recession (and a few cases of deflation, from Japan to Germany).

After the Shock (2008), the Monetary Policy Counter-Shocks (Since 2009)

The effects of the 2007–2008 crisis on the countries of the South and East were catastrophic, and none of them really escaped. Some were only affected a little later, such as India and Nigeria, and sometimes several times, as was the case for China, which was first affected in 2009 and then more severely and durably from 2012 onwards. In the Summer of 2008, however, Russia and the countries of the former Soviet Union once again experienced large capital outflows, as they had a decade earlier, which led to a reduction in their foreign exchange reserves and a depreciation of their currencies. The easing of the stresses on their banking systems allowed growth to recover after the spring of 2009, but with a *hysteresis* effect: economic indicators had improved, but remained less good than in the previous decade.

After the shock came the monetary policy counter-shock. From 2014 onwards, the end of Quantitative Easing in the United States, the recovery of the U.S. dollar and expectations of interest rate hikes by the

Fed combined to wreak havoc in countries in the South and East. Since 2009, trillions of dollars, either freshly minted or borrowed at near-zero rates, have flooded these economies. Washington's sudden tightening of monetary policy caused speculative capital to flow out of the "emerging" countries and back into the U.S. financial markets, destabilizing many developing countries—and also weakening some strategic rivals. It is absolutely clear that these shifts in monetary strategies were not expressly designed and implemented to affect directly, as a priority, the countries of the South and East; this is for the simple and decisive reason that the multiple internal disruptions that the current domination of high finance is causing in the U.S. economy are of such gravity that they needed to be addressed for their own sake and before any other objective. Nevertheless, the most immediate and brutal result of these prodigiously selfish changes in U.S. monetary policy is the destabilization of almost every economy on the planet. This is the fate of the world in the global monetary-financial chaos into which it has been plunged since the early 1970s by the government of a single country whose interest is, under the rule of the dollar, to serve the financial oligopolies and to maintain the status of the United States as a world hegemony.

Of all the factors that explain the abrupt changes in the foreign exchange market during the period 2014–2016, the inflection of the decisions taken by the Fed is certainly the most fundamental—even more so than the exchange rate regime adopted or the interventionism of the monetary authorities of the countries concerned. Since the middle of 2013, it was anticipated that Quantitative Easing 3 would be curtailed, which it was in fact in October 2014, and that the Fed would raise interest rates, which it finally did in December 2015. The result was a tightening of liquidity conditions at a worldwide scale, which the quantitative easing policies of the European and Japanese Central Banks only incompletely compensated for due to the relative tightness of the euro and yen financial markets. Net capital inflows then dried up in the so-called "emerging" markets—i.e., from countries that were themselves supposedly "emerging"—hampering economic growth and driving down commodity prices, starting with raw materials.

Since late 2013, the dollar had been strengthening against most flexible exchange rate currencies, whether the South African rand or the

Brazilian real, among many others. However, the currencies of numerous other countries, such as Mexico, Algeria and Indonesia, showed signs of a downward trend as early as the Summer of 2014, when the expectation of an upcoming contraction of Quantitative Easing in the United States was confirmed. The sharp depreciation of the Russian ruble against the dollar, which began in the first quarter of 2014, accelerated in July and again in October, to be exacerbated during the market panic in mid-December of the same year—with tensions continuing until February 2015. After a lull, the downward trend resumed in August 2015 and even extended into January 2016. These evolutions accompanied the fall in hydrocarbon prices, but in the case of Russia, the disorder of 2014–2016, like the previous crises of 1998–1999 and 2008–2009, can be interpreted as a phenomenon linked more to the capital account* than to the current account, since this economy, in spite of everything, regularly exhibited a trade surplus, when net private capital flows have almost continuously been negative, especially, and increasingly, since 2008. The Russian Central Bank's foreign exchange reserves were bled, with a loss of some 160 billion dollars in the 18 months between October 2013 and March 2015, marking the period of the ruble's most intense defense. Only 20% of the lost currency was replenished over the next year.

However, this configuration is also costing Washington's proteges—and Brussels' ones—dearly. In the turmoil, the Ukrainian currency, the hryvnia, also fell. Its depreciation is of course associated with the political crisis into which the country sank from February 2014, but the acceleration of this trend in November 2014 finds part of its explanation in a contagion effect coming from the East. Until the beginning of 2015, the local banking system recorded massive withdrawals of hryvnia and conversions into foreign currency, euros and especially U.S. dollars. Ukraine was soon forced to restructure its public debt owed to eurobond holders* and from late 2013 to early 2015, like its Moscow counterpart, its Central Bank lost three-quarters of its reserves. It was only the support of the IMF that allowed it to recover them.

The exchange crisis of 2014–2016 also affected the currencies of the countries of the former Soviet Union, as a result of the decline in trade, but also and above all through mechanisms linked to expectations of currency devaluations on the financial markets. This was particularly the case for the member countries of the Eurasian Economic Union, which found themselves unable to sustain the sudden nominal appreciation of their currencies against the Russian ruble and ended up falling as well. The currencies that suffered the most were the Kazakh tenge and the Azerbaijani manat, which were affected by the fall in oil prices, but also the Belarusian ruble. Between the end of 2013 and the beginning of 2015, these three currencies lost almost 50% of their value against the dollar. The Moldovan (leu) and Tajik (somoni) currencies, for example, lost a third of their value, but the currencies that held up better were those with limited convertibility, such as the Uzbek soum and the Turkmen manat.

The Dollar as a Deterrent Weapon

It must be recognized, however, that some currency-related measures have been taken by the United States to target and hit particular economies, and this has been deliberate. Events in the midst of what looks like a "monetary-financial war" should be seen in this light. Countries whose governments stand out for their firm determination to fight to recover what can be of a dangerously diminished monetary sovereignty have thus been attacked by speculative raids, quite identifiable, against their national currency. Others, or sometimes the same ones, have suffered from manipulations of the prices of raw materials weighing heavily in their exports or of imported commodities indispensable to their population. Most of the economies in question are deliberately given biased assessments by the major international rating agencies. The most influential agencies in the world (Standard & Poor's, Moody's and Fitch Ratings), let's not forget, have predominantly U.S. ownership. Some countries are even subject to extremely harsh sanctions under embargoes.

Banks in countries that are sure allies of Washington have sometimes been fined huge sums—or even banned from participating in the international banking system—for having carried out various transactions in dollars that the U.S. courts have deemed reprehensible. The latter have in fact granted themselves the privilege, which is actually staggering, of imposing the extraterritoriality of their legal rules. This is what happened, for example, to the French bank BNP Paribas in 2014–2015. As a matter of fact, a Manhattan court ordered it to pay an 8.9 billion dollars fine to the Department of Justice for commodity trading prohibited by federal embargo laws against Sudan, Cuba and Iran. For similar reasons, the (Dutch) ING and (British) Standard Chartered Bank had to pay several hundred million dollars to the U.S. administration a few months earlier.

Such weapons of deterrence are used to weaken potential rivals of the United States—allies in the North or competitors in the East and South—and to preserve its monetary supremacy over the capitalist world system. But the maintenance and protection of the privileged international status of the dollar is also a motivation behind wars, this time military wars, undertaken by Washington. The U.S. military-financial power means that in practice this generates a global demand for the dollar, the world's key currency for trade and reserves, which places in the hands of the United States, and of the United States alone, on the supply side, the prerogative to print as many dollars as it wishes. The dollars created, according to the amount of value that suits its interests, are injected into the international financial system and available, notably through the public debt, to finance the continuation of a lifestyle that is far beyond its means, of a mode of consumption that is dramatically destructive of the environment and, what is no less serious, of its imperialist wars or its armed coups from one end of the planet to the other.

The United States thus threatens or attacks countries whose monetary authorities express the wish to try to break free from the yoke of the dollar, and whose government is judged guilty of lèse-majesté. They have to force the world to respect the supreme status of the dollar, and thus the unipolar U.S. hegemony. Let us take the example of Russia again. We know that Vladimir Putin has repeatedly denounced the injustice—which is undeniable, whatever one thinks of this President of the Republic—of an international monetary system placed under the domination of the U.S. dollar. It is also known that this attitude of protest has gathered the conditions for this country, Russia, to see its economy hit by sanctions by the United States—and behind it the European Union—officially following the Crimean crisis in February 2014, its currency attacked by determined speculators, especially in March–April of the same year, and the price of its main export product (oil) manipulated by Washington, with the docile complicity of Saudi Arabia, in order to be maintained at artificially low prices. Not to mention the assessment of Russia's ability to repay its debt, which has been knowingly downgraded by the rating agencies. And, as if that were not enough, several governments of neighboring countries have been shaken by "color revolutions" orchestrated in collaboration with the West—sometimes successfully (in Ukraine), sometimes unsuccessfully (in Belarus)—and accompanied by thinly veiled threats of U.S. military intervention.

Box 2.2 Israel, 1985: An economy saved from monetary collapse by the United States

The government in Washington knows how to sabotage the development of countries it considers incompatible with its order, but also how to save others, such as Israel, whose economy would very probably be doomed without the United States. Long after the partition of Palestine in 1948, Israel's resource-starved but powerfully militarized economy continued to experience chronic difficulties, linked in particular to its defense burden and structural external current account deficit. These problems, combined with institutional characteristics (wage indexation to prices, the weight of trade unions, etc.), provided fertile ground for inflation and currency depreciation for many years. The shekel, which replaced the Israeli pound in 1980, in the context of the rise of oligopolies and the financialization of the time, saw its function as a store of value diminish in favor of the U.S. dollar. More and more financial assets were indexed to the exchange rate—as well as deposits—and even denominated in dollars. The economy was *de facto* dollarized, with the U.S. currency becoming the (illegal) unit of account for many transactions. In the early 1980s, the situation worsened: the intervention of the Israeli army in Lebanon led to a surge in military spending and arms imports, capital inflows became scarce, foreign exchange reserves melted away, the devaluations of the shekel followed one another, inflation accelerated, Israelis fled their own currency… A banking crisis broke out. The Tel Aviv Stock Exchange had to be closed.

The economy, on the verge of collapse, was only saved by massive support from Washington, which avoided a foreign exchange crisis, the smash of the balance of payments and hyperinflation *in extremis*. In 1985, the injection of nearly 1.6 billion dollars, divided between special emergency aid (750 million dollars) and a waiver of the Israeli government debt, immediately allowed the country's internal and external accounts to balance—the current account balance even turned positive for the first time in 30 years. By mid-1985, inflation (which by then had reached 445%) had subsided and the shekel had recovered. Without the assistance of the United States, this crisis would have been insurmountable, given the unstable exchange rates and liberalized capital movements.

This implicit integration of the Israeli economy into that of the global hegemony—which has sustained economic aid since 1986 and ensured that the effects of sometimes extremely serious crises, including the 2008 crisis, are cushioned—is also reflected in the ongoing support of the U.S. armed forces. Israel is the main beneficiary of U.S. military aid, which, cumulatively from 1945 to 2020, is officially close to 146 billion dollars (far ahead of Egypt, South Korea and Colombia). Nevertheless, other substantial funds also pass through certain "private" channels. At the end of December 2020, the United States Congress voted to grant 3.3 billion dollars in "security aid" to Israel, plus an additional 500 million dollars for Israeli-U.S. missile defense cooperation… without worrying about whether some of this money would also be used for illegal establishments of settlers.

Palestine, on the contrary, occupied, colonized and segregated, has been deprived of its own currency, as well as of any instrument of monetary policy or debt. It is the shekel and the U.S. dollar, or to a lesser extent the Jordanian dinar, that circulate in the fragmented territories of the West Bank, the Gaza Strip and East Jerusalem. To cover the financing needs of the local economy, the "Palestinian Authority" must rely on credits from international organizations, donations and, more incidentally, loans from small local banks.

This role of relaying U.S. domination played by Israel in this oil-rich and dollarized region is carried out in close partnership with Saudi Arabia and the Gulf Cooperation Council (created at Washington's initiative and bringing together, under the authority of Riyadh, the United Arab Emirates, Kuwait, Oman, Bahrain and Qatar). Beyond their differences, the monetary authorities of these countries are firmly attached to the dollar. This is the case of the Saudi Arabian Monetary Authority, which is both a Central Bank and a sovereign wealth fund, especially since, for the time being, Saudi Arabia remains the best Trojan horse for the United States in OPEC and the petrodollar system. Under these conditions, it is likely that the Saudi riyal's peg to the dollar will last as long as this economy has not diversified.

It is therefore understandable that, when it comes to defending the U.S. dollar and, beyond it, the capital it supports, the big owners know how to overcome their religious differences and behave like the best allies in the world. Since the Six-Day War, Israel has behaved as if its conquered territory was a Middle Eastern state of the United States, confident that Washington would intervene, including militarily, in case of serious economic and especially monetary problems. Saudi Arabia, for its part, has been committed since the Yom Kippur War to denominating its oil exports in dollars exclusively in order to enable it, when its link to gold was cut, to remain attached to oil so that its supremacy over the international monetary system can be prolonged, via petrodollars.

The United States Focused on Maintaining the Global Supremacy of the Dollar

More broadly, the "BRICS"—Brazil, Russia, India, China and South Africa—have at times attempted to loosen the dollar's grip on their economies through joint initiatives. This group was most active on the international stage during the period from the 2007–2008 crisis to the rise to power of reactionary, pro-U.S. forces in India (Narendra Modi, the leader of the Hindu Nationalist Party, became Prime Minister in 2014) and Brazil (Jair Bolsonaro, nostalgic for the dictatorship, was elected President in 2018).

In turn, China, whose GDP now rivals that of the United States and whose role is a driving force among developing countries, has been designated as a target of the "pivot strategy" implemented by the Obama administration in the early 2010s in order to point the bulk of the U.S. military strike force towards Asia. Since then, political destabilization campaigns have been stepped up, from the former British colony of Hong Kong (where the leaders of the "Umbrella Revolution" thought they could make Beijing back down by encouraging Hong Kongers to withdraw their deposits from the Bank of China in 2019) to the western provinces (from Xizang to Xinjiang), with the backdrop of a still potentially explosive conflict in the China Sea over Taiwan. In addition to this, Washington was also launching recurrent attempts to isolate China economically from its neighbors. This was the initial objective of the multilateral "Trans-Pacific Partnership" agreement, which was signed in 2016 and initially involved, among the Asian partners, Singapore, Malaysia, Brunei, but also Vietnam—before President Trump ordered the United States to withdraw from it a few months later.

While there are obviously a number of factors that contribute to explain the strategic line of U.S. hegemony, let us stress that, among them, monetary issues are absolutely essential. Let us look at another important example to illustrate this argument. After the crisis of 2008 had unleashed its destructive effects all over the world from the U.S. center of power of globalized finance, some of the highest political leaders of China and Russia saw fit to propose to the international community, as early as 2009, that the different governments of the planet should unite their efforts to free their countries from the domination of the U.S. dollar by substituting it with an international reserve currency, the issuance of which would no longer be controlled by a single, overwhelming country, as it is still the case today. They also suggested that the IMF's Special Drawing Rights (SDRs) could be used as a global currency free from the exclusive interests of the United States. This proposal was immediately torpedoed by Washington.

SDRs are in fact a "fatal product" of the crisis in the international monetary system that began in the late 1960s. At that time, the IMF had tried to respond to this serious exchange crisis—which was once again caused by the United States, seeking financing for its enterprise to annihilate Vietnam—by creating an international fiduciary currency composed of a basket of 15 currencies in 1969 (before being reduced in 1981 to five, and then to four in 1999) and intended to replace gold in international transactions (see Chapter 1). Washington really did not like the idea—SDRs being a potential threat to the dollar—and, not surprisingly, stifled it. This was just before the world's economies were thrown into total monetary disorder.

As a result, very few countries have pegged their currency to the SDR, and always for a short time. The Burundian franc was linked to the SDR between 1983 and 1992, after its earlier peg to the dollar had driven it up as the local economy deteriorated in the early 1980s. In the 1990s, the Bulgarian lev was also pegged to the SDR, and later to the German mark. Following the elimination of President Gaddafi in 2011, the Libyan dinar (called the *jni* in Tripolitania and the *jneh* in Cyrenaica) was also anchored on the SDR. The latter currently represents only a tiny portion, in fact a derisory one, of the world's foreign exchange reserves. This is because, since the early 1970s, successive U.S. governments have frustrated all attempts to strengthen the SDR, using their veto power in the IMF.

The rules for a transformation towards a greater international role for SDRs could be changed by a decision that would have to be approved by an 85% majority, but the United States happens to have a 17% quote-part—share of funding, and therefore of voting power—which puts it in the position of being the only country to have such a veto power within this institution. Sometimes, the IMF, despite its dependence on the U.S. Treasury, has been known to (politely) criticize the functioning of the current dollar-led international monetary "order," asphyxiating, and to (quietly) promote SDRs—or a new international reserve currency—as a possible alternative. However, nothing concrete has been achieved so far.

It is the very prospect of a reorganization of the international monetary system, going in the direction of its rebalancing, that seems dangerous to the United States. And this is not unrelated to the threatening, even outright bellicose behavior of the United States in many theaters of military operations and on many occasions. The U.S. takeover of NATO, the expansion of its facilities in Eastern Europe (from Estonia to Northern Macedonia, via Poland, Romania or Kosovo), the support for the overthrow of the government in Ukraine or the particularly hostile campaign against Belarus are all attempts to isolate Russia and separate it from Europe by keeping the latter in a subordinate position under Washington's thumb. Just as the Trans-Pacific Partnership project was intended to block the gigantic Silk Roads program driven by Beijing, the Transatlantic Trade and Investment Partnership (known as the "Greater Transatlantic Market") aims to prevent the creation of a unified economic space on the continental scale of Eurasia.

The weakening of Russia and China—or of the BRICS group in general—both in monetary (and economic) and in military (and political) terms, with some regime changes in prospect, is therefore a fundamental objective of the strategy followed by the United States to maintain its hegemony, and especially that of its currency. For the time being, Washington continues to enclose these two countries in its network of military bases and to harass them by various means. In such a context, it is understandable that the omnipresence of U.S. armies in the Middle East does not serve exclusively to ensure their access to hydrocarbon reserves in the region—particularly since they have significant shale gas resources that can be exploited (at the risk of terrible environmental damage)—nor to control the various routes leading to these energy reserves—the Chinese are already there. It also and above all intends to ensure that the perimeter of the petrodollar sphere is protected, so as to make sure that the international fossil fuel markets continue to denominate all their transactions in dollars. Iran—and the so-called "Shiite crescent" around it—has once again entered the U.S. "line of fire" since its government stated its desire to de-dollarize its oil exports.

The Dollar Again, Still a Global Problem

Nevertheless, the U.S. dollar is unfortunately again and still the world's problem. We have seen that from 2009 onwards, the Fed flooded the planet with dollars, granting several trillions to large banks and other institutional investors through "Quantitative Easing," at interest rates maintained at zero or close to zero. Unimaginable sums of money, measured in millions of millions of dollars, were then poured into the stock markets of the South and East. This was the moment that many (non-bank) companies in these peripheral economies chose to borrow in dollars at very low rates. Borrowing in dollars then cost almost nothing. Many anticipated that the Fed would maintain its easy money policy for a while, allowing those who took on debt to renew their credit lines. Yet, as we also saw it, the Fed came to limit the application of Quantitative Easing in early 2014, then ended it in the Fall of the same year and evoked the possibility of raising interest rates. The interruption of easy money, coupled with the expectation of higher rates, but also with the perception—illusory—of an economic recovery in the United States, all of this would result in some strengthening of the dollar and, concomitantly, a weakening against it of most currencies around the world. As a result, dollar-denominated foreign debt was more heavily serviced and access to the U.S. currency became more difficult.

At the same time, international investors, who had previously set up short-term speculative operations consisting of borrowing dollars cheaply to place them in currencies with higher interest rates and benefiting from higher returns (carry trade*), began to abandon peripheral markets and to get rid of negotiable corporate securities on their secondary markets, forcing these companies to buy dollars to repay maturing debt. These evolutions not only pushed up the U.S. currency, but also dried up the flows of capital available in the South and East, increasing the risk of recession there. In the United States, where these funds were hastily repatriated, few of these "reinvested" dollars were, however, directed towards the productive sphere.

Although economic growth in the United States is higher than in other Northern countries (Europe and Japan, where it is barely above zero), it remains low. It is certainly boosted by the consumer credit system, but undermined by imbalances, inequalities, violence... In total disconnection with reality, the dollar continues to attract, and the U.S. economy continues to be the hegemony that sets the tone for all monetary policies on a global scale. Risk-averse agents seek out "greenbacks" as a safe haven. This very fact helps to fuel its global demand and push its price up. The dollar remains attractive, not so much because of an alleged U.S. economic "recovery" as because of the demand for it, and it is not so much its quantity in circulation that tends to determine its "value" on the foreign exchange market as this demand, which remains very important internationally, due to the status of key world currency that it still enjoys. For, in the final analysis, its ultimate foundation rests on the military hegemony of the United States, the only area in which it retains an indisputable "comparative advantage" over economies that are on the "wrong side" of the dollar and that must operate under the supremacy of a currency that they cannot control, and even less print.

However, such a situation, at the origin of multiple monetary convulsions for the world, carries with it serious dangers, including for the United States. Not only because a strong dollar hinders U.S. transnationals, which see the price competitiveness of their exports diminish, but also and above all because, by boomerang effect, the turmoil in the financial markets caused by the Fed's changes in monetary policy could end up having repercussions on the U.S. economy itself if they precipitated a new episode of the systemic crisis. These markets are increasingly interdependent and the foreign exchange market is globalized. The economies of the periphery now account for more than half of world output, while those of the North, weakened, are moving back. We are all entering uncharted territory where the United States is issuing trillions of new dollars and trying to force the planet to continue to submit to its undivided domination, but we also understand that we are entering an era where it will no longer be able to succeed in exporting its problems—and its crises—with impunity.

For it is no longer tolerable to survive in a world devastated by a "currency war" where the U.S. government uses the dollar as a weapon of mass destruction and has infinite ammunition at its disposal, thanks to the power of the Fed to create it without limits. It is definitely no longer possible to accept that the only agenda to be discussed with Washington is the terms of surrender of the rest of the planet, namely the imperative implementation of neoliberal national policies and the required changes in nominal exchange rates. If it is undeniable that the U.S. economy has a diversified productive structure and is capable of adapting domestic supply to external demand in a much more flexible way than elsewhere, does this justify that country's right to shift onto others the burden of necessary adjustments that it refuses to bear itself? Especially since the slow devalorization of the dollar has recently resumed, to a large extent, under the effect of the huge injections of primary money decided by the Fed since the 2008 crisis; since the monetary policies followed by the interventions of the Central Banks (open market operations) or the fixing of the interest rate (as close to zero as possible) appear to be less and less efficient; and since the link between the exchange rate and exports is weakening, while the U.S. administration—wrongly—expects a depreciation of its currency to reduce the trade deficit and stimulate domestic production.

The fact remains that, despite everything, at the present time and on an international scale, it is the U.S. dollar that is still the most important key currency by far: the currency in which almost all raw material prices are measured, in which most economic transactions are invoiced and in which most foreign exchange reserves are held; the currency in which cross parities between currencies are calculated, in which interbank exchanges are made and in which the large majority of long-term issues are carried out internationally. It is also the currency that allows for the quantification of the pressure exerted on a national currency, which operators use the most on a daily basis on the foreign exchange market and on which the guarantee of liquidity and solvency provided by the monetary authorities to the financing systems ultimately depends. Under these conditions, there is still a long way to go before we are able to free ourselves from the supremacy of the dollar. However, given the current damage caused to the world by the global monetary disorder, is this liberation not the most desirable outcome from a collective point of view?

References

Amin, S., G. Arrighi, A.G. Frank and I. Wallerstein (1982), *La Crise, quelle crise?*, Paris: François Maspéro.

Brand, M. and R. Herrera (2015), "Dollar Imperialism, 2015 Edition," *Counterpunch*, 6 March, Petrolia (CA).

Chomsky, N. (2017), *Les Dessous de la politique de l'Oncle Sam*, Montreal: Écosociété.
Foster, J.B. and F. Magdoff (2009), *The Great Financial Crisis*, New York: Monthly Review Press.
Herrera, R. (ed.) (2003), *Cuba révolutionnaire: Histoire et culture*, Paris: L'Harmattan (collection Forum du Tiers Monde).
——— (2005), "When the Names of the Emperors Were Morgan and Rockefeller," *International Journal of Political Economy*, vol. 34, n° 4, p. 25–49, New York.
——— (ed.) (2020), *Imperialism and Transitions to Socialism*, Bingley (R.U.): Emerald.
Hudson, M. (2003), *Super Imperialism: The Origin and Fundamentals of U.S. World Dominance*, London: Pluto Press.
Marie, J. and S. Charles (2018), "Comment Israël a évité l'hyperinflation?," *Working Paper*, n° 10, Villetaneuse.
Zinn, H. (1980), *A People's History of the United States*, New York: Harper & Row/HarperCollins.

3

Europe, Between Aporias and Dead Ends: *From the Straitjacket of the Euro to the Logic of Every Man for Himself*

> *Unser Artillerie hat ein ordentlich Kaliber (…). Die Schweden, die haben verflucht schlechtes Geld, (…) Mit Pomade bezahlt den Franzosen sein König. Wer kriegt so prompt wie der Preuße sein Traktament?*
>
> Our artillery is of impeccable caliber (...). The Swedes cursed their bad money, (...) The French are paid by their king by buttering them up. Who gets his pay as quickly as the Prussian?
>
> Song of the grenadiers of King Friedrich II of Prussia (1837)

For more than 40 years that neoliberalism has imposed its diktats on monetary policies in Europe, no large-scale alternative experiment has really been attempted on this continent, except in France between 1981 and 1986. In this respect, this moment deserves special attention. However, even this original episode came up against the "wall of money," as we shall see, and in the end had to limit its ambitions and give up on real structural change. The financial markets quickly took over and dictated their law to the French executive—which, it is true, proved to be without genuine convictions. The main reason for this failure, in addition to the lack of consistency and firmness of political decision-makers,

R. Herrera, *Money*, Global University for Sustainability Book Series,
https://doi.org/10.1007/978-981-19-2848-2_3

was the choice to remain within the strict framework of Europe's monetary institutions. For the construction of the latter had seen their pace accelerated since the early 1970s as a consequence of the U.S. dollar's unpegging from gold and the tipping of the capitalist world system into the chaos of generalized floating exchange rates. At the time, the response of the member countries of the European Economic Community (EEC) was to provide a counterweight by forming a zone of relative exchange rate stability. But a Europeanist and neoliberal orientation has since presided over France's destiny. And it is this same direction that largely explains the trajectory taken by the socio-political convulsions in this country. Nevertheless, the process that eventually led to the establishment of the European single currency, the euro, is proving to be an unbearable straitjacket for the French people, as it is for a large majority of other Europeans.

Monetary and Financial Aspects of French "Socialism" (1981–1986)

From May 10, 1981, a "socialist" experiment was conducted in France. It took mainly the form of a policy to revive the economy, but this remained isolated. And for good reason, the international context was anything but tranquil. Faced with the recession following the second oil crisis, the Western European reaction was to implement austerity policies, under the impetus and leadership of the Federal Republic of Germany (FRG). The French left came to power only four months after Ronald Reagan's presidential term had begun in the United States, and Margaret Thatcher had been Prime Minister for two years in the United Kingdom. The U.S. and British governments had already begun to implement their neoliberal macroeconomic programs. The immediate effect of these measures, which were put into effect under pressure from high finance and directly inspired by the monetarist theses that were gaining ground, was a vertiginous rise in interest rates, to the benefit of rentiers. In May 1981, the Fed's funds rate returned to its highest level of 20.0%—an all-time record since the Second World War, previously reached in March and December 1980 (to combat a double-digit inflation rate of 14.2% and 12.6% respectively on those two dates), and again a third time in February 1981, as Paul Volker wanted to mark the occasion after the inauguration of President R. Reagan. Such heavy interest charges were deteriorating the financial situation of French companies, especially those indebted in dollars. After weakening almost continuously between 1973 and 1978, the U.S. currency was now rising, appreciating since the end of 1979 with each tightening of the U.S. monetary strategy.

Under President Mitterrand, the government of Pierre Mauroy clearly announced structural reforms. Nevertheless, the nationalizations were much more modest than expected. They still involved 39 banks and two financial companies. The balance of power at the top of the government, which was not very favorable to the progressives, had in fact led to the threshold of deposits and liquid investments that were to lead to the State taking control being raised to one billion French francs, when it had initially been set at 400 million—which would have involved 47 additional banking and financial entities. It is whispered that certain bankers, warned of the danger that was coming by some high-level connivances, hastily organized themselves in order to transfer the bulk of the "expropriable" assets to safe havens on the other side of the borders (in particular, the one that slips so nicely, and so discreetly, between the Alps and the Jura). The former shareholders of the nationalized banks received, as compensations, bonds guaranteed by the State and spread over 15 years. This was already good. But far from enough for them.

Fiscal activation, aimed at supporting public enterprises seen as the spearhead of development, increased spending and widened the deficit. Monetary control was loosened to accompany the revival's stimulus, but as the State needed more means of financing, taxes were increased without compensating for the additional costs, so that the public debt grew. While French domestic demand increased in 1982, demand from abroad decreased. Therefore, the trade deficit worsened, as did the current account deficit; hence a persistent pressure on the franc on the foreign exchange market. More fundamentally, the structural weaknesses of the French economy (including those related to dispersed specialization, narrow comparative advantages, lack of competitive clusters, etc.)

made price competition untenable for exporters at times of overvaluation of the national currency, while undermining all possible attempts at undervaluation.

Speculative attacks on the French franc—which pre-election uncertainties had dragged to the bottom of its fluctuation range against the deutschemark—were unleashed again after the victory of the left, consuming a significant part of foreign exchange reserves and causing a hemorrhage of foreign currency through capital flight and purchases of foreign securities by (rich) French residents. The government defended the franc so that its central rate would not diverge from the concerted floating margins of the European Monetary System (EMS*), which resulted in interest rate hikes (up to 19%) and tighter exchange controls. The strong appreciation of the dollar, which followed the Fed's funds rate hike and allowed the United States to attract permanent capital to its coffers, accentuated the price effect of higher oil prices on the deterioration of the balance of payments and thus increased the external debt of the State (long-term) and of the nationalized banks (short-term) to a worrying degree. The government launched an international loan in 1982, then another with the EEC in 1983—and even contracted, under the radar, a complementary "secret" loan to the Saudi royal family... Indebted, France had to change the parity of its currency.

The franc was devalued three times during the period 1981–1983, its effective exchange rate losing 20% of its value in the meantime. These successive currency readjustments were to increase competitiveness gains, and thus exports, and ultimately the profits of domestic firms. The June 1982 devaluation was associated with a freeze on prices and wages—with wages being de-indexed from prices. From then on, priority was given to fighting inflation in order to curb demand and reduce the external deficit—even though the impact of imported disinflation was in fact partly offset by the appreciation of the U.S. currency. The country's monetary policy returned to its course interrupted in 1981. The integration of the franc into the EMS—a system designed as a counterweight to the dollar—had marked the end of competitive devaluations, which was supposed to put an end to the spiral of currency depreciation-imported inflation-new depreciation; and, as a result, what was sought from then on was the chain of a "German-style" virtuous circle, i.e., currency appreciation-disinflation-new appreciation.

In the past, the logic of low growth, but enhanced by a strong franc, had never really worked in France, for reasons related to the structures of its economy and trade. However, it was on the path of such monetary orthodoxy that the left embarked. With its "strong franc" strategy, aiming to regain the confidence of the markets and placing the defense of the exchange rate at the top of the economic policy hierarchy, the government put an end to the revival stimulus, hardened liquidity controls, tightened the money supply bands, reduced the financing of the budget deficits through money creation, increased the influence of interest rates in regulating the economy, limited the demand for credit and—the last shame for "socialists" —generalized all-out market mechanisms. The return of the austerity policy accelerated in 1984. At the cost of causing a demand slowdown, the adjustment corrected imbalances by prioritizing the consolidation of the franc and corporate accounts by controlling price (and wage), as well as the quantity of money in circulation.

The Mechanisms of Regulation (of the State by the Financial Markets)

The paradox is that in France, the driving force behind the expansion of the financial markets was none other than the State. It was the State, historically very dirigiste as it is known in this country, that took the initiative to "modernize" the financing system. But one original feature of France is that neoliberalism was introduced by governments that claimed to be "socialist." They were the ones who chose not to go back on the European commitments, and first of all not to leave the EMS. And they were also the ones who promoted the rise of supposedly "efficient" financial markets—in particular to better manage Treasury issues.

The model followed was that of the process of deregulation and decompartmentalization of the monetary-financial market launched in the 1970s in the United States, from Chicago and New York, and the Big Bang of the stock market in the City of London. These "reforms" gradually subjected France to the domination of high finance. In Paris, the stock market was unified, the bond market was perfected, the short-term money market was reorganized, while the interbank or "monetary" market was opened to non-bank operators and expanded by the launch of new negotiable investment instruments that favored the raising of short-term capital, thanks to the "*billets de trésorerie*" for non-financial companies (the equivalent of U.S. commercial papers*) and the "*certificats de dépôt*" issued by credit institutions (copied and pasted from U.S. certificates of deposit*).

The aim was also to reduce "distortions of competition" within the financial sector. The way was paved by the implementation of the 1983–1984 banking law, which established a standardized regulatory regime for credit institutions, and by the creation of new tax-free vehicles. The accelerated growth of the markets was encouraged by a series of financial innovations. The provisions in favor of savings were consolidated. The sophistication of the equity and bond markets deepened: the first, with the arrival of options and the creation of the second market of the Paris Stock Exchange (1983); the second, following the model of the U.S. futures markets, through the opening of the futures market for financial instruments (in 1986), on which tools representing a wide variety of assets (currencies, Treasury bills, etc.) were traded by standardized contracts, with transactions giving rise to delivery at maturity, or to variable-rate formulas. Derivatives were in the spotlight.

Thanks to these "socialists," patrimonies remained largely untaxed. Dating from the 1970s, the privileges granted to owners of capital by the favorable tax regime for stocks and bonds were not called into question, and the interest rates paid were maintained at sufficiently high levels, in real terms, to guarantee comfortable yields. The markets were already saturated with speculation: it was enough to use the hedging solutions against risks (of exchange rate variations or others), which the deregulated, flexible and globalized markets had made necessary, to take a position without counterparty and hope to unwind an operation by multiplying one's stake… That is to say, in the strict sense, to speculate. The promotion of the financial markets resulted in a surge in transaction volumes and prices on the stock market. Bond issuance doubled between 1982 and 1985, with equity issuance doing almost as well. Returns on equity securities were +29% from 1982 to 1985 (compared to +2%

from 1977 to 1981, under the right), those on bonds +11% (compared to −1% over the five years before the arrival of the left in 1981).

State intervention was everywhere hampered by market mechanisms. Furthermore, the nationalized banking sector was never used as an instrument for redirecting financing towards the sectors deemed most strategic for national sovereignty. It was called upon to provide financial support to the ailing public industrial sector, but not much more. It kept its management autonomy intact and even had a free hand to reduce its workforce by laying off employees...

During the year 1985, as the dollar and oil prices fell, the disinflationary process in France was self-sustaining and the financial situation of domestic large companies began to recover, but not investment. Expectations of market outlets and opportunities continued to be hampered by a sharp contraction in demand and real interest rates that were falling but still high, which meant that the profitability of production projects was most often lower than that of financial investments.

From the "Strong Franc" to Frankfurt

West German Chancellor Helmut Schmidt's "theorem" that "today's profits are tomorrow's investments and the jobs of the day after tomorrow" had no chance of being realized in the neoliberal era. Especially since such a virtuous circle would be challenged as long as the "socialist" government applied a low-intensity "growth model" with disastrous socio-economic effects. The austerity policy left an economy with restored internal accounts, but weakened by external debt. Neoliberalism mobilized State interventionism, heavily, especially to consolidate the power of financial oligopolies. And this at the cost of a regression in the income of the working classes, mass unemployment and the crushing of social demands. As a matter of fact, the priority was clearly on the external component of monetary policy, that is, the exchange rate policy, the "strong franc" policy, placed at the top and commanding its internal component, i.e., liquidity control and disinflation. This was what allowed the rentiers to get richer thanks to very high interest rates in real terms. To curb inflation was, in their minds, to make the class struggle disappear…

It would have been possible, however, by relying on the popular mobilizations available at the time, to strengthen the means of the State to attack this "money wall" and to try to demolish it, to move towards social justice and to initiate a process of transformation of society—which would have implied at that time, very probably, an exit from the EMS. Instead, it was decided not to question European monetary integration. The French "socialist" governments that followed (1988–1991 and 1997–2002) continued, in parallel with privatizations and wars, the construction of this increasingly neoliberal Europe: from the Single Act in 1986, liberalizing capital movements, to the Maastricht Treaty in 1992, which, while the speculative fury of finance was testing the solidity of the EMS, opened the headquarters of the *Europäische Zentralbank* (European Central Bank [ECB]) in Frankfurt and established the European Union, providing for an economic and monetary union… and the creation of the euro.

In one way or another, all the popular resistances which, in the national framework, have been brought to struggle against the neoliberal steamroller bear the imprint of the anti-social and anti-democratic stiffening which characterizes the European Union, in particular in view of the formation of the euro zone. This was the case, for example, of the great strikes of November–December 1995 against the break-up of the pay-as-you-go pension system—strikes that were the most massive social movement in the country since May 1968. This "reform," intended to reduce public and social deficits, was part of the roadmap to "qualify France for the single European currency," as required by the Maastricht Treaty. This meant keeping a strict eye on administration accounts and wage trends, but also plugging the "holes" in social security and pension schemes. France was to be governed by an absolute austerity, in fact a German rigor, almost like that which had just engulfed the Democratic Republic (GDR).

From that moment on, monetary policy was no longer a domestic matter, to the point where it completely escaped French decision-makers, due to the implacable logic of the euro that was emerging. On October 25, 1995, Jacques Chirac, who had been President of the Republic for less than six months, forgot his election campaign promises ("to reduce the social divide") and went to Bonn to assure the Federal Chancellor of Germany, Helmut Kohl, of his determination to ensure that France respected, at all costs, the criteria dictated by the other side of the Rhine to adopt the single currency. Paris was moving into the era of Maastricht, the "Stability Pact" and the fight against internal imbalances. Soon after, speculators began to moderate their attacks on the franc.

Ten years later, in the referendum of May 2005, the French rejected by 54.68% the project to constitutionalize neoliberalism in Europe. Brussels, normally so prolix and quick to give lessons in democracy to the South and the East, found nothing to object to when in 2007 another French president, Nicolas Sarkozy, signed the Lisbon Treaty, taking up the previously rejected constitutional text. Before having it ratified in 2008, undemocratically, authoritatively.

Box 3.1 Germany haunted by its past: Hyperinflation, Deflation, Ordoliberalism and the Bundesbank

In 1918, Germany, which had came out of the First World War defeated, was in turmoil, and it was not much for significant parts of the demobilized army to side with the *Spartakusbund* insurgents and to turn the tide of the revolution. However, the Spartakists were finally crushed in blood in 1919, and the successive shocks of hyperinflation (which reached its peak in 1923), and then deflation (1930–1932), both painful for the German people, and caused by the brutality of its dominant classes, paved the way for fascism, with the consequences that we know.

At the time of the Treaty of Versailles (1919), the representatives of the French President of the Council, G. Clémenceau, tried to make Berlin collapse under the weight of reparations, just as O. von Bismarck, Chancellor of the German Empire, had in the past burdened the French people with a debt whose repayment was a condition for the withdrawal of the occupying troops (1870)—a debt that the reactionary government of A. Thiers had then committed to paying, thereby helping to hasten the outbreak of the Commune of Paris (1871).

The constraints linked to the settlement of reparations, as well as the cost of the occupation of the Ruhr—notably through the assumption by German employers and the State of the wages of striking workers during the episode of "passive resistance"—contributed to accelerating the post-war inflation rate. Nevertheless, the triggering of the exceptional and complex phenomenon of hyperinflation in 1922–1923 had to combine a number of factors, among which: the organization by the ruling classes of budgetary and tax laxity and the expansion of the volume of official means of payment (in a context of increased public war debts); the multiplication of private currency issues (including by large companies) and bank credits (the shareholders of these same firms often converting their loans into dollars or pounds sterling in order to speculate on the fall of their own national currency); the breakdown of confidence in the fiduciary money and government securities; and the use by the employers of wage increases in order to stem the revolutionary thrust... What is important to remember is the responsibility of these ruling and dominant classes—their frenzy for profits, exacerbated by the contradictions between their fractions (capitalists/rentiers, German capital/foreign capital, etc.)—in these events; those that sustained hyperinflation, as well as the extreme austerity that led to deflation in the early 1930s.

The man of the hour, as well as the one of the great German capitalist groups, was Hjalmar Schacht. President of the Reichsbank, he managed to break the inflationary spiral from November 1923. Ten years later, as Hitler's Minister of the Economy, he invented the "MEFO bonds," backed by a fictitious entity, by which he replaced gold exchanges by a system close to bartering and thus concealed, with the complicity of big capital (Krupp, Siemens...), the German rearmament, bypassing the foreign exchange market (and the accounting books) for almost half of the foreign trade of the Third Reich.

The current of thought on ordoliberalism (*Ordoliberalismus*), which emerged in the 1930s, was strongly influenced by this tormented history. Its proponents, attached to the principle of price competition and the non-alteration of market mechanisms, consider that money poses a particular problem: an efficient banking system—i.e., one that functions thanks to competing banking institutions—risks granting too much credit, in other words, creating too much money, and thus, in their view, causing inflation and, in the end, damaging the purchasing power of depositors. Traumatized by the chaos of the post-First World War years, ordoliberals expressed a marked distrust of the State and preferred a Central Bank, as guarantor of the general interest in monetary matters, that could not be manipulated by the government nor be used as the latter wished to finance its budgetary expenditures; in other words, that was independent of political power. The State, for its part, will have the fundamental mission of ensuring that the institutional environment of competition between economic agents is guaranteed.

In June 1998, the European Central Bank (ECB) took over from the European Monetary Institute (EMI), which had been created by the Maastricht Treaty with the intention of preparing for the establishment of a "transnational" Central Bank and a common monetary policy with a single currency. It was modeled on the German (federal) Central Bank, the *Deutsche Bundesbank*, which had been itself the creation of the ordoliberals—who had established the *Bank Deutscher Länder* in 1948 at the time of the unification of the sectors occupied by the Western armies and the introduction of the deutschmark. The reunification of Germany in 1990, when the mark was overvalued in the East, shattered the GDR's productive apparatus and heralded what awaited the Europeans of the euro zone a decade later. But in the end, is inflation still the curse waved by successive German leaders if the debt is well controlled, repaid by a fairer tax system and likely to boost economic activity? It is true that European debt is used for other purposes: the objective of these same leaders, who are in favor of austerity for their peoples, is above all to save the big banks by recapitalizing them with taxpayers' money!

The Euro, a Monetary Straitjacket

Let us be clear: the single currency does not stem in any way from the will of the French people, nor, besides, from that of the other nations of Europe—the "cradle of democracy," as one says. The vast majority of the governments of the countries that have accepted it have not wanted to organize referendums on the subject, with the aim of obtaining the assent of their respective populations, for the reason that it is very likely that their results would have been unfavorable, and therefore would have blocked entry into the euro zone, as happened in Denmark in 2000 or in Sweden three years later. The euro has been in circulation since 2002 in its fiduciary form (coins and banknotes), but since 1999 already in its scriptural use (writings in the accounts of banking and financial institutions). It is the culmination of the process of creating a single currency within the Union, and more precisely the Economic and Monetary Union. While this project was part of a logic of integration of the continent actively supported by the United States after the war, it was accelerated when the U.S. administration switched the international monetary system to exchange rate flexibility in the 1970s in order to maintain the supremacy of the dollar in a different way.

The euro took over from the European Currency Unit (ECU), which had been created in 1979 to stabilize the currencies of the EEC member countries, but was used mainly for trade between Central Banks and for financial investments. At present, this euro zone, in the strict sense of the word, includes 19 countries of the European Union, which have adopted the euro as their exclusive currency—plus a few (small, even tiny) States of the continent that also use it: Monaco, Andorra, San Marino and the Vatican City, as well as Montenegro and Kosovo, which are authorized to do so, and Bosnia-Herzegovina, which has replaced the "convertible mark' and by special agreement with Germany.

In reality, European integration has been very badly designed since the beginning and the 1957 Treaty of Rome. Conceived by the biggest capitalists, it was built without its citizens, and even, in fact, against them. Bestially bleeding Greece and the other "PIGS" (Portugal, Italy and Spain, according to the expression so graciously disseminated by the media at the behest of high finance), the serious problems experienced by the euro zone, from 2010 onwards, in the wake of the systemic crisis that started in the United States in 2008, are also and above all to be understood in their connection with the very foundations of the European construction: as a "fatal product" of the risks associated with fluctuations in the foreign exchange market and a defensive reaction to the disruptions caused by variations in the U.S. dollar, the ruling classes wanted to make believe that it was possible to create a single currency without a State, and without a political Europe really existing.

The initial mistake was to pretend to be able to force structurally heterogeneous economies to converge—under German tutelage—without any real consolidation of European institutions on a regional scale. As long as no effort is made to provide European budgets with the resources they need and to make the redistributions that are essential for such intra-regional convergence, as long as no serious consideration is given to homogenizing tax regulations, and even less to social harmonization "from the top" in the direction of progress, it does not take a seasoned expert to see that, without solidarity between countries, we will not have an "optimal currency area*."

The European Union is above all a space for the domination of the *Konzern*, the German oligopolies. In order to assert their interests, they defend this new deutschemark, which is *de facto* the euro. It is precisely for this fundamental reason—and also because of a strong Atlanticism—that the British have always wanted to stay out of this zone and that they have recently reactivated, despite sharp tensions and internal dissensions, the spring of their monetary sovereignty. The Union, which today constitutes a regional block of central power composed of 27 member countries, is a supra-State construction designed to maintain relations—not of equilibrium, but—of imbalance between its participants; in other words, to establish a system of deficits and surpluses aimed at transferring wealth to Germany through the mechanism of the single currency. Germany succeeded in getting most of the countries in the Union, and even some outside the euro zone, to ratify a budgetary treaty ("on stability, coordination and governance") which, by imposing structural deficits close to zero, prevents any revival or recovery policy.

The absorption of the GDR (by the monetary union of July 1990), and then (shortly after the fall of the Soviet Union) the conquest of the *Hinterland* corresponding to Central and Eastern Europe, only extended the sphere of influence of German big capital, institutionalizing its very special vision of neoliberalism on a continental scale. After the Cold War, German capitalists, led by Deutsche Bank (with the French following meekly behind), broke away from their national base and transformed themselves into financiers, in order to promote a type of indebtedness of the European Union's partner countries that would guarantee them in return full access to all local markets. The objective here was not to homogenize this regional bloc, but rather to "hegemonize" it. It was a question of imposing German domination on an economic area that became all the more heterogeneous as it expanded eastwards.

Imperceptibly, Germany benefits from a euro that is almost at parity with the old deutschemark, or perhaps even slightly undervalued, which favors its companies, whereas all the other countries in the euro zone, with a few rare exceptions (such as Luxembourg), are on the contrary penalized by a *de facto* monetary overvaluation, which handicaps their national production systems and hinders their domestic companies, less competitive in exports. In a context where a large majority of foreign trade takes place between E.U. member States (about two-thirds), German (plus Luxembourg) trade surpluses correspond to a very large extent to the deficits recorded by the other European countries, which weighs even more heavily on the economic growth rate of the latter. The resulting drop in their demand for imports from abroad is, in turn, detrimental to Germany itself. It is understandable that, in order for the Germans themselves to accept the absurdity of such a dynamic chain of events, the immediate benefits of crushing their neighbors must surely be substantial.

However, by construction, the countries that have adopted the euro are forbidden to adjust the exchange rate in such a way that they can absorb their trade deficits—something that was still potentially possible in the EMS era. This rebalancing must then take place through another form of "devaluation," this time not external, but internal, that is: the compression of domestic wages. This is most often achieved through wage austerity, which is accompanied by a permanent reduction in the purchasing power of indirect incomes (social benefits and assistance, pensions, etc.). And the height of absurdity, or cynicism, is reached when one knows that instead of being reinjected into Europe where, despite relatively high average living standards, social needs are obvious, the surplus savings generated by Germany are placed on the international financial markets, mainly in the United States, to finance the colossal deficits of the latter. Meanwhile, the deepening liberalization of capital transfers tends to condemn an entire continent to austerity, with its implications in terms of insecurity for the world of labor, a decline in the social functions of the State and generalized stagnation. This path is a losing one for Europe, including for Germany, which is exhausting itself trying to stifle the others. The control of the currency is thus confiscated by a technocratic Eurocrat elite that bends to German diktats. Despite timid attempts at autonomy, Berlin does not dare to encroach on the interests of U.S. decision-makers, who are themselves ultimately under the control of high finance, according to a relentless hierarchy of powers. Let us not forget this: the purse strings are tied in Frankfurt, but the German territory is still dotted with dozens of U.S. military bases...

Every Man for Himself as a Collective Operating Mode

In the early 2010s, the euro zone experienced its most serious crisis, which is often presented as a direct result of the excessive public debt of its member countries. Nevertheless, no one is unaware that the subprime crisis, which originated in the United States in 2007 and was linked to the unbridled speculative behavior of high finance, forced the governments of the North, which are usually so stingy when it comes to social budgets, to finance without limit the rescue of the large shareholders of the financial oligopolies, which everyone knows are responsible for the general disaster. These massive State interventions have increased public debt inordinately. Obviously, the idea was to pass on these burdens to their respective peoples, the very peoples on whom restrictive budgetary policies have been imposed for decades. These debts, which are unbearable for public finances, cannot be repaid, especially since between the launch of the euro (2000) and the outbreak of this "debt crisis" (2010), the performance of the European economies that have adopted the single currency has been disappointing, not to say mediocre, even (above all?) in Germany. GDP growth rates are very low and social indicators are not improving.

In Greece, against the background of serious initial imbalances in public accounts, the crisis reached a truly worrying scale. From there, it quickly spread to Southern Europe (from Italy to Portugal and Spain) and beyond (to Ireland), and almost took out the euro zone itself in 2011–2012. As early as 2010, the Greek government asked for emergency financial assistance from the IMF and the European Union bodies, i.e., the ECB and the European Commission—the three of them together forming the so-called "troika." In return, the country was required to implement an austerity program that would not only cut wages and social budgets, but also plunge the economy into a long and deep recession. However, what was at stake, beyond the survival of the euro zone, was the preservation of the interests of the financial oligopolies which were creditors of this country. To satisfy this priority, which is the antithesis of the search for the well-being of the population, a particularly inhuman policy was deployed. Of an inhumanity that is rare in Europe; or rather, let us say, which is traditionally reserved for the nations of the South of the capitalist world system. Therefore, the Greek citizens were brought to their knees, humiliated and supplicated. Without mercy. Under the eyes of all. As an example.

In 2015, the new government formed after the success of the left in the parliamentary elections and led by Prime Minister Aléxis Tsipras was only illusory for a short time and soon submitted to the orders of the "troika." It did not consider suspending payments on the public debt, nor did it make the slightest attempt to take control of the banking system—which the Greek State had recapitalized after the shock of 2008, but without granting itself voting rights. The intention here is not to give lessons, nor to suggest that the situation was easy to deal with. Our position is simply to say that, even in such a tense moment, and despite the constraints and difficulties that seemed impossible to overcome, it was possible to resist. Among the measures available at the time, because they could be envisaged even within the framework of the current European treaties, exchange controls and capital movements were the minimum expected. The head of government, assisted by his Minister of the Economy Yánis Varoufákis, did not even try to exercise the prerogatives that were theirs. They preferred to lay down their arms without a fight and abandoned their country, bloodless, bound feet and fists, to the cynicism of the Brussels technocrats and the plundering of the financial oligopolies.

However, this singular savagery of the European leadership (Commission and ECB) is only a reflection of the fact that within the Union, all member States are pitted against each other in a merciless competition: Slovenia, Croatia and the Czech Republic will play on the relative weakness of their labor costs; Poland, Slovakia and Romania on the regulation of posted workers; the Netherlands, Austria and Malta on the taxation regimes—without being able to compete with Luxembourg and Ireland, which are unbeatable in the matter. It is revealing, in this respect, that these last two countries, apart from Germany, are the ones where, according to opinion polls, citizens are the most in favor of keeping the euro. But there is a complete and shameful hypocrisy on the part of European leaders concerning tax havens, which are scattered all over the continent (especially in micro-States, with different statuses vis-à-vis the Union, and which function as latrines reserved for the use of the ultra-rich). These facts, which may be considered regrettable, are logical in the context of a Europe that only unites its people in the jails of neoliberal policies and by the chains of a single currency. Under these conditions, it is not surprising that the credibility and coherence of this regionalization—despite being the most advanced in the world—have been altered, and that political components of very different persuasions, but increasingly unifying, act as centrifugal forces in Italy, Poland, Hungary, Cyprus...

The uncooperative logic of the hardening of financialized neoliberalism was already at work within each country, especially in Germany. In 2010, the income of the poorest decile of German wage earners was almost 20% lower than in 2000, and 80% of Germans earned less than in 2000. Even the category of senior executives lost purchasing power in the first decade of the Twenty-First Century, with only CEOs and top managers seeing an improvement in their remunerations. This logic of every man for himself, typical of the environment of economies with a flexible exchange rate regime, is nevertheless the one that prevails within this island of fixed exchange rates that is the euro zone. More generally, the reactions of the various States to the COVID-19 pandemic, vying with each other in a competition of egoisms, have only confirmed the true face of intra-European "solidarity."

To see this, however, it was enough to take a closer look at the characteristics of the ECB—at least until very recently. For it is a unique institution, among the major countries of the North. It has not been satisfied with being independent of governments—in its case, of the governments of the euro zone—as the others are. On the strength of this "independence," the ECB has also prohibited member States from borrowing from itself, including through purchases of government debt securities when issuing these instruments on the primary market. When, in mid-2010, the ECB agreed to finance the Greek government, in particular through the Securities Market Program (SMP), it did so indirectly by buying public securities from private banks and financial institutions that were selling on the secondary market for sovereign debt. Moreover, it does not allow governments to finance themselves by creating money—by running the "printing press," on the pretext of the induced risks of inflationary drift. It even refuses to allow them to grant credit to each other. All of this gives it an exorbitant power: that of forcing governments to adopt the policies that it alone deems "appropriate," that is to say, exactly in line with the interests of the financial oligopolies.

The ECB's action is therefore clearly different from that of the Fed in the United States, the Bank of Japan, or the Central Banks of other European countries which are not members of the Union, such as the Bank of England. The ECB only intervenes in the euro exchange rate to achieve one objective: controlling the inflation rate (which has historically been contained at a maximum of 2%). Supporting economic growth is not its concern, and even less so that of employment. It has been much more obstinate in monitoring the evolution of real assets, which directly concern the purchasing power of households, than it has been vigilant in controlling operations on financial assets, which have multiplied and extraordinarily expanded in recent years, to benefit only a tiny minority of privileged rich people. Surprising, and clearly exceptional when compared to its counterparts, these tasks of the ECB—the exclusive guarantee of price stability, without any monetary policy support for growth—are those which were dictated by the German monetary authorities at the time of the creation of the single currency as a *sine qua non* condition for its existence.

The ECB, an Atypical and Ultra-Rigorous Institution

It is true that the ECB's interventions have changed and are now very different from what they were, if only in the near past. Faced with the ineffectiveness of measures to lower interest rates, they have moved towards "accommodative" policies, making increasing use of so-called "unconventional" instruments—which have, however, been used later and more moderately than elsewhere. The ECB's policy thus moved from "Qualitative Easing"—which relaxed its conditions for intervening in the markets and modified the composition of the assets held without increasing the size of its balance sheet—to "Quantitative Easing"—by which the purchase of securities became massive, and more precisely sovereign securities in the first instance, and private securities in the second, which correspondingly inflated the size of these accounts.

In 2012, the "Outright Monetary Transactions" succeeded the "SMP" and corresponded to unlimited repurchases of bonds issued by the euro zone States with the aim of lowering interest rates in Southern European countries (by pushing for the reduction of risk premiums associated with a possible explosion of the euro and the subsequent repayment of the securities in a national currency that would be re-established on that occasion). In Germany, some political leaders objected to this arrangement, which they considered "illegal" because, according to them, it would undermine the independence of the ECB. From 2015 onwards, the ECB decided also to buy back private debt, creating money for this purpose, as other Northern Central Banks had already done, first in Japan, then in the United States and finally in Great Britain, to name only the largest. The aim was to avoid the trend towards deflation by supplying transnational companies with liquidity in the hope that activity could be reactivated.

These operations, which amounted to several trillion euros between 2015 and 2019, all had to be carried out in derogation of the ECB's statutes—prohibiting them, in theory. In practice, however, despite the considerable amounts of money that were injected into European financial markets, the most immediate and tangible result of these interventions was the aggravation of asset price instability and the swelling of "speculative bubbles" (as in real estate, among other sectors). On the contrary, this torrential influx of liquidity has obviously not found its way to the real economy, nor the means to "trickle down," notably through credit provided to non-financial companies and households. Clearly, the ECB used QE-type repurchase operations to pressure governments tempted not to apply the neoliberal line, by blackmailing them into substituting their maturing securities with others issued by more disciplined countries, and thus increasing the cost of financing the public debt of recalcitrant governments. In addition, some private investors could have imagined transferring their carry trade* operations to the euro, given the ECB's new arrangements, but the European institution is unable to provide the dollars that were requested. In reality, European Quantitative Easing has helped fuel the rise in the value of the U.S. currency.

On May 5, 2020, the Federal Constitutional Court of Germany handed down a very important ruling. As a matter of fact, it deemed "unconstitutional" the policy of generalization of debt purchases pursued for the past five years by the ECB, which had exceeded its mandate by extending its influence to all macroeconomic activity, beyond the strict monetary perimeter. Maintaining interest rates close to zero and supporting public debt in the euro zone would have eroded the purchasing power of German savers. The confusion is even greater, since everyone knows that the ECB prevented the bankruptcy of the big banks—starting with Deutsche Bank—and accentuated the concentration of financial capital.

The exceptional crisis accompanying the COVID-19 pandemic in 2020 only worsened the worrying trends of recent years. By March 2020, the ECB authorized an extension of the previously implemented (both public and private) bond-buying programs. So, a very large-scale rescue plan for the economies of the euro zone, initially involving an envelope of 750 billion euros, was organized by the Pandemic Emergency Purchase Program (PEPP) and intended to guarantee to States and to a selection of transnational companies (through the component of the PEPP entitled "Corporate Sector Purchase Program") the continuity of their access to credit. The ECB's new interventions have further expanded the range of securities it can acquire, which now also includes short-term private commercial assets. The fact that the giant firms receiving this generous aid are shamelessly laying off workers and cynically polluting is of little importance to European decision-makers...

Single Currency... or Common Currency?

The violence of the austerity imposed during the sovereign debt crisis on the Southern European countries, especially on Greece whose economy is not recovering, has considerably altered the already weakened unity of Europe. And the pursuit of "integration" with a hard slap is not reassuring to the most skeptical. It is becoming clear that no alternative, whatever it may be, can be found in such a framework. The European project cannot be reformed from within, by the sole logic that drives it; it must be deconstructed in order to be torn away from the grip of finance and the confrontations it foments—against Russia, of course, but also against China—, because that is not the real interest of the European peoples. It is therefore urgent that Europeans imagine and debate alternatives likely to stop the trend towards the destruction of their societies under the effect of the dogmatism and voracity of the German *Konzern*. All the more so as it is difficult to rule out any risk that one day Germany, tired of indiscipline by its side, will decide—as usual: unilaterally—on a "Grexit" excluding Greece (or another "PIGS")... or even on a "Gerxit" by slamming itself the door to tolerate only solid and loyal vassals (Austria and the Benelux countries) around it.

In the interest of the European peoples, including the Germans, it would be necessary to get out of the single currency, whose polarizing functioning accentuates the inter- and intra-national inequalities of the euro zone, and to block the gear of neoliberal economic policies that are as destructive as they are absurd. If it were almost certain that a return to the old currencies of each of the member countries could lead to the alleviation of the difficulties that their economies are currently facing, the way would be clear. Nevertheless, this is far from certain, and the opposite could even happen. There is no doubt that the current balance of power, both within the Union and within the societies that make it up, is very unfavorable to the world of labor and to progressive movements. As soon as the speculators launch their attacks on the re-established national currencies, the popular resistance, on which the governments would rely, would prove fragile, so that, in the best case, only the national capitalists would come out on top. However, the actual choice of Europe's monetary future cannot be reduced to this alternative between maintaining the straitjacket of the euro and adopting national currencies doomed to collapse. The horizon of possibilities is much wider, and its magnitude is enough to give hope.

Among the various options that are now conceivable, it is in our opinion the solution of the joint issuance of a common currency and new, reinstated national currencies that would offer the most numerous and probably the most significant advantages—at the same time as preserving the precious historical heritage of a rapprochement between European countries. This system would allow for the coexistence of a common currency and the currencies of the member States; each of which would be convertible only into this "new euro," which would dissuade speculative behavior, and linked to it by fixed parities. The latter would be adjustable when necessary to compensate for imbalances (i.e., as soon as differences in inflation rates or trade balances become too great). This common currency, an obligatory point of passage between the currencies of the member countries, would be used for transactions within the zone, which are important. Trade with foreign countries outside the zone would be carried out using the common currency obligatorily, but according to the exchange rate quotes of third currencies on the foreign exchange market.

In this variant, adapted to the current complex situation, a regional Central Bank, with a role reconfigured in relation to the ECB, would manage the common currency and its respective conversions, while the national Central Banks would see their tasks broadened and regain full autonomy in the conduct of their own monetary policy. Each country would recover freedom to determine its interest rates and to use the complete range of monetary instruments available to protect and stimulate its economy. And to extricate it from dependence on the financial markets, a thorough reform of the way public debt is financed—allowing the government to borrow from its Central Bank, with second-tier domestic banks obliged to buy quotas of the securities issued—would be essential at the same time, as would be the introduction of exchange controls. Such an arrangement is not strictly prohibited by the European Union treaties. But the process by which a common currency would be combined with the rehabilitated national currencies to replace the euro as the single currency implies transformations which are so profound that it will certainly require a challenge to these European treaties, and probably even a questioning of membership in this Union, with all the uncertainties and risks that this entails.

Box 3.2 Switzerland, that island of (monetary and banking) happiness

If the Allies had some reasons for not approving its attitude during the Second World War, Switzerland had its own for not joining the international institutions set up at the end of the conflict. For this country did not sign the General Agreement on Tariffs and Trade (GATT, the forerunner of the World Trade Organization) in 1947, nor, three years earlier, the Bretton Woods agreement establishing the new international monetary order. Among these reasons was the apprehension of the Swiss monetary authorities about a possible internationalization of the Swiss franc if they had to grant credits—and thus create money—to countries with current account deficits, as provided for in the IMF Articles of Agreement. In addition to the risk of inflation, this entailed that of a relative loss of monetary sovereignty. There was also their refusal to limit the free movement of capital and, above all, to provide information on the identity of the owners of these funds—in other words, to question the principle of banking secrecy. The Confederation, a world apart, finally joined the World Bank and the IMF in 1992, and the United Nations in 2002.

The stability of the country's political institutions and the solidity of its economic structures only strengthen the role of the Swiss franc as a key international currency. The strength of its 7,000 powerful banking and financial institutions, to which large international "investors" flock, is the main reason why this currency has become a refuge for agents seeking safe and lucrative investments, especially in times of crisis. This strength, and the industrialization of tax evasion that they have been shaping for decades. Bank secrecy officially ended between 2009 and

2018, but in practice it continues to be applied, effectively. The lifting of anonymity from 1991 did not prevent the use of intermediaries, discreet professionals in charge of opacifying the reality of the transactions carried out. In the same way, the abandonment of banking secrecy, which was decided under international pressure and which implies automatic exchanges of information with certain countries, is circumvented by the use of cascades of offshore shell companies and the mobilization of front men allowing to hide the real beneficial owner (or holder of last resort) of bank accounts opened in Switzerland. As much as to say that the business remains prosperous and, as before, not very transparent.

The "Swiss franc" was introduced as a monetary unit in 1798, then definitively from 1848, replacing the old cantonal currencies which it unified. For a time, it was associated with the French franc, the Italian lira, the Belgian franc and then the Greek drachma, from 1865 (1868 for the latter) until the beginning of the First World War within the framework of the Latin Monetary Union. It remained, alongside the U.S. dollar, one of the few currencies convertible into gold after the Second World War, on the basis of the large gold stocks that the country had built up. It is also the official currency of Liechtenstein and of Italian and German enclaves in the Swiss Confederation, linked (or having been linked) to it by a customs union.

Switzerland does two-thirds of its trade with the European Union, which is why the Central Bank (Swiss National Bank, or SNB) wants to keep its currency stable against the euro through a reserve fund. The aim is to avoid a sharp rise in the value of the Swiss franc, which would expose the national economy by damaging the competitiveness of domestic companies, especially since the euro zone crisis of 2010. A floor rate had even been set from September 2011 (at 1.20 Swiss francs to 1 euro), but this mechanism was discarded in January 2015, which brought the two currencies back to near parity. Therefore, the SNB has to sell a lot of Swiss francs to curb the rise in value, which tends to exert an effect of relative monetary inflation. The value of the Swiss currency has appreciated further against the euro, but especially against the U.S. dollar, since the beginning of the COVID-19 pandemic—with foreign "investors" placing more capital in Switzerland, while domestic agents, for their part, keep or repatriate theirs.

Starting in 2007, a subsidiary of the French bank BNP Paribas (Personal Finance, now Cetelem) offered a new investment to individuals called "Helvet Immo." These were variable-rate home loans denominated in Swiss francs but repayable in euros. Nevertheless, between the subscription and the subprime crisis, the exchange rate of the Swiss franc appreciated, which led to an increase in the outstanding capital, until it exceeded the amount initially borrowed. In 2020, a Paris court condemned this bank for spreading "toxic loans."

In June 2018, the Swiss have been called upon to decide by citizen vote on a "full currency" initiative. The idea was inspired by the theses once defended by Irving Fisher (known as "100 per cent money") or by Maurice Allais (who considered "the creation of money *ex nihilo* by the banking system" [i.e., credits granted by private banks] as a process of "counterfeiters")—two economists who are not, however, known for being progressive. This project, which aimed to reserve for the Central Bank the monopoly of money creation and to limit the State debt—hence also the burden on the taxpayer—and against which the large local financial groups and the Federal Council itself had expressed their opposition, was finally rejected.

European Countries Whose Currency Is Not the Euro...

Besides, the tyranny of the euro is felt to be intolerable by many Europeans. Among them, of course, a majority of British citizens. This reality was made clear not so much by the "Brexit"—decided after the June 2016 referendum and effective since the end of January 2021—but by the fact that the United Kingdom has continuously refused to make the euro its currency, and has never even seriously considered abandoning the pound sterling. The British pound dominated the international monetary system for more than a century and was only supplanted by the U.S. dollar in the 1950s. Although it too had signed the Maastricht Treaty, this country was the only one, however, to reject any prospect of joining a monetary union from the start. In fact, from the outset, it remained one foot in and one foot out, in order to maintain its peculiar position as an outsider to the continent and always be ready to jump off the moving European bandwagon.

In 1957, the British project for Europe—which failed—was limited to the outlines of a free trade area, with no binding institutionalization. The United Kingdom's Atlanticism, which was inescapable and congenital, aroused France's hostility and, during the Gaullist period, motivated the refusal of its membership. The latter was, however, achieved in 1973, when the U.S. dollar depreciated and concern about international currency disturbances grew. The exit of sterling from the "European currency snake" in 1972 (barely a month after joining), and then from the EMS in 1992 (two years after joining), helped to fuel mistrust of the single currency. For a while, London pretended to believe in the alternative idea of a "common currency," but did not defend it energetically. And very recently, in this logic of ambiguity and "double-dealing," it is not just the euro zone, but the European Union that no longer seems desirable, necessary and still less vital to the U.K. The City had prepared for Brexit early on, even when it seemed unlikely.

The U.K. is a country with global weight and it is not easy to impress it with all kinds of blackmail, such as that which Greece had to endure, for example. The more so as the forces behind the Brexit have combined popular disgust at the social damage caused by neoliberalism, the disappointment of local employers who are not really interested in the continental European market and the adventurous ambitions of ultraliberals who have been seduced by the appeal of unfettered globalization. National sentiment and attachment to traditional institutions remain strong across the Channel, as does a certain confidence in the benefits of the old Commonwealth—bringing together countries such as South Africa, Nigeria, India, Pakistan, Guyana, Jamaica, Canada or Australia and even, in Europe, Cyprus or Malta. The U.K. is the former world hegemony, very closely linked to the current one (the United States), with a seat on the United Nations Security Council, a powerful military arsenal and the second largest economy in Europe, after Germany, ahead of France. For a country like that, therefore, national sovereignty matters. And we saw this again during the COVID-19 pandemic.

In addition to this, and for the moment, some members of the European Union are keeping their own currency, not pegged to the euro, in anticipation of adopting the latter soon, as soon as the conditions for participation in the European "Exchange Rate Mechanism" (in its second version, called "ERM II," since 1999) are met. Poland, Hungary, the Czech Republic and Croatia are in this situation, which implies a so-called "automatic" adoption of the euro—if these requirements, technically comparable to "convergence criteria," are met and if the process functions "normally." The integration process would take longer for Romania, but the same path is already set. Following their application to join the European Union, the governments of Serbia and Turkey have expressed on various occasions, albeit with reservations, their desire to eventually join the euro zone, but talks have been slowed down by a number of obstacles, including the fact that their monetary authorities do not yet have an issuance board to ensure the convertibility of the Serbian dinar and the Turkish lira, respectively.

Denmark, on the contrary, has so far preferred to keep its national currency, the krone (*kroner*). As early as 1992, the Danish government successfully negotiated an opting-out clause allowing the country to remain outside the (then) future euro zone. This attitude was confirmed in a referendum held in 2000, which decided against joining the euro zone. Unlike in France five years later, this result was respected, even if it provoked aggressive attacks on the single currency on the foreign exchange market at the time. Nevertheless, the Danish krone, which participates in ERM II, is still linked to the euro, since the Danish Central Bank maintains its exchange rate within narrow and tightened fluctuation margins (officially ±2.25%, in practice less than 0.50%). This arrangement is reminiscent of the one that pegged the krone to the deutschemark before the introduction of the euro (between 1982 and 1999). The Danish krone is also used in Greenland and, in a specific form, in the Faroe Islands—both of which remain dominions outside the European Union and thus, in any case, beyond the reach of the euro zone.

Sweden, for its part, accepts the euro as a means of payment on its territory, but is deliberately blocking its participation in ERM II so as to prevent the disappearance of its national currency (krone or *krona*), and thus *de jure*, strictly "compulsory" entry into the euro zone. Bulgaria has found itself in a similar situation, although it is only at the stage of applying for integration into the European Union. After attaching the lev to the deutschemark in 1999, then to the euro, with a currency board, and moving closer to the euro zone to join in 2009, the process was postponed during the crisis of 2010–2011, until the Bulgarian government made it known in 2012 that it no longer wished to give up its national currency—even though the European Union accession treaty does not provide for any withdrawal option and the domestic economy is *de facto* "euroised."

... or Which Are Not Members of the European Union

Apart from Switzerland, two other countries, subarctic, are also recalcitrant to the euro zone and refuse to join. Norway, the world's fifteenth largest oil producer and the largest in Europe (excluding Russia), is enjoying its rent income without having to go through the euro's wringer. The floating of the Norwegian krone, which began in 1971, was restricted only for brief interludes, when the country joined the European snake (between 1972 and 1978) or was explicitly linked to the ECU (from 1990 to 1992). However, the evolution of this currency against the U.S. dollar is mostly positively correlated with the price of hydrocarbons.

Iceland has experienced a more turbulent currency path in recent years. In the early 2000s, local private banks, carried away by a speculative madness, took on excessive debt, and very dangerously so: the four largest banks alone owed loans that exceeded seven times the country's GDP in 2007. Although the Central Bank was considered the "lender of last resort," it was unable to guarantee the repayment of such amounts. When the U.S. subprime mortgage crisis hit in 2008, they faced serious refinancing difficulties, so much so that in September–October of that year, the Icelandic authorities were forced to nationalize the three largest institutions (Kaupthing, Landsbanki and Glitnir) to avoid a total collapse of the banking system as well as the risk of bankrupting the State itself. The national currency (the *króna*) plunged, losing more than half of its value against the euro in the first 10 months of 2008, while inflation soared (to 17%) and, with it, the interest rate (to over 15%).

To get out of this situation, the aid provided by the IMF—the first in more than three decades in a Northern country—was not enough. It was necessary to "clean up" the mess (i.e., imprison bank executives who had caused the country's ruin, resign fraudulent and/or corrupt politicians, etc.) and then to find new, effective solutions—economic growth was quickly restored and was even the strongest in the OECD by 2011. The methods implemented resolutely turned their backs on the odious austerity that had bled the euro zone's most troubled countries dry: Greece, Portugal, Italy, Spain, but also Ireland...

To get out of the recession, Iceland's recipes were the devaluation of its currency against the euro and the U.S. dollar (as opposed to the countries of the Southern part of the Union, where the competitiveness of companies was undermined by a euro that was far too strong to encourage their exports), the imposition of controls on capital movements (and not the promotion of the liberalization of capital accounts), expansionary State budgets and a rise in social spending (the opposite of rigor policies), the unlimited protection of deposits of all individuals and the cancelation of credits of over-indebted households (but not the guarantee of all bank loans), and the supervision of the banking system and the enactment of stricter regulations (in particular the requirement to return to the State a fraction of the aid previously granted), but also the order to banks to support domestic enterprises and the strengthening of the Central Bank's tasks relating to the support of activity, etc. Certainly, the public debt has been diluted and the vulnerability of the economy (highly dependent on tourism) has not disappeared, but an "alternative" strategy has been tried here. And it succeeded, at least partially.

At present, the European Union is experiencing very strong tensions between its members because of the divergences induced by the euro, but also because of the inadequacy of budgetary compensations, which dramatically constrains the countries with deficit, now including France. The Union must face a redefinition of its relations with the United States—in particular in connection with the hard measures taken against Moscow and Beijing, or the sanctions imposed on Tehran. These changes are likely to lead to crises or even wars of a monetary-financial nature, potentially damaging to European interests, which seem to be widely despised by Washington.

Europe is losing ground and importance in the world at an accelerated rate, but it still remains a key player in the global balance of power. For the time being, U.S. plans are to confront Russia, striving to make Europe a battleground again. The States now without currency sovereignty that make up the European Union, all but Germany, are being subjected to the dictates of the latter, so that the continent's capitalists find themselves torn between the demands of military security, provided by the Anglo-Saxon axis, and major economic interests that call for closer ties with the emerging Far East. NATO's military deployment in Central and Eastern Europe (especially in Poland) and the economic warfare waged against Russia are designed to dissuade German capitalists from turning more to the East. The collateral damage to the Union is already there. The E.U. will probably not emerge from its deep crisis until it has established good relations with Russia, which it should regard as a partner, also a European partner, rather than as an enemy. It has no alternative in the short term but to come to terms with Moscow. In our view, the threat comes more from the U.S. "ally," whose worldwide monetary dictatorship is impoverishing Europe and putting it at great risk. The peoples of Europe may well come to regard such threat as too costly and dangerous.

References

Andréani, T. (2001 and 2004), *Le Socialisme est (a)venir*, 2 Volumes, Paris: Éditions Syllepse.

Arriola, J. and L. Vasapollo (2005), *L'Europe masquée*, Lyon: Parangon.

Bettelheim, C. (1946), *L'Économie allemande sous le nazisme*, Paris: Éditions Librairie Marcel Rivière.

Fonteneau, A. and P.A. Muet (1985), *La Gauche face à la crise*, Paris: Presses de la FNSP.

Harribey, J.-M. (2021), *En Finir avec le capitalovirus – L'alternative est possible*, Paris: Éditions Dunod.

Herrera, R. (2010), *Un Autre Capitalisme n'est pas possible*, Paris: Éditions Syllepse.
——— (2020), *En Lutte! Les Résistances populaires en France de 1981 à nos jours*, Paris: Éditions Critiques.
Husson, M. (2012), *Le Capitalisme en 10 leçons. Petit cours illustré hétérodoxe*, Paris: Éditions Zones.
Millet, D. and É. Toussaint (2010), *La Crise, quelles crises?*, Aden - CADTM - CETIM, Brussels-Liège-Geneva.
Mistral, J. (2014), *Guerre et paix entre les monnaies*, Paris: Fayard.
Morin, F. (2006), *Le Nouveau Mur de l'argent - Essai sur la finance globalisée*, Paris: Le Seuil.
Sapir, J. (2012), *Faut-il sortir de l'euro?*, Paris: Le Seuil.
Ziegler, J. (1976), *Une Suisse au-dessus de tout soupçon*, Paris: Le Seuil.

4

Africa Under Influence, but in Struggle: *Persistent Neocolonialism, Perpetual Debt and Neoliberalized Pan-Africanism*

Ceux qui nous ont prêté de l'argent, ce sont eux qui nous ont colonisés. (…) La dette, sous sa forme actuelle, est une reconquête savamment organisée de l'Afrique, pour que (…) chacun de nous devienne esclave financier (…). Nous ne pouvons pas être complices [de] ceux qui sucent le sang de nos peuples. (…). [N]ous ne pouvons pas payer la dette. Non dans un esprit belliqueux. Pour éviter que nous allions individuellement nous faire assassiner. Si le Burkina Faso seul refuse de payer la dette, je ne serai pas là à la prochaine conférence. [A]vec le soutien de tous, nous pourrons éviter de payer [et] consacrer nos maigres ressources à notre développement. (…) Produire en Afrique, transformer en Afrique, consommer en Afrique. [N]ous devons accepter de vivre en Africains. C'est la seule façon de vivre libres et de vivre dignes.

Those who lent us money are the ones who colonized us. (...) The debt, in its current form, is a cleverly organized reconquest of Africa, so that (...) each of us becomes a financial slave (...). We cannot be accomplices [of] those who suck the blood of our peoples. (...). [W]e cannot pay the debt. Not in a bellicose spirit. To prevent us from going individually to be murdered. If Burkina Faso alone refuses to pay the debt, I will not be there at the next conference. [W]ith the support of all, we can avoid to pay [and] devote our scarce resources to our development. (...) Produce

R. Herrera, *Money*, Global University for Sustainability Book Series,
https://doi.org/10.1007/978-981-19-2848-2_4

> in Africa, transform in Africa, consume in Africa. [W]e must accept to live as Africans. This is the only way to live free and to live with dignity.
>
> Thomas Sankara, Addis Ababa speech (July 29, 1987)

Considered in a general way and tolerating disparities, Africa is today, more than any other, a peripheral continent supplying raw materials to the centers of the capitalist world system, but also to certain peripheral or semi-peripheral countries of the South (especially Asian or even Latin American ones), in the process of industrialization. Such a position makes African economies considerably vulnerable, as they are prey to the games of international speculators on commodity prices and exchange rate differentials. As a consequence, they are permanently exposed to sudden and frequent drops in tax revenues, and therefore also in budgetary expenditures, due to the effects of fluctuations in the prices of exported (unprocessed) goods, amplified by exchange rate variations.

On the whole, the African continent remains highly dependent on foreign capital inflows and crushed under the weight of external debt, in addition to being left to the plundering of transnational corporations and bled by capital flight. With a few exceptions (South Africa, Maghreb), it is relatively under-banked—which is compensated for by informal or solidarity networks; monetization is far from being generalized; and the local financial system is not very developed. However, the sophistication of the instruments available on African stock exchanges is sometimes advancing rapidly, as, for example, on the Ethiopian Commodity Exchange in Addis Ababa, one of the commodity futures markets where derivatives are traded in Africa. But the main channel through which the impact of imported economic crises is transmitted remains the exchange rate, via trade and financial exchanges with foreign countries. Under these conditions, the choice of exchange rate regime is of decisive importance for a country.

Since the 1980s and especially the mid-1990s, marked by the multiplication of the structural adjustment programs (SAPs) imposed on most African economies by the IMF and the World Bank, market liberalization has been accompanied by a trend towards greater exchange rate flexibility, even if, from the beginning of the Twenty-First Century onwards, the move towards floating (and depreciating) currencies has been qualified by the adoption of mixed or intermediate systems—with administered interventions by the monetary authorities. Nevertheless, at present, more than half of African countries have adopted a fixed exchange rate regime, most often adjustable, which is proportionally much more than elsewhere in the world where flexible exchange rates, in their liberalized or managed versions, account for more than two-thirds of the regimes in force.

However, this predominance of fixed parities on the African continent cannot hide the fact that these countries remain prisoners of monetary dependencies from another age. As a matter of fact, the economies of the CFA franc zone, for example, will be disadvantaged by an appreciation of the euro against the U.S. dollar, both because their raw material exports are denominated in the dollar, which has depreciated, and because the pegging of their currency to the stronger euro affects the competitiveness and thus the margins of their companies.

Exchange Rates and the Vulnerability of African Economies

African economies, which are generally more extroverted and poorer than those of other regions of the world, are extraordinarily disrupted by the disorder of the international monetary system. And this, without exception. Not even South Africa, the only African country with fairly wide access to world capital markets and a banking system that is fully integrated into capitalist globalization, is immune. However, for the whole continent, exchange rate fluctuations are an inescapable problem, compounding and worsening the many problems of internal economic structures. These countries, like others in the South in general, but more so than them, can thus be violently destabilized by the downward pressure on their currencies at the time of sudden falls in raw material prices.

The links between the foreign exchange market, on the one hand, and, on the other one, the commodities market—two areas that are all the more conductive to speculation because they are relatively less regulated than the stock exchanges—are close, particularly on the grounds that, in most cases, in order to intervene in the latter, one must first have passed through the former. Countries with fixed exchange rate regimes are not themselves spared, as shown, for example, by the recurrent difficulties encountered by the cotton sectors of the "C4" group, which includes four cotton fiber exporters (Mali, Burkina Faso, Benin and Chad). These countries are suffering from the impact of disorderly and wide variations in the price of this product, in response to competition from new actors on the world markets or the arrival of synthetic materials, but also and above all with the pegging of the CFA franc to the euro and the induced behavior of speculators wishing to diversify their investments in various currencies in times of crisis.

Sometimes commodity prices are effectively manipulated by the oligopolies that dominate the various segments of these markets. As an illustration, this is what happened with the prices of hydrocarbons and mineral resources from late 2014 and early 2015. A few months later, this exogenous shock hit the GDP growth rate of several of the region's major economies hard, including Nigeria and Angola, which plunged into recession in 2016. After the fall of non-oil commodity prices, South Africa, which was also affected in 2016, only managed to rise above zero, while the growth performance of sub-Saharan Africa as a whole averaged just 1.1% that year. Therefore, between 2014 and 2016, the exchange rates of the Nigerian naira and the Angolan kwanza, which circulate respectively in Africa's two largest oil-exporting countries, but also those of the Mozambican metical and the Zambian kwacha, suffered significant depreciations—as did most other currencies on the continent, losing more than one-fifth of their value in three years, and consequently consuming considerable amounts of foreign exchange reserves to prop up their parities.

These effects of the slowdown in activity, in the short or medium term, caused by the turbulence of currencies on the foreign exchange market, themselves linked to variations in commodity prices, are amplified by a latent phenomenon of deterioration in these countries' terms of trade*. Such trends can then alter, over a longer period, the economic structures of the countries concerned by modifying those of relative internal prices. And from the point of view of domestic entrepreneurs, the weakening of the local currency leads to an immediate increase in the price of imported products, and thus to higher production costs, as well as an increase in the burden of the debt contracted in foreign currency. When combined with dollar liquidity shortages, as observed in Egypt (after 2011 and the "Arab Spring") or more recently in the Democratic Republic of Congo (DRC), business operations on the national territory are hampered—as are profit transfers abroad.

Often, the effects of commodity price changes on exchange rates reveal so-called *hysteresis* phenomena: when commodity prices revert to an upward trend after having fallen sharply, the value of the exporting country's currency may not recover by the same proportions as the previous depreciation. While rising prices in primary commodity markets in 2017 improved the exchange rate of the Guinean and Congolese (DRC) francs, or the Liberian dollar and Ethiopian birr, for example, there were nevertheless recurrent episodes of depreciation for these currencies in the foreign exchange market during the year, in part because of the fragile growth dynamics of these economies and their dependence on international capital.

To cope with the resulting pressure on their currencies, the monetary authorities are reacting in a variety of ways, within the framework and with the tools of the exchange rate regime they have adopted. Exogenous shocks can be absorbed relatively more easily by a floating exchange rate system, thanks to a depreciation of varying magnitude depending on the circumstances. Foreign exchange reserves will have to be mobilized more to defend the domestic currency if the regime has less flexibility—it is up to the Central Bank to replenish them as soon as net capital inflows become positive, that is to say, export earnings, foreign direct investment, profits from foreign investments, or private (remittances) or official (development assistance) transfers.

This is not as easy as it sounds, however, as over the 2014–2016 period referred to above, illicit cross-border financial flows out of Africa in three years amounted to nearly 100 billion dollars, i.e., roughly equivalent to the sum of development aid and foreign direct investment received by the continent. Thus, the cumulative amount of illegal capital flight between 2000 and 2015 would be greater than the total debt owed by all African countries today.

Box 4.1 Sanctions against South African apartheid and their circumvention by Western banks

The racial discrimination laws or "colour bar" implemented in the British dominion of the Union of South Africa from the end of the Nineteenth Century—with their segregationist variants in Africa (in Rhodesia [Zambia in the North, Zimbabwe in the South], Nyasaland [present-day Malawi], Kenya…), Asia (India, Malaysia, Singapore…), Australia (with its White Australia Policy) and of course the United States (with the Jim Crow Laws)—were systematized by the apartheid system imposed in 1948 by an alliance of the South African National and Afrikaner parties in power, and then after the foundation of the Republic of South Africa in 1961. More than 30 years after its abolition (1991), it continues to impede the progress of this society.

In November 1977—that is very late in fact—the members of the United Nations Security Council unanimously voted to impose an arms embargo on South Africa. Yet in September 1986, President Ronald Reagan vetoed the Comprehensive Anti-Apartheid Act passed by the U.S. Congress. Since the beginning of the Angolan conflict, Washington had supported, financially and militarily, the offensive launched by the South African army against the legitimately elected government of Agostinho Neto. Various official documents, including from the South African Central Bank, have provided evidence that the U.S. administrations of the time only partially implemented the apartheid sanctions.

Less well-known is the fact that during the period of the U.N. embargo, French arms companies, with the active complicity of their government and its secret services, also violated it on a massive scale. A branch of the Armaments Corporation of South Africa (Armscor), the South African State agency in charge of arms exports and imports, operated clandestinely within the precincts of the South African embassy in Paris—another cell of this institution was located in Israel. It was through Armscor that French arms exporters (in particular Thompson-CSF) supplied the apartheid regime, under the guise of unmarked trade, notably via West Germany and Zaire. Ultra-sophisticated Mistral surface-to-air missiles thus reached Pretoria, to be used by the South African armed forces…

Behind the ornate forced condemnations of the Swiss government, Swiss companies continued to do business with their South African counterparts right up to the last days of apartheid. Some of them appreciated that the arms embargo did not apply to trade in materials manufactured under license abroad. Banks, for their part, had only to split up their financing to their South African clients in order to comply with the ban on loans of more than 10 million francs. It is even possible that a Swiss ambassador in Pretoria, acting on behalf of the Federal Department of Foreign Affairs (then called the "Political Department"), succeeded in having the name of Switzerland removed from the statistics on international capital movements compiled by the South African Central Bank by merging it with the more vague title of "rest of Europe"...

The strategic importance of South Africa as a gold producer and exporter, as well as a relay for the domination of the central capitalist powers in Southern Africa, had motivated Western banks, especially European ones, to agree to reschedule South African debt and to stabilize a depreciating rand in the mid-1980s, when the apartheid system was on its last legs. Zimbabwe, as to it, chose a more radical path to emancipation through land reform, but did not enjoy the same favors from the major international banking institutions, which very strictly enforced the various financial sanctions against this country. Its monetary trajectory did not emerge intact.

A Variety of Monetary Policies Among the Countries with Flexible Regimes...

South Africa is, as we have said, the only African country that is not only deeply integrated into financial globalization, but also, and consequently, the only one that has a currency, the rand, that is both convertible and freely transferable. Although its GDP is only the third largest on the continent, behind Nigeria and Egypt, South Africa's economy is considerably more diversified than those of these two other countries—even if it remains dual, with masses of poverty surrounding pockets of prosperity. Obviously, South Africa, like the rest of the continent, also exports a lot of unprocessed or minimally processed natural resources, especially gold, diamonds and iron, but unlike the other economies, its industrial base is larger, fairly coherent, and many local firms export high value-added equipment. Furthermore, it has the most sophisticated financial services infrastructure and the largest stock exchange in Africa, namely the Johannesburg Stock Exchange.

Outside South Africa, the rand is also used by other countries. It is officially legal tender in the Common Monetary Area of Namibia, Lesotho and Eswatini (formerly Swaziland), alongside their own currencies, as well as in Zimbabwe (formerly Rhodesia) and, to some extent, Malawi, Zambia, even Angola, for Southern Africa, or as far North as Kenya. The Namibian dollar is pegged to it. The price of the rand is strongly influenced by the price of gold, of which the country is the largest producer in the continent (*ex aequo* with Ghana, ahead of Sudan, Mali, Burkina Faso and Tanzania) and has the third largest reserves in the world. The current exchange rate regime is floating, but "supervised"—as with the Ghanaian cedi or the Ugandan shilling—: the South African Reserve Bank, which is independent and sets an inflation target of between 3 and 6% per year, reserves the right to intervene on the foreign exchange market from time to time in order to influence the rand rate. Nevertheless, this currency still remains a quite vulnerable one. On June 24, 2016, the day after the British referendum in favor of Brexit, the rand plunged by 8%, the biggest drop since the subprime crisis, due to uncertainty about the trade-offs that large speculators were about to make between the U.S. dollar, the British pound and the South African rand…

Nigeria, the continent's largest oil producer and exporter, resisted pressure from the IMF until the second half of the 1980s, before giving in to the siren calls of liberalization. Therefore, it was the African country pioneer (or "laboratory guinea pig") for the launch of debt equity swaps*, refinancing operations through which debt holders can obtain property titles in exchange for debt cancelation, without having to advance money. The effect on the money supply and the price level will depend on the type of swap arrangement selected. Concretely, in the case of Nigeria, this scheme, encouraged by the World Bank and the IMF, has mainly allowed international capital to enter in force the ownership structure of companies that were previously State-owned. One of Africa's economic strongholds, home to its largest population, long conscious of its weight and jealous of its independence, was then taken over by Western transnational firms.

The naira, Nigeria's currency, was peeled off from the U.S. dollar in 2016 to become floating. But in the year 2020, marked by the pandemic and the downturn in hydrocarbon prices, its official exchange rate had to be devalued three times, despite emergency assistance from the IMF. The country's financing needs are mainly covered by the domestic market, which is more accessible and less expensive (the interest rate being negative on naira debt) than the global markets. To maintain its foreign exchange reserves, the Central Bank—from which the Nigerian Treasury can obtain financing—has significantly restricted access to foreign exchange for investors from abroad wishing to transfer profits from their local currency investments, whether direct or portfolio investments, into foreign currencies. Under these conditions, it is not surprising that international financial institutions are pushing hard for a more decisive disengagement of Nigeria's monetary authorities, including for the complete unification of the foreign exchange system and the removal of numerous State subsidies, particularly in the energy sector.

Under pressure from powerful donors at the world-wide scale, the Nigerian government decided in the Summer of 2018 to sign an agreement with China, the country's main supplier (India remains its main client for the time being), to open up the possibility of denominating some of their commercial and financial transactions in naira or yuan—and thus bypass the exclusive use of the U.S. dollar in hydrocarbon trade (or those, more secondary, of the euro and even the pound sterling for trade in other goods and services). For their part, the Angolan authorities had already granted the Chinese currency legal tender and liberatory power throughout their territory two years earlier (August 2016). It is true that, despite the consequent devaluation in April 2016, the kwanza continued to experience strong tensions in the foreign exchange market, which continuously reduced foreign exchange reserves and widened the differential between the official and parallel market rates. The depreciation of the Angolan currency has continued since the partial liberalization of the exchange rate regime in early 2018.

… but (Almost) All Subject to IMF Dictates

The currencies of the most important oil exporters, closely linked to hydrocarbon prices, therefore, expose their respective economies to the extreme and irrational volatility of these markets. However, this is also true for countries with a more diversified foreign trade structure, such as Egypt, which competes with Nigeria for the economic top spot on the African continent. In addition to receiving enormous U.S. military aid (less than Israel's, but still very significant), in 2016 Egypt benefited from a new IMF aid program (to the tune of 12 billion dollars), which included a series of privatizations and austerity measures at a heavy social cost.

To cope with the crisis, Egypt took its national currency off the U.S. dollar in order to let it float. The Egyptian pound, which is also used (unofficially) in the Gaza Strip, as well as in several parts of Sudan, has again become attractive in the foreign exchange market for hot money investments, attracted by high interest rates and massive issuance of public debt securities. Just as it happened in Tunisia, which also fell under the IMF's caudine forks, one of the most tangible consequences of the post- "Arab Spring" era was—in the absence of such hoped-for democratization—a decline in monetary sovereignty and an aggravated neoliberalization of the Egyptian economy. Controls on capital movements are now increasingly relaxed.

The Moroccan authorities have also locked their country in the trap of neoliberalism, especially through an ever greater flexibility of the national currency, the dirham. Led under the guardianship of the IMF, this "reform," accelerated since January 2018, is presented to the general public as a modernization of the financing system of the Moroccan economy and a means of increasing the competitiveness of the latter. The reality is quite different. Modernity is currently embodied by Abdellatif Jouahri, the old "*wali*" of *Bank Al-Maghrib* (the governor of the Central Bank of Morocco), the same one who, in 1983, when he was then Minister of Finance, established the first SAP of the IMF in Morocco. It is this same line of submission to international financial organizations and to high finance that has been followed ever since. And the IMF conditions its credits by liberalization in all directions.

In recent years, the Moroccan monetary authorities have focused their objective solely on controlling the rate of inflation. They refused direct financing of public expenditure by the Treasury, reinforced the weight of the U.S. dollar in the dirham's peg basket since 2015 and introduced terribly speculative derivatives on the Casablanca Stock Exchange, on the pretext of wanting to develop the risk hedging instruments available to economic agents. And when, in the midst of the COVID-19 pandemic, Governor A. Jouahri addressed the banks—many of which are subsidiaries of foreign establishments—to urge their boards of directors to moderate their dividend distributions, it is nevertheless necessary to note that it in no way prevented shareholders, whether national or international, from receiving record payments in early 2021—starting with those of Attijariwafa Bank, the first establishment in French-speaking Africa. Some media even sometimes made people believe in a spirit of frugality and one simulated good management (following the advice of the Central Bank to "conserve own funds to face the crisis of the pandemic") by distributing these dividends in the form of newly issued shares. It was quite tricky, but the strings could be seen with the naked eye.

In the current context, Algeria appears to be an exception: it has so far excluded any recourse to IMF financing, in the name of preserving its national sovereignty. It is an oil-producing country: the third largest producer on the African continent, with the fifteenth reserves in the world, behind Libya and Nigeria, but ahead of Angola and the Sudan (the South included). The fact of extracting more than nine tenths of its exports from hydrocarbons enables it to adopt a rather original monetary strategy. In force since 1964, replacing the French "new franc," the Algerian dinar depreciated markedly against the U.S. dollar in the second half of the 1980s during the oil counter-shock which seriously deteriorated the balance of payments, then in the beginning of the 1990s with the outbreak of the civil war and the (relative) opening of the economy. A major devaluation was decided in 1994. The downward slide resumed and continued during the 2000s, including against the Moroccan dirham and especially against the Tunisian dinar, until another official devaluation occurred in 2012 against the dollar, which accompanied sharp increases in civil servants' remunerations.

In the recent conjuncture of reduced oil revenues, and the COVID-19 pandemic, the finance law for 2021, which forecasts a budget deficit of 14% of GDP, organizes a controlled and gradual depreciation of the dinar over three years: 142 dinars for one dollar in 2021, 149 dinars in 2022, 156 dinars in 2023. Such a monetary strategy thus consists in inflating oil tax revenues by a mechanical effect linked to the conversion into national currency of income derived from exports denominated in U.S. dollars—to the detriment of the promotion of non-oil sectors or foreign investment, especially since imports remain very controlled. The government's objective is to continue to increase public spending, whether it be wage bills or social budgets, even as the revenue associated with the country's oil manna shrinks.

Like many African countries (oil Gabon, Morocco producer of phosphates, Botswana exporter of precious stones or Congo (DRC) of various minerals, as examples) and others of the rest of the world (from Azerbaijan to Norway, from Venezuela to Canada, via Saudi Arabia or Kuwait, and as far as Australia), Algeria falls into the category of economies struck by what is often called the "Dutsch disease." This is a paradoxical process, first evidenced in the Netherlands in the 1950s, leading to the deterioration of the situation of an economy which became rentier following the discovery of considerable reserves of natural resources. Among the mechanisms at work, those linked to the exchange rate occupy a decisive place. The emergence of new deposits leads to increased exports of raw materials and an influx of foreign capital come to invest in this highly lucrative extractive activity. These changes then cause the appreciation of the national currency. In other economic sectors, on the contrary, there is a deterioration in the competitiveness of local businesses, since their exports are now carried out in a strengthened currency. This chain of events can lead to deindustrialization and a decline in the agricultural sector of the country in question.

The CFA Franc, a French-Style Anachronism?

In view of these complex problems arising from floating regimes and specialization in the export of raw materials, one might think that fixed exchange rates represent the solution for the economies of the African continent. In fact, it is not the case, and perhaps even the opposite is happening, as the CFA franc shows. It is more appropriate to speak of the CFA francs, plus the Comorian one, since France is actually involved and linked to three distinct monetary zones in Africa: the West African Economic and Monetary Union (WAEMU, in French *Union économique et monétaire ouest-africaine* or UEMOA), the Economic and Monetary Community of Central Africa (EMCCA, in French *Communauté économique et monétaire de l'Afrique centrale* or CEMAC) and the Union of the Comoros. The first area uses the West African CFA franc ("CFA" here being the acronym for *Communauté française africaine*, that is, French African Community), the second one the Central African CFA franc (which in this case means *Coopération financière d'Afrique*, i.e., Financial Cooperation of Africa), and the third the Comorian franc. The first two francs are equivalent (one euro officially worth 655.957 rancs), without being however interchangeable or of comparable reputations (the West African CFA being considered relatively safer than that of Central Africa). The Comorian franc is managed separately (with a parity of one euro for 491.968 francs), but according to rules similar to those applied in the other two currency unions, more or less.

It should be noted that WAEMU brings together eight countries in the region (Côte d'Ivoire, Senegal, Mali, Burkina Faso, Benin, Niger, Togo, which were joined in 1997 by Guinea-Bissau, independent of Portugal since 1974) and relies on the Central Bank of West African States (CBWAS, in French *Banque centrale des États de l'Afrique de l'Ouest* or BCEAO), located in Dakar, while EMCCA, for its part, brings together six other countries (Cameroon, Gabon, Republic of Congo, Chad, Central African Republic, plus Equatorial Guinea, a former Spanish colony independent since 1968 which joined the Central African Customs and Economic Union [*Union douanière et économique de l'Afrique centrale*] in 1983) and is backed by the Bank of Central African States (BCAS, in French *Banque des États de l'Afrique centrale* or BEAC), located in Yaounde.

These different francs have formally replaced that of the "French colonies in Africa." More than six decades after formal political independence, the former French colonial metropolis still insists on keeping their peoples under guardianship, on the pretext of wanting to help them ensure the monetary stability of their economies. The CFA and Comorian franc system is the by-product of a monetary device that the French authorities once chose to establish in relations with their colonial empire (made up of colonized territories, under protectorate or mandate), then decided to extend in agreement with them the regimes set up during the accession to "independence," under the close control of the former metropolis.

On the contrary, the sterling area, which the United Kingdom had pragmatically instituted in order to protect the value of the pound sterling and to preserve the trade carried out with its vast colonies and the dominions which used the British currency as currency, anchor or reserve, was dismantled. Or rather it gradually disintegrated with the loss of influence on the international financial exchanges of this country, world hegemony before the United States, and of its currency, which the dollar did not replace definitively until 1945, or a little after. To quote only the African countries, left the sterling area, successively, Egypt in 1947, Sudan in 1957, Somalia (British Somaliland) in 1964, Rhodesia (Zimbabwe) in 1965, Libya in 1971, then in 1972—when London tightened its exchange controls vis-à-vis its partners—a large group including Nigeria, South Africa, Kenya, Ghana, Tanzania, Uganda, Zambia, Botswana, Namibia, Mauritius, Malawi, Swaziland, Sierra Leone, Lesotho, Seychelles, then finally The Gambia in 1978. This long list shows that, for most of these countries, some of which are very small size, the detachment of their currencies from the orbit of the pound did not lead to the imagined monetary catastrophe. The sterling area, emptied of almost all of its members, was to become inoperative as early as 1979, after Margaret Thatcher deregulated the U.K. exchange rate regime in record time—just over three months (July–October).

France has made an entirely different choice, and its African "partners," for the most part, have submitted to it. A franc zone had been created in the 1930s in order to attach to the franc of the metropolis all the currencies of the French colonial empire (or almost, since the rupee of the counters or "French establishments in India," remained pegged at that of the Indian Union). Thus, and among other examples, the Lebanese pound has lost value during a long time at the same rate as the devaluations of the French franc—that of 1969 was not, however, followed by the three Maghreb countries. During Second World War, several French territories were temporarily anchored to the sterling area. It was in 1945 that the franc of the French Colonies of Africa ("CFA") was created, but also, we will come back to this, that of the Pacific ("CFP"), in addition to the Indochinese piastre.

In 1949, the exits of the Syrian pound and the Djibouti franc (brought closer to the Ethiopian birr, itself pegged to the U.S. dollar) weakened the area of influence of the franc, but this zone continued. The divisions deepened during the waves of independence. On the one hand, several countries remained inside the franc zone, through the West African Monetary Union (Côte d'Ivoire, Senegal, Upper Volta [future Burkina Faso], Dahomey [now Benin], Niger, Togo from 1963 and, as we have just seen, Mali since 1984) or various cooperation agreements (with Cameroon, Gabon, Zaire [before the DRC], Chad and the Central African Republic). On the other hand, countries or groups of countries left the area: Indochina in 1954 (under the leadership of Ho Chi Minh), Guinea in 1958 (under that of Ahmed Sékou Touré), then Madagascar and Mauritania in 1973. Mali initially withdrew from the area in 1962 (thanks to Modibo Keita), but returned there again in 1984 (under the military dictatorship of Moussa Traoré). That same year, and the three following ones, Burkina Faso (by Thomas Sankara) did not find the means to tear itself away from this monetary heaviness, despite the radical nature of the revolutionary process initiated between 1984 and 1987. That is to say all the difficulty that there is a credible and practicable alternative to be considered.

Box 4.2 Rwandan genocidaires and their generous Western financiers
Perpetrated in 1994, between the beginning of April—following the assassination in Kigali of President J. Habyarimana, Hutu—and mid-July, the Rwandan genocide claimed the lives of 800,000 people, or perhaps a million, almost all of them of Tutsi origin, and with them tens of thousands of Hutus opposed to these massacres. Beyond the local implementers, belonging to extremist Hutu groups, Western leaders,

bankers and entrepreneurs bear responsibility in these events. This is overwhelming in the case of France, but it also engages—light will undoubtedly be made one day—an international organization established in Paris, which would have served as a cover to exfiltrate high-ranking Rwandan criminals.

Let us milit ourselves to point out that international financial institutions, the IMF and the World Bank in the lead, had supported the dictatorial, pro-Western regime of General Habyarimana with their loans, throughout the two decades preceding the tragedy. Less than 50 million dollars in 1973, when J. Habyarimana seized power, the country's external debt, mainly due to these two institutions, was close to one billion dollars on the eve of the genocide. After the establishment of the SAP in 1990 and the subsequent devaluation of the Rwandan franc by more than two-thirds of its value, IMF credits increased. Some of them enabled the government to increase its spending on defense and internal security and to import weapons. Faced with this situation, and while the genocide was in preparation, the IMF and the World Bank finally interrupted their aid during the year 1993, without however attempting to hinder arms purchases—as they could have done—nor to question the effective use of funds loaned to this reactionary regime, an ally of the United States in the region.

Most of the weapons supplied came from France. Different military equipment firms of this country, but also of other Western countries (such as Belgium), continued to supply genocidal groups, passing through the Zaire of President Mobutu Sese Seko, another ally of the United States, even after the arms embargo decreed by the United Nations in May 1994. Following the flight of the authorities responsible for the killings, the headquarters of the National Bank of Rwanda was transferred to Goma (capital of North Kivu in Zaire), under escort of the French army, in order to make payments for the final arms acquisitions in August, via European commercial banks, including Belgolaise (the former colonial establishment "Banque du Congo belge"), BNP Paribas and Dresdner Bank of Frankfurt. Besides, various trials then revealed that deliveries of arms had passed through Seychelles, that in addition to those of the Central Bank of the latter country, on these occasions accounts in Switzerland were used (at the Union Bancaire Privée in Lugano, in particular) and that South African intermediaries are also involved (including an arms broker converted after having been private secretary to the President of the Republic, Pieter Willem Botha, during the apartheid era).

From the end of 1994, the administration of the United States began to release funds destined for Rwanda, but with the sole aim of ensuring the continuity of the repayment of the debt service accumulated by the Habyarimana regime and due to international financial institutions. The latter, as the country emerged from the dictatorship and the human tragedy to which it had led, immediately demanded a tightening of budgetary austerity. Nine out of ten Rwandans were living below the absolute poverty line at the time. By agreeing to remain silent on these multiple and odious complicity, the new Rwandan government saw itself erected by high finance into an African "economic model," eligible for the Heavily Indebted Poor Countries (HIPC) program aiming to make its debt sustainable, and even associated with the military occupation of the Eastern provinces of the Democratic Republic of Congo, which the transnational powers of the North were placing in a regulated cut.

Effective Functioning and Alleged Advantages of the CFA Franc

To avoid any confusion, it is necessary to remember beforehand that the "franc" is also the name of other currencies used by countries which are not members of the three spaces of the franc zone. We thus speak of Rwandan, Burundian or Democratic Republic of Congo (DRC) francs, even if this name covers quite other realities. Burundi uses a system of multiple exchange rates, known as "at several counters." Dollarization has not prevented the DRC from experiencing several years of recession recently, and attempts to extricate itself from the grip of the U.S. currency have followed, to no avail. As for the success of the Rwandan economy, this should not be misled (Box 4.2).

So let us come back to the CFA franc. Since 1999, it has been placed in a fixed parity regime against the euro, which has replaced the French franc. The member countries of one of the areas in the zone are linked to France—and, through it, to the European Union—by a cooperation mechanism. First, the CFA franc benefits, unlimitedly and regardless of the foreign currency, from a convertibility guarantee*. The French Treasury—and not the European Central Bank (ECB)—provides it to these States on the basis of budgetary funds. In other words, it is this Treasury which acts as guarantor with Central Banks in the event of insufficient reserves in euros, imbalance in the balance of payments or inability to pay for imports. Then, the parities of the CFA and Comorian francs remain fixed with the euro. They are nevertheless adjustable, since the value in euros of these currencies can be modified. Finally, a principle of free transferability of capital is added to this: transfers relating to financial movements and commercial transactions enjoy complete freedom within each zone and to France and the European Union—while specifying, however, that, since 1993, transfers are no longer unlimited between the West and Central CFA areas, whose currencies, which are inconvertible to each other, now have more clearly differentiated statuses.

What compensation is required from African countries? This one: obligation is made—or was made until 2020, as we will see—for Central Banks to centralize part of the foreign exchange reserves that they hold in euros on transaction accounts recorded in the open books in their names to the French Treasury (up to 50% for the CBWAS-BCEAO since 2005 and for the BCAS-BEAC since 2007, and 65% for the Central Bank of the Comoros). These reserves, which are remunerated (but become chargeable when the account becomes debit), fluctuate according to circumstances and according to needs. In West Africa, for example, the widening external deficits during 2016 exerted such pressure that a significant fraction of WAEMU's foreign exchange reserves was consumed. But these reserves were able to recover in 2017, in particular thanks to the increase in gold production in Mali and uranium and oil exports from Niger.

It is often claimed that the monetary cooperation framework established by France contributes to the credibility of the exchange rate regime in force in these regions of Africa and, consequently, to the stability of their respective institutional environments because of the protection against currency fluctuations brought to agents, local and foreign.

The attractiveness of these national economic territories would also be improved for international investors due, in particular, to the very strict control of price movements, required by the peg to the euro. Inflation rates are thus systematically contained below 3%, or even 2%. Besides, the Central Bank—at least the CBWAS, not in the EMCCA—is also prohibited from carrying out any monetization of the budget deficits of the member States.

Under these conditions, individuals, considered in general, would see their purchasing power and savings better preserved, and the risks of national currency collapse and the currency race avoided, in principle. Consumption would thus be encouraged. If there were a few skeptical or recalcitrant minds left, then the specter of hyperinflation and "Zimbabwean" currency chaos would be waved before them to convince them. As regards entrepreneurs more specifically, they would benefit from an optimal growth environment, that is to say, reassuring their activity expectations and favoring investment decisions. This would be particularly true for raw material exporters whose revenues would be secured in this way, unlike those from countries with floating exchange rates who would be more exposed. More generally, the convertibility of the exchange rate being guaranteed by France, any balance of payments crisis could be bypassed. Finally, it is unnecessary to describe the deep satisfaction that free transferability provides to transnational companies, which can repatriate as they please, without risk or constraint, the abundant profits they are making on the continent. Nor the joy of the African ruling classes whose fortunes can flee unimpeded from national borders and hide discreetly far from their countries of origin.

Defenders of the CFA in West Africa put forward the argument of quite satisfactory results—according to them—recorded in macroeconomic terms by the WAEMU countries, just before the outbreak of the global crisis linked to the COVID-19 pandemic. Therefore, for the year 2019, the GDP growth rate was dynamic in the sub-region, at more than 6.0%, which is more than the average for all of sub-Saharan Africa. That same year, the increase in prices remained under control, at less than 1%, while the budget deficit had been reduced and the debt ratio limited in proportion to the wealth of nations, respectively, around 2.5% and 44.5% of the national wealth.

Limits and Criticisms…

However, the fact is that, by construction, the participants in the spaces of the franc zone see the autonomy of their monetary policy considerably undermined. To put it mildly. Concretely, they no longer have monetary sovereignty at all. They do not have in hand the instruments of devaluation, nor those of foreign exchange reserves, much less those of exchange control… The line in this field is dictated only by the French Treasury—and the ECB. The pyramid of submissions from African countries affected by the franc zone also cumulates submissions to international financial institutions—foremost among them the IMF—and of course, above all, to shareholders of the powerful global financial oligopolies.

If, in future, a devaluation should possibly occur—in particular with regard to the countries of Central Africa, as demanded by the IMF during the visit to Yaounde in 2016 by Madame Christine Lagarde (Managing Director of the Fund, before becoming president of the ECB)—, it is undoubtedly in Paris that the decision would be taken. On paper, nevertheless, a change in parities falls within the prerogatives of African heads of State and government. But the reality is quite different on the ground. For it was abruptly that they were told of the devaluations that have taken place until now (in 1948 and 1994). And this is despite the extreme violence of the impact these measures have had on the peoples. In 1994, some African political leaders were informed only through the French Minister of Cooperation. Loyal servants of Françafrique's interests had prepared the local conditions for the application of the oukaze of Paris and the IMF, as was the case, among others, of the Ivorian Alassane Ouattara who was the Prime Minister of President Félix Houphoët-Boigny just days before the devaluation of January 11, 1994. Is it necessary here to clarify that Africans had nothing to say during the changes in parities following the passages to the "new franc" in 1960 and to the euro in 1999?

It must be recognized that the CFA and Comorian francs are neocolonial currencies—in the sense that they have survived formal political independence and today prolong relationships of subordination vis-à-vis the former colonial metropolis, silencing their true nature—and which, as such, turn out to be totally unsuited to the real needs of African economies and societies. This, for several reasons.

First and foremost, the stability of the exchange rate stems essentially—less from what France would accept to bear this "burden" (as a Rudyard Kipling would say poetically) than—from the fact that the strategy imposed on African "partners" is the decal monetary policy followed in the euro zone. The currencies of these franc zones are only the current extensions of the euro on African soil, as they were previously those of the French franc, to the point that the top priority of pegging the fixed parity takes precedence over any other objective. Nonetheless, it is clear that the historical, geographic, demographic or socio-economic realities of Europe and Africa are, to say the least, different. Peripheral and even quarter-worldized in the capitalist global system, Africa has been dominated by Europe—central although having lost hegemony—and is continuing to be so today, even through the conditionality of public aid. In other words, such monetary stability mainly benefits foreign agents, from the management of transnational companies established on site to "expatriate" individuals, and this much more than to local actors.

It is European investors, and international firms more generally, and not the various small and medium-sized domestic enterprises, that benefit from the protection against the risk of exchange rate loss and the ease of fund transfers allowed by this device. Could we forget here that these zones were originally set up with the aim of providing French entrepreneurs (and adventurers) with both secure and profitable outlets in the colonial empire, within the perimeters of what formed in the past period French West Africa (*Afrique-Occidentale française* or AOF) and French Equatorial Africa (*Afrique-Équatoriale française*, i.e., AEF)? And the fact is that today, the fixed exchange rate regime does not serve even African countries in the CFA and Comorian zones to attract foreign direct investment flows. These are, for example, significantly less dynamic towards the Ivory Coast than towards Ghana, whose currency obeys a floating exchange rate regime.

To achieve this imperative of monetary stability, it is the control of price movements that is primarily targeted to the detriment of all other development objectives. The CBWAS-BCEAO is a "tropical ECB," tense by conservative reflexes and the (all German) obsession with an exclusive fight against inflation. Therefore, the monetary absurdity dictated by Frankfurt, then internalized by Paris, is reproduced in sub-Saharan Africa and imposed on its peoples. Yet it is the extreme poverty of large masses of Africans that explains the low level of consumption in the region. The purchasing powers of the populations are too weak for local enterprises to manage to sell their products, to generate sufficient profit margins and to create a large number of jobs.

Despite the situation of near-deflation observed in many West African economies, the fixed parity pegging of the CFA (and Comorian) francs on a currency as powerful as the euro harms the competitiveness of exporting companies and handicaps domestic producers. The sale of commodities invoiced in hard currency deters international customers from buying, while the lower cost of merchandises produced abroad encourages importation instead. Consequently, these changes contribute to deteriorate trade balance deficits, but even more, and more seriously, to hamper the conditions for the development of these economies. The combination of the CFA franc and the dismantling of customs tariffs cuts into the internal potential for agricultural expansion and industrialization (especially in the textile sector). Obviously, this currency, which is in fact a foreign currency, turns out to be far too strong for economies with such vulnerable structures.

Like the "strong franc" strategy formerly pursued by the *Banque de France* (French Central Bank), the "strong CFA franc" strategy currently pursued—especially by the CBWAS—has reached a dead end. The "solution" adopted is the same as in Europe: a substitute for monetary devaluation which makes exports more competitive is therefore found in a particularly destructive depreciation, in this case a fierce wage austerity, compressing all the other labor remuneration, and an increase in the rigor of public finances, with a zero budget deficit rule in the WAEMU. All this, in the extremely difficult context of African societies where the basic needs of the greatest number are far from being met.

... Limits and Criticisms Again

The mechanisms of monetary cooperation with France have in no way made it possible to develop national productions and to modify the international integration of these economies, still very largely specialized in the primary sectors of raw materials, whether agricultural goods or natural resources. The diversification of the productive structures of these countries is very limited and their extraversion exacerbated, as we have underlined. It is therefore understandable why trade relationships between members of the franc zones remain modest: it is towards the countries of the North that exports are mainly oriented. Intra-regional trade remains around 15% of total trade in West Africa and 10% in Central Africa (compared to over 60% in the euro zone).

In recent years, out of the top ten intra-African exporting countries, only two are part of one of the franc zones: Togo and Senegal (the others being Swaziland, Namibia, Zimbabwe, Uganda, Djibouti, Lesotho, Kenya and Malawi). Under such conditions, the regional integration of these economies turns out to be minimal, even though their heterogeneity is real and potential complementarities exist between them (with primary sectors [agricultural and mining] in Burkina Faso, Mali, Niger; secondary [industries] and tertiary sectors [services] in Côte d'Ivoire or Senegal; and import–export trade in Benin or Togo). What good is a single currency shared by these countries if they basically exchange so little with each other? But that does not make defenders of the CFA franc back down, who advocate more monetary integration and the promotion of financial markets at the regional level.

The supporters of the choice to abandon monetary sovereignty are clearly not hampered by the fact that the African countries of the franc zones are among the poorest in the world and that their progress in terms of per capita economic growth is very modest over the long period. More than three-quarters of a century after the establishment of the "modern"

CFA franc system (December 26, 1945), development remains evanescent in all the countries which have adopted it. Thus, of the 15 countries in the CFA zone, 11 are classified as "the least developed," while of the eight comprising the WAEMU, seven remain today in this same category. Among the many explanations contributing to this state of affairs, monetary lockout is one of the most decisive.

How can we not recognize the urgency of calling into question the mission of sub-regional Central Banks (CBWAS-BCEAO and BCAS-BEAC) which are not set any objective of accelerating growth and creating jobs? Often highlighted, the "dynamism" of these economies—in WAEMU much more than in EMCCA—remains, however, exceeded, on average, by the results in terms of GDP growth rates of countries located outside the franc zones. Especially since the recent growth of French-speaking West Africa—until the outbreak of the COVID-19 pandemic—seems to credit less the CBWAS than the boom in global demand, the surge in commodity prices and a (temporary) appreciation of the U.S. dollar against the euro, and consequently against the CFA franc.

How can we not admit the need to relax the current modalities of the functioning of the financing systems in these economies? In CFA franc zones, the real interest rates borne by loans remain very high (reaching in some cases 15%), which closes the access routes to loans for many agents, whether they are enterprises or households. Faced with low production and rigid economic structures, opening the credit floodgates could encourage imports, which are payable in foreign currency. Nevertheless, the risk is that a currency shortage could lead to devaluation. It is to avoid this chain of events that Central Banks in the zone are encouraging commercial banks to ration credit, lest it accelerate foreign currency outflows. The CBWAS and the BCAS prefer to defend at all costs the pegging of CFA francs to the euro, rather than offering their economies financing conditions adapted to their needs. The operations account agreements stipulate that the Central Banks of the two zones must ensure a coverage rate of 20% of the monetary issue. These minimum threshold contractual obligations are in practice more than honored, since African States generally build up foreign exchange reserves that range between 95 and 105%. The net external assets deposited by the BCAS are even proportionally the highest, while the use of these investments seems probably even more urgent in Central Africa.

The Eco... but Which One?

As we can see, the CFA franc turns out to be a resounding failure on these many fronts. So much so that many observers question the relevance of this device by insisting on the costs to be borne by member countries, which do not have an autonomous monetary policy. Voices are even heard within the spheres of high finance and IMF bodies to suggest the urgent need to end the fixed parity of the CFA franc vis-à-vis the euro and adopt a new currency, weaker, but better suited to domestic productive structures. The blockages remain important, however, both on the French side among the supporters of "Françafrique" and on that of the African ruling classes opposed to the end of the privileges that the CFA franc helps to give them, in particular by allowing them to import luxury goods at a lower price... and to send their assets abroad easily and free of charge.

Recently, however, changes have taken place in West Africa. It should be recalled beforehand that, in this part of the continent, an institution overlooks the WAEMU; this is the Economic Community of West African States (ECOWAS), which brings together 15 countries: the eight members of WAEMU plus, in decreasing order of economic weight, Nigeria, Ghana, Guinea, Sierra Leone, Liberia, Cape Verde and The Gambia. Six of the latter seven countries, none of which uses the CFA franc, form the West African Monetary Zone (WAMZ)—with the exception of Cape Verde, which has chosen not to belong to it. During one of their summit meetings, organized in June 2019 in the Nigerian capital, Abuja, the 15 ECOWAS economies revived an already quite old idea: that of the creation on a regional scale of a single currency, called the eco. A monetary institute supposed to prepare the tools of a future Central Bank was set up. This ambitious project, the horizon of which was initially planned for 2020—which was unrealistic, and moreover without a precise timetable—also intended to make the ECOWAS perimeter coincide with those of the two monetary unions whose merger was envisaged, the WAMZ and the WAEMU. The latter should therefore in theory abandon the CFA franc, but the explicit rules of the new exchange rate regime for the eco against the euro and the U.S. dollar had been voluntarily left in abeyance, and the 2020 deadline had itself been postponed, because the strict convergence criteria that had been set (in terms of limits on inflation, budget deficit and public debt) were not met by any of the economies in this group.

If serious difficulties obstruct the path of this monetary regionalization, in particular because the rapprochement of the ECOWAS countries has shown its limits (by instance, in the trade agreements concluded with the CFA zone), there is every reason to think that a single currency would act as a factor of integration. Especially since trade flows are much more intense in ECOWAS than in WAEMU (for example, between Nigeria or Ghana and their respective French-speaking neighbors). This process would also put an end to archaic neocolonial monetary rule in West Africa—and possibly elsewhere on the continent. However, such a prospect appeared inadmissible to the French leaders and their local acolytes who, hand in hand, bypassed the efforts of ECOWAS.

On December 21, 2019, French President E. Macron and his Ivorian counterpart A. Ouattara jointly announced a name change for the CFA franc; which will henceforth be called in the eight WAEMU countries… the eco! Just like the name of the currency previously chosen to be the future currency of ECOWAS, even if the two have nothing to do… It is decided to close the operations account on which the WAEMU had until then the obligation to deposit with the French Treasury at least 50% of the foreign exchange reserves of member countries—reserves which can henceforth be managed according to the goodwill of the latter—but also to put an end to the presence of French representatives within the governance of the BCEAO. France therefore says that it has removed the "political irritants" which too explicitly recalled its neocolonial domination, but forgets to add that it retains the reality of its control, since it is Paris who will of course ensure the convertibility of the West African "new currency."

Or how to try to reassure the financial markets and continue to oversee from Paris a very neoliberalized "pan-Africanism" which would endeavor to persuade that the right to have one's own currency, however effective in The Gambia, would be inappropriate in the Senegal which surrounds it, and that what countries the size of Cape Verde or Mauritius have managed to do—namely, to manage a national currency—would be beyond the reach of economies, much larger, such as Côte d'Ivoire or Cameroon... Absurd. The disapproval shown by Nigeria and Ghana, followed by Liberia and Sierra Leone, although very real, and indeed quite justified, remained moderate and contained within the framework of ECOWAS. At its extraordinary summit in February 2020, the objective of launching a West African common currency was confirmed, but its postponement ratified. The "reform" of the CFA franc would appear in this context as a step that does not conflict with the implementation of ECOWAS' eco.

In our opinion, it would be wise, in the fundamental interest of the peoples of the WAEMU countries, to be aware of the trap set for them and to firmly reject the current "makeover" of the CFA franc—with discreet, but persistent French tutelage. It is more realistic to envisage an exit from the CFA zone than to hope to "get France out of the CFA." The most relevant option for each of the economies concerned is probably to break free from these anachronistic shackles in order to support the ECOWAS common currency project. The same decision could be taken by the EMCCA countries. Such an orientation might not be the optimal solution, but rather, certainly, a lesser evil. Provided, of course, that Africans do not fall into the same trap that Europeans were unable to avoid with the euro zone.

If the limits of ECOWAS are visible, in particular through its insufficient distance from the neoliberal line, as also the risk of domination of Nigeria (oil producer), assisted by Ghana (gold exporter), could then be driven, decisively, a dynamic that would help promote a more authentically pan-African monetary sovereignty—especially if it is joined by other countries, even beyond those of Central Africa. For this new currency, which will be likely to gradually expand its area of influence on the African continent, the most appropriate would be a flexible exchange rate regime, but controlled thanks to the pegging on a basket of currencies reflecting, by its composition and weighting, the diversity of the foreign trade of member economies.

However, in this part of the world that some French leaders think it is their "private preserve," things are changing. Here, as everywhere else, the power of China is felt. Governments of countries in the CFA zones have recently become heavily indebted to it. This is the case, among other and numerous examples, of that of the Republic of Congo. Outside the franc zone, many other economies have also moved in this direction. More than half of Eritrea's external debt is currently owed to China. The latter has become the main supplier to neighboring Ethiopia, as now to a majority of African countries, which accumulate trade deficits against it. China entered into currency swap deals with the Central Bank of South Africa, when major Chinese banking institutions penetrated the capital ownership structure of their counterparts in Southern Africa. The Chinese currency, the yuan, is already used as a settlement and reserve currency in several economies on the African continent, including Ghana, Zimbabwe and Mauritius.

Since the Summer of 2016, as we have seen, Angola has legally accepted the yuan as a currency throughout its territory, which allows it no longer to make its oil revenues depend exclusively on the U.S. dollar. In August 2018, as we also said, it was Nigeria's turn to make an agreement with China to open the possibility of denominating transactions between the two countries in national currency or in yuan in order to bypass the dollar, but also the euro and the pound sterling.

The noise of criticism against the CFA francs resonates in Russia, and even in the European Union itself. Despite these major changes, the French leaders, who themselves gave up their own currency to adopt a European currency managed by Germany—in addition to having abandoned their army to submit it to the planetary military command of the United States via NATO, their industry to sell it off to the winds or relocate it to Asia, their medical research to bend it to the wishes of foreign transnational pharmaceutical companies, and even their language to convert to "Frenglish"—would like Africa to be "The last of the Mohicans" to keep a "revamped" franc. Thus, in Paris, monetary authorities with evaporated prerogatives try to make believe that they have some power left in the world. A strange way of exercising, by proxy, a monetary sovereignty ceded to whom we think to be stronger than ourselves in Europe by confiscating in Africa that of other peoples who we imagine to be "inferior."

At the start of the Twenty-First Century, it would only border on the ridiculous if this anachronistic French-style backwardness did not above all contribute to blocking the conditions for growth and development in 15 African countries. Countries which together represent nearly 200 million inhabitants—almost the demographic weight of Brazil, or the populations of France and Russia combined—and some 6.6 million square kilometers—the equivalent of the cumulative areas of India and Argentina, not so far from that of Australia. From then on, the countdown to the after-CFA franc began. A change of name, the movement of French advisers-controllers from the stage to the backstage and the affixing of delicate "distinctive identity signs" on banknotes will not be enough. When it comes to money, symbolism is very important, of course, but it is not everything. It does not remove the cruel reality of domination, exploitation, mass misery. The African peoples know it, but perhaps not all of their politicians have understood it yet...

References

Afana, O. (1966), *L'Économie de l'Ouest africain*, Paris: François Maspéro.

Alexandropoulos, J. (2007), *Les Monnaies de l'Afrique antique*, Toulouse: Presses universitaires du Mirail.

Amin, S. (1971), *L'Afrique de l'Ouest bloquée*, Paris: Éditions de Minuit.

——— (1976), *Impérialisme et sous-développement en Afrique*, Paris: Éditions Anthropos - Economica.

——— (1988), *L'Eurocentrisme - Critique d'une idéologie*, Paris: Éditions Anthropos - Economica.

Chossudovsky, M. and P. Galand (2016), "Le Génocide de 1994 - L'usage de la dette extérieure du Rwanda (1990–1994)," CADTM website (https://www.cadtm.org/), Brussels.

Coquery-Vidrovitch, C. (1985), *Afrique noire: permanences et ruptures*, Paris: Payot.

Herrera, R. and L. Ilboudo (2012), "Les Défis de l'agriculture paysanne: le cas du *Burkina Faso*," *L'Homme et la Société*, n° 183–184, p. 83–96, Paris.

Nubukpo, K., M.Z. Belinga, B. Tinel and D.M. Dembele (eds.) (2016), *Sortir l'Afrique de la servitude monétaire*, Paris: La Dispute.
Suret-Canale, J. (1987), *Afrique et capitaux*, 2 Volumes, Paris: L'Arbre verdoyant éditeur.
Tchundjang Pouemi, J. (1980), *Monnaie, servitude et liberté - La répression monétaire de l'Afrique*, Paris: Éditions J.A.
Toussaint, É. (2021), "Rwanda : les Créanciers du génocide," CADTM website (https://www.cadtm.org/), Brussels.

5

Oceania, Often Forgotten, but So Revealing: *Archaism of Peripheral Traditional Societies... or of the Forms of Central Monetary Domination?*

Registered sacred site. Beyond this point lies a site of traditional significance to Aboriginal people. Please respect the sanctity of this area. Penalty for unlawful entry up to $20,000.

Road sign (Nhulunbuy, North Territory, Australia)

"Island continent," distant, isolated on the blue limits of the planispheres, Oceania is too frequently seen neglected in debates on monetary and financial questions. This is regrettable, because this region, very sparsely populated (42 million inhabitants, including almost two thirds in Australia, i.e., 0.5% of the world population) and mainly maritime (5.5% of the land area, just over half the size of Antarctica, when the Pacific Ocean covers about a third of the earth's surface), reveals, perhaps more than anywhere else, a symptomatic contrast between the supposed archaism of the traditional societies of the periphery and that, quite real as for it, of the mechanisms of monetary domination exerted on them by the various great central powers of the capitalist world system.

R. Herrera, *Money*, Global University for Sustainability Book Series,
https://doi.org/10.1007/978-981-19-2848-2_5

An "Irrational" Attitude Towards Money?

The social formations of Oceania constitute one of the privileged fields of research of anthropologists, ethnologists and sociologists, among others and multiple themes, for the study of "primitive money." The interest of economists in this region is generally less—except for the paid experts recruited by transnational companies who come to exploit local natural resources. What mainstream economists most frequently question is the rationality of agents in societies that the outside observer tends to deem "archaic." The selfish calculations of *homo œconomicus*—scientific absurdity produced by the maximizing individualist ideology of the academic mainstream—would indeed run up against a so-called enigma of traditional Oceanian societies. The latter would be endowed with institutions perceived by many in the West as being brakes or obstacles to development.

This is the case with the persistence of ancestral "customary" rights over soils and subsoils. In many Oceanian societies, as in many other places in the South in general, and in particular on the African continent, land is only very exceptionally the object of private appropriation, as understood by modern (capitalist) law. The vast majority of land tenure systems are said to be "customary," based on possession of land not individually but in community, with joint ownership and the right of pre-emption of soils. So it is less a question of property than of access to the use of the land, linked to the exploitation of the land by a group. The relationship of human beings to land and their marked attachment to forms of collective property translate into a singularity of land law: its legal sources are twofold, deriving, on the one hand, from the Western tenure system, introduced by the colonial administration formerly and today managed by the modern State, and, on the other hand, from customary land tenure—or para-customary land tenure, where the gradual penetration of private property has degraded it.

Under such conditions, the institutions of traditional societies, structured on the basis of families, villages and clans, grouping together vast networks linked by actual or imagined lineages, are considered by most orthodox economists who have been interested in them as capable of confining the economic life of individuals to simple subsistence and self-consumption—therefore in spaces that are largely demonetized—or, *a fortiori*, as making it difficult for them to freely associate with a view to the production of surpluses intended for sold in the market. In societies which favor a principle of solidarity within them and do not allow an individualization of property and income, it would not be possible, it is argued, to envisage an extensive division of labor, nor to encourage personal initiative or technical innovation. All the more so as these institutions would be associated with visions of the world qualified—like their money—as "primitive," as well as with socio-cultural behaviors supposed to stifle any potential for progress. This is the case, above all, of a conception of work which perceives it as having to be oriented above all towards the immediate satisfaction of vital needs; or that of a time spiritualized and thought of as cyclical, which would require making a distinction between foresight, applying to a known reality, and forecasting, projecting action into a more uncertain future.

Nevertheless, according to standard economists, it is the attitudes that members of these traditional societies would tend to adopt towards "money"—money as it is understood in the current capitalist system—which is the most problematic. For there would still exist, here and there, parallel "currencies," with specific symbolic meanings and functions making them follow circuits distinct from those of modern money. Approaching barter, these networks are in fact dominated by cycles of prestige and honor competitions, and exchanges (of a ritual, ceremonial or commercial nature) between chiefdoms competing in splendor. As a consequence, money is seen as an instrument of measurement and exchange, but little as a store of value turned towards the future. The way of understanding money leads to disassociating it from market prices, hoarding and the accumulation of capital. In these circumstances, "economic agents" would be led to get rid of "good money" (that is to say, the official or State one) as quickly as possible, as opposed to "bad money" (i.e., the traditional or "archaic" one), according to an original version of Gresham's law (cf. Appendix B).

Box 5.1 An example of "primitive money" in Oceania: The rai or fei of Yap Island

A spectacular example of "primitive money" is that of the *rai* or *fei*, this monumental stone coin from Yap Island in the Palau Archipelago, located in Western Micronesia (off the coast of the Philippines). The size of these stone blocks was usually 30 to 50 cm, but they could be smaller (a few centimeters) or much larger (up to 3.6 m). Their shape is rounded, or oval for the larger ones, with a hole in the center, or two on either side. The *rai* or *fei* was used locally (the first in the North of the island, the second in the South) until the 1970s. These objects have been known to the West since the beginning of the Eighteenth Century, but are probably very old. These enormous stones, which can weigh between one and two tons, were cut in calcite extracted from quarries in the Palau archipelago, then transported once carved for nearly 450 km by canoe to the island of Yap, to be used there as primitive currencies. Their value and the prestige given to its owner were linked to the efforts expended during the manufacture of these stone discs (the work carried out, even the suffering caused on this occasion). Due to the difficulty of moving them, these stones, when exchanged, most often stayed with their original owner.

These impressive "currencies" have given rise to various interpretations by specialist researchers and by economists as well. In *A Treatise on Money* (1930), John Maynard Keynes takes this example to describe the evolution by which settlements between Central Banks are no longer effected by changing the location of gold stocks, but by modifying the name of their owner—the material support no longer changing places and the money distancing its links with physical assets. With reference to the gold standard system, neoliberal economist Milton Friedman, for his part, compares the nature and rationality of the belief in the value of these stones to those attached to gold in his book *Money Mischief* (1992). With this in mind, many authors have made it an illustration of fiat money*, or fiduciary money without assets. However, others insist on the contrary on the intrinsic value of these stones, of religious, aesthetic or "utilitarian" nature (use as a jewel or a throne, for example). Some anthropologists even refuse to consider them as money, instead likening them to diamonds. Recently, economists have seen a resemblance between the *rai* or *fei* and crypto-currencies, such as Bitcoin, in particular because of the way they are made (the "mine") or the registration of properties.

If the *rai* or *fei* was a traditional means of exchange of importance in Yapese society, other primitive "currencies" were also used there, such as cetacean teeth, shell necklaces, mother-of-pearl shells, ropes in coconut fibers, banana leaf mats, turmeric tubers, etc. In the rest of Oceania, one observed in great detail, not so long ago, the complexity of inter-tribal exchanges in the highlands of the central cordillera of Papua New Guinea or on the islands surrounding this archipelago, from the Trobrian *vaygu'a* (necklaces and bracelets), studied by Bronislaw Malinowski, to the bayura "salt coins" of the Highlands, interpreted by Maurice Godelier.

Nevertheless, money in the modern sense of the term is, of course, now widely used in all Pacific Island societies. And this, even if in each of them, except for the cases of Australia and New Zealand, a significant part of local production is still currently performed outside the market—therefore without being monetized. The reality of the functioning of these peripheral countries, with their postcard landscapes, is however far removed from the slogans of tourist brochures. The peripheral Oceanian economies present similarities (island and fragmented territories, narrow internal markets, etc.), and they face common challenges (improvement of communication and transport infrastructure, protection of the environment in the face of excessive exploitation of mining resources and climate change, surveillance of very large maritime areas, control of tourist activities and of the fishing, etc.). These economies are above all very vulnerable, because they are dependent (for those that remain colonies) on the flow of transfers from their respective metropolises intended to cover the payment of the salaries of local civil servants and the cost of military installations, or (for the others, which have now become free States, at least formally) on their relationships maintained, specifically, with Australia and New Zealand.

A Special Space: Scattered but Hierarchical and Placed Under the Thumb of the Dollar

Although its countries and territories are spatially dispersed, Oceania is a region of the world "unified" in that its economic space is largely dominated by the dollar. Let us say dollars instead, because, in addition to the U.S. currency, which is very present, the currencies of the two main regional powers are the Australian and New Zealand dollars, with floating exchange rates on both sides. Australia, a strategic ally of the United States—which grants it a very extensive national defense perimeter (the Pakistan/India, East Russia/China, Indonesia/Pacific triangle)—, is "authorized" to pursue its economic interests in a sphere of influence covering much of the Central and Southern Pacific, in this case: almost all of Melanesia, Eastern Micronesia and Western Polynesia—plus Timor-Leste in South-East Asia and some small territories in the Indian Ocean. The recognition of this "precinct" by its U.S. guardian and its Northern allies does not exclude certain occasional rivalries and tensions, especially with France, which retains possessions in the region, and to a lesser extent Great Britain, still influential on its former colonies. Australia is assisted in this task by New Zealand, whose radius of action is in Polynesia. And the United States encloses it all in a huge arc stretching from the Northern Mariana Islands to American Samoa, via Hawaii.

Apart from these two central countries which, although located in the Southern hemisphere, are to be included in the Northern triad (United States/Europe/Japan), a large majority of the Oceanian economies share the common trait of not issuing own currency and to use, instead, that of another country. The currency in question is most often the U.S. dollar, or, failing that, the weight of history requires, the currency of their former colonial rule. As a matter of fact, in the region, many territories remain colonies to this day. Are thus "administratively attached," as it is said in diplomatic language: to the United States, Hawaii, Guam, the Commonwealth of the Northern Marianas, American Samoa, but also the atolls Johnston, Wake and Midway (placed under military command), as well as the Line Islands; to Australia, Norfolk and Lord Howe; to New Zealand, Kermadec and Tokelau; to the United Kingdom, the Pitcairn Islands; and to France, New Caledonia, Wallis and Futuna and French Polynesia. Among the peripheral countries that are now officially independent, are part of the zone of the Australian dollar: Nauru, Kiribati and Tuvalu; that of the New Zealand dollar: the Cook Islands and Niue; and that of the U.S. dollar: the Marshall Islands, the federation of the States of Micronesia and Palau, to which must also be added East Timor, which in 2000 replaced the Indonesian rupee by the U.S. dollar. U.S. and New Zealand dollars also circulate, simultaneously, in the British Pitcairn Islands.

To put it simply, let us say that in the Oceania region, only six independent States have their own currency: Samoa, with the tala (since 1963); Tonga, with the pa'anga (since 1966); the Fiji, with the Fijian dollar (since 1969); Papua New Guinea, with the kina (since 1975); the Solomon Islands, with the Solomon dollar (since 1977); and Vanuatu, which issues the vatu (since the year 1981). The last four countries are economically very dependent on Australia, while the first two are in the New Zealand zone of influence. Before the adoption of their respective national currencies, most of these economies were dollarized, partially or totally, in one way or another, then they maintained sometime after independence an anchor on the currency which was previously legal tender on their soil. To stabilize their multilateral exchange rate*, five of these States ended up adopting a fixed exchange-type regime (Samoa and Solomon Islands) or allowing fluctuations within narrow margins (Tonga) or regular adjustments (Fiji and Vanuatu) with respect to baskets of specific currencies—in this case, the U.S., Australian and New Zealand dollars, and marginally the pound sterling, the yen and the euro. Fiji maintains some capital controls, authorizing the repatriation of profits from foreign companies and banks, but under fixed ceilings and after payment of tax obligations.

Papua New Guinea, the region's largest peripheral economy, is the only one to resort to a *de jure* floating exchange rate regime. In reality, however, its monetary system is *de facto* "intermediate" insofar as its Central Bank tends to intervene constantly to counteract the depreciation of the parity of the kina, which is slippery, certainly, but with an implicit anchoring on the U.S. dollar. This country of nearly 10 million inhabitants and 465,000 square kilometers deserves attention.

It is symptomatic of the archaism of the forms of monetary and financial domination of the central powers, first and foremost of course its former colonial power, Australia. The latter now directs its capital flows primarily to Asia, but those invested in Melanesia remain profitable, especially in the Papua New Guinean mining and energy sectors. Today, this economy ranks thirteenth in the world for gold production (with the third largest gold reserves on the planet), as well as for copper, and also exports oil and gas.

Papua New Guinea, or the Direct Passage from Colonialism to Neoliberalism

It was until 1975, so very late, that Papua New Guinea remained a colony of Australia—which took over from Great Britain and Germany (while the western part of the great island had been Dutch, before choosing Indonesia). Colonization led to an interweaving of local productive and commercial structures in those of its metropolis, with the effect of the advance of the monetization of traditional society inside and, outside, a slow integration into the capitalist world system, in subordinate position. By the end of the Nineteenth Century, colonial plantation and trading companies had arrived, first in the coastal plains and on the surrounding islands, then inland as far as the Highlands, to transform some of the natives into small peasants or in agricultural workforce, especially for the production of palm oil, coffee and timber which gained ground and gradually directed the economy towards the market, and with it towards the money. As for integration into world capitalism, the most vigorous impetus was to be given, from the end of the 1960s, by the penetration of new big investors (including Conzinc Rio Tinto of Australia) and the intensification of the exploitation of mining deposits (especially gold and copper).

The requisition of community lands in order to integrate them into capitalist logic was therefore a permanent priority of the colonial administration. And the fact is it is also for successive governments since independence. For in a country where—still today—95% of the land of the national territory is governed by customary law and collective property, and where more than three-quarters of the workforce is still devoted to food crops, these singularities were problematic. The State had to "alienate" these soils so that it could be used by transnational mining, oil and agribusiness companies. Therefore, if the State recognizes the customary rights of groups of landowners or traditional owners of land everywhere, even where the subsoil is rich, it in fact preserves the integrity of land only where transnational corporations have no interest, nor overdraft of resources. Elsewhere, it seizes the soils and subsoils by spoliation to cede their use to private big capital.

Nevertheless, after the economic context of the early 1980s of strong dollar and soaring precious metal prices boosting exports of minerals and hydrocarbons, then external shocks occurred (with the sudden downturn in commodity and raw material prices), as well as internal ones (closure of several mines following conflicts with indigenous populations), which worsened the financial situation. The budget deficit widened, foreign exchange reserves melted, the State went into debt. The 1989 structural adjustment program (SAP) tipped the country into the neoliberal era: in addition to cutting public spending and privatizing State-owned enterprises, the government devalued the kina and set a draconian anti-inflation target. The drastic constraints that the restrictive stance of monetary policy placed on the economy were suffocating. Public finances deteriorated further, prompting political leaders to lock themselves a bit more into the IMF's trap. In 1995, a second SAP increasingly subjugated the country: liberalization of prices and of capital movements, abolition of customs duties, new reduction in wages... In accordance with neoliberal dogmas, the exchange rate became floating. These tough decisions did not improve the economic situation. A third SAP was implemented in 1999, to attract foreign capital. In the early 2000s, the financial sector was abruptly liberalized, the independence of the Central Bank was consolidated, a pack of credit institutions but also insurance companies were transferred to powerful private owners—including all newcomers in the region: pension funds, with predatory behaviors.

Pressure was increasing to register community lands, establish cadastres and guarantee individualized land titles in accordance with capitalist modern law. Each of these SAPs included a component of "land reform" to facilitate private appropriation of land and the exploitation of their natural resources as a condition for the granting of loans from the IMF and other institutions, including the Australian aid agency (Ausaid), but also that of the United States (Usaid) or the Asian Development Bank. The process of privatizing and monetizing customary lands in order to form a real land market was to play a key role in Papua New Guinea in this virtually direct transition from colonialism to neoliberalism. The conservation of a national currency may have given the illusion that a certain monetary sovereignty was preserved, but this latter is in fact largely fictitious given the country's extreme monetary and financial dependence. We need to study the mechanisms to fully understand it.

Mechanisms of Monetary and Financial Dependence on Australia

Currently, the Papua New Guinean economy finds itself tightly embedded in a regional free trade system within which it remains tied to that of Australia. The latter is omnipresent in the capital ownership structure of large mining and hydrocarbon consortia, as well as in foreign trade flows. Half of Papua New Guinea's imports come from Australia, to which in turn goes more than a quarter of the country's exports. The exported merchandises are almost exclusively primary: unprocessed raw materials (oil and gas, gold, copper, silver, nickel, cobalt, etc.) for two thirds, and non-processed agricultural products (wood, coffee, cocoa, palm oil and copra oil…) for about a quarter. Oil refined in Australia is re-imported for the needs of the Papua New Guinean economy; most of the gold imported by Australia is refined there and then re-exported to the world market…

So what are the mechanisms of this monetary and financial dependence? When a SAP is adopted under the aegis of the IMF, the State privatizes its public enterprises and opens its markets. Foreign transnational corporations and private banks, mostly Australian, can enter in force in the structures of ownership of capital thus offered, invest massively to exploit to the maximum the natural resources—and the underpaid labor force—then repatriate the profits realized and pay dividends to their shareholders. This results in a double external imbalance for Papua New Guinea: on the one hand, a surplus in its trade balance and, in the other one, a deficit in financial accounts. The first is explained by the dynamism of foreign capital on its soil, and the second by the flows of repatriation of profits on foreign direct investments (or on portfolio investments) and by those of interest payments on the external debt. Under these conditions, it is the inflows of official aid that rebalance the balance of payments and, unsurprisingly, it is Australia which again plays the main role here—far ahead of Japan. An obligation is imposed: Australian "cooperation" funds are not released until the Papua New Guinean government agrees to renew the credit agreements signed with the IMF.

The circle is complete. Papua New Guinea can boast of its status of the first country to receive public aid from Canberra (more than half of the total envelope granted, at the expense of Australian taxpayers, it should be remembered). However, the amounts in question represent little in comparison with the enormous profits which foreign transnational firms and banks derive from this peripheral country, and whose transfer to the central powers contributes to destructuring its external accounts. The imbalances also have repercussions on public finances, since the State of Papua New Guinea guarantees investors, on the tax revenue side, a very accommodating tax on dividends and, on the budget expenditure side, the financing of infrastructure to support private big capital. And since the official aid received remains even lower than the external debt service flows, more debt is needed.

Domestic debt has therefore grown significantly, especially through the issuance of Treasury bonds. These government bills were acquired by financial institutions from abroad, but are also held by local investors, in particular senior officers of the Papua New Guinean army. It should be noted in this regard that the sovereign function of national defense has been delegated more and more explicitly to Australia, while that of maintaining public order was "outsourced" for the benefit of private military companies, especially for the protection of mining and oil sites. The scale of military aid and "special transactions and confidential items" of defense from Australia persuaded domestic authorities to adopt a line subject to the strategic interests of Canberra—and Washington. It is understandable, in such a context, why the role of fractions of the army was so decisive in the neoliberal change in policy followed in recent decades.

Box 5.2 "Commodity currencies" in the shadow of transnational corporations

The prices of Fijian sugar at the New York Mercantile Exchange, Solomon Islands wood at the Chicago Mercantile Exchange, Samoan cocoa at the Intercontinental Exchange Futures in Atlanta or New Caledonian nickel at the London Metal Exchange are quoted in U.S. dollars. Nevertheless, the price of some currencies is strongly influenced by that of raw materials and commodities, to the point that some call "commodity currencies" currencies issued by major countries exporting one or more commodity(ies) and whose exchange rates appear to correlate with fluctuations in the prices of these commodity(ies)—and even more closely with variations in the prices of the stock markets of transnational corporations which dominate the sectors concerned.

Australian dollar and Papua New Guinean kina are often classified in this category of "commodity currencies." One of the mining giants operating in these two economies is the Anglo-Australian firm Rio Tinto. To get a sense of its might, let us just say that in 2019, its total turnover was more than twice Papua New Guinea's GDP. In general, when the prices of minerals mined by Rio Tinto are on the rise, due to strong demand or a contraction in supply, the value of the company's shares tends to appreciate and, with it, the rate of the Australian dollar. Conversely, the exchange rate of this currency tends to weaken when these prices go down. These correlations are observed frequently, even if they are not systematic, because they also depend on exchange rate regimes, the economic weight of the country or the period studied, among other elements. Very often, the Australian dollar has been presented as an investment currency, because the rates of bonds denominated in this currency have long remained relatively high.

However, scandals and rampages, human as environmental, for which Rio Tinto is held responsible are legion in Papua New Guinea. And in Australia, his last "feat" was committed in May 2020: it consisted in blowing up, outright, a 46,000-year-old Aboriginal sacred site in the prehistoric caves of Juukan Gorge (Pilbara region, Northwest of country). The firm's management has issued a vague apology to the media, along with an official business license issued by the State authorities of Western Australia. The latter, barely three days after having themselves deplored the facts, gave their agreement for the BHP Group, another mining transnational firm, also Anglo-Australian, to destroy new aboriginal sacred sites.

We remember that in 1988, to protect the properties of Rio Tinto on the island of Bougainville, the Papua New Guinean State preferred to come to the aid of the mining giant and choose war against the local populations—triggering a conflict that lasted ten years and was the deadliest in Oceania since Second World War. It should be noted that the inhabitants of Bougainville voted in favor of independence during the referendum of December 2019. In September 2020, a complaint was filed in the Melbourne court against Rio Tinto by a human rights association acting on behalf of a group of citizens from around Panguna. In this area, the largest open-cast copper mine in the world was established in the 1970s and 1980s, at the origin of the Bougainville war. Indeed, more than three decades after its closure in 1989, the uncleaned toxic waste from this mine continues to pollute the environment and poison the people living around it.

The history of this transnational company had set the tone. Already in 1888, when one of the branches of the Rothschild family had bought the copper mine located in Minas de Riotinto in the province of Huelva (Andalusia, Spain) from a consortium led by Deutsche Bank, the miners demonstrating against the harsh working conditions imposed on them, and joined by peasants protesting against the damage caused to surrounding crops by mining, saw their strike movement repressed by the army. The shooting killed several hundred people. It had been five years since the Rothschilds had taken over the Société Le Nickel in New Caledonia.

Monetary Compensations

Generally speaking, when a new oil, mining, or cash crop exploitation program is launched by a transnational company, compensation solutions are considered. They most frequently take the forms, on the one hand, of monetary compensation payments intended for landholders, and on the other hand, of the payment of royalties returned by the State—at the cost of harsh costs negotiations—to these same customary owners of land affected by this investment project. In certain configurations, which are less and less rare, it may even involve distributions of listed shares (equities); a process that has sometimes been able to switch community groups directly from the virtual absence of the use of money to the universe of fictitious capital…

While the law does not require the prior identification of all landholders, the allocation of royalties and compensations is, on the contrary, subject to the legal obligation to precisely identify the beneficiaries. In recent years, land jurisprudence has favored competition between community groups seeking to be recognized as customary owners by the State, as well as by transnational firms, which has led many clans to enter into this logic of compensation and adopt rentier strategies. This is to say that even in a society where traditional structures have remained very much alive, as in the case of Papua New Guinea, many individuals have been receptive and responsive to such monetary incentives.

Nevertheless, it is clear that the process of monetization associated with compensations did not necessarily lead to the collapse of ancestral social systems, for the reason that its effects were very contradictory. The market penetrates previously preserved relationships; more products arrive in commercial exchanges where money comes to play its role; more social relationships are monetized. Obviously, social inequalities have worsened and the attitude of "every man for himself" has gained ground, which has caused very strong tensions and the breakup of numerous families, especially due to the separation of brothers, or of entire clans. The division of collective lands leads to a weakening of community authorities over their soils and a loss of influence of ancestral values. But, at the same time, groups recognized as landholders have repeatedly drawn from it, in addition to tidy sums of money, renewed grounds of consideration and prestige. As a result, Papua New Guinean traditional social structures have not been destroyed, as one might have imagined, but rather adapted.

Over the past decades, the distribution of royalties paid by transnational corporations to the central State, various local governments and landowner groups, respectively, has tended to shift in favor of the latter. And if we observe that the number of complaints relating to land disputes which have been brought before the courts by indigenous groups has increased significantly, what we also notice is that most of the claims mainly concern the compensation amounts to be paid, much more than the principle of customary land ownership as such. Only a few groups have made the demand to do away with the modern kina in order to revert to the old, "primitive" shell money also called "kina." The fact remains that despite the converging pressures that transnational firms, Northern States and international financial organizations have exerted in the direction of the commodification and monetization of land, successive Papua New Guinean governments have not achieved to question collective property, nor to establish a "free" land market. And the crucial reason for this state of affairs lies in the fierce resistance and the permanent mobilizations of a people drawn up against the "reforms" (in fact the scandal) of the privatization of their customary lands, and more generally of all their natural resources, under or on floors. Indeed, the reserves in forests and water, consequent, also interest more and more openly the Australian investors...

Meanwhile, the most immediate social needs of the population are being sacrificed and indicators of life expectancy and literacy rates are among the lowest in the world. The influence produced by the extension of capitalist land relations is destructive on the survival of ancestral bonds of solidarity. Despite frequent nutritional deficiencies, malnutrition remains quite rare. The cause is to be found in the maintenance of the access of a very large majority of the inhabitants of rural areas to community lands and in forms of collective organization of subsistence crops, but also in the persistence of a traditional system of solidarity, called *wantok*, materialized by distributions in kind (food) or in currency (income). This system of community support has undoubtedly cushioned the devastating impact of neoliberal policies, in particular by limiting the risks of individual forfeiture. However, the effectiveness of such solidarity networks diminishes over time, especially in urban areas where mutual aid links tend to weaken, crumble, or even break. In cities, provincial capitals as well as Port Moresby, nearly three-quarters of the population are believed to be living below the poverty line today.

The CFP Franc: "Financial Community" or… "French Colonies" in the Pacific?

Among the Oceanian economies, the cases of New Caledonia, Wallis and Futuna and French Polynesia are interesting to examine, in particular as an extension of the reflections on the CFA franc. These are in fact the three French overseas communities still using the "CFP" franc today, an acronym which means "Change Franc Pacifique" or franc of the "*Communauté financière du Pacifique*" (Financial Community of the Pacific)—but it seems although the metropolitan authorities did not deign to replace in the official texts the original terminology of "*Colonies françaises du Pacifique*" (French colonies of the Pacific).

It is the *Overseas Emission Institute* (Institut d'Émission d'Outre-Mer, IEOM) which strikes this currency today—for which a private institution, the Banque d'Indochine, was in charge until 1966—and applies in these territories the monetary policy of France, under the supervision of the European Central Bank (ECB). The value of the CFP franc does not have to be defended by the IEOM (which does not have its own reserves and over which the New Caledonian, Wallis and Futunian and Polynesian representatives sitting on its council of surveillance have no influence), because its exchange rate regime, guaranteed by the French Treasury, is fixed—and has remained unchanged since the years after Second World War, vis-à-vis the French franc until 1999, then the euro from the year 2000. Such a framework, even more restrictive than that of the CFA franc zones in Africa (Chapter 4), therefore favors trade and financial relations with the countries of the euro zone, but leaves exchange risks to persist with the rest of the world, since the rate of the CFP franc evolves against all other currencies when that of the euro varies against them.

This monetary stability is obviously valuable for these territories which, despite their differences (and the notable exception of nickel in New Caledonia), share common points. They are those of having very narrow productive structures and local markets—which are based on a few sectors sheltered from competition (public and non-market services) and consumption boosted by a high purchasing power maintained by the metropolis, with levels of costs and prices clearly higher than those of the independent Oceanian countries—but also a deficit of foreign trade. This situation does not, however, exclude the need to reflect on avenues that would allow these territories to consider various possibilities of refocusing on their trade with neighboring Oceanian economies—and especially with a view to possible future independence.

At least three alternatives to the current situation do indeed exist. First there would be the adoption of the euro by New Caledonia, Wallis and Futuna and French Polynesia. Nevertheless, the main advantage of this option, that of monetary stability, is already provided by the peg of the CFP franc to the euro. On the contrary, its major drawback, namely the dependence on abroad and the renunciation of the autonomy of monetary policy, would be aggravated, because of the choice to endow the economy with an exchange rate much too overvalued in relation to the real capacities of the productive structure, by ruling out—in addition to the idea of independence—the choice of a devaluation, that is to say an adjustment which would however improve the price competitiveness of exports. Could then be imagined the option of selecting a currency that would be modeled on the African device of the CFA franc. On the positive side, the credibility of these territories would be strengthened, at least in the eyes of local elites and foreign investors, who could release their profits as they see fit. But on the negative side, the management of the currency would be largely dictated by the supervisory powers, France and the ECB, and if devaluation there were to be, such a decision would be the responsibility of these powers. This strong constraint, which would require on the part of the metropolis the extension of the guarantee of financial transfers and the free movement of people to be bearable, would nevertheless be unfavorable to the financing needed by the development of these territories.

So why not aim, ultimately, the objective of creating a new currency, sovereign, that is to say issued by a local Central Bank and having its own foreign exchange reserves? Obviously, the minimum conditions are not met to achieve this goal in the near future. However, it is not unreasonable to think about it in the longer term (especially if independence is obtained…) by accompanying a process tending to the creation of a common currency between peripheral Oceanian economies—and by relying on some positive points of existing cooperation frameworks, such as that of the Melanesian Spearhead Group or, more recently, that of the Pacific Islands Forum, in particular the revitalization of trade that these spaces allow.

The ambition of this project, the purpose of which is to reduce the dependence of these Southern economies on both central powers and international donors, as well as to promote the beneficial effects for these countries or territories of deepening regional cooperation in monetary matters will undoubtedly require progressivity. In the immediate term, it would be advisable to demand a more active participation in the governance exercised by the IEOM and within the various current regional levels of decision-making, then to prepare the constitution of substantial foreign exchange reserves thanks to net inflows of capital, in order to be able to set up the institutions of national currencies. On this basis, and in this transition, an intermediate exchange rate regime, anchored on a basket of currencies, chosen from among the main trading and financial partners, would probably be recommended. While allowing (relative) stability of the multilateral exchange rate inside the zone, it would ensure softness in monetary policy by allowing the necessary parity readjustments against the outside. The ideal would be to make converge the compositions of the baskets of the different sovereign currencies of Oceania towards a similar structure, in order to maximize the chances of the emergence of a future regional common currency. Thus, the fact that the Australian and New Zealand dollars are now under the growing influence of the yuan—these two central economies being increasingly dependent on China for their respective exports—could it facilitate this evolution towards more monetary sovereignty in Oceania?

References

Godelier, M. (1982), *La Production des Grands hommes*, Paris: Fayard.

Herrera, R. (2007), "*Australie* : l'*impérialisme oublié*," *Afrique Asie*, p. 58–61, July-August, Paris.

Herrera, R. and P. Tetoe (2012), "Papouasie Nouvelle-Guinée / Australie: des relations ambivalentes," *Journal de la Société des Océanistes*, vol. 2, n° 135, p. 201–214, Paris.

——— (2015), "The Papua Niugini Paradox: Land Property Archaism and Modernity of Peasant Resistance?," *in* R. Herrera and K.-C. Lau (eds.), *The Struggle for Food Sovereignty*, p. 119–135, London: Pluto Press.

Malinowki, B. (1963), *Les Argonautes du Pacifique occidental*, Paris: Gallimard.

Watts, M. (2007), *Chronology of Bougainville Civil War*, *mimeo*, Sydney.

6

Latin and Caribbean America on the Way to Its Second Independence: *Monetary Lessons from a Region in Rebellion*

> *Lo que queremos es desmitificar el dinero y no rehabilitarlo. Nos proponemos incluso abolirlo totalmente. La ley del valor tiene un sentido en una sociedad capitalista donde la economía se funda en la ganancia. No tiene ninguno en una sociedad socialista.*
>
> What we want is to demystify money, not rehabilitate it. We propose ourselves even to abolish it completely. The law of value makes sense in a capitalist society where the economy is based on profit. It has none in a socialist society.
>
> Fidel Castro, Interview with K.S. Karol (September 1967)

Today, we are very far from that time when the leadership of the Cuban revolution sought a way to abolish money, as some of the Bolshevik economists had attempted to do nearly half a century earlier. After the end of the Soviet Union, Cuba even had to dollarize its economy, but recently managed to de-dollarize it, we will see how. Across the rest of the continent, all countries, to varying degrees, are dominated by the U.S. dollar. Several Caribbean and Central American economies, such as Panama, have chosen to substitute their currencies for that of the United

R. Herrera, *Money*, Global University for Sustainability Book Series,
https://doi.org/10.1007/978-981-19-2848-2_6

States, outright. This is also the case for Ecuador, which has nevertheless undertaken an experience of "citizen revolution." Others have so far failed to tear themselves away from the US orbit, such as Mexico, thrown into the whirlwind of crises of global hegemony, or Colombia, grappling with local speculative "bubbles," particularly in the real estate sector.

However, in this backyard of the United States that constitutes the region, resistance is trying to extricate itself from the surrounding monetary quagmire. After having been ultraliberalized, dollarized, and offered as food to foreign capital, Argentina declared itself insolvent at the end of 2001, but managed, despite the voracity of vulture funds*, to open up margins of maneuver. The giant Brazil, for its part, attempted a reformist step which has so far failed, stumbling, among other things and many things, on the issue of exchange rate. In spite of a grueling external constraint and multiple internal contradictions exacerbated by the pursuit of their "extractivist" economic models, advances are possible, as the very different examples of Ecuador, Bolivia and Venezuela show. Cuba, an exception in Latin America and the Caribbean in that it represents by far the most in-depth experience of socialist revolution to date, must be examined in detail, as it best illustrates political voluntarism in the reconquest of monetary sovereignty.

The Other America of the Dollar: From Caribbean Tax Havens to Mexican Turmoil

Various economies in Latin America and the Caribbean are currently dollarized. For some of them, they legally and exclusively use the currency of the United States, as is the case of Panama (as regards only paper denominations, alongside the balboa—since its detachment from Colombia in 1903, at the instigation of Washington—), Ecuador (since the year 2000), El Salvador (since 2001), as well as several tax havens, such as the British overseas territories (the Virgin Islands, the Turks and Caicos Islands) or Dutch overseas territories (the Caribbean Netherlands, comprising the islands of Bonaire, Saint Eustatius and Saba). For others, they have a currency closely pegged to the U.S. dollar. The currencies concerned by these fixed parities are the Guyanese, Belizean, Bahamian,

Barbadian, Bermudian and Caymanian dollars, the East Caribbean dollar (which is in force in Saint Lucia, Grenada, Saint Vincent and the Grenadines, Antigua and Barbuda, Dominica, Saint Kitts and Nevis, in addition to the British territories of Anguilla and Montserrat), as well as the Aruban guilder and the Netherlands Antillean guilder (circulating in Curaçao and in the Dutch part of Saint Martin).

Putting aside micro-states or small economies turned into tax havens (from the British Virgin Islands to Panama), amongst the larger countries on the continent, only Argentina was once dollarized. As we will soon see, however, this period has shown that dollarization does not guarantee the stability of domestic prices or the balance of payments, and that it ensures even less economic growth, the reduction of unemployment or that of poverty.

Although not (officially) dollarized, the Mexican economy has found itself since the debt moratorium of 1982, by recurrence, at the heart of chains of very serious currency crises. The reason lies in the contradictions that arise from the close ties that attach Mexico to the United States, especially since the integration of these two countries, with Canada, within the North American Free Trade Agreement (NAFTA). Less than a year after the signing of this treaty, on January 1, 1994, when the Zapatista rebellion broke out, the anchor of the Mexican currency on the U.S. dollar nevertheless shattered: the peso was sharply devalued on December 20 of the same year, and carried in its fall the most important of the economies of Spanish-speaking America.

What had happened? A set of factors, combined, would have to be mobilized in order to respond. But which was, of all, the most determining? Here it is: the Fed, which then anticipated an inflationary slippage in the United States—a slippage which, moreover, did not happen—raised its interest rate throughout 1994 (five times, of a quarter point each time), then a little more abruptly in November (bringing it to 5.5%). This was enough to make flow back some of the roughly 180 billion dollars that had been invested in Mexican capital markets between 1990 and 1994—two-thirds in the very short term, magnetized by positive Mexican interest rate differentials and secured by the fixed parity of the peso on the dollar.

In fact, the dollarization that operates undercover in Mexico, torn between a north orbited by its powerful neighbor and a marginalized and abused south, makes it one of the weak links in the United States' system of monetary domination in the region. At that time, Washington rushed to rescue its new NAFTA partner, which it itself had previously shattered—by rallying the IMF in the process. By contrast, the United States did not move a finger to come to the aid of other countries hit by the repercussions of the Mexican crisis (or what has been called the "tequila effect"*), from Brazil to Chile, and up to in the Phillippines. And it did not react either five years later when the Argentinian currency was in its turn in danger.

Nevertheless, this foreign exchange crisis of 1994–1995 also and above all reflected a worsening of the economic situation in the United States itself. First, because the rescue plan deployed by Washington, to the tune of more than 20 billion dollars, disbursed in order to guarantee the financial markets an assumption of responsibility for Mexican liabilities and to prevent them from a new episode of suspension of payments, weighed even more heavily on the U.S. external debt, already very fat—not to say obese. Then, because the loss of more than half of the value of the Mexican peso against the dollar between November 1994 and March 1995 did not strengthen the U.S. currency, however undervalued, against the deutschemark and the yen. On the contrary. Finally, the depreciation of the dollar, which had been observed since the beginning of the 1990s, took place in a paradoxical situation of a new rise in Fed interest rates and of moderate inflation (2.7% in 1994, 2.5% in 1995). To explain these phenomena, we had to go back to the origin of the problem: the gigantic external payments deficits of the United States, whose economy is encountering increasingly obvious structural weaknesses, but which still today have the means to impose on the whole world that the U.S. citizens (especially the richest) live on its hooks.

Box 6.1 Colombia trapped in mortgage loans, ten years before the subprime crisis

In 1990, under the presidency of C. Gaviria Trujillo, Colombia liberalized in an accelerated way its economy. Within months, many financial establishments were privatized, restrictions on capital movements lifted, customs duties reduced to a minimum. Exchange controls were abolished, as was deleted the Central Bank's monopoly on the purchase and sale of foreign currencies, within the framework of a new very flexible exchange regime where a (partial) floating of the national currency was substituted for the administered rate. This liberalization was thought out much more in the interest of the United States than in that of Colombia. The latter is rich in natural resources (at the time 60% of the world production of emeralds, the first coal reserves and the fourth production of gold and platinum from the Western Hemisphere, the fourth largest oil producer in South America...) and very close to the Panama Canal, a zone strategic for trade with Asia. All the more so since the service of the Colombian external debt, contracted largely at variable interest rates and in dollars, was considerably heavier since 1979 and the policy of increasing interest rates of the U.S. Federal Reserve, resulting in an appreciation of the dollar. Washington found the arguments to push for the economy's opening by a Colombian government constrained by the lack of foreign exchange, and what more is complicit of the drug traffickers and threatened by revolutionary guerrillas.

The liberalization of capital flows in the 1990s triggered a spiral of speculation in the local real estate market—in addition to a decline in agriculture and industry. Against a background of a favorable exchange rate differential, large U.S. investors acquired mortgage-backed securities, contributing to the formation of a real estate bubble. With house prices soaring, (privatized) domestic banks also rushed into the mortgage market to multiply loans, often by refinancing themselves with short-term foreign capital that liberalization encouraged, but which made the national economy vulnerable.

Nevertheless, the scale of capital inflows from the beginning of the 1990s pushed the Colombian peso to appreciate, which worsened the trade deficit and deteriorated the level of foreign exchange reserves, against a backdrop of weak competitiveness of the economy. Faced with the risk of disruption in external debt service flows, the Colombian monetary authorities decided to raise their interest rates in 1994 in an attempt to attract new international capital. The effect generated was not only to slow down economic activity, but also to pass this rise on to mortgage rates, plunging indebted households into the inability to repay their loans, the amount of which often exceeded the value of the housing (which served as collateral guarantees with banks). This quickly resulted in a cascade of foreclosures for unpaid debts, transfers for dations of payment and sales of housing by households in difficulty, which caused a fall in prices on the real estate market, as soon as 1995 in Medellin or Cali, in particular. Despite these worrying signals and the generalization of the fall in these prices throughout the country in 1996, starting with Bogotá, the banks continued to grant mortgages even more vigorously.

During the Asian crisis of 1997 and the moratorium on the Russian debt in 1998, Colombia, like many other countries of the South, was victim of the arbitrage of portfolios of financial assets operated against it by big international speculators, which restricts external financing and increases its cost. Therefore, capital flows reversed and net outflows dried up the resources available to banks and savings and housing companies (*corporaciones de ahorro y vivienda*), worsening the contraction of mortgage loans and the drop in real estate prices. Bad debts then multiplied, as did the bankruptcies of financial institutions—the State overwhelmingly supporting the largest of them. Despite the limited size of the Colombian capital market, the gravity of the problem was such that a credit crunch* occurred, well beyond the construction sector. In 1998, a further increase in interest rates also proved ineffective in attracting foreign capital and only further exacerbated the recession (which averaged −4% in 1999).

Less than a decade before the subprime mortgage crisis in the United States—which plunged millions of households into a catastrophic situation, causing them to lose not only part of their savings, but also the ownership of their homes purchased with loans—the neoliberalized Colombia of the 1990s had served as an experimental laboratory for high finance for its speculative arrangements on mortgage loans.

Argentina of the "*Kirchnerismo*"

The presidency of Carlos Menem (from 1989 to 1999) carried out a brutal sacking of Argentina and the complete subordination of its economy to globalized high finance. It was then the time of dollarization and the currency board*—i.e., the system introduced by the British in India and their other colonies in the Nineteenth Century. The Argentine peso was managed by an issuance fund (or currency board) that modeled and mapped its value to that of the U.S. dollar, the latter alone being used for international settlements. Argentina is the only large country in the world to have adopted such a monetary regime—under the pretext of stopping inflation, the flight from the national currency and the race for dollars. The explosion of the system at the turn of the Twenty-First Century revealed the extreme constraints imposed by such a device, involving the abandonment by the Central Bank of its issuing power. Indeed, the creation of the new pesos was carried out according to the inflows of dollars into its coffers and, in the event of outflows, the money supply contracted as much.

The fate of the exchange rate was based on the reference currency, with variations unrelated to the domestic economy and its international trade or monetary relations, which risked leading to inconsistent turmoil. The collapse of the currency board plunged the country into a deep crisis between 1999 and 2002: decrease in GDP, soaring debt, deflation, reduction in wages, cuts in social assistance, rise in unemployment and poverty, bank rushes, insurrectionary climate, etc. It occurred from the end of 1998 during a shock following a persistent rise in the U.S. dollar, the implications of which were amplified by the devaluation of the currency of Argentina's main trading partner, the real Brazilian. The appreciation of the dollar blocked all economic dynamics by hampering exports and reducing the money supply, while the devaluation made inaccessible imported goods (especially from the United States), which had become too expensive.

At the end of 2001, when its presidents succeeded one another at a rapid pace, Argentina was declared in default of payments. Nearly 95 billion dollars was at stake, 80% of which was government debt. The return to the peso caused its sudden devaluation in January 2002, and a simultaneous loss of wealth from bank deposits. Defying the predictions of orthodox economists, the evolution of the economy did not bring back the hyperinflation that had characterized the second half of the 1980s. Under the Duhalde presidency, the government of the time (which did not have much of a progressive one) had resolved to put an end to the peso-dollar parity, but refused that domestic prices—in particular, it is to its credit, those of food and public services—be forced to keep pace with the increase in the dollar-to-peso exchange rate. It thus resisted the pressures both from foreign transnational corporations, present in force since the privatizations of the 1990s, and from local enterprises, especially agribusiness, demanding to sell at world prices (in dollars) while buying their inputs and paying their employees at national prices (in pesos).

Néstor Kirchner, who was able to appropriately criticize the debacle of the neoliberal model and meet popular aspirations, was elected president in 2003. He made the choice to renew the incumbent Minister of the Economy, Roberto Lavagna, whose policy was beginning to bear fruit, despite a context in which the international standard rate loan market was deteriorating and closing. The takeover by the monetary authorities of the issuance of the peso made it possible to revive public expenditure, while the stimulation of credits granted by the banks which remained in the bosom of the State helped the local producers to restart their activities. GDP growth became strong again in 2003 and, thanks to the multiplication of redistributive measures, internal tensions subsided. The State carried out (re)nationalizations. These, as well as social policies, were further amplified in 2007, after the election of Cristina Fernandez, wife of N. Kirchner. One of the most important reforms of this era was to broaden the powers of the Central Bank, beyond controlling changes in the money supply, to allow it to purchase certain volumes of Treasury bonds.

The difficulties were mounting, however. Inside, with the revitalization of economic growth was also reactivated the spiral of inflation, under the effect of the raised cost of imports, but also of price increases decided by the employers, followed by wage revaluations, themselves quickly caught up by further rises in price… It was necessary to avoid the return of the race for dollars which risked to generate an acceleration in inflation. Externally, the strategy adopted—it was already that of Néstor Kirchner—was to continue deleveraging the country in order to restore its international credibility in the eyes of backers, and to make it depend on them as little as possible. The repayment at the agreed maturity of a tranche of the loans contracted with the IMF in 2004 had avoided the suspension of payments vis-à-vis this institution and reestablished a somewhat more cordial relationship with it. During the first ten years of the Kirchner terms of office, the deflation of the total debt in foreign currencies (especially in dollars) was impressive, going from more than 150% to less than 10% of the GDP.

To do this, the government took advantage of the situation of rising raw material export earnings to devote a large part of the trade surpluses to honor the repayment of its loans. The successive negotiations relating to the private debt resulted in the restructuring of almost all of its amount, which was replaced by new securities—with a discount*, but also with indexation on future growth; this allowed their holders to recover their stake on the scheduled dates. Nevertheless, some 5% of creditors refused to join in signing its agreements. These were vulture funds*, which had bought debt securities at dirt-cheap at the time of the 2000–2002 disaster and then demanded repayment a decade later at face value. The aggressiveness of these financial predators took the Argentine State to court. On this occasion, U.S. judges demonstrated their partiality by taking up the cause of these vulture funds, which however hindered the various cycles of renegotiations and, consequently, the access to international credit of a now "normalized" Argentina.

"*Petista*" Brazil

When the Workers' Party (*petista* for PT, *Partido dos Trabalhadores* in Portuguese) candidate Lula took over the presidency in 2003, most of the neoliberal program, from the liberalization of the capital market to the privatization of banks and State-owned enterprises, had already been established by his right-wing predecessors in the early 1990s, F. Collor de Mello and F.H. Cardoso. The Real Plan, applied from 1994, had beaten hyperinflation—by resorting to a semi-flexible exchange rate, sharply raising interest rates and opening up the domestic market to foreign capital—, but it also quickly reached its limits. Marked by a persistent imbalance in current payments and growing indebtedness, the country had even experienced an exchange rate crisis and a financial collapse in 1998. Before the election, Lula therefore endeavored to reassure the markets with a *Letter to the Brazilian people* which, in mid-2002, proclaimed its refusal of a rupture and the "need" to respect external commitments and to conduct the internal reforms demanded by globalized capital. Soon after, the IMF authorized the signing of a new financing agreement.

The first important step that President Lula adopted was to allay financial markets' fear of "political intervention" in monetary matters, by guaranteeing the Central Bank extensive operational autonomy in the use of its "inflation targeting" instruments. The overall logic was laid down as soon as 1999, with the floating of the real and the hardening of the fight against inflation. The new progressive government wanted to strengthen the country's credibility and macroeconomic stability. Monetary policy renewed orthodox dogmas, at home (setting annual targets for price movements, strict control of liquidity, very high interest rates) and abroad (floating exchange rate regime, overvaluation of the real, financial liberalization). This implied further increases in interest rates, already very high (26.5% in February 2003), to limit fluctuations in the real and restore the external accounts. The top priority was to ensure that payment of external debt service was not interrupted. Efforts were redoubled to bring public finances under control and raise the primary surplus (that is to say, the surplus of tax revenues over budget expenditures), with cuts in social and infrastructure programs.

The results were mixed. On the one hand, the inflation rate was brought back below 10%, the real recovered against the dollar, the external accounts also recovered (by reducing the cost of imports and valuing exports) and the debt burden lightened. However, on the other hand, austerity contracted consumption and with it private investment, resulting in very weak GDP growth of 0.5% in 2003. In 2004, real wages increased by 2%; and the value of listed companies by 33%. Rather than seeking GDP growth, the Brazilian monetary authorities preferred to confirm the option of rigor. As soon as consumption and investment started to boost growth, monetarist stubbornness broke the springs. The Central Bank tightened the inflation target for 2005 and raised interest rates further, which revalued the exchange rate. But servicing the public debt required additional efforts. The Central Banker had to raise the interest rate once more and increase its reserves. High finance had succeeded in domesticating the leaders of the left of the largest country in Latin America. Neoliberal policy prohibited growth which, in 2006, remained half that in the rest of the continent, while the exchange rate, as to it, continued to rise.

During Lula's two terms of office (2003–2010), the Brazilian currency appreciated more than 100% against the U.S. dollar. However, this revaluation of the real—and therefore that of the GDP calculated in dollars—led, through an optical effect, to a marked improvement in the country's external vulnerability indicators. On Brazil, nevertheless, the trap of the financial markets was closing in; financial markets which demanded more and more: a sustained real, high interest rates, tighter inflation targets, an acceleration in the liberalization of the capital market, etc. The government complied with a new set of measures in favor of big capital: unification of foreign exchange markets, lifting of various constraints on foreign exchange transactions carried out by banks, authorization to open exempt accounts, reduction in the tax on financial transactions, protection of foreign investors against double taxation, exemptions from income tax and from provisional contribution on financial transfers for foreign capital holding public debt securities, improved taxation for pension funds, liberalization of the insurance sector, and even reform of pension schemes...

The "decommissioning of Union resources" procedure, which allowed the government to grant itself, at its discretion, up to 20% of federal revenues, was extended. Put in place during the *Plano Real*, this device had made it possible to circumvent some "rigidities" introduced by the Constitution of 1988 (obliging to allocate a part of the resources generated by the tax to the financing of public expenditure) and to divert funds from the accounts of national education or social protection to use them to secure debt service payments. As a result, the primary surplus kept climbing, in order to maintain the confidence of creditors.

Paying off the debt was still the goal. At the end of 2005, the Brazilian Treasury chose to anticipate the repayment schedule for debts owed to the IMF and to the Paris Club*, while announcing at the same time that it was putting new external debt securities on sale in order to be able to pay them! Raising taxes and cutting public spending, accentuated by the "fiscal responsibility law," freed up enormous resources transferred to high finance and the pension funds it controls. The priorities of the federal budget then reflected the privileges reserved for them: the item of "special charges," which includes the service of external and internal debts, represented 43% of State expenditure in 2005, against less than 20% ten years earlier.

The Central Bank had to increase its official reserves in an attempt to stabilize the exchange rate, domestic prices and external accounts. A very large chunk of the debt was turned into fictitious capital, while the bulk of these foreign exchange reserves were converted into loans and drained to the United States, covering its abysmal deficits. At the head of a country very dependent on external capital movements and where terribly powerful ruling classes have braced themselves on their privileges, the Lula administration has failed to stem the destructive logic of neoliberalism. The economic and social cost to be borne is exorbitant. This, while, despite its vulnerability, Brazil could, given its size and weight, consider modifying the neoliberal monetary order that imposes such a submission on it.

After the election of Dilma Rousseff (2010), this Lulist action program continued its course. However, in an international context degraded by the effects of the financial crisis of 2007–2008, the "recipes" which had made it possible to containing the damaging effects of this crisis on the Brazilian economy proved unable to curb the slowdown in economic growth. The anti-crisis policies applied used the methods and tools previously mobilized by Lula's teams since 2009, following those of the Central Banks at the center of the world system. The Brazilian monetary authorities supported the restructuring of the local financial sector and revitalized bank lending in order to push for massive recourse to debt. No more than in the countries of the North, however, the fall in the interest rate was not able to revive activity during the first 12 months of the

Dilma mandate; and even less the following year, when inflationary pressures increased. The finance law continued to generate a primary surplus, revised downwards, but still comfortable for creditors. It did not matter that the government's goal was to boost the economy; because for international high finance, the essential remained the intangible principle of fighting inflation.

In early 2013, the Central Bank of Brazil reversed the trend and raised the interest rate again. But faced with disappointing GDP growth, the Rousseff government did not change course. It relaunched privatizations, multiplied tax gifts to transnational corporations, turned the State against public services, without moderating criticism of the financial markets against it. It sank deeper into the trap: the real interest rates of Banco Central do Brasil were too high to stimulate activity, and their declines ineffective to turn it around. For, in general, upstream of the decisions of the monetary authorities, these same rates are influenced by those set by the most powerful financial oligopolies which maintain them at the levels required for the continued draining of the country's resources.

Furthermore, the swelling of Brazilians' indebtedness made economic growth quite artificial and worsened the imbalances of an economy which, on the outside, continues to import manufactured products and to remain specialized in the export of primary goods—all the more so as the exchange rate of the real, one of the currencies that have appreciated the most in recent years, hampered the competitiveness of local businesses. Thus, the country's dependence is felt with each contraction in global external demand for raw materials (for oil, iron, soybeans, sugar, meat, etc.) and debt, the weight of which had been reduced, but involving the payment of a still very heavy service (4.8% of GDP in June 2013), amplifies the country's vulnerability to exchange rate and interest rate fluctuations. Therefore, many entrepreneurs argue that the performance of the industry is disadvantaged by the excessive valuation of the real and by the "Brazil cost" (that is to say, high real interest rates) which would dissuade them from investing. An illustrative example: the leading coffee producer in the world, Brazil exports coffee beans and imports industrial coffee from Northern countries (especially from Switzerland), and ultimately records for this product… a trade deficit!

Monetary Aspects of Three Revolutionary Advances: Ecuador, Bolivia, Venezuela

Before President Rafael Correa took office in January 2007, it was the decision to dollarize the economy that had hit Ecuador's independence the hardest. It dates back to 2000, when the dollar replaced the sucre, just a year after the Manta base was handed over to the United States military under Plan Colombia. Serious blows struck against national sovereignty, these two facts are moreover linked, since Washington had interfered in the electoral campaign of 2006, evoking in covert words the option of a military intervention in the eventuality where the future leader of the country would have ventured on the path of de-dollarization. The leftist candidate then contented himself with justifying dollarization by the importance of remittances from Ecuadorians living abroad (which at the time amounted to one third of GDP). Maintaining such a submission to the dollar, however, could only arouse apprehension insofar as this situation placed constraints on the "citizens' revolution" which exceeded it, and which condemned its deployment in advance.

Nonetheless, a very positive aspect of R. Correa's action concerned the shifting of the lines of the monetary and financial debate, but above all of the political one, towards the external debt. The former Ecuadorian president indeed emphasized the issue of "odious" debts, that is to say, debts which are illegal and/or illegitimate. As we have said, at the start of the 1980s, in a context of high interest rates, Latin American governments decided to "nationalize" part of the private debts owed by the local bourgeoisies in order to make bear the weight of these debts to their respective peoples, through the State budget. This conversion was carried out, most frequently, under the yoke of neo-fascist military dictatorships which were already preparing the conditions for the introduction of neoliberalism. So it was in Ecuador. And one of the effects of these measures has been the rise of this type of "odious" debts, contracted against the general interest. Financial globalization then transformed many of these debts into securities traded on international capital markets, which made the calculation of the drain much more complex. In this discussion, a prerequisite is to conduct a debt audit allowing to identify the magnitude of its "odious" components in order to come to the decision to cancel them.

Such initiatives have been taken by Ecuador, which appeared to be a pioneer among debtor States in their establishment. A complementary legislative apparatus subsequently came to make these debt cancelations effective.

In addition, as early as 2008, the government of the "citizens' revolution" dared to confront foreign backers. At the end of this arm wrestling, it had managed in a few months to largely free the country from the grip of its creditors: more than 90% of the debt was thus bought back on the secondary market*, with an average discount* of around 20%, the rest being canceled unilaterally, very courageously. The balance of power within the country, however, did not make it possible to end the dollarization of the Ecuadorian economy. A process of social transformation that makes the U.S. dollar its only national currency and gives up its power of issue could therefore only be minimal. Herein lies part of the explanation of the coming political setbacks.

The major changes that followed the election of Evo Morales as President of Bolivia in 2006 resulted, first and foremost, in a (re)nationalization of the oil and gas sectors. The most direct consequence was a considerable increase in State revenues, which the government chose to devote to financing public investment programs, but also social policies and redistribution of income—very urgent measures in the poorest country in South America. The efforts to support production and employment were aimed at promoting the internal market. These advances were only possible because the new most senior political leaders decided to override the injunctions of the international financial organizations, which were fiercely opposed to State ownership of hydrocarbons. Before a progressive government came to power, two decades of IMF lending did not prevent Bolivia from declining per capita GDP.

The Central Bank played a decisive role in supporting the strategic capital expenditure plans of State-owned enterprises. Credit policy was revitalized and favored productive sectors to which more incentive interest rates were granted. The receipts from hydrocarbons made it possible to rebalance the accounts of the balance of payments and to stabilize the prices of the boliviano, the national currency. The Bolivian monetary authorities also organized a de-dollarization of the local financial system, in particular by dissuasive measures which brought about a reduction of the share of the U.S. currency in the domestic deposits during the last years.

From the year 2010, when the impact of the global crisis was felt the most, an unconventional device called "Quantitative Easing" was going to be applied, consisting in mass buying of government bonds and securities issued by public companies (these assets representing almost half of *Banco Central de Bolivia*'s balance sheet at the end of 2018). Inflationary slippages have so far been avoided. Serious problems remain, however, such as those linked to the persistence of the extractivist model and the concentration of exports, the occurrence of current account deficits, the increase in public debt denominated in foreign currencies or even the importance of stocks of Bolivian financial assets deposited abroad. Nevertheless, the main "lesson" that the Bolivian experience has given the world, however, is the following one: a State takeover of natural resources and the most strategic sectors of the economy is likely to rule out severe balance of payments difficulties and to mitigate exchange rate instability.

At least since 2012, an "economic war" has escalated against Venezuela. It led, from 2017, to a situation of hyperinflation which has still not been stopped. Today, the pace of inflation is essentially determined by the exchange rate. The prices of goods and services are constantly adjusted according to the prices of the bolivar, or more precisely its quotations not so much official as illegal. Its value in the informal market is being "organized," day by day, by anti-government political forces, in particular through specialized websites and social networks which amplify the echo. These manipulations, deliberate, tend to destabilize the national economy, mainly through the depreciation of the national currency, in order to undermine the popular bases for the revolution.

The attacks targeting the Venezuelan bolivar lead to weaken the latter, and therefore to increase the cost of imports, which causes the contraction of domestic supply, but also, by contagion effect, the acceleration of the rise in domestic prices, the whole being materializing at the end by the deterioration of the purchasing power of real wages and, therefore, of the living conditions of workers. Moreover, this scheme locks the Bolivarian government into a trap, since its interventions to support the volumes of production and employment widen the budget deficit and oblige to finance the latter by an increase in monetary liquidity, this in a particularly tense international context. Hence new pressures on internal prices, all in an economy based fundamentally on the oil sector, which ultimately leads to rampant dollarization...

As we have said, the price level results from social conflicts for the appropriation of the surplus—or, in other words, from the class struggle, according to the Marxists. The fact is that at the present time, Venezuela, although leading an important process of social transformation, retains an economy whose features remain capitalist; and, what is more, largely dependent on the petroleum sector. Since 1999 and the coming to power of President Hugo Chavez, the local dominant classes have remained in place and have kept the bulk of their property over the (largely private) means of production, and therefore foundations of their powers—unlike the revolutions of the past. Nevertheless, they transferred their immense fortunes abroad and continuously challenged the Bolivarian government to implement its exchange rate and inflation rate regulations. This battle, in which the advantage has often gone to a counter-revolutionary bourgeoisie denying the people's choice to initiate an alternative development strategy, was carried out on the legal ground (via property rights)... or by fraudulent means, to say the least.

As a matter of fact, until the end of the 2000s, it was very common for the black market to be stimulated with the aim of artificially overvaluing the exchange rate and accelerating capital flight—which, for their illegal components, can be approximated by the "errors and omissions" line of the balance of payments. Other times, the big local employers did not hesitate to reduce (or stop) the productions (even to store and hide goods rather than to sell them) in order to create shortages, knowingly, to push the domestic prices on the rise and to dry up the inflows of dollars in order to bring about a depreciation of the national currency.

And when, in April 2007, President Chavez made public his desire to withdraw Venezuela from the institutions of the IMF and the World Bank, which he described as "*mechanisms in the hands of U.S. imperialism,*" the dominant classes of the country were unleashed and raged against him. The one they had accused of having "*amputate the Caracas stock market*" by taking control of the oil, electricity and telecommunications sectors, repeated in vain that the repayments of the service of the external debt would not be interrupted, the fury of the financial markets immediately caused the value of government-issued securities to drop and country risk to jump.

To this day, the influence of the counter-revolutionary forces has remained strong, with their ideological values and their old ways of managing within the Central Bank of Venezuela. It is the latter which, in theory, is supposed to master the mechanisms that link fiscal and monetary policies, allowing the exchange rate to be fixed as well as the use of exchange controls. Nevertheless, in reality, it was not until nearly ten years after the start of the revolution that the government finally came to suggest calling into question the "autonomy" of the Central Bank—recognized by the 1999 Constitution, and that the IMF recommends—in order to strengthen State control over official reserves as well as interventions on the foreign exchange market, but also to finance public expenditure or to curb capital flight. For too long, the monetary policy conducted by the Central Bank, devoid of very explicit rules, has been limited to implementing inflation "targeting" and traditional interest rate regulation aimed at controlling the level of prices through the monetary base—besides, without meeting the same success as in other economies, including the South.

It is that, in the intensity of the internal political conflict, inflation cannot be rigorously contained by monetary authorities largely beyond or even escaping revolutionary power. The Central Bank could however constitute a powerful tool to induce the necessary changes of the socialist transition, in particular the transfer of oil revenues in favor of the poorest layers of the population. In our opinion, it would therefore be appropriate for democratic control to be exercised over it, via the new bodies of popular power in particular, but also for the government to increase the weight of public enterprises (and those of social production) and include them in a system of planning which would be both coherent and homogenizing budgetary, monetary and exchange rate policies.

These difficulties of the revolution in ensuring minimum loyalty at the top of the hierarchy of monetary and financial institutions, like those of the senior administration in general, explain to a large extent why the financing of "social missions" sometimes had to resort to acrobatic accounting arrangements. It is in fact from various special social development funds, connected directly to the accounts of the public oil company PDVSA (Petróleos de Venezuela SA)—which the government managed to take control after five years of relentless internal struggles—that such missions could be financed. The latter, deployed on a large scale, especially in the fields of health and education thanks to Cuban solidarity, now concern a whole range of public services provided to the population, and which have very concretely and positively changed the lives of the poorest Venezuelans.

Box 6.2 Haiti, debt vs. development

In the French colony of Saint-Domingue, on August 22, 1791, a slave armed insurrection began which would culminate in the abolition of slavery (in 1793) and the independence of the Republic of Haiti (in 1804). This, the French reactionaries have never forgiven. Besides the loss of the profits of the slave plantations (sugar, coffee, etc.), such a liberation also entailed a considerable fall in budgetary revenues for the metropolitan State. In 1825, Haiti was forced to pay France 150 million gold francs (that is, approximatively the annual budget of France at the time) as "compensation" for the former settler owners, in exchange for recognition of its existence as a new State. Illegitimate, this debt was imposed (by the vanquished on the victor!) under the threat of a military invasion of Port-au-Prince, which left the risk of a possible restoration of slavery in the event of disobedience and defeat. Somewhat reduced in 1838 by a "Treaty of Friendship," it was reimbursed in 1883 for what concerns its principal and in the middle of the Twentieth Century for its arrears of interest and agios. In the meantime, it had condemned generations of Haitians to a life of misery, bowing under its invisible but crushing weight.

Shortly after President Jean-Bertrand Aristide affirmed, in April 2003, that it is France which is indebted to Haiti, and not the other way around, and asked for "restitution and reparation" for the damage suffered (estimated at 21 billion dollars), he was overthrown by a politico-military intervention of the United States and France (February 2004). And no politician spoke about it again afterward. After the earthquake of January 2010, 56 million euros were deducted from the bilateral debt owed to the Paris Club*, a minimal portion of the capitalization of the amount of this odious debt.

Rather than accede to this demand for reparations, the French government saw fit to grant the status of "political refugee" to the Haitian dictator Jean-Claude Duvalier, whose crimes go unpunished—and personal fortune would have made it possible at the time (1986) alone to pay off the country's external debt.

The Cuban Experience

The partial and temporary dollarization of the Cuban economy is an original and complex phenomenon. Since the beginning of the "special period" in 1990, Cuba had equipped itself with new engines of economic growth and rebalancing of its balance of payments (tourism, foreign investments, remittances or *remesas*), which were also vectors of dollarization. The latter, consequence of the extremely serious crisis experienced after the disappearance of the USSR and the CMEA (or COMECON), was decided in 1993. It took the form of a decriminalization of the holding of dollars, but also of the authorization to open accounts, to purchase goods from State stores or to receive funds from abroad in that foreign currency. It was manifested by the simultaneous circulation of three distinct monetary units on Cuban territory: (*1*) the Cuban peso (CUP), national currency, inconvertible; (*2*) the dollar, the world reserve; and (*3*) the convertible peso (CUC), the internal equivalent of the dollar which expressed, as a measure of value, the level and dynamics of U.S. productivity relative to the rest of the world. This multiplicity of currencies was associated with a double exchange system (1 dollar for 1 peso at the official rate, but 1 dollar for 26.5 pesos at the semi-official rate of the time), with a compartmentalization of the local economy into monetary circuits which were interconnected, but sealed and tight, within which the price structures of similar goods could be differentiated.

The Cuban public authorities therefore decided, under constraint, to partially dollarize, but by integrating this contradictory process within the framework of a strategy of "recovery" that they managed to control. Thanks to this scheme, the revolutionary government partially achieved its objectives of increasing foreign exchange inflows, reducing external imbalances and securing recovery, while shifting the economy's center of gravity from the sugar sector to that of tourism. And above all, it finally allowed it to preserve the social system of the country, as much as possible. Its maintenance is due to the establishment of an inter-sectoral transfer mechanism using two exchange rates: one overvalued (official rate), the other (semi-official) very probably undervalued. Direct State subsidies to public production units were reduced and relayed by various inter-company equalizations. Dollarized entities (in the tourism sector, joint ventures, emerging sectors, etc.) have benefited from priority investments and management autonomy of the foreign currencies at their disposal. In return, they drained income in dollars to the State by transferring their surplus currency balances to the *Caja Central de Divisas* (Central Foreign Currency Fund), by collecting wages in dollars from their employees (paid in pesos), or by resorting to the fiscal route.

Dollarization has involved the placing of products of domestic units in competition with imports at world prices. Historically an exporter, the sugar sector also helped to drain dollars, but without the same freedom in their use, because its mutation had to be controlled to orient the "factors" of economic growth towards new engines. The system was designed so that all fundamental entities (food, social services, infrastructure...) could finance their acquisitions of inputs by buying dollars at the *Caja Central de Divisas* with pesos at the official rate of 1 to 1, and continue to provide the bulk of their goods and services free of charge (education, health) or at extremely low prices (consumption, housing, water, electricity, telephone, transport, culture). With the recovery of the economy, the semi-official exchange rate of the peso, very depreciated in 1994 (95 pesos against the dollar on average), revalued quickly enough to stabilize at 21 pesos from 1996 to 2001, before slipping to 28 pesos after the sharp post-September 11 contraction in tourist activity, then to return to 26 pesos. In 1996, the exchange rate appreciation represented a transfer of over a billion pesos from dollar holders to the rest of the population. Dollarization also had an influence on planning, which was not abandoned, but changed its instruments, now monetary and financial in nature, and more decentralized. Even dollarized, the socialist system was much more than a simple Welfare State in the tropics.

However, these monetary reforms have not had positive effects only—far from it. Among their undesirable consequences, it should be noted that the situation created a wedge between those who had and those who did not have access to sources of income in dollars, which resulted in social differentiation. Being paid only in pesos, workers performing functions essential to society (among others, industrial workers, peasants, doctors, teachers, researchers, etc.) were penalized compared to others who could access to the dollar. The equality of the structure of domestic remuneration and the existence of a large system of public services, recognized at the international level, constitute the success and one of the justifications of the revolutionary process. This could only be destabilized by the fact that part of the population's income was no longer based on work or on social rights, but came from remittances (*remesas*), conversions in exchange offices or the informal sector. The "parallel" circulation of the dollar made it more difficult to control these phenomena, especially as the different circuits of the economy remained interconnected through the exchange rate. The incentives to work and to increase productivity were themselves blurred. Inequalities were most evident in the concentration of bank deposits.

The rise of a much richer social stratum with accumulated funds in foreign currency sharpened internal contradictions. Its expansion risked consolidating anti-socialist forces hostile to the program carried by the revolution. Dollarization was likely to fuel both economic and political instability. The threats weighing on society were such that the authorities repeatedly recalled their desire to decide to remove it as soon as conditions allowed them to do so. The question was to agree on what these conditions entail. The part of the population that benefited from this situation was unwilling to see de-dollarization engage, which posed a political problem for the feasibility of these measures. The fact that the monetary authorities did not want to introduce a sophisticated financial market made it possible, however, to always consider the reversibility of the process with realism. Cuba is not part of the IMF and the World Bank, so it has no debts to these international organizations nor adjustment constraints dictated by them. Room for maneuver therefore existed for recovery and—even if the blockade undermines them—it must be recognized that this leeway was judiciously used, in the service of the people, to overcome the crisis.

From Dollarization to De-dollarization, the Challenge of Cuban Monetary Sovereignty

In mid-2003, the government began to restrict foreign exchange transactions by announcing that State enterprises were no longer allowed to mobilize the dollar to trade with each other. The use of the convertible peso (CUC) became compulsory and exchange controls was tightened. On October 25, 2004, Central Bank Resolution No. 80 stipulated that the dollar should no longer circulate in Cuba, in reaction to the decision of the G.W. Bush administration to tighten the blockade on financial transfers. The change of monetary system chose to give a central role to the CUC. Revalued in the process, it replaced the dollar and was to be used in all domestic commercial transactions at the 1 to 1 exchange rate. Dollar accounts remained available and guaranteed by the banking system. Remittances of "greenbacks" from abroad were only accepted once converted into another currency (e.g., euros).

This reform did not mean banning the possession of the dollar, which remained a store of value for Cubans, who could keep it or deposit it in local State banks; nor that the economy was fully de-dollarized, because the CUC, to which a key role was assigned, remained an equivalent of the dollar. Maintaining the convertible peso as a means of internal circulation, replacing the dollar, made it possible—at least during a transitional period—to modify the inter-firm subsidy mechanisms as the supply of national producers diversified, and to increase the importance of income in national currency. De-dollarization was accompanied by a redistribution of income, including increases in remuneration and pensions, but also the widening of the range of consumer goods incorporated in the *libreta* (that is to say, the basket of food products guaranteed by the State to the population). Progress towards monetary reunification, these measures had the advantages of extending the control of the foreign exchange market and the inflow and outflow of currencies, of increasing the mass of dollars collected by the Central Bank and of deflating the black market. Cuba thus affirmed its will to recover its full monetary sovereignty.

The important thing was to extend de-dollarization beyond replacing the dollar with the CUC as a medium of circulation. Pursuing de-dollarization was fundamental to strengthening the planning and financing system of the economy in national currency. It was also imperative to prevent the internal credits granted in dollars by local banks to national companies inducing a risk of financial crises. In any case, the de-dollarization agenda had to be carried out in line with the amount of foreign currencies at the disposal of the Central Bank—a condition to guarantee internal circulation, the balance of external accounts and the increase in financial capacity of external payments.

One of the two currencies then in circulation, the CUC or the Cuban peso, was to disappear. The selection of the latter as the only currency in force in the national territory was the solution that presented the most advantages. To do this, measures had to be adopted: that Cubans and foreigners use one and the same currency, the Cuban peso, for all their transactions carried out on the island; that the assets and credits in CUC of enterprises and banks be converted into Cuban pesos, at the prevailing exchange rate; but still that the Central Bank sees its missions reinforced in order to maintain the stability of the exchange rate without conducting an excessively rigid fixed rate policy, to manage deposits and foreign currency reserves, to regulate the monetary base, to supervise the banking system, internal loans in pesos and the interbank credit market, to control internal monetary capital, to guarantee deposits in current and savings accounts, and of course to perform its function of lender of last resort. On January 1, 2021, monetary unification finally became law and the CUC was abolished.

The exchange rate policy decided upon makes it possible, by consolidating the State's monetary control, to prevent the risks of speculative behavior. This role differs from what is done in capitalist countries where the interests of banking and financial oligopolies prevail over all other considerations. However, the difficulties of de-dollarization are far from negligible. They relate firstly to the amount of foreign currency reserves that the Central Bank must maintain in order to guarantee internal circulation and meet conversion needs, by controlling the external accounts under the pressure of import demand. They then concern the determination of the exchange rate and the corresponding (internal and external) price structures—even if, after years of experience with the CUC, a certain compatibility has been possibly established between these two sets of variables. They may also be linked to the redistributive non-neutrality of this reform, which made it necessary to activate new income distribution mechanisms (by strong revaluations of remuneration and pensions, improvement in the quantity of products making up the *libreta*, etc.). Finally, an internal difficulty is to convince the population of the fundamental importance of State control over money and credit, in order to avoid any speculative behavior, and of strengthening socialist planning. The opposition of foreign banks and companies, which would withdraw their confidence in the Cuban authorities, is also a still worrying risk. However, this threat has been defused by the State, which is committed to guaranteeing foreign investors that they will not suffer any losses as a result of the reform.

At the time of writing, despite real concerns related to the economic impact of the COVID-19 pandemic (on tourism revenues or inflation in particular), the risks associated with de-dollarization, outside or inside, seem to be relatively contained: no race for foreign currencies, no squandering of reserves, no serious depreciation... The management of the process is for the moment under control, as had been the interlude of dollarization itself. Monetary sovereignty regained, with a Cuban peso substituted for the CUC and recovering all the characteristics of a national currency—including that of being unique—also requires a more efficient productive apparatus and additional productivity gains, a self-centered development strategy and modernized planning—but certainly not through liberalization of markets, privatizations of national heritage and a "transition" to capitalism. The revolutionary government will therefore have to be ready to face the implications of a possible tightening (or loosening...) of the blockade that the United States is imposing on Cuba and which hinders the possibilities of its economy to access international capital and currency transfers from families living abroad.

The dollarization that was applied until recently in Cuba has very little to do with those implemented in Latin American capitalist countries with neoliberal exchange rate regimes. During this period, Cuba was less dollarized than economies where the U.S. dollar does not yet circulate, but whose monetary policy has no real autonomy vis-à-vis the United States. Unlike these other countries, in Cuba, dollarization was intended to provide the State with the means to continue its social interventions and cushion the effects of the crisis. Monetary reform differed from those carried out in countries also under the leadership of communist parties, such as China or Vietnam. The Cuban State always retained the impetus for capital accumulation, which escapes the private sector, through ownership of the means of production largely dominated by the public or collective form. In Cuba, dollarization did not imply the creation of a financial market. The dollarization of 1993 also had little to do with that of pre-revolutionary times, when the reality of power was totally beyond the control of local monetary authorities. The dollarization of the 1990s was suffered by the revolution as a *de facto* situation linked to the disappearance of its external markets, but it was able to be incorporated into the heart of a coherent set of reforms consisting in admitting market mechanisms, while at the same time controlling them firmly. Their penetration is undeniable, but much more limited than in China or Vietnam. All this without forgetting, or course, that Cuba is under U.S. blockade…

References

Calcagno, A.E. and A.F. Calcagno (2015), *El Universo neoliberal*, Madrid: Akal.

Guerrien, B. (2014), "La Situation en Argentine: information et désinformation," website http://bernardguerrien.com/.

Herrera, R. (2004a), "FTAA Dangers and the Necessity of an Alternative for Development," *Written Statement for the United Nations Human Rights Commission*, E/CN.4/2004/NGO/122, January, Geneva.

——— (2004b), "Why Lift the Embargo?," *Monthly Review*, vol. 55, n° 8, p. 49–54, New York.

——— (ed.) (2006), *Cuba révolutionnaire: Économie et planification*, Paris: L'Harmattan (collection Forum du Tiers Monde).
——— (2010), *Les Avancées révolutionnaires en Amérique latine*, Lyon: Parangon.
Herrera, R. and P. Nakatani (2003), "Reflexiones para una desdolarización en Cuba," *Revista Venezolana de Análisis de Coyuntura*, vol. 9, n° 2, p. 277–296, Caracas.
——— (2004), "Dollarization in Cuba," *International Finance Review*, vol. 5, p. 115–134, Oxford.
——— (2008), "Structural Change and Planning in Venezuela," *Review of Radical Political Economics*, n° 40, p. 292–300, New York.
Herrera, R. and M. de Souza Sabadini (2008), "France 0–0 Brésil: l'échec du réformisme," *La Pensée*, n° 355, p. 69–80, Paris.
Marques, R.M. and M. Ribeiro Jansen (eds.) (2010), *O Brasil sob a nova ordem - A Economia brasileira contemporânea*, São Paulo: Editoria Saraiva.

7

Asia in Search of a Better Future for It (and for the World): *From the "Asian Crisis" to Controlling Monetary Policy*

子曰。 篤信好學、守死善道。危邦不人、亂邦不居、天下有道則見、無道則隱。 邦有道、貧且賤焉、恥也、邦無道、富且貴焉、恥也。

(*Zǐ yuē. Dǔxìn hào xué, shǒu sǐ shàndào. Wēi bāng bù rén, luàn bāng bù jū, tiānxià yǒu dàozé xiàn, wúdàozé yǐn. Bāng yǒu dào, pín qiě jiàn yān, chǐ yě, bāng wú dào, fù qiě guì yān, chǐ yě*).

The Master said: Be of unshakeable faith and love to learn. Whatever the cost, stand firm in the pursuit of the Righteous Way. Do not enter a country in peril, do not reside in a country in chaos. When the Righteous Way prevails in the country, show yourself. When not, hide. When the Righteous Way prevails in your own country, then being poor and obscure is a shame. However, when this Righteous Way does not prevail, it is being rich and honored that is a shame.

Confucius, *Analects* (Lún Yǔ, Tai Bo, VIII-13)

To counteract persistent deflation since 1997 and overcome an even older stagnation, the Central Bank of Japan decided to reduce its key interest rate to zero, then developed in 2000, and applied between March 2001 and March 2006, and again from 2010 to 2012, a monetary policy

R. Herrera, *Money*, Global University for Sustainability Book Series,
https://doi.org/10.1007/978-981-19-2848-2_7

described as "unconventional." On this occasion, it invented "Quantitative Easing" (QE) consisting for the Bank of Japan to massively increase liquidity by creating credit money by allowing the direct purchase of public debt securities (bonds of the Treasury, among others) or assets—including of questionable quality—of commercial banks and domestic private companies. As we know, this method flourished and was replicated, from 2008, by the Fed and the Bank of England, then by the European Central Bank, before being generalized throughout the world. Nevertheless, initially, in the case of Japan, the new process did not really lift the country out of the doldrums. Besides, the era was that of the aftermath of the so-called Asian monetary crisis of 1997–1998, the implications of which had already spread durably and widely to Russia and the economies of the former USSR, or even Mongolia, and beyond, on other continents.

This crisis has swept through most of the countries in the region, starting with Thailand, Indonesia and the Philippines, where its socioeconomic effects have also provoked certain geopolitical upheavals, locally or regionally. We remember the former president Soeharto forced to sign—seated, humiliated, with behind him, standing, arms crossed, the director of the IMF—the letter of intent that this institution imposed on Indonesia… before being pushed out by the uprising of his people. Washington, which had always supported the dictator, refused to participate actively in the rescue plans of the many Asian countries affected by the crisis and pressured the Japanese government to do the same. That is to say, to do the bare minimum. The Chinese authorities, on the contrary, did not play the worst-case strategy by seeking to take advantage of the situation (for example, by devaluing their currency), even as their country's exports suffered from the fall of neighboring currencies. Indeed, the Chinese provided substantial financial assistance to the region and asserted themselves as a responsible partner, behaving in solidarity.

It is South Korea, a highly industrialized country among those affected in the region, which has seen its GDP decline the most under the impact of the crisis; also the one whose government most ostensibly preferred to follow the line of neoliberal orthodoxy—and it was going to pay dearly for that choice. In contrast, experiments in the State's reappropriation of a certain power of political decision over money, carried out not without courage and difficulties, have nevertheless helped some economies to extricate themselves from the quagmire in which they were stuck. As such, Malaysia certainly deserves our attention. Taiwan held the shock. Vietnam also resisted quite well.

The fact remains that today much of Asia is still facing an ongoing challenge: that of trying to limit the repercussions of the monetary disorder imposed by the continued hegemony of the U.S. dollar. This is true from Turkey to India, passing of course through the Middle East, the oil reservoir over which the United States retains control. Under the supervision of the latter, the dollarized oil monarchies of the Gulf have for their part been militarily bunkerized. A few islands of stability remain, however, such as Singapore. In Asia, whose economic and demographic weight will count decisively in the inflection of the trajectory of the whole world, only the People's Republic of China seems to have the means and ambitions to put an end to the monetary and financial domination of the United States, thanks to an effective public control of its currency. We will explain for what reasons.

An "Asian" Crisis... Which Does Not Really Have Its Origin in Asia

The "Asian" crisis was above all a currency crisis. It broke out in Bangkok on July 2, 1997. Less than a year earlier, the World Bank had published a report devoted to the "Thai miracle." Its publication followed that of a famous work by the same institution attesting to another "miracle," even more impressive because collective, Asian in general—but which strangely did not mention neither of the two countries with the fastest GDP growth rates, namely, neither China (the People's Republic) nor Vietnam (also led by a Communist Party). Why then did these "experts" in Washington need to invoke divine intervention to speak about these facts, when the "God" who threw down the course of the baht, the Thai currency, was none other than a green note whose name everyone knew? The United States dollar. Nor was it about predicting the future—who could do it, if not charlatans? It was more a question of understanding the sequences at work. And, if possible, to go back to their main cause(s).

The decade before this crisis had been marked by accelerated GDP growth in many countries in the region. Apart from the yen, the strongest currency in this space and which appreciated against the U.S. dollar during the period 1985–1995, numerous Asian countries officially or unofficially anchored their national currencies to the U.S. currency. For their part, a lot of international investors, whose pursuit of profits was mainly guided by changes in interest rate differentials at the center of the global system, borrowed in dollars at the time—i.e., at a time when the United States was in recession and when the Fed lowered its funds rate (from 9.75% in December 1988 to 4.0% in December 1991, and even 3.0% in September 1992)—in order to invest huge funds in Asia. Not so much in Japan, where interest rates were low, and where big speculators came to raise money, but rather in the markets of so-called emerging Asian countries. Especially since the governments of these countries had for the most part opened their capital accounts*, under pressure from the U.S. Treasury and the IMF, both concerned to find more outlets for the oligopolies of globalized high finance. Free float capital thus flocked to Asian markets, rushing wherever profitability was high, particularly in the real estate sector. And at the same time, the relatively good performance of the region's currencies, pegged to the dollar, tended to penalize exports, increase the cost of imports and therefore widen current account deficits, covered by short-term financing which made these countries vulnerable.

It had been several months since the yield on money in the United States had risen again above the 5% mark when, in the Spring of 1997, the Thai real estate bubble burst. The defense of the national currency—and of the Bangkok Stock Exchange, in the midst of frenzied speculative behaviors and all kinds of fraud and corruption scandals—required that local monetary authorities part with large amounts of U.S. dollar reserves, until to finally force them to let the baht float. The fall was almost immediate and vertiginous. Within weeks, as the dollar continued to appreciate, panic spread to other Asian countries, whose fixed exchange rates were going to explode. Their currencies also unscrewed, with the ebb of floating capital: the rupiah of what officials at the Davos Forum liked to call the "Indonesian Goliath," but also the South Korean won, then the Malaysian ringgit. The Taiwan dollar, those of Hong Kong (British until July 1, 1997) and Brunei, but also the Laotian kip, the Philippine peso and the Indian rupee were also affected, although less violently. This regional collapse in exchange rates caused a meltdown in the stock markets. The indices of the places of Bangkok, Manila or Kuala Lumpur lost more than a third of their values over the first nine months of 1997, and the movement accelerated even during the last quarter of the year, to represent between two-thirds and nearly nine-tenths of capitalizations (for example, in Bangkok: −84%). In 1998, GDP levels had fallen by −7.0% in South Korea, −10.1% in Thailand or −14.2% in Indonesia...

The flight of capital redoubled. This weakened banking systems, themselves very often lacking rigorous (and honest...) supervisory institutions. Bad debts abounded, deteriorating the mistrust of international investors. The continued depreciation of local currencies accelerated capital outflows, as well as the difficulties of financial systems having to cope with loan repayment deadlines demanded by foreign banks. In an attempt to slow the fall in exchange rates, the domestic Central Banks raised their interest rates and tightened credit conditions, which affected local productive systems—the credit crunch* phenomena first hitting small and medium-sized enterprises. While China's GDP growth rate fell from +9.2% in 1997 to +7.8% in 1998 (against, respectively, +6.8 and +4.7% in Taiwan, +5.0 and −5.1% in Hong Kong and −0.7 and −2.1% in Japan, over the same period), the largest country in Asia, by maintaining the exchange rate of its national currency against the U.S. dollar, then held a role of real dyke for the region.

By 1997, the Russian economy had its first year of positive GDP growth since 1991 and the creation of the Russian Federation, but its fixed exchange rate regime did not withstand the shock. The currency crisis hit it in mid-1998, triggering a sovereign debt crisis and a banking crisis, then spreading to ex-Soviet Central Asian countries. The latter, much less indebted, and less financially developed too, had not received, like East Asia, huge amounts of free-float capital and were not as exposed as it to the risk of these flows being reversed. Nevertheless, the channels of transmission of the crisis, via the foreign exchange market, were quite similar in these two parts of the continent. Responses differed by country. The more liberal Kyrgyzstan did not apply protective measures and remained open. Uzbekistan, on the contrary, imposed foreign exchange and trade controls. The direction taken by Kazakhstan, mapped out between the two preceding ones, accepted sprains of the market, in a partial and temporary way. The Central Bank of Tajikistan sharply devalued its currency, then intervened massively. That of Turkmenistan preferred to try to maintain its monetary parity against the U.S. dollar and rather let slip the budget deficit.

South Korea, or Neoliberal Relentlessness

The specificities and varieties of the national framework cannot obviously be underestimated, but their importance can be seen more in the assessment of the internal consequences of the crisis than in the identification of its causes. For, in any case, the primary origin of this crisis was the opening of economies insufficiently endowed with protective and regulatory institutions within a liberalized and flexible international monetary system placed under the domination of the U.S. dollar. The same goes, of course, to South Korea, and does not change anything fundamentally the fact that this country, for years, therefore before the date when it was affected (September 1997), showed obvious signs of shortness of breath. These signs were perceptible through the phenomena of over-indebtedness, sectoral overproduction, but also chain bankruptcies of conglomerates, or *chaebôl*, closely linked to local private banks, especially those of "medium" size in the sectors of construction, steel, automotive, clothing or food. Only a few weeks before the stall in the Korean financial markets, which took place precisely from November 21 on, an IMF mission concluded, again, that the success story of South Korean development was not going to be disrupted by the monetary turmoil that swept away its neighbors of South-East Asia… It was well seen, ladies and gentlemen experts: at the beginning of December, the country was on the verge of default.

Against the dollar, the value of the won was halved during the month of November 1997 alone. The currency crisis, which quickly degenerated into a liquidity crisis, then a solvency crisis, became the deepest that South Korea had suffered since its formation at the end of the 1950–1953 war. The country came out of this crisis transformed. By mid-1999, when a recovery took hold, the ownership structure of its industries—which the nation had taken nearly half a century to build—was pervaded by Western financial oligopolies and their transnational corporations; society was ravaged by new disorders; the pact of national union even appeared to be called into question. The restructuring process itself remained fragile, as illustrated by the bankruptcy of Daewoo, the country's second largest *chaebôl* (crumbling under hundreds of millions of dollars in debt), and the difficulties faced by number one Hyundai. The Fed worked to convince commercial banks to reschedule their loans. The extent of the emergency financial aid released at the end of 1997 by the IMF (21 billion dollars, the largest support ever provided at the time to a member country. or just the equivalent of the amount of capital flight that same year, however), as well as by the World Bank and the Asian Development Bank, was commensurate with the severity of the shock suffered. In return for this, a very harsh austerity policy was put in place.

On the labor market, the crisis had the effect of accentuating the flexibility of wages and worsening the dualism of jobs—traditional phenomena in South Korea—but also—unprecedented facts—the appearance of mass unemployment and growing inequalities. Before the 1997 crisis, South Korea was of all the OECD countries the one with the highest rate of GDP growth in real terms (+8.7% on average from 1985 to 1995) and the lowest unemployment rate (2.0% of the active population in 1996). The decline in per capita GDP, from 10,550 dollars to 7,970 dollars between 1997 and 1998 in purchasing power parity, brought the country down from 24 to 55th in the world. The unemployment rate quadrupled between the end of 1997 and the beginning of 1999 to exceed 9.0% of the active population at the latter date. The hardest hit were young people, the unskilled, temporary workers, women and the elderly. Employment contracts have become more precarious, with many workers moving from high-paid, permanent jobs to lower-paid, fixed-term jobs. Many slipped into informal, agricultural or intra-family work, inflating underemployment. The contraction of real wages was −12.5% between mid-1997 and the end of 1998. The share of wages in national income fell from 55.0 to 50.8% between 1997 and 1998, while that of profits leaps.

Under these conditions, purchasing power fell in 1998, as did household consumption (−8.6% for food). Gini's income inequality coefficient rose from 0.28 to 0.32 over 12 months. The number of very poor people, whose per capita consumption is below 80% of the poverty line, tripled in the country between 1997 and 1998. In urban areas, the poverty rate doubled, to approach 20% of population in 1998. By that date, all urban household quintiles had experienced declines in income—except the better-off, whose wealth continued to increase, in particular thanks to high real interest rates. The crisis was felt even in the education system: decline in primary and secondary enrollment due to economic difficulties, record abandonment of studies in higher education, decline in public spending… so many unprecedented changes for South Korea. These harmful impacts were mitigated by transfers within the traditional family, but the latter itself was quite damaged: increases in domestic violence, divorces, mistreatment and abandonment of children. In summary, we have: initially, the drop of the national currency against the U.S. dollar and, upon arrival, very concretely, the aggravation of human suffering.

The government did little to alleviate this pain. It responded to the crisis with an austerity plan that fiercely slashed public spending and subsidies, and raised taxes. It drastically liberalized, deregulated and privatized. It was ruthless, without mercy in the banking sector, not hesitating to shut down the least profitable establishments—the IMF demanding the elimination of half of the jobs there. It further tightened competition in the private sector, but took over part of the debts contracted by large companies. It opened the economy wide to foreign capital, which had long stood ready to step into the breach. To restore "*financial market confidence*" in the won, the monetary authorities deepened the liberalization of the capital account and reaffirmed their priority given to strict control of inflation and of the money supply by tightening credit and rising interest rates. At least initially, and temporarily, until the won's stability is consolidated and a relative easing can be considered.

Despite its own reluctance, and the hostility of the big employers, the South Korean State admittedly adopted some assistance measures for the workers most exposed to the crisis, but these measures were derisory in view of the social tragedy the country was going through. Example: unemployment insurance. When the crisis erupted in 1997, the country was one of the few in Asia, along with Japan, the People's Republic of China and Mongolia, to have a system of unemployment benefits—the direct result of workers' struggles in the 1980s against the dictatorship. Nevertheless, the device, incomplete, in the ambient "social laissez-faire," was submerged by the explosion of unemployment, so that at the height of the crisis, 90% of workers who lost their jobs did not receive compensation; and for the others, the allowances paid have remained modest. This social cover, granted by the big employers and implemented by the State (in March 1998), was the compensation for the prior "acceptance" by the trade unions (in February 1998) of the abandonment of job security—as advocated by the OECD. But if the flexibility of the labor market quickly became a reality, social security remained a project in limbo.

Resistances in 1998: From Malaysia to Vietnam

Most of the governments of Asian countries severely affected by the 1997–1998 crisis, including South Korea, Thailand, Indonesia and the Philippines, have resolved to implement IMF structural adjustment programs (SAPs) with violent social impacts for their peoples—except for the wealthiest decile, for whom the crisis was the opportunity to get richer, including in times of extreme financial market volatility. Of course, IMF programs had a component of privatizing State-owned enterprises in these countries. Western transnational corporations, foremost among them U.S. (and European) companies, then gave themselves to their heart's content, taking advantage of the windfall to acquire property titles ceded by the State at slashed prices.

Yet it was possible to act differently, even from leaders attached to capitalism. Several countries were relatively protected in 1997 by the virtual absence of a financial market on their soil, as in Myanmar, for example, or in Cambodia (where the opening of the Cambodian Securities Exchange was not considered until ten years later, and under South Korean supervision). However, with the exception of the socialist economies, which deserve a specific and in-depth analysis, most other Asian countries were and still are exposed to the fluctuations of the U.S. dollar and the erratic movements of capital that they imply. In such a context of international instability, certain monetary authorities—this was the case of those of Taiwan, among others—chose to control portfolio investments and to oppose any liberalization of the capital account, and the firmness of their position, contrary to what experts from the IMF and the World Bank recommend to do, probably explains why their economy was able to weather this crisis without serious incident, or at least without major damage. In October 1997, in Hong Kong, retroceded for three months to the People's Republic of China, Beijing's government allowed the local monetary authorities to tolerate an exceptional violation of their status in order to proceed with massive purchases of shares in order to avoid the collapse of the Hong Kong Stock Exchange... even if it means having the cost borne by speculative hedge funds*.

The Malaysian government, meanwhile, dared to challenge the IMF. In 1998, it refused IMF funding and set limits on the injunctions of this institution by taking anti-crisis measures deemed preferable in the national interest. First, from December 1997, a completely orthodox, neoliberal anti-crisis program had been applied at the initiative of the Deputy Prime Minister and Minister of Finance, Anwar Ibrahim, supported by the senior officials of the Central Bank. It consisted of letting the ringgit float, and allowing the interest rate to rise under the effect of market forces, as well as reducing public spending. For what results? The national currency continued to lose value, and the Kuala Lumpur Stock Exchange continued to fall (despite the establishment of a support fund); the credit crunch pushed many local businesses into bankruptcy, which in turn further weakened the domestic banking sector. The recession deepened. Faced with the inability of the Ministry of Finance and the Central Bank to halt the deterioration of the country's economic situation, Prime Minister Mahathir bin Mohamad—who is not strictly speaking a "progressive" and who did not hesitate to *manu militari* dismissing supporters of pro-U.S. alignment and allegiance to IMF diktats—changed course.

Supporting the nationalist expert group of the National Economic Action Council, led by ex-Finance Minister Diam Zainuddin, the Malaysian head of government ordered, from mid-1998, a new policy to be implemented, radically different of that followed previously. It was now a question of trying to revive the dynamic of economic growth—as well as stabilizing a society fragmented by inter-communal conflicts. It was then decided to lower the interest rate and inject liquidity into the economy, but also to impose certain restrictions on the movement of capital, both at the entry of the country (by obstacles placed at the penetration of foreign investors in domestic companies) and at the exit (through the temporary ban on repatriating short-term investments within one year). Assets that were held in national currency abroad, mainly in the Singapore offshore market, had to return to Malaysia to be deposited in local accounts or reinvested in the stock market. To control the evolution of the debt, institutions were created whose missions were to recapitalize the balance sheets of the banks and to clear their accounts of doubtful or unprofitable loans.

This ambitious and courageous "National Economic Recovery Plan," which also provided for, in addition to these massive State interventions in monetary and financial matters, to boost major public infrastructure works, produced its positive results from the end of 1998. The ringgit exchange rate, which had been forcibly pegged at 3.80 to the U.S. dollar, stabilized, and the economic recovery was vigorous in the first quarter of the following year. These devices, which effectively protected the country at the height of the crisis, were however released, slowly, between February and October 1999. In the meantime, Washington had succeeded in blocking the initiative of Japan—with which the Malaysian leaders had asked for help in order to escape the IMF's ukases—aiming at the creation of an Asian Monetary Fund...

Vietnam was not directly affected by the 1997–1998 crisis; and this for the essential reason that its government, which still claims to be socialist, has kept total control of the national currency, the dông. The latter, which is non-convertible, admittedly recorded a slight *de facto* depreciation in October 1997 (by about 5%), but it has held up rather well against the U.S. dollar, probably even remaining overvalued. However, it is above all indirectly that the Vietnamese economy has suffered from this crisis; the fall in the currencies of its neighbors, Thai and Indonesian in particular, penalizing its exports (rice, peanuts, etc.) and reducing its foreign exchange income. Added to this, the flow of foreign investment, particularly Japanese and South Korean, has declined markedly. Despite everything, overall, the growth of the Vietnamese economy, although weakening, remained quite strong, at +5.76% in 1998, compared to +8.15% in 1997, and again +4.77% in 1999.

Box 7.1 Lebanon, prisoner of the rapacity of its bourgeoisie... and of the U.S. dollar

Lebanon is now going through the worst economic crisis since the end of the civil war in 1990. Its currency, the pound, which was pegged to the U.S. dollar by a fixed rate (just over 1,500 to 1 officially) since 1997, has depreciated sharply in recent months, crossing 23,000 pounds per dollar in July 2021 on the black market. In this dollarized economy, the shortage of "greenbacks," extremely rare at automatic teller machines, is severely felt in everyday life, from small businesses to gas stations, including food stores and pharmacies. Foreign currency inflows are drying up (especially since the war in Syria), but the money supply in Lebanese pounds is increasing dangerously. Between 2019 and 2020, more local banknotes were printed than since the start of the civil war in 1975. This situation reflects a phenomenon of hyperinflation; the rise in prices (especially of basic necessities) has been accompanied by a loss of purchasing power of wages, but also of business failures and waves of layoffs. Since the Fall of 2019, social revolts have multiplied, exacerbated by mass poverty and the limitation of cash withdrawals by banks. It is the latter, and a corrupt and incompetent political class, that concentrate the criticism.

The country's productive base being very narrow and economic growth slowing, the scale of imports widens the trade deficit, like that of current accounts, which is generally rebalanced by remittances from the diaspora. But this is not enough to avoid the increase in external debt, which is reaching world records. Total public debt is said to be approaching 250% of GDP today—even though the Central Bank (Bank of Lebanon) has a large stock of gold, among the 20 largest in the world. To cover its recurring budget deficit, the State issues bills (Treasury bonds*) on the primary market*, but the downgrading of the rating of Lebanese bonds tends to push the Central Bank's interest rates upwards in order to attract capital, which further increases debt service and hinders activity. The local bourgeoisie, which lends to the State, has every interest in seeing the dynamics of public debt self-sustaining. The profits it derives from its juicy investments are akin to organized looting: all it has to do is borrow abroad very cheaply in dollars and make this money grow in Lebanon at extremely high rates (sometimes around 20%), in the same currency or by benefiting from an official exchange pegging of the pound on the dollar, guaranteed by the Central Bank, which makes this its priority mission.

In March 2020, for the first time in its history, the Lebanese State was in default of payments. It declared itself unable to repay a maturity of Treasury bonds that it had issued in dollars (eurobonds) and a month and a half later requested IMF assistance (of nine billion dollars, ten times its quota within this institution), negotiated against the promise of a package of economic reforms, including the liberalization of the monetary regime and the floating of the pound, but also the restructuring of the debt (nearly 100 billion dollars) and of a banking system (rich in fifty commercial establishments). The recommendations of the Lazard investment bank, responsible for advising "reformers," did not disappoint them: first of all, the standard of living of the population should be drastically reduced! As early as 2018, under the auspices of the French government and its Economic Conference for the Development of Lebanon through Reforms with Businesses (*Conférence économique pour le Développement du Liban par les Réformes avec les Entreprises*, CEDRE), globalized high finance had come to the aid of this Lebanese bourgeoisie by dangling an additional 11 billion dollars, but conditioned by the same "reforms." Nevertheless, political life is stuck in an institutionalized communitarianism and a game of alliances between ruling classes which keep it inactive, to the detriment of the general interest.

It is clear that the line followed by the Bank of Lebanon, buying currencies to increase its foreign exchange reserves and defend the parity of the pound, contributes to dry up the local market, hampering the access to dollars of agents—including to acquire inputs essential to production or vital consumer goods. But it is quite likely that the current shortage of dollars is the result of a deliberate will of the United States, putting pressure on the political components of the country with the primary aim of isolating the allies (starting with some Lebanese banks) of the forces hostile to Washington and helping them to circumvent the sanctions imposed in the region—or to envisage cooperation freed from dependence on the West… and trade not denominated in U.S. dollars. In the meantime, wealthy Lebanese continue their extortion of public funds: 24,000 bank accounts, belonging to the local "1 per cent," would have siphoned off a good quarter of the 82 billion dollars paid in respect of the debt service of the State since 1993. Logically, in this country which is one of the most unequal on the planet and where three-quarters of the hundred billion dollars that entered from 2005 to 2015 went to invest in real estate or wasted in imports luxury goods, who should pay the bill if not this top percentile?

The Domination of the U.S. Dollar, Again

The Association of Southeast Asian Nations (ASEAN) and the Asia–Pacific Economic Cooperation (APEC) Intergovernmental Forum have proven incapable of helping countries affected by the "Asian" crisis. The lack of support and the difficulties that some States have caused their neighbors by not coordinating their actions have created great tensions between them. In May 2000, during the meeting held in Chiang Mai (Thailand), the members of ASEAN +3 (that is, the ten ASEAN countries plus China, Japan and South Korea) agreed that they could swap and buy back reserves from their Central Banks to weather the coming financial crises. The "Chiang Mai ASEAN +3" initiative is therefore an enhanced regional cooperation that would allow countries in difficulty to obtain foreign exchange from their neighbors through swap and buyback agreements. China, Japan and South Korea have said they are prepared to work not only with ASEAN, but also and most importantly together—without IMF intervention. Measures could therefore be expected to minimize future dangers to their economies.

Yet less than a decade later, Asian countries, this time without exception, like the rest of the world, were again in turmoil. In 2009, in real terms, the GDP growth rates were −2.4% in South Korea, −3.3% in Singapore, −3.5% in Thailand, −3.6% in Malaysia and even −5.4% in Japan. The Indian economy was much more affected than in 1998. These were the effects of the 2008 crisis, which had shaken the pillars of the capitalist world system and had started from its hyper-center, namely the U.S. financial markets. It was before everyone's eyes, but the chain of repercussions connecting the fluctuations in the dollar or the Fed's interest rates to concrete economic variables is only seen by insiders—who are generally reluctant to provide the general public with the elements of explanation which would enable it to truly understand that at the origin of such destructive chains are, again and again, the ultimate responsibility of globalized high finance, especially from the United States.

Nevertheless, at the present time, a large part of Asian countries remains under the sway of the U.S. dollar, to which their currencies are more or less closely pegged, formally or not. This is of course also the case in the Middle East, an oil and therefore dollarized region—since the hydrocarbon market operates using almost exclusively the U.S. currency. Not only. Cambodia, for example, is informally but effectively dollarized, in parallel with the official circulation of the national currency, the riel. In fact, almost all deposits, as also almost all loans processed by local banks, are denominated in dollars. Economies as different as those of Nepal, Yemen, Myanmar, Azerbaijan, Singapore, Georgia, Taiwan, Tajikistan, Laos or especially Turkey, as well as, we have seen it (Chapter 5), that of East Timor, have accepted or continue to accept that the U.S. dollar circulates widely alongside their respective national currencies. In this large and dispersed space, few "islands" of stability manage to float, as is the case with the Singaporean dollar, anchored in a basket of currencies whose composition incorporates weightings according to the importance of the main trading partners.

What about the Gulf oil economies? Behind their black gold reserves, they are obviously the most dollarized. The Qatari riyal has been pegged to the U.S. currency since mid-2001. The other countries of the Gulf Cooperation Council—created, let us repeat, at the invitation of Washington—made the same choice, applied for most of them in the months following its founding. All of them, Saudi Arabia, Qatar, United Arab Emirates, Kuwait, Oman and Bahrain, must build up huge foreign exchange reserves so that their respective Central Banks are able to defend their anchor regimes, which consequently forces them to align with the Fed's monetary policy decisions. This is the case, for example, with regard to the Saudi monetary authority, to the tune of 450 billion dollars in 2019, or two-thirds of national production and more than two years of imports, without taking into account the assets of the public investment fund which may have exceeded 350 billion. Besides, it is to this opulent Riyadh that Iraq, struggling with dramatic economic problems, has just turned in 2020 to demand additional financial support to that provided by the IMF. Pakistan and Sri Lanka, too, had requested assistance from the same international financial institution the previous year.

India, which nevertheless has a national currency remaining non-freely convertible and which pursues a monetary policy concerned with maintaining restrictions on the movement of capital, has recently experienced serious problems in connection with a vast demonetization operation. In early November 2016, far-right Prime Minister Narendra Modi ordered major banknotes withdrawn from circulation, catching a shocked and panicked population by surprise. The usual denominations of 500 and 1000 rupees (that is, about seven and 14 dollars), the largest ones and representing more than 85% of the total amount of cash in the country, suddenly ceased to be legal tender. The exchange of the old banknotes for the new ones was carried out in haste (in just a few weeks) and confusion (the rules being obscure and moreover changing).

The reasons by which the Indian government justified this decision have also themselves evolved, ranging from the desire to fight against "dirty money" and corruption to an incentive to switch to a dematerialization of the economy, and even the alleged objective of drying up the sources of financing of terrorism. This measure caused indescribable chaos in the country, to be measured in the movements of hundreds of millions of people, in queues in front of the automated teller machines (insufficiently supplied, the new denomination of 2000 rupees not having been printed on time) or at bank counters (the limitation of weekly withdrawals having had to be lowered several times) and migrations from the countryside to the cities (because of the scarcity of banks or withdrawal points in the area rural). It is an understatement to say that the disorganization of the economy was complete, starting with trading activities, including for basic goods.

The failure is obvious. None of the targets were met. The Modi government imagined that mafia networks would not dare to show up at banking establishments to bring their banknotes. However, the conversion reached almost 95%, so much so that the remaining and ultimately canceled denominations (potentially resulting from illegal activities, *de facto* covered by the Indian monetary authorities) represented only small amounts, relative to the size of this economy. This suggests that in this country, assets derived from corruption are clearly not kept in cash, but rather invested in gold or real estate, among others. As for the modernization induced by the disappearance of monetary cash species, we are still far from it. Even though electronic payment methods are advancing (with credit cards, Internet payments, etc.), the use of cash is still omnipresent. And, as if that were not enough, a few months later, the Indian rupee was dragged to the bottom—carrying other currencies pegged on it, like the Nepalese rupee and the Bhutanese ngultrum—notably by the swirls that the Turkish lira was undergoing, plagued by speculative assaults in 2017–2018.

Box 7.2 The unpleasant surprises of microcredit

Microcredit usually targets poor populations wishing to undertake an economic project, but lacking the necessary start-up capital and hoping to escape traditional local loan sharks. It consists, for an institution specializing in microfinance, in granting loans, most often of relatively small amounts, to debtors whom the creditor has taken care to bring together in a group, which can reach several dozen people. Deceptively sympathetic, this mode of operation is intended, in the event of repayment difficulties, to trigger reactions of mutual solidarity, but also pressures affecting the reputation of each member of the group. The latter must in fact, prior to obtaining their loans, build up common savings, which subsequently make them interdependent on each other, and undertake to respect a code of good conduct with regard to their "collective."

It is in Bangladesh where microcredit is most important today (with almost a quarter of the world market). The most famous agency is the Grameen Bank (which means "village bank"), created in 1976 by Muhammad Yunus—who received the Nobel Peace Prize for the 30 years of this initiative. Since 1983, the Grameen Bank has had the status of a banking institution, but its activities have diversified (to include the textile industry, telecommunications or energy). It has served as a "model" for other private microcredit banks, whether in Bangladesh (with BRAC Bank or ASA Microfinance, to name only the first two institutions dominating the sector in this country) or in the world (in Pakistan, Nepal, Sri Lanka, India, but also in South Africa, Morocco, Colombia or Eastern Europe). Nevertheless, many standard commercial banks have also opened departments or branches specializing in credit to microenterprises.

At present, there are approximately 130 million borrowers using microcredit for a total of 90 billion dollars (that is to say, an average loan of about 700 dollars per person, but with large disparities between the customer files). These are frequently women, most of them living in rural areas in landless peasant families, others working in the informal sector in urban areas. Innumerable are the complaints addressed to the various microcredit establishments, and revealing of the practices usually put in place. The most widespread criticism relates to the interest rates that are actually charged by these agencies: the contracts generally provide for commissions of 15%, but, in reality, the adjustments, rescheduling or penalties for delays lead to rates of around 35 to 50%, or even 60 to 75% (and even greater than 100%, when the initial contribution fund is seized). There have been many cases of mistreatment and threats from intermediaries responsible for debt collection. Even for sums that may seem derisory, these situations have led many people already plunged in extreme poverty to over-indebtedness, flight or even suicide. Dramatic examples abound on the Indian peninsula.

At the same time, Muhammad Yunus, accused by foreign non-governmental organizations, associations for the defense of borrowers and the Bangladeshi government itself of embezzling and misappropriation of a hundred million dollars in aid received (in the direction of a fifteen companies of which he is also the owner), was dismissed from his functions and expelled from the Grameen Bank in March 2011. A parterre of celebrities of high finance or transnational firms, as well as some of their more fervent public supporters, from James Wolfensohn, former President of the World Bank, to Hillary Clinton, former Secretary of State of the United States under the mandate of Barack Obama, came to his rescue.

China (I): Facing the Power of the Financial Markets

Seen from the West, China's financial system is very frequently viewed as obsolete, and its modernization deemed necessary for the continued expansion of the economy, especially if the power of financial markets is strengthened. It is accused of a failing legal system, difficulties in enforcing contracts, overly lax accounting documents, the scarcity and vagueness of information concerning creditors, unfinished banking regulations and of course the "excessive weight" of public banks. This would introduce "uncertainties," despite some "progress" made towards partial privatization of State-owned banks or reform of the contract regime, among other examples. Obviously, the argument that it would be essential to relax the "*financial repression*" of the Chinese model is finding adherents within this country, where certain senior politicians sometimes claim that such "modernization" would prove inevitable. Nevertheless, this "modernization" should not be confused with the adoption of capitalism, or the renunciation of socialism. For it is far from clear that a choice in favor of market finance has been definitively made, so massive are the interventions of the monetary authorities within the financial system, and the pragmatism of their approach is noticeable.

It is true that in China, reforms of the system of financing the economy, which have accelerated since 2005 and have taken the form of opening up the capital of State banks and the creation of stock exchanges, had followed those, which occurred previously, of public enterprises. The latter had been autonomized, empowered, transformed into joint-stock companies, encouraged to apply market management criteria, to draw inspiration from market finance methods or to develop partnerships with outside investors in special export zones. The initial public offering of large banking establishments, such as the Industrial and Commercial Bank of China, the China Construction Bank Corporation or the Bank of China, was preceded by the entry into their capital structure of first-rate foreign banking and financial oligopolies (in the examples cited here, UBS, Bank of America and Goldmann Sachs, respectively) in order to encourage learning about "corporate governance."

However, the system of financing the Chinese economy is still largely based on banking intermediation*—even if it tends to move away from it, on the grounds of seeking a certain balance between recourse to the financial markets and calls for credit banking. This persistent predominance of intermediation partly explains the importance assumed by the main Chinese banks, and the power acquired at the international level, whether the measure is the amount of assets or the level of market capitalizations, compared to their foreign counterparts.

The Chinese public authorities are moving forward and backward, in a context of ever deeper—but also very contradictory—integration into the world system. This is especially the case during each phase of slowdown in growth, such as after 2007–2008, marked by an activation of bank loans intended to correct failures in finance. At the turn of the 1990s, banks that had engaged in operations that were a little too adventurous (of a financial or related nature, especially in the insurance or real estate sectors), had been prohibited from doing so between 1992 and 1995, following the crisis in the domestic economy in 1989–1991—but they have since been authorized to conduct mixed operations that combine bank loans and financial markets.

However, in the post-2008 period, the monetary authorities were led to react vigorously with the aim of mitigating the destabilizing impact of the imported global crisis—which is commonly referred to as "financial" crisis, but which is in reality, as we have already underlined it, a systemic crisis, since it touched the center of world capitalism under the domination of U.S. high finance. The public authorities made changes to the existing institutional framework, by equipping themselves with extremely powerful control instruments and by consolidating the coherence of their national development strategy. Will these measures be sufficient? Will the chosen path turn out well? The challenges to be met are indeed sizeable, as illustrated by the recent difficulties of the Evergrande Group, a giant conglomerate and number two among Chinese real estate developers.

Nevertheless, the thesis of the "efficiency" of financial markets does not only have supporters in China. Chinese officials not only know that financial markets are dangerous, lacking in recall forces and plagued by speculative practices; but they also understand the numerous advantages of intermediation and therefore prefer to keep most of the banking system under State control, while striving to continuously improve its functioning. They are reluctant to abandon the universal banking model and are moving towards a scheme that tolerates mixed operations, but to be carried out within the strict framework of specialized subsidiaries, separated from the rest of the holding company (still with public status) and kept under the vigilance of a Banking Regulation Commission.

Besides, it is also the Securities Regulatory Commission, a non-profit institution placed under the supervision of the government, which manages the financial markets. The latter see their prices closely controlled by the State and the regulations it enacts and, if necessary, supported through interventions by the Central Bank, the various public banking institutions, and several investment funds. This applies to the Treasury bond market, which is very active, as well as to the two compartments of the equity market, that of quotes in dollars, initially the only one accessible to foreign actors, and that of quotes in yuans, which was opened, in order to attract foreign capital, only very carefully, first of all, through a restrictive system of share subscription quotas, to "qualified" institutional investors, then, more recently, to individuals, thanks to the connection established with the Hong Kong Stock Exchange. The risk of contagion effects of possible shocks appearing on internal financial markets and spreading to the rest of the economy is considerably limited by the fact that the largest public companies listed on the stock exchange have only opened their capital very little.

On the contrary, at the present time, it is rather the expectations of the various international actors as to the evolutions of the "fundamentals" of the Chinese economy, starting with those relating to the pace of the growth rate of its GDP, which tend to cause erratic fluctuations in the world's main stock exchanges.

China (II): Building a Great Monetary Wall

The danger of strong stock market convulsions, linked to the intrinsic irrationality of the financial markets, was clearly perceived in the Summer of 2015, when the bubble that had formed in the Shanghai and Shenzhen markets burst. While the Chinese Central Bank had increased bank liquidity and lowered its interest rates during the previous year, the government had seen fit to simultaneously stimulate financial market activity by authorizing transactions to buy securities from credit. The main point here was to allow State-owned companies to get out of debt by obtaining cash through the sale of shares whose value was rising and by carrying out capital increases. The surge in securities prices, notably thanks to investments made from household savings—which are very abundant in China—was going to be meteoric. Equally brutal, however, were the reversal of prices and the deflation of this bubble, as soon as the mirage of promises of large dividends dissipated. Immediately, the government deployed its monetary arsenal to stem the stock market crash and preserve what might be the earnings of small holders. What it decided then was to multiply the credits and to push the Central Bank to create more money so that the public banks and the institutions dependent on the State could buy securities whose prices were falling and thus try to redirect them on the rise. It goes without saying, nevertheless, that these new resources would have been immeasurably better spent if they had been devoted to investing in productive projects.

In such circumstances, it is understandable that it is extremely difficult to succeed in harnessing or taming the power of the financial markets, and even more so in controlling derivatives, even for a country which is currently competing with the United States for the place of the world's largest economy. And this even when the officials in charge of monetary authorities use great means, because it is not only finance, but also the stock market regulator itself that must be monitored. One conclusion is clear: without the slightest doubt, the rise of the financial markets is not the path to choose to improve the financing system of the national economy—at the risk of losing control and refraining from implementing a self-centered development strategy. It has been realized in China that the most important thing to do is to improve the internal credit circuits, continuously, and, vis-à-vis the exterior, to regulate the movement of capital very firmly.

The Chinese government does not allow the yuan to float freely, the price of which it wants to control. It thus established an intermediate regime, adaptable according to the needs of the economy and going beyond the limits of the simplifying dichotomy between fixed and flexible exchange rates. The monetary authorities act on the price of the currency by using the foreign exchange reserves (reserves which are out of the ordinary, probably in excess of 3 trillion dollars) that they have accumulated and by ensuring that the recurring trade surpluses do not push up its exchange rate too much—while avoiding a devalorization or even a depletion of these reserves.

The People's Republic of China has always protected itself from financial globalization through the use of exchange controls. Financial transactions are strictly controlled; capital flows, both outgoing and incoming, are subject to authorization above ceilings. And where these constraints are relaxed, in particular to attract foreign investors to special economic zones, it is because other protections are implemented, in the form of bans in sectors considered strategic, of limitations on participation in the capital in large banks or State-owned enterprises, and of incentives for joint ventures. To renounce this exchange control, as some suggest, would prove to be a disaster; the country would then be disarmed in the face of speculation and the flight—legal or not—of capital. Everything militates in favor of maintaining, or even tightening, the monitoring of capital flows, so as to subordinate the interests of shareholders to the logic of the development of the whole society. And what we can observe in the case of China is that the State controls capitalism there, rather than the other way around. At least so far.

With good reason, the monetary authorities have desecrated the myth according to which the Central Bank should be "independent" from political decision-makers—a hypocritical myth, since that amounts to placing this institution in the hands of high finance and its most powerful oligopolies. The People's Bank of China is not autonomous as it is an integral part of the State, and even directly of the government. In China, the missions of the Central Bank are broad and important, but cover only the regulation of the internal components of monetary policy, namely—in addition to the supervision of domestic banking establishments—the adjustment of changes in the money supply, fixing of interest rates and determining the volume of credits, and this according to the objectives of economic growth decided by the strategic orientations of the planning. In other words, these functions go in practice well beyond the control of the inflation rate, like what falls to the European Central Bank or, to a lesser extent, to the Fed (because the latter is concerned about the growth and employment, in addition to the inflation rate). What is more, even the monitoring of inflation is very different from what it can be in Western countries, since it is above all not a question of breaking the dynamics of demand in China, but of reasonably adapting the price evolution at the rate of growth of the activity. As for the external components, that is to say, the management of the exchange rate regime, as also those of foreign exchange reserves, the external debt and the balance of payments, they are placed under the responsibility of the State Administration of Foreign Exchange, closely associated with the People's Bank of China. Furthermore, sovereign wealth funds come under separate agencies.

These public institutions, which are not subject to financial markets, have so far been very efficient in preventing any serious risk of a banking or real estate crisis. All the more so since the dynamics analyzed here can also be explained by the effects of the land (1988) and tax (1993) reforms, which pushed up the prices of real estate, but also by those, in the context of opening up in international trade, from the compulsory reserve system. The latter, called the "compulsory foreign exchange settlement system", was imposed from 1994 to 2012 on Chinese exporting companies, which were forced to deposit their foreign currencies—at a determined administered exchange rate—with a specific network of public banks, thus facilitating their drainage by the Central Bank. In return, a mass of liquidity was issued and circulated in the national economy, fueling inflationary pressures, but also the formation of real estate bubbles.

Chinese monetary policy is, as we can see, extremely proactive, voluntarist, and its use is very intensive. This fundamental feature manifests its effectiveness in particular in terms of reserve requirements, a traditional tool for securing the financing system by which the Central Bank obliges banking and financial institutions to deposit a certain proportion of their outstanding deposits in accounts with it. As far as interest rates are concerned, they are admittedly no longer fixed independently of changes in money supply and demand, but they are still fairly largely administered by the State, or let us say semi-administered—despite a recent trend towards their easing. For "liberalized" rates, the volume of credit remains controlled by the Central Bank, among other instruments by reserve requirements. Limiting the ease of banks having cheap savings and curbing rate liberalization are in themselves far from bad things, given the ongoing financial disasters observed at a world-wide scale. In China, variation margins are tolerated around a floor rate or a ceiling rate for the remunerations of savings and of loans to companies and households, which makes it possible to influence the money supply in a way adapted to the needs of the economy. The result is a success. Uncertainty is limited and speculation under control.

One of the reasons for the success of China's development strategy lies in the facts that market forces are never left "free" to determine the price of money as they see fit, and that the monetary authorities keep the upper hand on the credit supply. All this is very difficult to control, but vital for the nation. Only the State, which has a macroscopic view of the risks, is able to guide the economy as a whole, in accordance with the major strategic choices of central planning. However, as interventionist interest rates do not really allow the rapid adjustment of the financing needs (of companies) to the financing capacities (of households), it is therefore a semi-administered rate regime that is preferred, endowed with ceilings for the supply of credit and floors for the remuneration of savings. To abandon this interventionism on the interest rates of savings as well as for credit would be very risky. Left to the vagaries of the financial markets, the domestic economy would then be confronted with uncontrolled capital flows; the credit system becoming sometimes too restrictive, when expectations would be pessimistic, sometimes too expansive, with an excess of debt—for example, in the real estate sector and for consumption.

China (III): Placing Money at the Service of Development

As we know, China's economic strategy largely mobilizes public investment with the aim of reviving State spending, as a key driver of internal demand. To finance itself, the Chinese State has found a method to get into debt prudently and at a lower cost: it does so with its own Central Bank—in a moderate way, let us insist—without resorting to printing money in order to limit the risk of inflation. The European Central Bank (ECB) does not allow itself to do this, alas. Added to this, in China, the State is indebted, not on international markets, as the United States is accustomed to doing, but, for most of the borrowings taken out, from its own second-tier banks. This is also the way the State acts in Japan, with the huge difference that the most important banking institutions in China are public and strictly controlled by government authorities. In the end, the debt can thus be subscribed under optimal conditions.

Nevertheless, it must be recognized that the indebtedness of Chinese State-owned enterprises, numerous and omnipresent in all strategic sectors of the economy, is imposing. The crucial role of these public behemoths for the rest of the domestic production units, particularly the small and medium-sized enterprises of the industrial fabric, could see its stimulatory effects significantly reduced. Especially since the banks, which fund them amply, have on their balance sheets many doubtful debts—which mainly emanate from opaque private firms. To cope with this delicate situation, China has advantages that other countries do not.

A large majority of these debts, whether public or private, are denominated in national currency and owed to domestic creditors. Dependence on foreigners is limited. In addition, Chinese banks are powerful institutions that belong to the State, which has the means to recapitalize them if they would struggle to recover the bad debts they hold in their portfolios, in the event of difficulties encountered by the companies concerned. Regardless, the Chinese monetary authorities have sounded the alarm; they are now forcing major banking and financial institutions to reduce their debts and clean up their accounts by tackling "shadow finance." The shift is noticeable, and China's total debt has already started to fall.

A remarkable feature of the Chinese economic system is its planning which, although it has changed a lot in its objectives and instruments in recent decades, continues to be used today. Since the mid-1990s, Chinese planning has undergone quite decisive transformations. Previously, producers were assigned directly—and free of charge—specific objectives to be achieved for their productions along with all of the physical resources needed for their achievements, through the Plan. The results of these productions were then distributed through a vast allocation system made at prices set by the State authorities. But, in such a scheme, excessively centralized, whoever received a product had to accept it, regardless of its quality or the actual cost at which it had been previously manufactured. This mechanism considerably limited the initiative of enterprises, as also the efficiency of the productive sector taken as a whole. As a result, quality and cost became "administrative" or "technocratic" problems, and no longer factors arising from a system of predominantly economic incentives. The constraints and limitations of production were then expressed by a recurrence of crises in the availability of material resources.

With the gradual transition to more "flexible" planning, both monetary and decentralized, but still led by a central macroeconomic authority, from the end of the 1990s, a certain "self-management" in foreign currency was able to take place; the final recipient has been given the capacity to decide on purchases and sales autonomously, and better competition is now possible, including from outside suppliers, while the activity levels of the production units have ceased to be strictly limited by the physical assignments of the Plan. These changes, which are liable to undergo further improvements, have allowed to rectify certain deficiencies which remained insoluble in the previous too rigid scheme of the regulatory mechanisms of producers, and made possible a gradual evolution towards economic reproduction of a more intensive type—and respectful of the environment. Such strategic planning, which is very powerful, and whose techniques have been softened, modernized and adapted to the requirements of the present—which makes it extremely effective (in particular, through decisions relating to subsidized interest rates and price controls)—is a distinctive feature of a socialist path. The takeover of the national currency and all the major banks is a *sine qua non* condition of development, as is the close monitoring of the activities of financial institutions and of the behavior of foreign firms operating on China's territory.

References

Andréani, T. (2018), *Le "Modèle" chinois et nous*, Paris: L'Harmattan.

Andréani, T., R. Herrera and Z. Long (2021), "Is China Transforming the World?," *Monthly Review*, vol. 73, n° 3, New York.

Gazier, B. and R. Herrera (2003), "Active Labor Market Policies in the Republic of Korea and Europe," *in* K. Marshall and O. Butzbach (eds.), *New Social Policy Agendas for Europe and Asia*, p. 405–417, Washington, DC: The World Bank.

Herrera, R. (2014), "Some Problems (and Paradoxes) Related to the Internationalization of China's Economy," *in* R. Herrera, W. Dierckxsens and P. Nakatani (eds.), *Beyond the Systemic Crisis and Capital-Led Chaos*, p. 237–251, Brussels: Peter Lang.

Herrera, R. and Z. Long (2019), *La Chine est-elle capitaliste?*, Paris: Éditions Critiques.

——— (2021), *Dynamique de l'économie chinoise: Croissance, cycles et crises de 1949 à nos jours*, Paris: Éditions Critiques.

Herrera, R., Z. Long, Z. Feng and B. Li (2020), "U.S. Trade War: Has the Real 'Thief' Finally Been Unmasked?," *Monthly Review*, vol. 72, n° 5, p. 6–14, New York.

——— (2021), "¿El que pierde gana? La guerra comercial sino-estadounidense en perspectiva," *El Trimestre Económico*, vol. LXXXVIII (4), n° 352, October–December, Mexico.

Lanzarotti, M. (1992), *La Corée du Sud: une sortie du sous-développement*, collection IEDES, Paris: PUF.

Seo, I.-J. (2000), *La Corée du Sud - Une Analyse historique du processus de développement*, Paris: L'Harmattan.

Wen, T. (2021), *Ten Crises: The Political Economy of China's Development (1949–2020)*, New York: Palgrave Macmillan.

World Bank (The) (1993), *The East Asian Miracle*, New York: Oxford University Press.

8

The March Towards Currencies at the Service of the Peoples: *Systemic Crisis and Currency Wars or Alternatives of Sovereignty in a Multipolar World?*

La Commune ne voyait pas les vrais otages (…): la Banque, la Caisse des dépôts, etc. Par là on tenait les glandes génitales de Versailles; on pouvait rire de ses canons. Sans exposer un homme, la Commune n'avait qu'à dire: "Transige ou meurs." Le Comité central avait fait une grande faute en laissant filer l'armée versaillaise; la Commune en commit une cent fois plus lourde. Toutes les insurrections sérieuses ont débuté par saisir le nerf de l'ennemi, la caisse. La Commune est la seule qui ait refusé. Elle (…) resta en extase devant la caisse de la haute bourgeoisie qu'elle avait sous la main.

The Commune did not see the real hostages (…): the Banque, the Caisse des Dépôts, etc. By this they held the genital glands of Versailles; one could laugh at its cannons. Without exposing a man, the Commune had only to say: 'Compromise or die.' The Central Committee had made a great mistake in letting the Versailles army slip away; the Commune committed one a hundred times heavier. All serious insurgencies start with grabbing the nerve of the enemy, the cash register. The Commune is the only one which refused to do it. It (…) remained in ecstasy in front of the high bourgeoisie cash register it had on hand.

Prosper-Olivier Lissagaray, Histoire de la Commune de 1871 (1876)

R. Herrera, *Money*, Global University for Sustainability Book Series,
https://doi.org/10.1007/978-981-19-2848-2_8

The dynamics of wealth production in most countries of the North, whether in Japan, Germany or even the United States, to name only the main ones, has been characterized for several years by economic growth rates of very low intensity. In 2020 and until the first months of 2021, the COVID-19 pandemic only worsened an already pronounced recession or near-recession situation. We have seen that, to face the risks of serial bank failures caused by the accentuation of the 2007–2008 crisis, the Fed, the Bank of England, the European Central Bank (ECB), among others, and before them the Bank of Japan, had made the decision to create money on a massive scale. The measures adopted in the context of successive Quantitative Easing rounds in the United States (QE 1, 2, 3) and in other Western countries have enabled monetization amounting to several trillions of dollars—thus inflating Central Bank balance sheets by the same amount. Simultaneously, these monetary authorities lowered their interest rates to almost zero.

However, the fact is that these devices did not have the expected consequences: their effects have vanished into a "liquidity trap" like floods of money being dumped in an endless pipeline. Neither this creation of extraordinary amounts of money, nor the reduction in interest rates that complemented it, succeeded in increasing the efficiency of capital, in significantly shifting capital flows into the productive sphere, or in straightening out investment—and even less in preventing transnational corporations from laying off workers and polluting environment. How would it be otherwise when public budgets are strangled and wage policies crushed by obsessive, oppressive austerity, which slows down the engines of economic and social progress, while at the same time condemning the ecological transition programs? Nevertheless, finding solutions to this systemic crisis—in the sense that it will not find a way out by resorting to the logic of the capitalist system, let us insist again on this point—becomes urgent. Let us say it: it has become an absolute emergency.

Systemic Crisis and Currency War

If the situation does not improve, what we have observed in the foreign exchange market is rather a devaluation of the dollar—already weakened for a long time by the decline of U.S. hegemony; a devaluation which was confirmed, at an accelerated pace, after the 2008 crisis. This downward trend was accompanied by a new surge in prices on the markets of energy commodities (hydrocarbons, in particular, with what some have called the "third oil shock" which peaked at the beginning of 2008 but which had started at least three years ago) and of agricultural products (such as cereals, e.g., hence the world food crisis of 2007–2008). Combined with a worsened budget deficit in the United States, this policy of massive currency issuance practiced by Central Banks has exacerbated a "currency war" and resulted in attempts to thwart the depreciation of the dollar or to mitigate its negative impact—which was reflected in particular in the deterioration of the external current account of some countries that trade with the United States. Everywhere it has been realized that, in an environment of generalized flexible exchange rates, the undivided domination of the U.S. dollar over the international monetary system is seriously disrupting all foreign economies; whether its price is high, floating capital then being magnetized towards the places of New York or Chicago, or whether it is low, which makes exports of U.S. products more competitive. Either way, the United States finds itself in a position to be able to impose terms of surrender on the rest of the world—as well as the pursuit of neoliberal policies. And the United States does not hesitate to crush all foreign countries, rather than to dialogue and negotiate with them.

From the 1990s, the countries of the South and the East therefore believed they could extricate themselves from the external debt crisis and protect themselves against speculative attacks by the accumulation of official reserves, while Washington continued to enjoy, without restriction (or almost), of the exclusive privilege of issuing the key currency of the world monetary system. The result was then the constitution of dollar reserves, mainly concentrated in China, India, Russia, Brazil and Japan. These reserves correspond *de facto* to loans granted by these States to the United States, and which moreover serve to boost consumption by stimulating credit in this country. The simultaneous effect has thus been to further increase the U.S. indebtedness which, if we add up the levels of the federal State, the federated States and the local communities, now stands well above the amount of the wealth produced annually there. This immense pyramid of debt is built by the creation of dollars by the Fed as well as by the international credit system. Holders of reserves in dollars, the Central Banks of the South and the East however see themselves trapped and hesitate to divest themselves of this key currency in order not to risk precipitating its devalorization and depreciating their own foreign currency reserves.

In a context of strong uncertainties, this "currency war" is for the moment won by the dollar, for the simple reason that Washington has a federal reserve system (Fed) which can itself create money accepted by other countries, which allows the United States to force the whole world to undergo the exchange rate that best suits its strategy of global domination. Successive U.S. administrations have believed that a depreciated dollar could reduce their trade deficit and boost domestic production. This is a mistake. For years, these variables have reacted little, and less and less, to declines in the dollar. In fact, economic growth is weakening in the United States—despite slight upward inflections—and even more so in Europe and Japan. And the situation is deteriorating, as the problems are now linked to the financing systems, taken as a whole, of the capitalist economies.

As we recalled, bankrupt private financial institutions were nationalized after the 2008 crisis in many Northern countries, including some of relatively small or medium size: ABN-Amro in the Netherlands; Fortis, Dexia and Belfius in Belgium; Bankia in Spain; Banco Espirito Santo in Portugal; Kaupthing, Landsbanki and Glitnir in Iceland, as examples. The State rushed to the aid of the big shareholders, without nevertheless exercising its rightful prerogatives, and by re-privatizing these banks after having bailed them out and cleaned up. Consequence: a hyper-centralization of banking and financial oligopolies. The crisis is in fact that time during which less productive or less innovative fractions of capital are incorporated into a more concentrated ownership structure. Behind these large-scale State interventions, it is necessary to discern the fundamental trend that is coming: that of the collapse of the financialized section of globalization. Neoliberal policies continue to be carried out under the command of high finance, thanks to a "management" of the debt—that is, the continuous payment of its service—and to a succession of structural adjustment programs (SAPs). They are applied to debtor countries by force of international financial institutions under U.S. control. This strategy seeks to manage the crisis of the expansion of big capital in the face of insufficient possibilities of profitable investments for the profits drawn from productive activity, and this by always trying to broaden the outlets of surplus floating capital in order to avoid its devalorization. Although they have failed to find a way out of the crisis, these policies have offered capital the opportunity of a permanent headlong rush in liberalized markets into ever more speculative investments, extremely profitable for it.

Speculation, which is generally legal, is not a corporate governance "mistake." It is the magic potion against the structural evil of the capitalist system, that is to say, the tendency to fall in the rate of profit, by offering and widening outlets to the masses of capital no longer finding to invest profitably in the productive sphere—the bursting of bubbles being the price to pay for it (by the peoples). The problem is not just speculation, but above all the extreme concentration of private property and the money-for-money gear. Since high finance is driven by a relentless quest to maximize individual and immediate profit which borders on madness today. And which threatens capitalism itself with death.

Spontaneously, the financial markets pour into the self-fulfilling prophecy, are frequently disturbed by mimetic runaway, animated by the temptation to make gains at the expense of others. Or to cheat. We remember, among other examples, the Lehman Brothers bank which embellished its balance sheet by an accounting manipulation (nicknamed "Repo 105" or "100 plus 5 per cent" and consisting in selling securities to an accomplice establishment to buy them back immediately afterward having published its accounts), in the complacent silence of financial auditors which were nevertheless aware. Such a perpetual flight into these speculative practices, which divert hedging instruments from their primary function, and banks from their fundamental mission, is obviously an illusory solution, as illustrated by the 2008 crisis when the entire system was about to collapse. To want to "regulate" speculation (e.g., through a "Tobin tax"), is to believe that one can treat the symptom without addressing the root causes of the disease. A disease whose deep origin is to be diagnosed in the current disproportionate imbalances in favor of big capital.

The urgent conversion of States to interventionism—anti-democratically actuated and aimed at making peoples pay the price of saving high finance—must not be misleading: in the policies currently followed, the predominance still goes to neoliberal measures in order to save the maximum amount of financial wealth accumulated in the form of fictitious capital. Therefore, it is still and always the giant financial oligopolies which dictate their laws to fix interest rates, to create money. or even to (self-)nationalize. Neoliberalism continues to prevail, and its proselytes are far from being extracted from dogmas that have yet been shattered. However, the high finance in power is not willing to make any concessions, even though the essential contradictions of the capitalist system have not been resolved. For the current "currency war" itself results from the deployment of these contradictions unsolved by policies of liberalization of international capital flows as also of the structures of national economies.

At the present time, the "reformist" measures have become utterly incapable of solving the extremely serious problems associated with the over-accumulation of capital actuated by high finance. Social inequalities and unemployment have not disappeared in the South, or even in the North, where phenomena of great poverty are resurfacing everywhere—since long before the COVID-19 pandemic. At the center of the world system, the advanced capitalist economies, United States/Europe/Japan, stuck in stagnation, seem to have reached an almost stationary stage, where economic spaces for productive investment are disappearing. Nevertheless, if the financialization of capitalism is not a lasting solution to get out of the crisis and raise the rate of profit, the only thing such a system can offer is the slow worsening of living and (when there will be jobs) working conditions for the greatest number. Is this the desired society?

Aware of the peril, even certain mainstream authors believe in a possible collapse of capitalism by quite ordinary sequences (via the fall of the U.S dollar due to an increase in the public debt, itself due to a widening budget deficit) or, more abruptly, by the dislocation of the foundations of the global financial system. Some harden the criticism of trends dangerously deteriorating global imbalances and suggest the need for changes deeper than orthodox banking regulation, i.e., the end of this singular form of capitalism that is neoliberalism. But all "reformisms" argue, in one way or another, that the capitalist State has the means to resolve the systemic crisis, and many of them dream of returning to a regulated society like that of the post-war "golden years." At the start of the Twenty-First Century, nevertheless, we are faced with a considerably greater degree of contradictions in the process of over-accumulation of capital than in the previous century. Contradictions that have exacerbated the social tragedies caused by the COVID-19 pandemic and to which climate change and environmental deterioration require immediate, radical and progressive solutions.

However, in the face of these emergencies, several fractions—minority, but restless—of the neoliberals become more fanatic and joins the ultra-liberal ideology. Their analyses of the crisis are based on a faith in the automatic rebalancing of the markets. According to them, one should put an end to State regulations that would limit the freedom of agents. Much more influential than we often think, these ultraliberals are therefore against any anti-crisis plan of the public authorities, in particular against the regulation of interest rates by the Central Bank. The most extremists go so far as to demand the abolition of State apparatus, starting with the dismantling of monetary institutions and policies, and thus with a privatization of the issuance and management of money.

Box 8.1 The tottering monetary and military pillars of U.S. hegemony

Crises and wars are intrinsically intertwined and their links have important monetary implications. Over-accumulation is a chronic disease of capitalism from which it cannot escape and which marks its long-term structural tendency to enter into crisis. To avoid it, a "solution" exists, drastic and dramatic: the devalorization of capital through its massive destruction. In order to successfully restart a cycle of accumulation at the center of the system, the current crisis would have to destroy additional enormous amounts of fictitious capital—including through new wars. However, the contradictions of the capitalist system have become so serious that such devalorization risks pushing it towards collapse. Since 1929, institutions and tools of monetary policy have been established, linked above all to the intervention of Central Banks, which have cushioned the most devastating effects of crises—without removing the deep contradictions of the system. Militarization is the modality of existence of financial oligopolies. Backed by the U.S. military, finance capital is trying to keep control of the petrodollar, even if this means more wars. Hence the continuing conflicts in the Middle East, a *de facto* dollarized and highly coveted oil region.

Today, much of the U.S. military-industrial complex has fallen under the clutches of high finance. The latter's hold over the arms transnationals is manifested in the control of the ownership of their capital by institutional investors, themselves owned by banking and financial oligopolies. The same is true of private military companies, passing into the hands of finance as defense activities are outsourced by the State. In a context where high finance's strategy imposed on the world is militarization as a condition for the reproduction of its power and where government agencies award astronomical military contracts to armaments firms, military spending becomes a source of profitability, transforming unproductive capital, financed by public debt, into fictitious capital.

Recall that the 2000s began with the attacks of September 11 (2001) and ended with the subprime crisis (2008); two dates of intensification of the U.S. wars in the Middle East. Those in Afghanistan and Iraq were launched at a time of changing monetary policy in the United States. The year 2001 saw the explosion of the "new economy" bubble. Faced with the slowdown in economic growth, the U.S. Central Bank reduced its interest rate or Fed funds rate (from 6.00% to 1.75% between January and December 2001) in order to get out of the crisis, while military spending was on the rise again after the "peace dividends" episode of the post-Soviet era. This interest rate will remain low until 2004 (and will even be negative in real terms in 2003), before rising to 4.25% in December 2005 to finance external wars. This context had given impetus to the real estate market, with strong risk-taking. The mechanisms that were going to lead to the subprime crisis were in place.

The Iraq war prompted the Fed to hike its rate to 5.25% in June 2006 to attract even more capital to the United States, when the housing bubble swelled and mortgage defaults multiplied. A few months later, masses of debtor households in default of payment had to interrupt their repayments. The crisis was already there and yet the Fed kept a rate above 5% until August 2007. It was only then that it began to grant banks huge amounts of zero-interest loans, without however succeeding to avoid the panic that was mounting. In the meantime, the economy had entered a depression. The 2008 crisis erupted at a time of worsening external and internal imbalances in the United States: the first to be seen in the balance of payments, due in part to industrial relocations; the second (budget deficit and public debt) can be explained by several causes, the most decisive of which was the pressure of increased financing needs due to the wars that Washington was waging to control the planet militarily.

With high interest rates inhibiting credit and growth, one "solution" has been to create billions of dollars in new money out of thin air and buy sovereign securities by reducing those rates—to zero. If the contraction in demand leads to deflation, then money will be issued in the form of government bonds, with which one will finance, in particular, mega-armaments projects. Since the fall of the USSR, the bulk of U.S. military expenditures has been carried out through debt in dollars, materialized by the issuance of Treasury bonds, that is, via fictitious capital—partly borne by third parties (Arab countries of the Persian Gulf especially).

Nevertheless, the militarization of high finance's neoliberalism is a dead end. Current U.S. military spending exceeds 1 trillion dollars. And if we integrate the amortization and interest of the associated debts (fictitious capital category), the burden is heavier. The crisis of U.S. hegemony seems insurmountable. Its ability to support its armies is running out, and it will be worse if the petrodollar's anchor slips its way and escapes Washington. The destabilization of the dollar, pillar of this hegemony, could indeed unbalance the other, the military pillar, depending on the indebtedness capacity of the country. If the Treasury bonds were no longer in demand, funding for the military-industrial complex would dry up; and if the United States were no longer able to maintain its worldwide network of military bases, its unipolar world would be called into question.

Some Nice Solutions, but Limited (or False)

The loss of effectiveness of monetary policy tools, whether traditional (by money supply control and setting the interest rate) or "unconventional" (with debt buybacks as part of the device of Quantitative Easing and their variants during the COVID-19 pandemic period, such as the ECB's Pandemic Emergency Purchase Program), has led to a proliferation of suggestions for "solutions." The latter are admittedly generally much less ambitious than the previous ones—which aimed to mitigate what is fearfully perceived as a risk of outright collapse of economies, including "advanced" ones—but they offer various parallel financing packages. Their "popularity" and, for some, their sympathetic and "ethical" character, invite us to examine for a moment these proposals, sometimes presented as "miracles," even if they are not always very original, nor conceived with coherence and seriousness, and even less up to the situation. Note, nevertheless, that, in this category, all these reforms remain fully compatible with the foundations of the economic system as we know them today.

The first of these proposals is the so-called helicopter currency. Out of the imagination of the neoliberal economist Milton Friedman (but already sketched out by the followers of "social credit" or the "monetary dividend," before being recently taken up by supporters of "universal income"), the idea consists in having banknotes printed by the monetary authorities and in distributing them—by metaphor, as if they were thrown in the street from a helicopter—to all the agents, households and companies, with the aim that this money is spent and allows, by revitalizing activity and pulling the economy out of recession, to raise prices and avoid deflation. This mechanism has recently aroused the enthusiasm of many experts, to begin with officials of Western Central Banks, including Ben Bernanke, the former president of the Fed, from 2002, or, in 2016, that of the ECB, Mario Draghi. Both have spoken of the possibility of implementing it in order to counter the recessive and deflationary tendencies observed over several decades of neoliberalism and the bitter (and indeed monomanic) fight against inflation. But nothing concrete happened.

And for good reason: there was, from their point of view, better to do. As a matter of fact, even if it means injecting newly created money into economic circuits, you might as well do it, if you remain attached to neoliberal policies, as are these senior leaders, for the benefit of high finance's giants. This is how the Quantitative Easing programs have worked. The repurchase of financial assets by Central Banks, from reserves created for the occasion, closely resembles the use of a monetary large helicopter (or rather a squadron of canadairs), but whose targets were only banks, insurance companies, pension funds and other financial institutions, leaving public services and consumers to their fate. How can one fail to see that these floods of liquidity thus poured out have mostly watered speculators and inflated the bubbles that threaten to burst? This defense of the exclusive interests of high finance by commanding monetary authorities pushes economies to the brink of the abyss.

Besides, it is illusory to believe that the helicopter money mechanism does not generate any additional public debt, as its promoters claim, on the pretext that there is no direct counterpart in the form of assets. Printing banknotes is indeed equivalent (as we pointed out in Chapter 1) to a singular type of debt creation and, since the Central Bank is a cog of the State, the indebtedness that this institution has to contract must be accounted for and ultimately integrated into the total public debt. The cost of such an operation will depend on the interest rate differentials that will be applied during arbitrage between financing methods (by new issuance or repurchase of securities, among others...).

The principle of helicopter currency is called by its supporters "quantitative easing for people." However, although it mobilizes the Central Bank to "distribute money to people," this device is in reality demagogic and contrary to the interests of the working world. Such a decision is meant to be an *ad hoc* one-off measure—otherwise, its renewal would damage the credibility of monetary authorities, and therefore also the value of the national currency. It is thus intended to replace State subsidies, which are transferred through fiscal policy and are more effective because they are better targeted; as it also risks replacing wage increases by companies, the effects of which would however be more regular and significant on demand. In this, this helicopter money proposal presents an anti-democratic aspect: it actually entrusts the Central Bank, an entity without an elective mandate and without the slightest legitimacy—to say nothing of the influence exerted on it by high finance—the responsibility for implementing a decision which usually falls to political leaders, who alone are in charge of collective choices. Example: organized by U.S. Presidents D. Trump and Japanese Presidents S. Abe, distributions of, respectively, 1,000 dollars per person and 300,000 yen (that is, 2,500 euros) to ten million households to help them through the period of COVID-19 pandemic are in reality nothing more than budgetary measures, and certainly not "money helicopter," contrary to what some media have said.

A second proposal that has recently been formulated to break the debt deadlock and circumvent the constraints imposed on the financing of public administrations is that of "fiscal currency." According to its initiators, these would be Treasury bills of low face value (not-remunerated), of limited duration (but renewable) and denominated in national currency, which would be issued in order to be used by the State to pay for purchases' government, civil servants' remunerations and social benefits, as well as by taxpayers (households, enterprises) to pay their taxes and social contributions. However, the multiple ambiguities of this project compromise its implementation and its logical inconsistencies disqualify it. First of all, the contours of the liberating power* of this "complementary" pseudo-currency remain unclear and, if restricted, it is not obvious why banks and merchants would accept it. Second, let us not forget that the issuance of Treasury bills by the State necessarily leads to an increase in the public debt—which is in opposition to the desired objective. Finally, if the evolution towards a heterogeneous monetary system is not necessarily problematic, it would become so if the Central Bank were not able to guarantee the homogeneity of the release powers of the different means of payments required to legally circulate on the national territory.

A third proposal is now relatively famous: "local currencies." They tend to proliferate today, just as in the past in times of crisis or war. In the case of France, for example, the one that has grown the most is, in the Basque country, the eusko, which has existed since 2013 in the form of denominations of one to 20, without divisional coins, or online since 2017. The issuance is provided by a non-profit association, Euskal

Moneta, whose maxim is "Eusko in everyone's hands." In general, the objective of local currencies, meritorious, is to revitalize social links, in particular by relocating production and trade and by rehabilitating short circuits. Their aim is also to dissuade speculation or hoarding, especially thanks to the principle of "melting money." The latter is then programed to devalue itself little by little, by convention, so as to encourage its holders not to keep it and to make it circulate as much as possible. Nevertheless, we have to admit that such experiments, very estimable, let us repeat it, are of limited significance; especially since these complementary currencies are not obtained by monetary creation, but by simple conversion (in the case of the eusko, at parity of 1 to 1 with the euro).

Another proposal is based on the belief that it would be possible to bend and change the behavior of the world of finance by establishing "alternative banks" which would undertake to respect the criteria of "business ethics." By way of illustration, some of these institutions will not charge interest on the loans they grant and/or will direct the investments they finance towards projects whose purpose meets the requirements of social justice or environmental protection. Most of these banks (or their specialized subsidiaries) are fully incorporated into the standard financial system, less concerned with "ethics"—and, of course, listed and publicly traded. This "niche" is also perceived as attractive by the large financial oligopolies which have all opened specialized departments in an attempt to attract new clienteles obeying moral principles. One variation of this approach is "Islamic finance," obviously more widespread in predominantly Muslim countries. And it is Malaysia that is today in the lead for the diversity of products offered and for demand. In practice, many tricks are employed in order to circumvent religious prohibitions and/or to make them reconcilable with the current process of financialization, as we observe ostensibly it in the Gulf countries or even, more discreetly, in Iran, with the informal financial system of so-called "charity funds" or "interest-free loan" (called "*sandogh-e gharz ol-hassaneh*").

Fifth proposition, among many others that it is impossible to review here exhaustively: microfinance. However, we have seen previously (in Chapter 7) some of the harmful effects of microcredits. In extreme cases, these devices are real scams, akin to usury. The fact is that, as with "ethical finance," many large traditional institutions have integrated these modes of financing into the range of services they offer to their customers. The goal, of course, is to try to bring into the universe of monetization the nearly two billion adults in the world who do not yet have personal bank accounts. Incidentally, in contexts where modern institutional frameworks are lacking, it is a question of absorbing the traditional networks of "tontines," these informal mini-banks—widespread in the countries of the South, in different forms and with multiple advantages—collecting voluntary deposits from members of a community and distributing the savings thus pooled or mutualized among them in turn.

Recent Changes in Money and the Responses to Them

It is clear that despite its appealing aspects, the "solutions" presented above are not really attractive. According to those considered, they call for reasonings which either introduce confusion between monetary and budgetary policies (helicopter money), are poorly designed (fiscal money) or turn out to be far from up to the challenges to be met (local currencies), either play a double game by serving two parties at the same time (ethical banks), or ultimately conceal their real motivations (microfinance). Nevertheless, their common weakness is to imagine that it is possible to change the order of things without questioning the productive base and the ownership structure of society, nor either altering the political base of money or the current course of financialization of the capitalist system. Yet it is this financialization, especially through the rise of fictitious capital, that is at the root of the crisis.

As capitalism develops, money appears more and more fetishized and comes to be converted, under the domination of capital, into the main expression of wealth, just like a talisman or an idol, until to camouflage capital itself. However, the forms that money takes have changed considerably in recent times. Today, money's hold over contemporary economies has grown to such an extent that… some people have it under their skin! In Sweden, where the will to abandon coins and banknotes has been displayed by the public authorities for several years, individuals have agreed to have a subcutaneous electronic chip implanted with which they can make certain purchases. Like features available on smartphones (from various brands, including Apple), payments by biometrics or facial recognition of customers have also been experienced in many countries, including the United States, Denmark and Nigeria. Recently, the transnational e-commerce company Amazon tested a method of payment by identification of the palm of the hand.

The bank account tends to become an integral part of the identity of individuals, a monetary extension of their physical person, establishing an ever closer link between them and their money; while money seems simultaneously, and paradoxically, to separate itself more and more from human labor, and that the amounts of fictitious capital increase and its forms become more complex. As a result, transactions are made more instantaneous, easy, "painless," but also more intrusive and less controlled by agents. The disappearance of physical currency is announced for soon, but it is difficult to implement because of some of its drawbacks, in particular the inequalities that this development introduces with regard among others to the elderly, to modest families and to technologically under-equipped households, who cannot live without any cash. In the meantime, the share of coins and banknotes continues to decline and uses are changing at an accelerated rate. The digitization of transactions is progressing: through smart cards, by "contactless" payments, via mobile phones with quick response (QR) codes or with other types of bar codes, etc. All the more so as the traceability of monetary flows is infinitely easier in a digitized world than with cash.

The so-called electronic currencies, which, although supplied by cash or transfers, are neither fiduciary nor scriptural, but stored in digital memories without a bank account, have developed considerably in recent years, and in a very competitive environment. An example of this success is provided by the case of M-pesa, launched in 2007 in Kenya by the telephone operator Safaricom, a subsidiary of the Vodafone group. This is mobile money (pesa meaning "money" in Swahili, appended to "M" for mobile), which allows users to easily make small money transfers or pay bills from their mobile phone. In a decade, this firm—initially supported by IBM and the British Cooperation Office, among others—has attracted some 30 million users in more than ten countries (neighbors, such as Tanzania and Mozambique, or distant, such as Albania and up to Afghanistan) and now provides a wide range of services, from providing loans to international transfers. Other private companies have replicated this technology in various places in Latin America, in Paraguay, Honduras, El Salvador… At the origin of such innovation, there was the observation of informal practices; in this case, those consisting in ceding telecommunications credits within solidarity networks. This practice is frequent in many countries of the South (in Uganda or Botswana, among many others) and particularly adapted to the repayment of microcredits (e.g., in India, in Egypt or in Romania). Nonetheless, it mainly diffused when infrastructure or financial regulations were lacking, and performed significantly less well in more banked environments, such as in South Africa.

Crypto-Currencies*: New Forms of Fictitious Money… and of Power Relations

In reaction to a growing mistrust manifested towards banking establishments, but also towards State institutions themselves, recently emerged crypto-currencies, or "digital currencies," also called "electronic" or "virtual"—even if the terminology, which is not yet fixed in the matter, covers distinct facts. Their main originality is that they allow their users direct contact, whether between buyer and seller or between creditor and debtor; this by going over the banking centralization mechanisms and, what is more, by escaping the national tax regulations, thanks to the anonymized and ultra-secure procedures which are employed.

The first crypto-currency, bitcoin, was introduced in 2009 by an individual (or a group) whose identity is unknown. The creation of bitcoins sets in motion a complex technique called, not by chance, "working the mine" or "mining." This is data processing in a decentralized network, operating on a global scale and connected around open source software (where each member receives two keys, one "public," known to all, and the other private, kept secret). To be created, bitcoin uses a technology known as a "blockchain"* of encoded and authenticated transactions that are added and articulated with each other. The "miners," who are individuals and now mainly companies and specialized data centers, are encouraged to enter the bitcoin network not only by the valuation of the course, but also by the existence of a reward: like the protocol codes of this cryptographic currency foresee it, they receive bitcoins at regular intervals if they prove their participation in the "mining" by solving, thanks to the use of powerful computers which generate the blocks, equations of increasing complexity over time and production (the total amount of bitcoins to be issued being limited). After the meteoric success of bitcoin, thousands of other crypto-currencies were launched (e.g., litecoin created in 2011, ripple introduced in 2012, dogecoin which dates from 2013, dash [in 2014], ether [2015], lisk [2016], aave [2017], etc.). It now appears every day. Many of them are intended to serve as a means of circulation or payment between the various national currencies themselves.

Rather, crypto-currencies should be qualified as "crypto-assets," as they are still far from fulfilling all the functions of currencies. They are characterized by a very great instability of their prices, which tends to exacerbate the risks considerably. Nevertheless, these innovations are extremely important, in the sense that they carry potentialities, most of which certainly remain to be explored—in terms of "smart contracts" or data confidentiality, among other examples—but which open up to future radical transformations of money. Since they are denominated in their respective national currency units, it is necessary to establish between these crypto-currencies and the currencies considered exchange rate correspondence tables. And in this process, from the moment when bilateral conversion rates are determined and allow economic transactions to be denominated in crypto-currencies, with a decimal measurement standard, the crypto-currencies could replace national currencies. A crucial problem to be solved here arises from the calculation of these exchange rates, precisely because of the effects of the extreme volatility of their prices and of their exchange rate regimes which are defined in virtual markets. An extreme volatility which is in fact indicative of highly speculative assets. Illustration: in 2017, the price of bitcoin took off from 1,000 to 20,000 dollars, then fell below the 10,000 dollar mark in early 2018. This yoyo movement was replicated in 2019, with less amplitude, before the new boom in 2020. In 2021, bitcoin exceeded 60,000 dollars in March, but fell below 50,000 dollars in September. And this decline was even further accentuated thereafter.

These impressive fluctuations, however, did not deter Salvadoran President Nayib Bukele Ortez from adopting bitcoin as the official currency, alongside the U.S. dollar, as of September 7, 2021—much to the chagrin of his fellow citizens. Nor do they frighten the tens of millions of Africans who use crypto-currencies, in contexts of high inflation or institutional failures, to reduce transaction costs, obtain funds or preserve the purchasing power of their savings. Besides, Nigeria is also the third country in the world in terms of the number of users of bitcoin, behind the United States and India. By launching in 2018 the crypto-currency called "afro," whose tokens* can be obtained on various exchange platforms from bitcoin or ether, among others, a Geneva non-governmental organization, the Afro Foundation, has even the ambition to pave the way for the first pan-African currency…

Crypto-currencies tend to be used more and more frequently globally as a means of circulation and payment, that is to say, they come to participate in the final metamorphosis of capital—in this case, in the transformation of commodities into virtual currencies. Under these conditions, this process pushes more and more for the creation of credits in these virtual currencies freed from any regulation and any constraint. A crypto-currency could replace national currencies, or even become a global currency—if it had an economic base and/or a political will behind it. To this end, a condition would be that the virtual currency that would take on this role, or the fundamental attribute of the standard of value, succeeds in exercising it permanently, on a daily basis, as a medium of circulation, money capital and global money, in place of the currencies which already fulfill such a function within the international monetary system. Difficulties of both an economic and geopolitical nature would then arise, stemming from the United States' interest in preserving the status of the dollar as a world currency, and from that of other capitalist countries which might wish to assist it in this task.

Crypto-currencies are to be located at the crossroads between (*i*) individual (or let us say rather interindividual) initiatives, (*ii*) renewed strategies of high finance (and other private actors, such as "Big Tech" [with the largest U.S. digital transnationals: Google, Apple, Facebook/Meta, Amazon, Microsoft]) and (*iii*) organized responses from States. It is not just about computer programs and financial technology. In addition to corresponding to new forms of "fictitious money," crypto-currencies are also and possibly above all a reconfiguration of social relationships of power. We insisted on it, from Chapter 1: any form of money is a social construction, and therefore the expression of socio-economic interests and of power relations.

The success of crypto-currency markets thus tends to become exponential lately, but in a context that is still quite largely anarchic (and sulfurous, because criminal finance is also in the game, for the laundering of dirty money…) where neither regulations and definitions themselves are not stabilized in any country in the world, and where the power of individuals seems to take precedence over that of governments. The libra, a virtual currency presented in 2019 by Facebook/Meta and its CEO Mark Zuckerberg, was torpedoed by the Central Banks of the Northern countries, in the wake of strong criticism against bitcoin made by Janet Yellen, while she was chairman of the Board of Governors of the Fed—before becoming secretary of the Treasury of the President Joseph Biden. This had caused the withdrawal of transnational firms like Visa, Mastercard, Ebay or PayPal (but not Uber) from the libra support consortium. But this crypto-currency project bounced back with its reformulation under the name of the diem in 2020… In early February 2021, the South African-Canadian businessman Elon Musk, at the head of the companies Tesla and SpaceX, bought for a billion dollars worth of bitcoins. In May, he disseminated concise messages on social networks that could be interpreted as taking a distance on his part; statements which brought down sharply the price of bitcoin which he bought at a low price immediately after. He also bought ether and dogecoin, among others. Accused of trying to manipulate the prices of virtual markets, he calmly asserted that he had never divested himself of these portfolio assets… and just thought about solutions to reduce the enormous energy consumption required for the production of crypto-currencies…

Towards a Multipolar World of Currencies… and of Crypto-Currencies

The geopolitical battle between the main fractions of capital at the international level takes on a special dimension with the arrival of crypto-currencies. By their introduction, starting with bitcoin, the monetary system expanded considerably. So this has translated into a new version of the currency war: that of crypto-currencies. The latter are in fact part of the divisions and contradictions at work within the great financial empires that currently exist, and more precisely between the dominant fractions of high finance which are at grips in the United States. This is in particular the case between (*i*) those of the "globalists," whose epicenter has been the leadership of the Democratic Party for several years and which is working to constitute a multilateral network of financial power (from oligopolies like Citigroup Inc. in New York, Barclays, HSBC, Lloyds in London, or the Dutch-British ING Barings and also Santander, the first Spanish bank, listed in New York, London and Madrid, among others of their "financial cities"), and (*ii*) those of the "continentalists" (with JPMorgan, Bank of America, Goldman Sachs, etc.), which remain more attached to the national territory and were for a time gathered around former President Donald Trump.

Nevertheless, what makes crypto-currencies potentially so different from what we have known so far is that they assure their users to obtain (almost) total independence from the international monetary system as it currently operates, under the domination of the U.S. dollar, but also from the interbank system of standardized messaging, transfer and payment platform SWIFT* (for Society for Worldwide Interbank Financial Telecommunication) at the global level, whose original matrix is of Belgian design, but over which the United States has kept the upper hand since the 1970s. For some analysts, crypto-currencies could make it possible to carry out the evolution towards a profoundly different social construction, as a renewed mediation in the relations of production and power, by offering an incredible opportunity to extricate oneself from traditional economic and political institutions. Such a transformation cannot, however, be achieved and unfold to its full extent without a battle being waged between the forces which rise and conquer new positions of power and those which decline and cede ground geostrategically.

Globalist oligopolies recently entered the crypto-currency market with all their might, notably through the issuance of bitcoin-denominated futures from December 2017, when the world's largest derivatives market, the Chicago Mercantile Exchange, inaugurated this innovative trade. With this launch, a large-scale manipulation of the prices of virtual currencies became possible at the same time. The giant transnational corporations registered on Wall Street, which buy and sell these futures contracts in Chicago in the form of bitcoins, therefore propelled these "digital assets" into the sphere of high finance. Banking establishments and financial institutional investors can trade derivatives expressed in bitcoins, but only a few of these operators, the most powerful (e.g., the U.S. asset management firm BlackRock in New York), are able to place orders in bitcoins and hold significant stocks of such crypto-assets in portfolios, while retaining effective power in this market. In 2018, the NASDAQ, the second stock exchange on the planet specializing in new technologies and the first electronic stock market, announced that the implementation of a bitcoin platform was being prepared, and published the prices in its 2019 index of the two most active crypto-currencies (bitcoin and ether).

The globalized financial elite, in conjunction with its relays acting within the executive boards of Central Banks and up to the Bank for International Settlements in Basel—the "Bank of Central Banks," partially controlled by large private shareholders—, was not delay in formulating the project of establishing an international crypto-currency on which it would have control. This materialized in September 2017 with the creation of the Utility Settlement Coin (USC), designed and driven by banks like Barclays, HSBC, Santander, Crédit Suisse and Deutsche Bank, among others. The objective was to prepare the ground so that in future, the Central Banks of the Northern countries could be able to manage crypto-currencies, which would make it easier for these entities to perform a variety of transactions among themselves through the use of assets that can be guaranteed by blockchain-type technologies.

We can thus understand that globalized financial capital is impelling a new phase of the "currency war:" that of crypto-currencies. State digital currencies of Central Bank would transform into an extension of the current global debt-based system, but no longer centered on the U.S. dollar. Whoever manages to have power over these crypto-currencies would then dominate the whole, because this is a matter of the geopolitics of power. China also entered this battle for virtual currencies in the same month of September 2017. The use of these assets was initially strictly prohibited for administrations and public banks—the People's Republic being the first country in the world to do so—in order to allow the State to retain control over capital operations and flows; even if individuals were left free to use them, but solemnly warned against the risks involved. And advancements in blockchain technology applications were accelerating (with Neo, for example, the first decentralized open-code blockchain platform launched in China). But quickly, the People's Bank of China, or Central Bank of China, decided to issue its own digital, public and sovereign currency. Originally, the aim was to guarantee a secure registration and transfer system against tax evasion and money laundering. The very first tests had already been carried out at the end of 2016.

In this context, the official Chinese digital currency acquires an openly geopolitical dimension as a fundamental means of exchange in the construction of the New Silk Road, insofar as it is intended to replace the U.S. dollar and, even more, would stop the attempt of globalist private oligopolies to introduce their own crypto-currencies. These same financial oligopolies are also simultaneously confronted with the interests of their continentalist rivals in the United States, which for their part are discussing the project to launch the "Fed-Coin." Even more so than JPMorgan, shortly after its CEO declared that "bitcoin is a fraud," was in February 2019 the first U.S. bank to create its own crypto-currency, linked to the dollar and called "JPCoin." And at the same time, the management of Goldman Sachs announced that it intended to implement as quickly as possible services to satisfy its customers wishing to carry out transactions in crypto-assets. Nevertheless, even though China has already become a leading country in the race for State digital currencies, and it still seems far from being ready to attack the dollar head-on, the U.S. currency appears to be on the verge of making a great leap back. It is also known that the Chinese Central Bank has taken the initiative to integrate crypto-currencies into its foreign exchange reserves. So we are slowly moving away from the initial configuration where crypto-assets had neither a productive base nor a political support.

This trend has already materialized in Latin America with the introduction in February 2018 of a national crypto-currency in Venezuela, the petro, whose value is guaranteed—for the first time in the world—by basic products, in this case the country's abundant and internationally certified oil, natural gas, gold and diamond reserves. Six months later, in August, it was on this digital currency that the sovereign bolivar was indexed, the new Venezuelan official currency substituted (at the conversion rate of 1 per 1,000) for the strong bolivar, which had itself been put into circulation in 2008 in an attempt to curb the rate of inflation. The creation of petro was primarily aimed at escaping the economic and financial sanctions imposed by the United States thanks to the authorization of the Bolivarian government to denominate exports (especially of hydrocarbons) outside the scope of the U.S. dollar. To explain this choice, there is, at the origin, the decision taken by Washington to block the possibilities of access to international credit, with the determined intention to suffocate the Venezuelan economy. The purchase by the Chinese monetary authorities of large quantities of Venezuelan Treasury bonds and the restructuring of this country's debt negotiated with Russia had, in recent years, been strong and positive decisions for Caracas. The arrival of the petro, which has its own blockchain, a legal framework inspiring confidence in investors, as well as centralized supervision by the State and special public institutions (without however being issued by the Bank Venezuelan Central), obviously helps to open up room for maneuver in Venezuela, since this digital currency cannot be subject to the control of the U.S. administration or international financial institutions.

Shortly afterward, several other countries, including Iran and Turkey, revealed their willingness to acquire digital currencies as well, also backed by the guarantee of their public authorities. While many Central Banks remain cautious, that of Sweden, the Riskbank, quickly declared itself in favor of issuing an electronic crown. As of August 2013, Germany was the first country to recognize bitcoin as a "private currency unit." Some time later, this crypto-currency was legalized in Japan as a means of payment. In this same direction, under different regulations and classifications, followed the governments of Australia, Switzerland, the Netherlands, South Korea, Estonia, Ukraine, South Africa, Belarus… As we can see, the base on which the domination of the U.S. dollar had been built for decades is slowly slipping away.

The Chinese Yuan, Finally a Major Opponent to Face the Dollar

But let us come back to classic currencies. After the exacerbation of the systemic crisis in 2008 and the global risks associated with it, the question arose of the advisability of internationalization of the Chinese currency, the yuan—i.e., the monetary unit of the renminbi, the official currency of the People's Republic of China—to make it one of the international reserve currencies. As early as 2012, Japan, then the second largest U.S. Treasury bond holder behind China, became the first economy in the North to acquire Chinese yuan-denominated State bonds. At the end of 2016, after the approval of the IMF Executive Board, the Chinese government succeeded in having its currency included in the basket of Special Drawing Rights (SDRs), alongside the dollar, the euro, the yen and the pound. This recognition is, nevertheless, a poisoned gift for Beijing.

The trap is indeed set: the international financial institutions tirelessly plead in favor of the liberalization of capital movements. However, convergence towards the objective of internationalization of the Chinese currency would require the adoption of a series of very strict conditions. These include, first, a critical size to be achieved by the economy in terms of levels of domestic production and export power, which may justify this particular status of the national currency. This criterion has obviously been met: China's GDP is now second in the world, almost on par with the United States, and its exports of goods and services place China well ahead of the latter country—and even ahead of the European Union. Another condition would be the reorientation of macroeconomic policies in a direction that would make it possible to gain the "confidence" of the globalized financial markets, in particular in terms of controlling the rate of inflation, limiting public debt and ensuring the stability of the exchange rate regime. This criterion also appears to be met, insofar as the application of anti-inflationary measures, limitation of public accounts and control of the yuan price have borne fruit in recent years. While the trend in inflation is the subject of constant attention from the Chinese monetary authorities, the price stability index is better in China than in the other "BRICS" countries (Brazil, Russia, India and South Africa), public administrations debts remain contained at lower levels than in most Western countries themselves, and national currency variability indices also show a much less volatile yuan than the real, the ruble, the rupee and the rand.

An additional requirement to internationalize the yuan would be, in addition to the accelerated growth of stock exchange activities, the opening of the capital account and the flexibility of the exchange rate regime. This would imply further integration of Chinese financial markets into the global capitalist system. Despite the current use of multiple market mechanisms in the management of the currency and a gradual relaxation of the various regulations relating to the capital account and the determination of the parity of the yuan, the Chinese monetary authorities continue to have powerful instruments of control. Likewise, and without being absent from these markets, the use of the yuan is still very limited (because it is closely watched) in derivatives trading, and relatively concentrated on fairly traditional hedging tools.

Internationalizing the yuan would certainly bring benefits to China—starting with the seigniorage right* it could capture. Nevertheless, such a fundamental orientation would undoubtedly mean a damaging submission of the country to globally dominant finance, and therefore also, to a fairly large extent, a loss of control over its monetary policy. How could China, as a new rising superpower—but not hegemonic, because that would imply that its national currency be a global key currency—manage to benefit from an internationalized yuan without being forced at the same time to pay a heavy price through the erosion of its national sovereignty and the renunciation of its autonomous development strategy, remarkable for consistency, coherence and efficiency?

Today, in China itself, the pressures are strong in favor of a deep liberalization of financial markets, but they can still be attenuated by the firmness and the credibility of official speeches which are interventionist and reassuring about the effective control of the reforms in process. The highest Chinese political leaders are generally qualified, nuanced and cautious, which indicates that they are aware of the positive consequences, but also and above all of the dangers for the future of "Chinese market socialism" that a convergence towards an internationalized yuan would imply. In the meantime, China has chosen to consolidate its strategic partnerships with its Asian neighbors, as well as with many countries of the South and East, therefore foreshadowing the construction of a multipolar world. However, the march towards the latter will not be smooth, as illustrated by the recent trade war launched against Beijing by Washington, under the mandate of D. Trump, and added to a currency war that pre-existed it. These U.S. pressures, partially maintained since President J. Biden took office, have not pushed back China as Japan was forced to do in the 1980s when the U.S. administration, under the Reagan administration, pushed for the internationalization of the yen. Today, the very tight monetary entanglement of the world's top two economies—one superpower in decline, the other in the ascendant—poses tail risks to the global system. As we know, part of the dollars collected by China via its trade surpluses return to the United States when the Chinese monetary authorities make massive purchases of Treasury bonds issued by Washington in order to finance its own balance of payments deficits.

Box 8.2 Dollar and yuan in the currency war

The present configuration of value chains shows a China occupying a key position in the globalized supply networks of many activities. The trade war against China was launched by the United States in a context where the latter had exerted, for decades, through their national currency—and world reserve currency—very strong pressure on other currencies. Aimed at trying to improve the price competitiveness of exports, the outbid in weak currencies accelerated when China reacted to U.S. sanctions by allowing the yuan to depreciate in August 2019.

The boom in exports, on which the Chinese growth "model" relied in part—only in part—has crystallized a major point of tension in international relations. The yuan would have been significantly undervalued for a long time, we hear in the dominant media in the North, and this undervaluation would even have been at the origin of the worsening of the U.S. trade deficits, because the exported Chinese goods, already cheap, would be made even more competitive on world markets by a yuan kept artificially depreciated. Hence, the pressure from Washington in the direction of an appreciation of the Chinese currency against the dollar which led, despite the reluctance and resistance of Beijing, to the revaluations of 2005 and 2012: between the time when the Chinese monetary authorities decided to no longer link variations in their currency to the dollar (July 2005) and that of the last revaluation carried out (April 2012), the real value of the yuan has increased by 32% against the dollar.

The debates between economists on the "fair value" of currencies are controversial. But we note that, among the criteria discussed, it is above all the ratio between the balance of the current account* and the GDP that is used by advisers to the U.S. governments (under Presidents Trump and Obama). The benchmark used to define the so-called "equilibrium" exchange rate would be a ratio of surplus or deficit of current payments to GDP of between ±3 or 4%. However, if we apply this criterion to China, marked by the importance of bilateral relations with the United States, we see that the Chinese ratio fell from 10.6% in 2007 to less than 2.8% in 2011 and only 1.4% in 2012. This criterion continued to be respected thereafter, settling just above 3.5%, therefore in the "shooting window." China thus succeeded at the start of the 2010s in reducing its ratio to a level deemed "reasonable," compatible with the exchange rate of the yuan against the dollar. The share of exports in GDP has been brought under control: after soaring to over 35% in the mid-2000s, it fell below 20%, or 10 percentage points of GDP below the world average. This export/GDP ratio is now lower in China than in the OECD (28%) and the euro zone (45%). It is also this openness control that has guaranteed China more stable exchange rate (and inflation) conditions than other countries. Consequently, when we refer to the criterion most used by the U.S. administration itself, the undervaluation of the yuan is not so obvious as it is said. This is unlike the deterioration in China's terms of trade, which is very real, but generally overlooked. Nevertheless, this did not prevent the United States, despite the abysmal external and internal imbalances that characterize its economy, from continuing a currency war on the foreign exchange market through the depreciation of the dollar.

The Sino-U.S. monetary conflict, triggering the spiral of a weaker dollar (or a weaker yuan), pushed the euro to appreciate simultaneously, penalized European exports accordingly (by deteriorating their price competitiveness) and thus aggravated the stagnation in Europe. However, it is China that the Western media, run by a handful of billionaires, blame for all the evils. Could it be because it has managed to deploy a development project that is both non-financial and non-warlike, challenging the power of high finance which, fed on fictitious capital, no longer offers the world anything but economic crises and military wars?

Cooperate Between Southern and Eastern Countries to Loosen the Hold of the Dollar

Today, more and more governments are questioning the dominance of the dollar, which they perceive as an obstacle to their own sovereignty and to a better integration of their country in the world economy. This challenge is yet another demonstration of the deep crisis in U.S. hegemony. Faced with the serious dysfunctions of the global monetary system, one of the solutions that can be envisaged involves the development of cooperation between the countries of the South and the East, by basing it on regionalizations that are no longer transmission belts of globalization. The last few years have seen a succession of events of continental significance that are decisive for a better future for the Global South, and for the world in general. The power of the financial oligopolies in the center is therefore increasingly in conflict with the interests of new actors rising to power at the peripheries of the world system.

In Latin America and the Caribbean, a step forward towards an international order based on equality between partners was the creation in

December 2004 of the Bolivarian Alternative for the Americas (ALBA), spurred by Cuba and Venezuela. These two countries were joined by others whose governments had shifted to the left: Bolivia, Nicaragua, then, for a time, Ecuador. It is within this framework that in 2009, a monetary agreement established a system of unit of account between members, the Sucre (meaning "single regional payment compensation system"). Its success is still very limited. The challenges are nevertheless to perpetuate the ALBA as a "federation of nations," strengthening their sovereignty as a counterweight to the hegemony of the dollar, and to extend an alternative regionalization by trying to activate complementarities with the processes of integration of the South. At the same time, other initiatives have involved States in order to draw a regional front and to conserve their monetary resources, not in U.S. debt securities or in Northern currencies, but within multilateral institutions on which these Southern countries refusing to submit to high finance would retain control. This is the significance of the creation in December 2007 of Bancosur, the Bank of the South, with which Brazil and Argentina, among others, are associated. Bringing together 12 South American countries, the Union of South American Nations (UNASUR) was also launched in mid-2008 in Brasilia, with the aim, in particular, of establishing a common currency—in addition to a passport and a transnational parliament. If the advances that can be made remain unclear and if it is not possible to affirm that its orientations will all be progressive, their initiation represents in itself an event of historic significance that could contribute to changing relations between these countries from South.

South-South cooperation projects have made great progress, especially between "emerging" countries. Before the political shifts that brought the far-right to power in India and Brazil in 2014 and 2018, respectively, the countries of the BRICS group had stepped up their efforts to march towards de-dollarization. This rapprochement was manifested by their intention to explore the conditions for the feasibility and viability of a multilateral credit institution managed by themselves. The New BRICS Development Bank, officially created in mid-2014, was conceived as an alternative to the IMF and the World Bank. It had to be able to finance, in the South and in the East (and perhaps even in the North), sustainable development and infrastructural projects involved in a search for autonomy and, for this, to issue a currency likely to compete with the dollar in the long term. One of the objectives was to weaken the role of the U.S. currency as an international payment and reserve currency. One way to achieve this goal was to boost bilateral trade, between the BRICS, but also with the rest of the South and East, denominated in their own currencies. The yuan was thus promoted as a regional currency for intra-Asian trade and foreign exchange reserves, while the Eurasian Economic Union, which brings together Russia, Belarus, Kazakhstan, Armenia and Kyrgyzstan, was considering on its side issuing a common currency, the altyn. The Kazakh government even openly declared that it was already engaged in a process of de-dollarization.

Russia announced in February 2015 the launch of an alternative to the dollar-dependent SWIFT system, in response to U.S. threats to disconnect the country from that network, and following revelations that the National Security Agency (NSA) is closely monitoring these interbank transactions. In September 2017, President V. Putin issued instructions for the U.S. dollar to cease to be the currency of payment in all Russian ports. And in February 2018, his government announced that Russian financial institutions were ready to operate without resorting to the SWIFT system. Insofar as the latter makes it possible to block international bank payments, and thus to strike individuals, companies and/or States considered as non grata by Washington, Moscow is trying by these measures to neutralize the effectiveness of the sanctions that have been imposed against its economy.

China has also successfully launched several initiatives, such as the establishment of the Asian Infrastructure Investment Bank (AIIB) in October 2014, with the aim of expanding infrastructural programs throughout Asia by circumventing the dictates of the IMF, dominated by the West, and without resorting to funding from international financial organizations, such as the World Bank and the Asian Development Bank (ADB), controlled by U.S. and Japanese interests. Forty-seven countries had applied to be founders, including Germany, Great Britain, France, Italy, Switzerland, but also South Korea and even Taiwan, despite pressure to the contrary by Washington; and 86 countries are officially members to date. Furthermore, and as we have had the opportunity to point out (especially in Chapter 4), China has been able to make its currency prevail in trade with many partner countries, well beyond Asia.

On December 16, 2014, the Russian and Chinese Central Banks activated a 24 billion dollar swap line*. Russia and China, the two giants which cooperate militarily and have signed gigantic agreements between their energy sectors, have reduced the share of U.S. Treasury bonds in their official reserves, and bought massive amounts of gold. These two countries have built up huge reserves to support the yuan. In November 2014, China had already presented a financial reform plan including a redeployment of its foreign exchange reserves: instead of recycling them by buying Treasury bills in the United States, they should be directed as a priority towards the support for the domestic economy and the development of foreign markets for high-end Chinese equipment and productions.

As we know, in recent years, relatively small States, such as Iraq or Libya, have been invaded and plunged into the chaos of war for claiming to trade their hydrocarbons outside of the zone of influence of the U.S. dollar. And it still persists at the present time a threat of invasion on Venezuela which has also defended the right to negotiate its oil without resorting to the "greenback." Nevertheless, most raw material-producing economies cannot set the price of the commodities they export, but a (group of) countries could influence how such prices are formed. China has understood this and intends to question the order that currently reigns in the oil market—where it is itself the world's largest importer. This is the reason why it has decided to launch, from March 2018, oil futures* contracts, denominated in yuan and accessible to foreign investors on the new market of the Shanghai International Energy Exchange, in order to compete with the—until then uncontested—global references that are the London Brent and the New York WTI (or West Texas Intermediate, the oil standard for defining the prices of crude and the futures contracts on this commodity at the New York Mercantile Exchange of Wall Street).

It is under these circumstances that the highest political leaders of China and Russia—countries which constitute an economically dynamic (and militarily dissuasive) alliance likely to represent a credible counterweight to the United States—have decided to launch a new currency, called "petro-yuan-gold," and to try to open up prospects for setting it up as a world reference alternative and for replacing the dollar with it as the dominant currency. The petro-yuan-gold is a global currency project that relies on the key commodity, oil, and is also pegged in gold—a feat no longer within Washington's grasp. China's advantage lies not only in the high rate of growth of its GDP, but also in the fact that it happens to be the main producer and buyer of gold, with Russia coming third in the world, behind the Australia, but ahead of the United States. In March 2018, Beijing took the initiative to promote a large petro-yuan-gold trading facility on the world energy exchange. Then, the following May, it was the metal-yuan-gold's turn to see the light of day. Thus, China intends to exchange yuan received in gold for deliveries of oil and purchases of metals. The Hong Kong Stock Exchange will also issue yuan futures contracts supported by oil and metals, that is to say, derivatives convertible into gold. Besides, oil exporters will even be allowed to withdraw these gold certificates outside Chinese territory.

These events are very likely to have a considerable impact on the international monetary system. In addition to oil, natural gas and metals which enter into this new global arrangement, other raw materials will also be affected very soon. Under these conditions, one could then expect that the Chinese monetary authorities would come to question the advisability of getting rid of U.S. Treasury bonds for dollars, to then exchange the latter in turn for yuans. The fixing of the price of hydrocarbons in yuan—at the same time as the mechanism of the Hong Kong Stock Exchange allowing the sale of physical gold contracts denominated in yuan—sets in motion a scheme through which a country could be able to bypass the global banking system, including the global dollar-linked interbank payments network (SWIFT), and even all international financial institutions.

To avoid what happened to the dollar at the start of the 1970s, when the United States had to abandon the gold standard, it is already advisable to anticipate that China will gradually introduce the yuan as currency of exchange (of raw materials for raw materials) in order to maintain a sufficient volume of gold as a counterpart. As has been said,

China's strategy is not to tackle the petrodollar head-on, but rather to see the yuan progressively occupy a space large enough to be able to function with a sovereignty which finally tends to draw the contours of a multipolar world of currencies. Just as China participated in the restructuring of sovereign debts during the euro zone crisis of the early 2010s, there are also agreements between the Central Bank of China and the European Central Bank to allow direct exchanges between yuan and euro and that these two currencies reinforce each other—but in an autonomous way—by promoting the interpenetration of their respective financial systems. Could this be interpreted as a sign that the European Union intends to keep a door open to join in future, possibly, this multipolar world under construction? It is therefore understandable that China has tangible plans to push the U.S. dollar out of its way. All of these measures have been taken so that at last the countries of the South and the East can now say to the United States: "The dollar is your currency, and it is also your problem."

The Money Is Ours: Alternatives to Democratize Monetary Policy

Clearly, great strides have been made recently in the direction of a more balanced, multipolar world of currencies as a response to the challenges of neoliberal globalization. This implies the formation, beyond the States, of regional organizations with both economic and political content. If it is part of a renewed perspective of cooperation intended to encourage solidarity and complementarity between partner countries, regionalization will prove to be an effective means of combating the polarizing effects of financial oligopolies and of engaging in collective negotiations at the inter-regional level which make it possible to organize a controlled interdependence—and to try to strengthen the social positions of the dominated peoples and the disadvantaged classes in order to improve their participation in production, as well as their access to better working and living conditions.

Still underway and with largely uncertain outcomes, these fundamental changes, which should lead to the building of regionalized exchange rate stabilization frameworks and arrangements and their articulation on a global scale, obviously call for a profound modification of the rules and regulation mechanisms of the international monetary and financial system—which would inevitably involve calling into question not only the dollar standard and "free" exchange rates, but also the functions (and perhaps even the existence) of the IMF and the World Bank, to abolish the obstacles that financial institutions impose on countries having recourse to them and to assert the primacy of the right of nations to sovereignly determine their economic path. The application of structural adjustment programs (SAPs) has proven to be totally ineffective in resolving the imbalances faced by countries of the South and East and has even caused and/or propagated very serious crises. Among the main transformations necessary to build a fairer international order, efforts should primarily focus on: (*i*) the establishment of international taxation of large fortunes, the profits of transnational corporations and financial capital flows; (*ii*) the eradication of tax havens and the elimination of their entire networks of activities; and (*iii*) the resolution of the external debt problem.

With regard specifically to this last proposition, it should be borne in mind that since the debt crisis—triggered by the Fed in 1979—, the countries of the South and the East have paid disproportionate cumulative amounts in respect of the service of their external debts, whereas the balances of the latter have not ceased to increase. In addition to other forms of surplus transfers from the South and East to the North (through unequal exchange, repatriation of profits on foreign direct investments, profits from the valuation of securities recorded as investments of portfolios in the balance of payments, etc.), this considerable drain on resources accentuates the dependent status of these peripheral economies and contributes to concentrate wealth at the national level—for the benefit of the dominant classes in the South—and globally—in favor of the Northern countries. The transformations, on the one hand, of debts into financial securities and, on the other hand, of external debts into internal debts, conceals perverse effects, in particular higher interest rates to be borne on the domestic market, which makes more difficult to calculate the size of the actual drawdown associated with total indebtedness. The weight and dynamics of the debt reveal that it is not used to finance the engines of economic growth, but that it increases in order to allow these countries to repay amortization of capital and interest on debt, by operating as a self-sustaining mechanism for blocking development at the periphery of the capitalist world system.

The external debt of the countries of the South is not just a financial problem. It was created under conditions and according to interests which were those of the dominant countries of the North, in collaboration with the local elites. These political alliances have produced very complex situations, often illegitimate, even illegal, as is the case with "odious" debts. The countries of the South and the East have already paid their creditors in the North their foreign debt, in full, and it is the rich countries that in fact owe a debt to the poorest countries. A general public audit, renegotiations and a partial (but massive) cancelation of public debts, including by calling into question certain external commitments made, are the only means likely to pave the way for development. However, neither the central countries of the North nor the international financial institutions that they control, or the groups of creditors, whether public (the Paris club) or private (the London club, bringing together the most powerful banks in the world), have an interest in seeing the external debt problem solved, because it constitutes one of the means of maintaining the South and the East in perpetual dependence.

However, it is at the national level, first and foremost, that changes must be driven. Changes which tend towards the primary objective of making money a public good—in other words, the production and management of which would be public—and which could thus be envisaged to serve the interests of the society as a whole, and no longer a tiny minority of the ultra-rich. It is impossible to review here—a single book chapter is not enough—all the politico-economic reforms that would be necessary for the popular classes and underprivileged countries to improve their working and living conditions. In the lines that remain, let us stick to the essentials, and to the heart of our subject: the actions to be adopted in monetary and financial matters, without which the room for maneuver of a government with a progressive direction would be reduced to a minimum. What alternatives to democratize monetary policy? The importance of three key measures should be emphasized: (*i*) establishing exchange controls, (*ii*) taking over the Central Bank, and (*iii*) socializing private banking establishments.

First, the country absolutely needs to protect itself through the establishment of strict limitations on the international mobility of capital flows. These regulations are essential to avoid sudden (legal) outflows or (illegal) flight of capital. On closer inspection, it is really not easy to identify a viable option other than a capital control to insulate the economy from exogenous shocks, most often directly caused by the violent ups and downs of unilateral decisions by the U.S. Federal Reserve Bank.

It is then necessary to regain complete control of the Central Bank and to refound its political role within a national framework. This institution is a fully fledged component of the State apparatus, but which at the present time is still maintained almost everywhere, for its monetary choices, "independent" from the orders emanating from those responsible for the political conduct of the country, whereas it has in practice lost its autonomy of action vis-a-vis the real masters of the monetary strategies followed, and more precisely: the powerful private financial oligopolies. This illusion of "independence" must be revealed and exposed. Likewise, should be rehabilitated, where necessary, the crucial function of the Central Bank as lender of last resort—not just of second-tier banks, but of course also—of the State, local communities and the entire public sector, so as to finance, at all levels, the effectiveness and continuity of budgetary expenditure which has been democratically adopted by the national representation, without submitting to the dictates of financial markets dominated by these giant oligopolies. The Central Bank must be able to finance the fiscal deficit and guarantee public debts; especially since the process of indebtedness by which the State falls into dependence on these same oligopolies results in part from the concessions it has made to them through the neoliberal policies implemented: general deregulation, tax gifts to the ultra-rich, to the transnational corporations and more broadly to the owners of big capital.

Finally, let us end with a very crucial point and yet still singularly taboo: the socialization of private commercial banks. It is not just a matter of delegitimizing the activities of autonomous creation of credit money, which give financial oligopolies exorbitant power in society—both over the State and, through it, over all citizens. Nor only of refusing to save the bankrupt establishments, of denouncing their responsibility in the outbreak of the crisis, or even of demanding that their owners and managers be brought to justice for the misdemeanors they have committed (so as not to reclassify them as crimes against community). What we absolutely need to talk about—because social demand and ecological transition require it, more than any ideology—is the urgent and inescapable necessity to set up a banking and financial sector which is fully public, including credit, insurance and finance. We prefer to use here the expression of "socialization" which goes well beyond "statization" (limited to the entry of the State in a majority position in the structure of property of the establishment concerned, but within a society which is maintained under the aegis of high finance), or even "nationalization" (symbolically implying a takeover by the "nation," but retaining the rules of the game and conserving the criteria of capitalist management). The socialization process corresponds to the expropriation of the largest shareholders of banking establishments, financial institutions and insurance companies (with or without compensations), their full transfer to the collective sector and the democratic foundation of worker participation and citizen control, at all levels (up to the highest). If we take seriously the imperatives of bringing the big private shareholders into line—and bringing down the dictatorship they impose—of stopping the destructive logic of finance capital and of regaining real and sovereign control of monetary and financial policies, it is the only solution, the most effective and reasonable, to think about it, the only one which is genuinely democratic, because it is collectively satisfactory. This path will of course involve a series of activity bans—from the abolition of speculative operations to that of the stock exchanges themselves, among others—, but also certain duties for public banking establishments: compulsory reserves, the acquisition of a determined volume of government borrowing, etc.

References

Amin, S. and R. Herrera (2000), "Le Sud dans le système mondial en transformation," *Recherches internationales*, n° 60–61, p. 87–99, Paris.

——— (2005), "Towards a Revival of the Solidarity Between the Peoples of the South?," *Inter Asia Culture Studies*, vol. 6, n° 4, p. 546–556, London.

Carcanholo, R. (2009), "Capital ficticio y ganancias ficticias," *in* Observatorio Internacional de la Crisis (ed.), *La Gran Depresión del Siglo XXI*, San José de Costa Rica: DEI.

Carcanholo, R. and P. Nakatani (2000), "Capital especulativo parasitario *versus* capital financiero," *in* J. Arriola and D. Guerrero (ed.), *La Nueva Economía política de la globalización*, Bilbao: Universidad del País Vasco.

——— (2015), "O capital especulativo parasitário," *in* H. Gomes (ed.), *Especulação e lucros fictícios*, São Paulo: Outras Expressões.

Cockshott, W.P. and M. Nieto (2017), *Ciber-comunismo. Planificación económica, computadoras y democracia*, Madrid: Trotta.

Dierckxsens, W. (1998), *Los límites de un capitalismo sin ciudadanía*, San José de Costa Rica: DEI.

Dierckxsens, W. and W. Formento (2016), *Geopolítica de la crisis económica mundial*, Buenos Aires: Fabro.

——— (2018), *La Crisis Mundial. Continentalismos, Globalismo y Pluriversalismo*, Buenos Aires: Fabro.

Foster, J.B. and R.W. McChesney (2010), "Listen Keynesians, It's the System!," *Monthly Review*, vol. 71, n° 11, New York.

Global Europe Anticipation Bulletin (2017), Global Systemic Crisis 2017–2021, n° 114, 16 April.

Harribey, J.-M. (2020), *Le Trou noir du capitalisme*, Lormont – Bordeaux: Éditions Le Bord de l'eau.

Harribey, J.-M., E. Jeffers, J. Marie, D. Plihon and J.-F. Ponsot (2018), *La Monnaie, un enjeu politique*, collectif pour Les Économistes atterrés, Paris: Le Seuil.

Herrera, R. (1995), *Statistics on Military Expenditure in Developing Countries*, Paris: OECD Development Centre.

——— (2004), "Good Governance Against Good Government?," *Written Statement for the United Nations Human Rights Commission*, E/CN.4/2004/NGO/124, 60th session, July, Geneva.

——— (2013), "Crise et guerre sont-elles liées?," *Innovations*, vol. 3, n° 42, p. 175–194, Brussels.

——— (2014), "A Marxist Interpretation of the Current Crisis," *World Review of Political Economy*, vol. 5, n° 2, p. 128–148, Shanghai.

Herrera, R. and P. Nakatani (2007), "What Rich Countries Owe Poor Ones," *Monthly Review*, vol. 59, n° 2, p. 31–36, New York.

Magdoff, F. and J.B. Foster (2017), *Ce que tout écologiste doit savoir à propos du capitalisme*, Paris: Éditions Critiques.

Observatoire international de la Crise (2019), *Le Capitalisme face à son déclin*, Paris: Éditions Critiques.

Piqueras, A. (2017), "El Capital ficticio especulativo-parasitario se pone al mando del capitalismo," *Áreas - Revista Internacional de Ciencias Sociales*, n° 36, p. 11–23.

Sterdyniak, H. (2021), "Nouvelles variations sur la dette publique et la monnaie," blog: https://blogs.mediapart.fr/henri-sterdyniak/.

Toussaint, É. (1999), *La Bourse ou la vie*, CADTM - Luc Pire - CETIM - Syllepse, Brussels-Geneva-Paris.

Conclusion

> *Lenin is said to have declared that the best way to destroy the capitalist system was to debauch the currency. (…) [He] was certainly right. There is no subtler, no surer means of overturning the existing basis of society than to debauch the currency. The process engages all the hidden forces of economic law on the side of destruction, and does it in a manner which not one man in a million is able to diagnose.*
>
> (John Maynard Keynes, *The Economic Consequences of the Peace*, 1919)

In the current international context disrupted by a loss of ground of State supremacy, the dominance—much contested, but persistent—of the U.S. dollar over the world system and the effects of unpredictable fluctuations in exchange rates and stock prices, the demand for a reconquest of national monetary sovereignty in the face of the power of high finance acquires an absolutely fundamental importance. A people who have lost this sovereignty, that is to say, whose government and the financing system of its domestic economy are not able to freely use incentive mechanisms through the intermediary of its currency, places itself in a critical, even unmanageable situation. Its citizens will run the risk of seeing their country submit itself entirely to centers of concentration of

R. Herrera, *Money*, Global University for Sustainability Book Series, https://doi.org/10.1007/978-981-19-2848-2

wealth and of power which will completely escape its control, or subordinate itself to random and irrational movements in the financial markets, without any correspondence with the real variables of production.

It is on the condition of daring to challenge the power of high finance head-on and effectively, by reaffirming the primacy of political decision-making over the economy, by socializing the banking system and by making money a public good, that it will be conceivable to reopen freedom of maneuver for economic policy, to put a development strategy on its feet and, above all, to place this strategy in the perspective of building credible and unifying alternatives. Credible alternatives, because they promote productive dynamism, job creation, income distribution, social progress, democratic participation, international cooperation, more equitable exchanges, food sovereignty, ecological transition and truly sustainable development. Unifying alternatives, because capable of massively rallying the progressive forces of the world and allowing them to become powerful enough to implement principles which impose on the accumulation of capital strict limits to its exclusive logic of maximizing individual profit.

Democratic control of the Central Bank and socialization of banks are essential requirements to find new modes and channels of financing serving the people. However, let us understand that, while regaining control of monetary policy is fundamental, in its internal and external components, it is not the miracle solution that will solve all problems. Socialization of the credit, insurance and finance system only makes sense if it is integrated at the heart of a program to transform the foundations of society. This profound transformation can itself only result from changes in the balance of power produced by organized social struggles, but the outcome of which is never known in advance. However, an exclusive focus on monetary and financial questions risks relegating to the background the importance of all the other dimensions of economic policy (that is to say, budgetary and tax, social, foreign trade policies, etc.), but also and above all forgetting the need to deeply modify these social relationships and the structures of the national economy.

All of these proposals for action certainly deserve to be discussed, and very widely—well beyond the circles of specialists in these issues. The democratic imperative demands that the populations be involved and associated with these reflections, as well as in the decision-making that will follow. How could such debates not also concern the public decision-makers in charge of what is called "official development assistance", who too often see their projects swept aside by a sudden turmoil affecting the foreign exchange market or their efforts ruined in an instant by the selfishness of commodity price speculators?

This reflection should also lead to a questioning of the global monetary system. For succeeding in depriving the U.S. administration in the service of high finance of its arsenal of privileges, including that of having the key global currency, will require that the peoples of the planet, including that of the United States, unite. In fact, is it acceptable for the government of any country, whatever it may be, to arrogate to itself the right to conduct an accommodating, not to say lax monetary policy for several years, then, always at its whim, to abruptly impose its tightening, crushing the rest of the world's economies in an extraordinarily violent way? Is it satisfactory, fair and rational, that the rulers of this unique country control the world's reserve currency in this way? All of this generates obstacles that are terribly difficult to overcome for a government, especially of a progressive orientation, which would like to free itself from the grip of the U.S. currency, or even which would initiate a process of de-dollarization.

A preferable solution would be to consider creating a new global reserve currency, which would not substitute for national currencies, but would only crowd out the dollar in its hegemonic role and end such injustice—a currency that would be managed by an international institution much more neutral than those currently in existence. Emancipating the world from the scourge of the dollar would open up a new era for the peoples of the South and East to live better, but would not truly deliver them from the evil which overwhelms them and from which they suffer: the undivided domination of capital. The proposal to create a new global reserve currency would be nothing more than returning to the Bancor imagined at Bretton Woods by J.M. Keynes. Nevertheless, in the face of the violence of current capitalism and the dictatorship of financial oligopolies that towers over it, Keynesian reformism will not be enough. Why? Because behind the dollar is capital.

Besides, the dollar does not really fulfill the role of foreign exchange reserves, which instead use forms of debt, such as securities issued by States or transnational firms—alongside gold. Likewise, dollars that function as international means of circulation in trade are not created by the Fed, but by the international banking system, like credit—destroyed at the end of cycles. Analyzing credit is therefore crucial, because it is a creation of money that can be converted into capital. In this way, we understand that the majority of the problems which are, apparently, generated by money are, in reality, generated by capital itself. Foreign direct investment and investment of portfolios do not exactly equate to "money"; they are, in fact, forms of money capital. The U.S. dollar is only a support of globally dominant capital. To create a new currency in a capitalist world system that would remain intact would amount to changing the name of the currency in the service of this capital in order to extend its domination on the universal market.

We must therefore realize, as quickly and as fully as possible, that the future will not have the face of the better world so hoped for as long as we are not in a position to impose on the financial oligopolies the obligation to public, participatory and democratic control.

Appendices

Appendix A: Some Chronological Markers of (World) History of Facts on Money

~ −3300, Iraq/Syria: Emergence of handwriting, used especially for accounting (and credit).

~ −2600, Egypt: Abstract unit of account, the *shât*, used as a standard of value.

~ −2500, China: Use of shell currencies in central China (for offerings and exchanges).

~ −2300 to −2200, Iraq/Syria: Use of the *mine*, a unit of account for the administrative management of claims and debts in the Akkad Empire in Mesopotamia.

~ −1800 to −1750, Iraq/Iran: Tablets of the Laws of Eshnunna found near present-day Baghdad fixing price matches between means of payment and basic products (barley, silver, copper, oil, etc.) (~ −1800). Code of Hammurabi, stele discovered in Susa with paragraphs devoted to "money and trade affairs":

R. Herrera, *Money*, Global University for Sustainability Book Series,
https://doi.org/10.1007/978-981-19-2848-2

interest loans, commercial loans, debt repayments, etc. (~ – 1750).

~ **−1500 to −1050, China**: Use as a means of payment of shells-cowries (or their variants in bone, wood or metal), but also of stamped and authenticated pieces of fabric, very distant ancestors of banknotes. Bronze coins (or "bronze shells") under the Shang dynasty.

~ **−1300, Indian Ocean islands**: Circulation of cowries (*cypraea moneta*) serving as a means of payment.

~ **8th Century BC, Greece/Turkey**: Reference to head of cattle as exchange currency in *The Iliad*.

−722 to −481, China: Circulation of the first bronze coins, in the form of tools (pikes, knives, shovels, etc.) in various parts of China.

−610 to −546, Turkey/Greece: Creation of metallic money (creseide coins or stater in electrum, natural alloy of gold and silver) in Asia Minor, under the Mermnades dynasty and the kings of Lydia, Alyatte II and Croesus.

~ **6th Century BC., India**: First coins in circulation on the Indian Peninsula.

~ **−550, China**: Extension of trade in the Chinese world and intensification of the use of money, with the appearance of round coins with a square hole, made by casting molten metals (bronze, copper, iron, etc.) and hot molding. Use of gold coins in Chu State (South of the Yellow River).

−520 to −510, Greece: Minting by Athens of the first silver coins (extracted from the Laurion mines), recognized in many places around the Mediterranean, with Athena on the right and an owl on the reverse.

−425 to −400, Maghreb/North Africa: First issues of Carthaginian coins.

~ **4th Century BC., India**: Mention, in the Sanskrit work *Arthashâstra*, of the currency *rūpyarūpa* (from *rūpya*, which means "metal silver," and *rūpa*, "piece"), but also of credit and the interest rate.

———, Libya: Issue of Greek gold staters in Cyrenaica.

−221 to −210, China: Standardization of the system of so-called "ban liang" monetary units within the framework of reforms to unify weights and measures, under the reign of the "First Emperor" Qin Shi Huang, who united politically and administratively Chinese Empire.

Copper sapeques, round coins with square holes in the center, strung by the thousands on ligatures—and on which taxes were levied.

−218 to −202, Italy: Monetary crisis of the Roman State which resorted, during the Second Punic War against Carthage, to monetary manipulations devaluing bronze and silver coins.

−44, Italy: *Senatus-consulte* granting to Julius Caesar (in possession of the gold reserves of the Public Treasury) the privilege of issuing a metal coin (the *aureus*) in his effigy to finance his military conquests and symbolize his absolute power, in a context of monetary disorder characterizing the end of the Republic.

−25 to 23, Maghreb/North Africa: Coinages of the Berber kingdoms of Numidia and Mauretania, with in particular the coins (*denarius* and *aureaus*) of King Juba II (current Algeria).

162, Italy: Writing by the jurist Polyen for the emperors Lucius Verus and Marcus Aurelius of a book on historical accounts relating to the financing of wars by resorting to stratagems, including monetary manipulations (strikes in base metal of a currency whose use is imposed to replace an old one).

3rd Century AD., Iran: Coinage of the Parthian Empire with a trimetallic monetary system.

———, Italy: Economic crisis in Rome. Reductions in the silver content of the denarius, decided by the emperors, then depreciation after the issue of the *antoninianus* (215) and rise in the price of wheat.

294–301, Italy: Monetary reform under Diocletian with a trimetallic system (continued issuance of the *aureus* [gold] and creation of *argenteus* [silver] and bronze coins). Maximum edict capping both the prices of consumer goods and the wages of workers in order to curb inflation.

310, Serbia/Turkey: Reform of the monetary system by Emperor Constantine to restore stability after the high inflation of the 3rd Century in the Eastern Roman Empire. Creation of the *solidus*, a gold coin marking a desire for firmness and becoming the pivot of the monetary system of the 4th and 5th Centuries (with an unchanged weight until the 10th Century).

7th Century, China: Invention of paper money, called "flying money" (*fei qian*) for trade in the Tang dynasty—later taken over by the State; the basic monetary unit remaining the copper coin.

675, France: Replacement of the gold penny (*sou d'or*) by the silver denier (*denier d'argent*), taking various forms in Gaul.

692, Syria: Introduction to Damascus by Caliph Abd-el-Malik of the gold dinar, a currency that established itself as a reference in the Muslim world and part of the Mediterranean borders for centuries.

696, Muslim world: Monetary reform with overhaul of coins and references to the Hegira and the Koran.

8th–10th Centuries, Muslim world: Minting of gold dinars accompanying the development of trade between Damascus, Baghdad and Cairo, or towards the Indus valley. To avoid expensive and risky gold transportations, use of deferred payment methods (similar to checks and bills of exchange).

708–958, Japan: Manufacture and put into circulation by order of Empress Genmei of *wadōkaichin*, the oldest official Japanese currency, in the shape of round coins with a square hole in the middle.

754–781, France: Unification of the weight and shape of the silver denier by Pépin le Bref after years of disorder (754–765). Monetary reform by Charlemagne (777–781), who restores the royal monopoly of minting money and imposes the silver denier (of which the *sou* is a multiple, as well as the *livre*) as the currency of the empire. A duodecimal system that lasted over a thousand years, until the French Revolution.

788–791, Morocco: Minting of coins, silver dirhams, by Emir Idris I.

864, France: Creation by Charles II of the *Monnaie de Paris*, workshop attached to the royal crown.

968, Vietnam: Replacement of Chinese coins by a first Vietnamese currency.

10th–13th Centuries, Europe: Credit boom after the introduction of Indo-Arabic numeration (instead of Roman numerals), which simplified the calculation of profits, interest and conversions using different bases (decimals, duodecimals, etc.), thanks to authors such as Gerbert d'Aurillac, or Leonardi Fibonacci from Pisa.

11th Century, China/Asia: First printing of paper money by the State under the Tang dynasty (1024), when dominated copper coins (in the North) and lead or iron coins (in the South, notably with the coin of heavy iron in Sichuan). Diffusion of Chinese currencies in Central, South-East and Far-East Asia (Japan).

———, **Africa/Europe**: Issuance of the Almoravid dinar in Morocco and Spain (*Al-Andalus*), currency minted from West African gold (Ghana), obtained through the control of trans-Saharan trade.

12th Century, China: Trade expansion calling for the need for a unified monetary system. Completion of reunification during the Song Dynasty. Large-scale circulation of paper money, under many names (the most famous of which is *jiaozi*).

———, **India**: Extension of banking activities in the Indian Peninsula and issuance of bills of exchange by bankers (*hundis*) for cross-border exchanges.

———, **Japan**: Chinese coins used as referents (until the 17th Century), after having been obtained by trade, piracy or import from Annam (modern Vietnam) or Korea.

———, **Europe**: Period of strong economic expansion, which culminated in the late Middle Ages with the progress of agriculture, techniques and trade (fairs, distant exchanges, etc.), disseminating currencies.

1192, Italy: *Grosso veneziano*, a type of silver ducat, currency of the Republic of Venice used in trade with foreign countries.

1214, Serbia: Put into circulation by the first king of Serbia, Stefan I, from the Nemanjić dynasty, of the Serbian dinar (in silver), one of the oldest European currencies still in circulation.

13th Century, Sub-Saharan Africa: Development of prosperous commercial empires in Africa, South of the Sahara, with diversified monetary systems (copper bars, gold powder, dinar, salt, etc.).

Second half of the 13th Century, Italy: Creations of the *genovino d'oro* by the Republic of Genoa (1250), then of the *piccioli* in Pisa (1251). Minting of the *fiorino* or golden florin in Florence (1252), widely accepted in Europe. Issue of the *ducato d'oro* of the Republic of Venice (1280), which became later the *zecchino veneziano* or gold sequin and circulated throughout the European continent and in the Levant (from 1283 to 1284 and until the 17th Century century).

———, **China**: Unification of monetary systems under the Yuan dynasty. In a context of high inflation, issue of the *jiaochao*-paper (1287), a fiduciary money not based on a guarantee in gold or silver.

———, **Russia**: Appearance of the ruble in the Novgorod region, in the form of ingots or pieces of silver (*grivna*).

1262–1270, France: Monetary reforms by Louis IX, with assertion of the king's monopoly on the creation of money (which has "forced course" on the whole of the royal territory and whose imitation is prohibited), guarantee of the quantity of precious metal, and reintroduction of gold alongside silver—therefore a return to bimetallism (at the time in force in the two great economic and political spaces dominated by Byzantium and Islam).

1290–1360, France: Monetary manipulations to cover royal expenses under Philippe Le Bel, which reduced the precious metal content of created coins without changing their face value (until 1314). Continuation of these practices in the first half of the 14th Century to finance the Anglo-French Hundred Years War.

14th Century, Mali: Trans-Saharan caravan trade in gold, copper, salt and fabrics, centered on an empire stretching from the Atlantic to the Niger River, with Timbuktu, Gao and Djenne as economic poles, which reached its peak under the reign of Mansa Kankou Moussa (1307–1332).

———, **Japan**: Mintings of Chinese currency Chinese imitations (especially Ming), until the beginning of the Edo period when a new monetary system was put in place.

———, **Europe**: In a context of agricultural crises (great famine of 1314–1317), destructions caused by the outbreak of the Hundred Years War (1337), epidemics (black plague of 1347–1351, recurrences until 1370), falling food prices, bankruptcies of many banks and State failures.

1339–1345, Europe: Bankruptcy of two Florentine families, those of the Bardi and of the Peruzzi, leading to a cascading financial disorder so important in Florence that it resulted, as a consequence, in the default of the King of England Edward III (1345), very indebted to them to finance the wars against France.

1360, France: Birth of the franc following the payment of a ransom to "proclaim franc," that is to say, to free King Jean II, prisoner of the English. Establishment of a tax for this purpose and promulgation of an ordinance creating the "*franc à cheval*" (franc on horseback), a new gold currency with guaranteed value without monetary manipulation

(Charles V for his part striking, in 1365, the "*franc à pied*" [franc on foot], representing the sovereign standing).

1372, France: Charter for the creation of the *Société des moulins du Bazacle* (Bazacle mills company) by the owners of the mills of Toulouse, the first joint-stock company (with shares transferable at market price, shareholders' liability limited to the level of their participation, profits returned to shareholders, annual meeting approving the accounts, voting on decisions and electing a board of directors which appoints the manager from among its members).

1409, Belgium: Creation of the first stock exchange in Bruges, facilitating the exchange of securities by allowing buyers and sellers to meet in one place (in front of the home of the van der Beurze family).

15th Century, China: Silver coins declared legal tender for the payment of taxes in (present-day) Guangdong (from 1423). Suspension of paper money issues under the Ming dynasty (1450), after a new inflationary episode.

———, Europe: Appearance of the first large banks, in particular those founded by the Medici family (in Florence) or the Fugger family (in the Holy Roman Empire) or by Jacques Coeur (France), with increasingly diversified and extensive operations (conversion, discount, etc.). Creation (as a pawnshop) of the Banca Monte dei Paschi di Siena (1472), the oldest European bank still in operation.

1497, Spain: Royal ordinances of Medina del Campo and monetary reform by the Catholic Monarchs, fixing the parity of the *real de plata* (the "silver royal"), initially circulating in the territories of the Crown of Castile; a parity that will remain unchanged for more than three centuries, until the beginning of the 19th Century.

16th Century, world: Influx into Europe of precious metals extracted from the colonies of the "New World" (mines of Hispanic America, including that of silver from Potosi especially) and "triangular trade" between Europe, Africa and America. Growth in monetary exchanges between Europe and Asia.

———, Czech Republic: At the beginning of the century, acceleration of the extraction of metal silver from the mines of Bohemia (current Czech Republic), discovered in the middle of the Middle Ages, for the minting of thalers in the Holy Roman Empire.

———, **The Netherlands**: Beginning of the minting of the rixdale (*rijksdaalder*), a silver currency which spread in Northern Europe (16th Century), then with the Dutch colonists on American counters (17th Century) and in Southeast Asia (18th Century) and into the Boer republics of Northeastern part of South Africa (19th Century).

1500, Portugal: Beginning of the colonization of Brazil and the circulation of the Portuguese real in these territories.

1534, Russia: Monetary reform fixing the equivalence of the Russian ruble with 100 Novgorod denga and 400 polushka.

1535, Spain/Mexico: Put into circulation in New Spain of the *real de a ocho* or *real de plata* (metal silver). First true international currency, which will gradually be accepted on all continents (from Africa to Asia and Oceania). In circulation in North America until the 19th Century.

1540, France: Opening in Lyon of the first French stock exchange, specializing in negotiable instruments and discounts, and wishing at the time to compete with that of Antwerp, very important.

~ 1540–1545, India: Monetary reform of North India (from Bihar) and introduction of the first silver currency called "*rupiyah*" during the reign of pādichāh (Afghan) Fahrid Khan, said Sher Shâh Sûrî.

1543–1551, England: Devaluation of the currency (Great Debasement) under King Henry VIII, due to the reduction in the silver content of the coins (1543), leading to inflation and a currency crisis (1551).

Second half of the 16th Century, China: Influx of silver metal from the Philippines after the establishment of the Spanish Empire in Manila (1571), in the form of coins (*real de a ocho*) or ingots (*yuanbao* or *sycee*, weighing a *liang*, or a Malay *tael*). End of the circulation of paper money (1573). Beginning of the dissemination of Spanish coins (mainly the *de plata* eight-real coin, from which the first yuan was heavily inspired), alongside traditional Chinese copper coins (until the 19th Century).

1566, Europe: Decision of Charles V (Charles Quint) to make the silver *reichstaler* the unit of account of the House of the Habsburgs' Holy Roman Empire. International circulation until the 18th Century and currency in Germanic countries until the 19th Century.

~ 1600, Japan: Issue of the first Japanese banknote, the *yamada hagaki*.

Beginning of the 17th Century, Africa: Spread of the use of cowries on the West coast, including as a means of payment by Europeans in their slave and gold trade.

———, **The Netherlands**: Transformation of goldsmiths' offices into deposit banks, notably in Amsterdam (1609), with the creation of certificates of deposit denominated in local currency allowing holders of deposited goods to recover them on sight. Issuance of cash vouchers or bills against cash deposits by the Bank of Amsterdam to merchants, allowing them to trade without having to physically transfer metal coins.

1636–1637, The Netherlands: "Tulip Crisis," considered the bursting of the first speculative bubble in history. Crisis in the market for tulip bulbs, after a surge in their prices due to the exoticism of these plants objects of speculation and at the origin of the opening of a futures market, until a turnaround and panic causing massive sales and economic collapse.

1640, France: Introduction by Cardinal Richelieu, Minister of Louis XIII, of the *louis d'or*. Safe investment.

———, **England**: Seizure by King Charles I of gold and silver deposited in the Tower of London. Transfers by the aristocracy of its wealth in ingots, coins and powders of precious metals in offices of goldsmiths.

1643–1645, China: Resumption of the issuance of paper money at the end of the Ming dynasty.

Mid-17th Century, Northern Europe: Acceleration of the process of creating credit money over an area covering the territories from Stockholm to Hamburg and London.

1661–1668, Sweden: Issue of the first bearer banknotes redeemable in cash (1661) by the Bank of Stockholm, a private institution with public privileges founded by the merchant Johan Palmstruch, but in quantity greater than that of the precious metals held in deposits, which led to the bankruptcy of this bank. Creation of the first Central Bank in Europe (1668), the Riksens Ständers Bank (Bank of the States of the Kingdom), without issuance of notes, due to the recent bankruptcy of the Bank of Stockholm.

1663–1665, France: Decision of Colbert, principal Minister of State to King Louis XIV, to reduce the interest rate on accrued annuities

(1663), substitutes for bank credit and declared distinct from usury (1665).

1685, Canada: Use of playing card money by the French administrators of New France (first "notes" printed in North America).

1694–1698, England: Creation of the Bank of England (1694). Flight of capital and monetary crisis (1695). Opening of the first English stock exchange at Jonathan's Coffee-House, London (1498).

1695, Brazil: First production of the *real* at *Casa da Moeda* in Bahia, under the authority of Lisbon.

1704, Russia: Monetary reform under Tsar Peter I the Great, establishing the first silver ruble (divided into 100 kopecks).

1708, England: Obtaining the monopoly on issuing banknotes by the Bank of England.

1716, Scotland: Competition between banks, organized in branches, with a system of weekly exchanges, clearing of banknotes and balancing of accounts. Significant growth in deposits and loans.

1716–1720, France: First issue of paper money ("*billets de monnoye*") by the Banque Générale created by the Scottish banker John Law (1716), with guarantee from the regent Philippe d'Orléans (1718), but in excessive quantities against gold reserves, leading to panic, a bank run* and bankruptcy (1720).

1720, England: Crisis of the South Sea Company, one of the first stock market crashes in history, when this company, created in London in 1711 and having a colonial monopoly with Hispanic America, had to face the collapse in its share price; a collapse which bankrupted many British investors.

1724, France: Opening of the Paris Stock Exchange at the Hôtel de Nevers (located Colbert and Richelieu streets today).

1739, Germany: Creation of the Berlin Stock Exchange.

1742, England: Use of the check as a means of payment by the major English banks.

1750, Austria-Hungary/world: Putting into circulation of the *konventionstaler* (or "thaler of Empress Maria Theresa"), silver piastre which will become one of the world currencies of circulation, including in the Spanish and English colonies or in East Africa.

1762–1765, England: Founding of Barings (1762), the oldest English investment bank, then of Lloyds Bank (1765).

1769, Russia: Appearance of Russian banknotes, coupons of rubles of assignment, pledged on raw materials and issued by the Assignment Bank of Saint Petersburg and Moscow established on that date.

1772, England/India: Financial crisis following difficulties encountered by the East India Company after speculation on the London and Amsterdam Stock Exchanges.

1775, United States: Putting into circulation, during the War of Independence against England, of the "continental currency dollars," in coins (inspired by the model of the Spanish *real de a ocho*) or in banknotes (until 1781).

1785–1787, Mexico/United States: Adoption of the eight-real coin minted in New Spain as the basis of the U.S. monetary system (1785). Issue of the *fugio* cent, copper coin worth one cent (1787).

1788, France: Crisis of the *Caisse d'Escompte*, threatening with bankruptcy the Royal Treasury itself.

1789–1795, France: Issue of assignats or "assigned" bills (that is to say, pledged) on the property of the clergy nationalized by the Revolution (1789), claims on the State owner equivalent to gold and silver coins, then became paper money after the removal of the interest they carried (1790), but printed without relation to the value of the initial goods in order to finance the war effort (1793)—and massively distributed in false bills by the English; hence their loss of value and suppression by the Directory (1795).

1790–1792, United States: Opening of the Philadelphia Stock Exchange (1790), notably to raise State loans and restructure the debt of the former Thirteen Colonies. Creation by the government of the First Bank of the United States, 20% State-owned and acting as a Central Bank, to create a new currency and regulate the credit system (1791). Panic caused by the rise in interest rates, pushing many borrowers into bankruptcy. Birth of the dollar, declared the country's official currency under the presidency of George Washington by the Coinage Act (April 1792). Opening of the New York Stock Exchange, Wall Street in Manhattan (May 1792).

1797, England: Following the Battle of Fishguard and rumors of a French invasion, panic of individuals who demanded that their assets be withdrawn from local banks, many of them bankrupt. Fall of the reserves of the Bank of England, which suspends cash payments. Passage of the Bank Restriction Act, establishing the forced course and inconvertible notes (February).

———, France: Law closing the public securities market and canceling two-thirds of the State's debt.

1798, Switzerland: Creation of the "Swiss franc" as the monetary unit of the Helvetic Republic.

1800, France: Creation by Napoleon—then First Consul—of the *Banque de France* (January), private bank, whose regents were J.-F. Perregaux (banker of Swiss origin) and his associates, and who therefore had the privilege (initially limited to Paris) of issuing banknotes payable on sight and to bearer, by receiving capital from the public body responsible for collecting taxes, the *Caisse d'Amortissement*. Granting of credit to encourage activity. Use of banknotes from the *Caisse de Comptes Courants* (with the endorsement "payable to the Bank of France") of high face value to be reserved for large manufacturers and traders.

1803, France: Birth of the germinal franc by the monetary reform (from "7 germinal year XI," that is to say, March 28, 1803) granting a monopoly of emission to the *Banque de France*, stabilizing the value of the national currency (until 1914) and establishing a bimetallist gold and silver system (in force until 1928).

———, worldwide: Participation of the British bank Barings and of the Dutch one Hope & Co. in the financing of the purchase of Louisiana by the United States from France.

1806, Germany: Foundation by financier Mayer Amschel Rothschild of the banking dynasty of the same name in the Holy Roman Empire.

1810, United Kingdom: Crisis in the credit system, at a time when the Napoleonic blockade, inflation, the rise in debt and the undocking of the pound sterling from gold combined their negative effects.

1816, United States: Establishment of the Second Bank of the United States, taking over from the First Bank, in an attempt to curb the inflation following the War of 1812 and to unify the various regional currencies.

1819–1821, United Kingdom: End of bimetallism and beginning of the adoption of the gold standard system. Act for the Resumption of Cash Payments (1819) organizing the return to convertibility (effective in 1821).

1820, Germany: Opening of the Frankfurt Stock Exchange.

1822, Brazil: Putting into circulation of the new *real* of independent Brazil.

1823, Mexico: Issue of the first Mexican banknotes, denominated in peso.

1825, United Kingdom: Increase in the number and capitalization of companies listed on the London Stock Exchange, in particular under the pressure of the railway companies. Bankruptcy of banks and of numerous firms following speculation on the securities of South American mines. Fall of many stock market prices. Wave of requests to convert banknotes into gold. Increase in the discount rate by the Bank of England.

———, United States: Total capital of U.S. banks more than twice that of England.

———, Senegal: First coin (in bronze) minted for the French colony of Senegal.

1826, France: Installation of the Paris Stock Exchange at the Palais Brongniart. Introduction by the *Banque de France* of "blank money orders," a form of checks allowing customers to withdraw funds deposited in their account.

1828–1843, United States: Gold rush in Georgia, the first movement to search for gold mines in the country.

1830, United States: Capitalization of U.S. stock exchanges equivalent to those of England.

1831, Spain: Foundation of the Madrid Stock Exchange.

1833, United Kingdom: Adoption of Bank of England notes as legal tender. Bank Charter Act promoting the creation of banks capitalized in the form of joint-stock companies listed on the stock market.

1834, Egypt: Monetary reform of the wali Mehemet Ali, introducing a bimetallic system and substituting the qirsh (equivalent to the Ottoman piastre) by the Egyptian pound as currency of exchange.

1835, India: Adoption of a monometallic monetary regime based on the silver rupee in British India.

1836, France: Foundation by Jacques Laffitte of the Caisse générale du Commerce et de l'Industrie, the first bank to grant long-term loans to companies (before its liquidation in 1848).

———, **United States/United Kingdom**: Edict of the Specie Circular making payment for the purchase of land in precious metals compulsory, which helped to slow down land speculation, but also to provoke a stock market crash in London, where U.S. banks were heavily indebted.

1837, United States: Burst of a speculative bubble and banking crisis (May), New York banks halting payments in gold and silver coins. Loss of confidence in paper money. Authorization of the free minting of metal silver in currency.

1844, United Kingdom: New Bank Charter Act, a law adopted at the instigation of R. Peel, which limited the growth of the money supply driven by the proliferation of banks, adopted the "currency principle" by which the issuance of banknotes was made in exact proportion to gold stocks held to avoid inflation, and enshrined the gold standard. Strengthening the role of the Central Bank and prohibiting second-tier institutions from issuing banknotes.

———, **United States/France**: Creation in New Orleans of Lazard & Co., future investment bank.

———, **Turkey**: Introduction of a gold currency, the "Turkish lira," in order to unify and make more coherent (in vain) the monetary system in force in the various territories of the Ottoman Empire.

1847, United Kingdom/France: Fall in stock prices of railway companies in London and Paris, due to a credit crunch after new calls for funds for investments. Bankruptcy of banks.

———, **Russia**: Gold rush of the Ural and Altai mountain ranges.

1848, France: Monopoly of the *Banque de France* for the issuance of banknotes in metropolitan territory. Declaration of legal and compulsory tender of these Bank of France notes. Stock market panic caused by the victory of the revolution.

———, **United States**: California's gold rush that begins East of Sacramento and sees tens of thousands of gold-digging adventurers arriving from around the world. Consolidation of confidence in banknotes.

———, **Switzerland**: Definitive introduction of the Swiss franc replacing the old cantonal currencies that it unified.

1850–1875, United States/United Kingdom: Acceleration of the diffusion of technical advances which favor banking and financial activities (electric telegraph, transatlantic telegraph cable, etc.).

———, **France**: Abolition (1850), then definitive restoration (1870) of the legal tender of the Bank of France notes. Creation of large banking establishments: French branch of Rothschild bank by James de Rothschild; Crédit mobilier by the Pereire brothers and Crédit Foncier (1852); Crédit Lyonnais (1863), Société Générale (1864), Banque de l'Indochine (1875), etc.

1850, Switzerland: Foundation of the Geneva Stock Exchange, the oldest in the Swiss Confederation.

1851, Australia: Beginning of the Australian gold rush (in Victoria, South-East Federated State).

1856, China: Reappearance of paper money, with the introduction of *wen* banknotes.

———, **Russia**: Devaluation of more than 20% of the paper-ruble following the Crimean war.

———, **United Kingdom**: First law on Joint-Stock Company limited (the law on limited companies dating in France from 1863).

———, **Switzerland**: Creation of Crédit Suisse (*Schweizerische Kreditanstalt*) in Zurich.

1857, United States/United Kingdom/France: Financial crisis of international scope, having its origin in the crash of the New York Stock Exchange of August 22 and in the banking panic which followed in the United States (with suspension of payments by many banks in New York, Philadelphia, Boston, etc.). Sharp increase in the discount rate. Interruption of trading on Wall Street on October 13. Currency crisis and credit crisis, which propagates the falls in stock prices to Great Britain and France. Economic recession.

———, **United States**: End of legal use of the Mexican *real de a ocho* as an official means of payment.

1858, world: "Unequal Treaties" (officially called "Treaties of Friendship and Commerce") imposed on China by Western countries (including the United States), with complete freedom of capital movements.

———, **Japan**: Trade treaty with the United States and establishment of a fixed exchange rate with the dollar.

1859, United States: Rush for silver from the Comstock Lode deposit (Utah, now Nevada).

1860, United States: Beginning of the activities of Henry Poor, at the origin of the future Standard & Poor's agency.

———, **Finland**: Issue of the Finnish markka, replacing the Russian ruble.

1861, India: Introduction of paper money.

1861–1865, United States: Issue of "greenbacks," in the form of notes printed in green on the back and called demand notes (1861–1862), then U.S. notes (1862–1865), authoritative paper money, or fiat money*, by the States of the Union (North) during the Civil War against those of the Confederation (South). Codification of banknote issuance by the National Banking Act.

1863, Mexico: Entry into force of the monetary system in "decimal *peso*" (worth 100 *centavos*).

1865, Europe: Creation of the Latin Union, a common currency area based on bimetallism between France, Switzerland, Italy, Belgium and Luxembourg allowing the currency of each member to be legal tender in the others signatory countries.

———, **China**: Foundation in Hong Kong by Scottish banker Thomas Sutherland of the Hong Kong and Shanghai Banking Corporation (HSBC), to help finance opium trafficking in the Far East.

———, **Australia**: Australian gold rush.

———, **France**: Passage of a law officially creating the check.

1866, United Kingdom/Europe: Black Friday stock market crash (Friday May 11), following the generalization of the law on limited liability in the banking and financial sector and the bankruptcy of the discount house Overend & Gurney, itself due to defaults from railway companies. Liquidity crisis. Diffusion of the banking and financial crisis towards the places of Paris, Berlin and Milan, among others.

———, **Mexico**: Issue of the first peso (silver) coins during the Second Empire.

1870, Germany: Foundations of Deutsche Bank (in Berlin) and Commerzbank (in Frankfurt).

1871, France: Non-takeover by the Paris *Commune* of the *Banque de France*, which it allows to finance its enemies (the Versailles army and government) and from which it requires only a few advances to cover its expenses and pay the national defense citizen guard.

———, Germany: Issue of the gold mark, in part thanks to the war indemnities paid by France in gold francs. Monetary unification of the Reich which puts an end to the fragmentation (seven spaces, 33 banks of issue) and seals the reunion of German States, demanded by business circles and organized by Bismarck.

1871–1872, Japan: "New Currency" Law creating the yen and adopting an international model gold standard (1871). National Bank Act (1872), promulgated by the Meiji imperial government and establishing a modern banking system inspired by the United States.

1873–1896, world: Wave of real estate speculation and series of bankruptcies of railway companies and banks having invested there in Europe at the beginning of the 1870s leading to the crash of the Vienna Stock Exchange in Austria (May 1873), which is transmitted to Central Europe, then reverberates in the United States. Depression ("Great Stagnation") in Europe and the United States, which lasted until 1896 and was characterized by recurrent deflation and a general decline in economic activity.

1873, United States: Coinage Act (February) changing the monetary regime from bimetallism (gold and silver) to monometallism (gold). Beginnings of the demonetization of the silver metal and the establishment of the gold standard partially implemented due to the monetary instability and deflation of the time. Financial panic (September) following the bankruptcy of the bank Jay Cooke & Co. Closure of Wall Street for 10 days.

———, Germany: Law making the gold mark the only official currency of the Reich.

———, Northern Europe: Scandinavian Monetary Union, a system based on the gold standard with fixed exchange rates between the currencies of Sweden and Denmark (1873), then of Norway (1875), which will last until 1914.

———, **Southern Europe**: Adoption of the gold standard by the Latin Union.

1875, Germany: Creation of the Reichsbank, the Central Bank of the empire, which minted gold money, issued banknotes, administered the exchange rate and the discount rate, and completed German unification.

———, **United States**: Bank of California bankruptcy and subsequent crash of the San Francisco Stock Exchange.

1878–1890, United States: Gradual regulatory limitation on silver purchases, in value (Bland-Allison Act of 1878) and in volume (Sherman Silver Purchase Act of 1890).

1881, Morocco: Manufacture of the Moroccan currency, the Hassani rial, inspired by the Spanish eight coin.

1882, France: Stock market crash in Paris and Lyon, causing an economic crisis lasting several years, following the bankruptcy of the Union Générale, a bank with very risky investments in Central Europe and the Balkans.

———, **Japan**: Foundation of a Central Bank, the Bank of Japan, to stabilize the value of the national currency by centralizing the issuance of convertible notes.

1885, France: Legal authorization of speculative operations.

———, **Japan**: Issue of the first banknotes by the Bank of Japan, the *daikokusatsu*, convertible into silver.

———, **Egypt**: Adoption of the gold standard for the Egyptian pound.

1887–1890, Congo (DRC): Appearance, at par with the Belgian gold franc, of the Congolese franc (1887), the new currency of the "independent State" of the Congo, whose sovereign was King Leopold II of Belgium. Decree making the *mitako*, a local copper currency in the shape of a U-hook, another official currency.

1889, China: Definitive replacement (from Guangdong) of the old imperial monetary unit, the wen, by the yuan (subdivided into 10 jiao, 100 fen and 1000 wen) as the official currency of the Republic of China, launched at parity with the "Spanish dollar," as with the Mexican and Philippine pesos.

1890s, world: Rise of gold production (South Africa, Canada, Alaska), precipitating the end of bimetallism, which had declined since the adoption of the gold standard in Europe in the previous two decades.

1890, United Kingdom: Bankruptcy of Barings Bank, after Argentina and Uruguay defaults, then bailout by a consortium organized by the Bank of England, backed by the Bank of France. Transmission of the stock market panic to New York.

1892, Panama: Financial scandal, involving corrupt politicians and journalists, exposed following the bankruptcy of the Panama Canal Company three years earlier (in 1889).

1893, United States: Financial crisis, stemming from a strong demand to convert federal securities into gold.

———, Ethiopia: The birr, official currency of the country where the thaler of Maria Theresa and the salt bar circulated.

1896, United States: Creation of the first stock index*, the Dow Jones, built from the stock prices of 12 companies listed on the New York Stock Exchange.

———, United Kingdom: Merger of several London banks to found Barclays.

1897, Russia: Monetary reform and adoption of the gold standard (against bimetallism) decided by Tsar Nicholas II's Minister of Finance, Serge Witte. Raising of loans abroad, especially in France and Belgium.

1897–1899, Japan: New "law on the currency" (1897) adopting the gold standard, after the abandonment of silver as a reference for currencies and with fixing of the weight of the yen at 0.75 g of gold. Gold convertibility of banknotes. Declaration of the monopoly on the issue of money by the Bank of Japan (1899).

1898, Mexico: Reintroduction of the peso as official currency (after that of the Republic in 1869, then its abandonment in 1874).

1899, South Africa: A quarter of the world's gold production coming from South African mines.

1900, United States: Gold Standard Act formally adopting the gold standard, suspended in 1914 and reinstated in 1922.

1900–1901, India: Failure of the experiment to use gold coins in monetary circulation and reshipment of remaining gold stocks to the Bank of England.

1901, Senegal: Transformation of the *Banque du Sénégal* into the *Banque de l'Afrique-Occidentale française* (bank of French West Africa), a limited company with the privilege of issuing money.

1902, Cuba: Dollarization of the economy of the Republic of Cuba, which had been created—under U.S. military occupation—without national currency.

1903, West Africa: Circulation of the franc of French West Africa (Senegal, French Sudan, Guinea, Ivory Coast…).

———, China: First coin issued by the central government in the yuan monetary system.

1904, Japan: First appearance of the "military yen" during the Russo-Japanese war.

1907, United States: Bank panic started from New York (bankruptcy of the Knickerbocker Trust) and generalized to the whole country, with bank rush and fall of the stock market followed by a bailout plan (on J.P. Morgan's own funds) restoring the confidence, but stressing the need for regulation of the financial system.

———, Congo (DRC): Mint of the Congolese franc of the Belgian Congo.

1908, United States: Beginning of the work by the National Monetary Commission of Congress to prepare for monetary and banking reform.

1909, United States: Founding of the rating agency Moody's.

1910, South Africa: Production of almost half of the world's gold by South African mines.

1911, China: Circulation of regional currencies after the Xinhai revolution that overthrew the Qing dynasty.

1912, Switzerland: Foundation of the Union de Banques Suisses from the Winterhour and Toggenburg banks.

1913, United States: Promulgation of the Owen-Glass Federal Reserve Act creating the Federal Reserve Bank (Fed, placed under the authority of the government) and the system of federal reserves in lender of last resort in order to regulate the creation of money, the functioning of banks and the management of inflation, in particular. Creation of the rating agency Fitch.

1914, world: Widespread abandonment of the gold standard and of the convertibility of currencies into gold at the start of the First World War. Acceleration of international indebtedness and gold transfers from Europe to the United States.

———, **China**: Issue of new official currencies, first in silver (1914), then in copper and nickel (1936), or in aluminum (1940), by the government of the Republic, with the gradual disappearance of most of the regional currencies (from the years 1920–1930).

1917, Central Africa: Putting into circulation of the franc of the *Afrique-Équatoriale française* (French Equatorial Africa, in a geographical area including the French Congo, the Oubangui-Chari and the Territory of Chad), replacing the French franc and the private coins of the colonial trade companies (zinc tokens, etc.).

1917–1918, Russia: Nationalization of banking establishments by the Soviet government after the Bolshevik revolution by expropriation and cancelation of shares. Cancelation of peasants' debts (1917). Repudiation of foreign debts (illegitimate and odious) contracted by the Tsarist government (1918).

1919, Russia (Soviet Federative Socialist Republic of): Introduction of "Soviet Treasury units" (*sovznaks*) serving as money, replacing the Russian imperial ruble (until 1924).

———, **Egypt**: Alignment of the Egyptian pound to the pound sterling (with unchanged parity until 1962).

1920s, world/China: Beginning of the appreciation of the price of silver on the international market. Massive outflow of capital from China and multiplied issuance of different currencies by provincial commercial banks. Abandonment of the silver standard by the Chinese central government.

1921, East Africa: Release of the East African shilling, into circulation in the territories under British administration.

1922, world: Genoa Agreement establishing the gold exchange standard. Definition of the value of most currencies against gold—but only the pound sterling (until 1931), the U.S. dollar (until 1933) and the French franc (until 1936) will be convertible into gold.

———, **Soviet Union**: First issue of Soviet rubles, in banknotes and at the rate of 1 new ruble for 10,000 *sovznaks*.

1922–1924, Germany: Period of hyperinflation during the Weimar Republic, with a climax in 1923, when the evolution of prices got out of control and the value of the mark fell on the foreign exchange market (the Papiermark, indexed to gold denominated in dollars reaching 4,200 billion marks on November 23, 1923, against 1 on July 1, 1914). Containment of the phenomenon by strong measures: ban on private agents from printing banknotes, strict limitation of bank credit to reduce the money supply, creation of the *rentenmark* as a transitional currency with a value pledged on the industrial and land capital of the country…

1923, USSR: Creation of Gosbank, equivalent to the Central Bank in the Soviet Union, alongside Gosplan (State Planning Committee) and Gossnab (State Committee for technical supplies of equipment).

1924, Germany: Hjalmar Schacht appointed President of the Reichsbank (January). Creation of a new official currency, the *reichsmark* (August), together with the "rent-mark." Sharp slowdown of the rate of inflation over the year.

———, **Turkey**: Monetary reform replacing the Ottoman Empire pound with a new currency, the republican pound bearing the likeness of Mustafa Kemal Atatürk.

———, **China**: Last mint of silver coins.

———, **Soviet Union**: Monetary reform, with the introduction of, among other things, the "gold ruble."

1925, United Kingdom: Return to the gold standard by the Gold Standard Act.

1925–1928, France: Sabotage of the *Cartel des Gauches* by the Bank of France (1925) which allows the franc to slip away and the capital to flee in order to accelerate the return to power of the right, led by Raymond Poincaré. Replacement of the germinal franc by the Poincaré franc, devalued by 80% of the gold counterpart of the germinal franc (1928). Partial restoration of the gold convertibility of the banknotes, known as the "gold bullion standard."

1926, Saudi Arabia: Creation of the silver riyal of the kingdom of Hedjaz, divided into 20 qirshs and backed by the Ottoman pound (*kuruş*).

1929, United States: Stock market crash on Wall Street, after a period of economic boom, but with speculation by many agents in the stock market, including by going into debt as the uptrend portended high profits. Darkening of the economic conditions (early 1929) and multiplication of profit taking (September), causing a reversal in prices (October). Sudden panic triggering a collapse of the Dow Jones index (with drops of 25% on Thursday, October 24, of almost 40% in mid-November, and then again for the next three years). Serial bank failures, ruin for many savers.

1930, world: Beginning of the Great Depression of the 1930s. Foundation in Basel (Switzerland) of the Bank for International Settlements (BIS), the oldest international financial institution, with a capital made up of shares of 60 Central Banks (nearly half of the stocks belonging to those of the United States, England, France and Germany), and with the initial mission of applying the financial terms of the Treaty of Versailles, before its role evolves to serve as a Bank of Central Banks in the management of foreign exchange reserves, ensure monetary stability and promote international cooperation.

1931, United Kingdom: Suspension of the gold standard and abandonment of the convertibility into gold of the pound sterling, devalued by almost 40%.

———, **Austria**: Bankruptcy of Austria's first bank, Creditanstalt, heavily dependent on U.S. capital caught in the turmoil of the 1929 crisis. Consecutive collapse of the Vienna Stock Exchange.

———, **Ethiopia**: Transformation of the Bank of Abyssinia into the Bank of Ethiopia by Emperor Haile Selassie. Decimal monetary system.

———, **world**: International standardization of legislation on bank checks.

1932, Soviet Union: Declaration of non-convertibility into gold of the Soviet ruble, the national currency.

———, **Japan**: Devaluation of the yen by 32% to deal with the Great Depression.

———, **Iraq**: Establishment of the dinar as official currency, replacing the Gulf rupee.

1932–1933, Austria: First experience of "local" (and "melting") currency in Wörgl, municipality of Tyrol, and in the region of Innsbruck. Prohibition of this currency by administrative court ruling (1933).

1933, United States: Banking crisis (March). Decision of President F.D. Roosevelt to close the banks (for a week) and then to consolidate them. Banking Act or Glass Steagall Act imposing a separation between deposit banks and investment banks. Guarantee of deposits for customers of banking establishments. Reduction of the freedom enjoyed by financial and banking circles, regulation of stock market activity. Devaluation of the dollar and abandonment of its convertibility to gold.

1934, United States: Prohibition for individuals of U.S. nationality to own gold. Creation of the first public defeasance structure, the Home Owner Loan Corporation, responsible for redeeming defaulting mortgages from banks.

———, **Switzerland**: A parallel currency system, the *wir* (which still exists today), launched by Zurich business owners to alleviate the lack of liquidity.

1935, China: Limiting the issuance of money to a few government-controlled banks. Prohibition of private possession of silver. Issue of a new currency (Kuomintang *fabi*). End of the peg to the U.S. dollar of gold customs units, generalized to payments. Hyperinflation.

———, **Saudi Arabia**: Creation of the Saudi riyal, soon aligned with the Indian rupee.

1936, France: No decision by the Popular Front to fully nationalize the Bank of France, whose capital remains private. Abandonment of the gold convertibility of the franc.

———, **USSR/Spain**: System of transferring Soviet financial aid to republican Spain.

1939–1940, world: Sharp rise in the general level of prices and that of loans on a world scale (the United States becoming the main creditors of the countries of Western Europe).

———, **France**: Putting into circulation of "necessity notes" (*billets de nécessité*), bills issued to replace fiduciary money where the branches of the *Banque de France* no longer operate. Control of trade between France, its colonies and the rest of the world (decree of August 28, 1939).

1941, Japan: Diffusion of the military yen in the occupied areas of Asia–Pacific, including Hong Kong

1942, Brazil: Adoption of the cruzeiro as official currency (known as "cruzeiro *antigo*").

1944, worldwide: Bretton Woods agreements (New Hampshire, United States) signed by 44 countries and aimed at organizing the post-war international monetary system in an attempt to avoid recourse to inter-war methods (devaluations, protectionism). Against the British position wanting to create a supranational institution issuing a world currency, imposition of the U.S. line, leading to a system based on the gold exchange standard, in which the U.S. dollar and it alone was convertible into gold at the rate of 35 dollars the ounce of gold (other currencies being convertible into dollars). Creation of the International Monetary Fund (IMF) in order to come to the aid—initially—to countries whose currency depreciated, and of the (future) World Bank to contribute—theoretically—to reconstruction and development.

1945, world: Ratification of the Bretton Woods agreements. First declarations of parities to the IMF.

———, **Japan**: Announcement by the Japanese Treasury that the "military yen" was becoming worthless (September).

———, **Yugoslavia**: Adoption of the dinar as the official currency of the Federal People's Republic, replacing the seven currencies which circulated in the territory during the war (November).

———, **France**: Nationalizations by the National Council of Resistance of the *Banque de France*, as well as of several large deposit banks, including Crédit Lyonnais and Société Générale (December 2).

———, **Africa**: Creation of the CFA franc for the "French colonies in Africa," with a parity of 1.77 against the French franc, as well as the CFP franc for the "French colonies in the Pacific" (December 26).

———, **Korea**: Replacement of the "Korean yen" by the won, quickly linked to the U.S. dollar (October).

1945–1948, China: Replacement of the currencies of pro-Japanese puppet States in the Northeast (including the "Manchoukuo yuan") and of collaborationist regimes by a new Kuomintang currency, then by the yuan-gold—the latter not being effectively backed by gold (hence the continuation of hyperinflation).

1946, United States/Japan: Reform of the Japanese monetary system decided by the U.S. government.

———, **Vietnam**: Introduction of the dong as official currency to replace the French Indochinese piastre.

———, **Indonesia**: Entry into circulation of the first Indonesian rupees under the Sukarno presidency.

1946–1979, United Kingdom: Issue of the "British armed forces pound sterling," a currency unit of legal validity used in Germany, Austria, Trieste (Italy), Japan, Singapore and Egypt.

1947, Soviet Union: Revaluation of the ruble, at the rate of 1 new for 10 old.

———, **India**: Independence of India, which chooses to peg its currency to the pound sterling and to keep the old British divisional system (1 rupee worth 16 annas or 64 paises).

———, **Pakistan**: Adoption of the Pakistani rupee as official currency by the Islamic Republic.

———, **North Korea**: Introduction of the North Korean won, issued by the Central Bank of the Democratic People's Republic of Korea.

1948, world: Creation of the Organization for European Economic Cooperation (future OECD) in charge of the Marshall Plan—refused by the USSR and the Eastern European countries, which created the Council for Mutual Economic Assistance (CMEA or COMECON).

———, **Germany (Federal Republic of)**: Creation of the deutschemark to replace the *rentenmark* (by the United States in the occupied zone).

———, **Africa**: Devaluation of the CFA franc, its value dropping from 1.77 to 2 against the French franc.

1949, Japan: Dodge Plan (equivalent to the Marshall Plan), deflation, pegging of the yen to the U.S. dollar.

———, **China**: Return to the silver standard with the issuance by the Kuomintang of silver yuan certificates backed by the U.S. dollar. Order made by Chiang Kai-Shek for the purpose of minting money in the United States to pay the salaries of the soldiers of the nationalist army (in Mexican pesos made in the workshops of San Francisco, California). Replacement of the Kuomintang currency with the renminbi-yuan issued by the People's Bank of China (created from several provincial banks and established in Shijiazhuang, Hebei), in the mainland areas liberated after the victory of the Communist Party and the end of the hyperinflation.

———, **United Kingdom**: Devaluation of the pound sterling by 30.5%.

1949–1959, United States: Process of merger of regional stock exchanges, notably around those of Chicago (to form the Midwest Stock Exchange), as well as of San Francisco and Los Angeles (Pacific Coast Stock Exchange).

1953, South Korea: Devaluation of the South Korean won, then substitution by the hwan (100 won = 1 hwan).

———, **Cambodia**: Replacement of the piastre of French Indochina by the riel (named after the Spanish *real*).

1955, China: Renminbi-yuan revaluation (with four zeros removed). Fixed parity with the dollar.

1956, world: Creation of the Paris Club, an informal forum of public creditors responsible for restructuring the debts of over-indebted developing countries.

———, **United States**: Ford company listing on Wall Street organized by Goldman Sachs bank, for a record amount of 700 million dollars at the time.

———, **Malaysia**: Creation of a bank fund specially intended to finance the *Hajj* pilgrimage.

1956–1957, USSR: Creation of Eurobank (Commercial Bank for Northern Europe), owned by and representative of the Soviet Central Bank (Gosbank). Conservation (especially in British banks) of dollars held by the USSR outside the United States for fear of freezing its assets for political reasons.

1957, world: Beginning of the expansion of the Euro-currency markets.

———, **India**: Decimalization of the monetary system (1 rupee now worth 100 paises).

1958, Africa: Change of name of the CFA franc, which becomes the "French Community of Africa."

1958–1961, Europe: Return to the convertibility of several European currencies.

1959, Cuba: Ernesto *Che* Guevara appointed President of the Central Bank of Cuba in an effort to affirm the importance of controlling monetary policy and the banking system in the socialist transition.

———, **Africa**: Creation of the Central Bank of West African States (CBWAS, in French BCEAO for *Banque centrale des États de l'Afrique* *de l'Ouest*) and the Central Bank of Equatorial African States and Cameroon (in French *Banque centrale des États de l'Afrique équatoriale et du Cameroun* or BCEAEC). The dirham (silver), the official currency of Morocco.

———, **Iraq**: Abandonment of the alignment of the dinar on the pound sterling and pegging on the U.S. dollar.

1960s, United States: Appearance of securitization, operating on increasingly complex financial products.

1960, France: Entry into circulation of the new franc, prepared by a stabilization plan (Pinay-Rueff) aimed at restoring budgetary balance.

———, **Africa**: Redefinition of the parity of the franc (at 50 FCFA for 1 French franc). Guinea's exit from the franc zone.

1961, South Africa: Creation of the rand, which replaces the South African pound, when the Republic of South Africa is founded and the latter withdraws from the Commonwealth.

———, **Egypt**: Creation of a Central Bank after the nationalization of the National Bank of Egypt.

1962, Africa: Devaluation of the Egyptian pound and alignment with the U.S. dollar. Creation of the West African Monetary Union (WAMU, in French UMOA or *Union monétaire ouest-africaine*) by six countries of the franc zone (Côte d'Ivoire, Dahomey [Benin], Upper Volta [Burkina Faso], Mauritania, Niger, Senegal) and signature between France and WAMU of new monetary cooperation agreements replacing bilateral texts. Mali's exit from the franc zone.

———, **South Korea**: Replacement of the hwan by the South Korean won (at the rate of 10 hwans to 1 won).

———, **Brazil**: Financial crisis. Weakening and depreciation on the foreign exchange market of the national currency, the cruzeiro, whose difference between the official rate and the parallel rate is widening considerably.

1963, USSR/CMEA: Creation of the International Bank for Economic Cooperation (BICE) between CMEA countries for multilateral payments in transferable rubles.

———, **United States**: Restrictions imposed on transfers of dollars by the U.S. administration.

———, **Samoa**: Adoption of the tala as official currency.

———, **Egypt**: Opening of the first Islamic bank, with an explicitly religious reference, granting interest-free loans. Closed by the Nasser government in 1968 and replaced by a State social bank.

1964, Algeria: Issue of the dinar, the currency of the People's Democratic Republic of Algeria.

1965, Japan: Declaration of convertibility of the yen.

———, **Ghana**: The cedi, official currency of Ghana.

———, **Yemen (South)**: Replacement of the dinar of the Federation of South Arabia by that of South Yemen.

1966, United States: Contraction of bank liquidity in a period of restrictive and anti-inflationary policies of the Fed (rise in interest rates). Credit crunch. Fall in stock prices. Slowdown in GDP growth. The first general-purpose credit card (not restricted to specific transactions) launched by the group of U.S. banks, Interbank Association.

———, **France**: Continuation of General de Gaulle's strategy of converting dollars into gold, a metal representing more than 90% of the reserves of the *Banque de France*. Creation of BNP (by merger of BNCI and CNEP).

———, **Tanzania**: Replacement of the East African shilling by the Tanzanian shilling as the official currency.

———, **Australia**: Introduction of the Australian dollar which replaces the Australian pound, with a decimal system.

1967, United Kingdom: Devaluation of the pound sterling by 14.3%.

———, **France**: Creation of the Carte Bleue group by the banks BNP, CCF, CIC, Crédit du Nord, Crédit Lyonnais and Société Générale to launch a French credit card that can be used on payment terminals.

1968, world: Appearance of the word "monetarism."

———, **South Africa**: Boom in gold production from South African mines, thanks to high-depth mining.

1969, world: Implementation by the IMF of the SDR (Special Drawing Right), an international reserve asset whose value depends on a basket of key currencies.

1970, Mexico: Launch of the first Mexican peso coin not containing silver metal.

1971, United States: End of the Bretton Woods system following the abandonment by the United States administration of the gold convertibility of the dollar (August 15), due to the strong tensions undergone by the latter under the combined effects of the insufficient gold reserves at Fort Knox in relation to the mass of "greenbacks" circulating internationally and the widening internal (budget deficit) and external (trade deficit) imbalances of world hegemony (at war in Vietnam). Dollar devaluation of 7.89% to 38 dollars per ounce of gold (December). Creation of the NASDAQ (National Association of Security Dealer Automated Quotations).

———, **worldwide**: Rise of offshore centers (in the Bahamas, the Cayman Islands, Panama, Bahrain, Singapore, etc.).

———, **Japan**: Revaluation of the yen (by 16.88%).

———, **Pakistan**: End of peg of the Pakistani rupee to the pound sterling and choice of peg to the U.S. dollar.

1971–1974, France: Double foreign exchange market (with a "commercial franc" and a "financial franc").

1972, Europe: Entry into force of the "European Monetary Snake" system between Central Banks of the European Economic Community (EEC), making it possible to limit exchange rate fluctuations between the currencies of member countries. Exit of the pound sterling from the European Monetary Snake and floating.

———, **Africa**: Monetary cooperation agreement between France and the Central African States members of the franc zone.

1973, United States: Devaluation of the dollar by 10%, the parity of which drops to 42 dollars per ounce of gold (February).

———, **Japan**: Closure of the foreign exchange market in Tokyo, after the devaluation of the dollar. When it reopens, new revaluation of the yen (after that of 1971). Floating regime.

———, **world**: Serious international exchange rate crisis, leading to the general floating of currencies (March). The first oil shock occurring at the time of the Yom Kippur War (October), with Arab oil-producing countries embarking on an embargo against the United States—and OPEC quadrupling the price of oil. Accentuation of the fall in the profit rates of the Northern countries. Rise of the Eurodollar markets, as well as the speculation activities of the big banks.

———, **Belgium**: Launch of the SWIFT company for interbank messaging and payments.

———, **United Kingdom**: Unification of the English and Scottish stock exchanges.

———, **France**: Approval of the law on the capping of assistance provided by the *Banque de France* to the Treasury.

———, **Africa**: New monetary cooperation agreement between France and the West African countries linked to it. Exit of Mauritania and Madagascar from the franc zone. The naira, the official currency of Nigeria.

1974, Germany: Bankruptcy of the Herstatt bank, causing a crisis in the foreign exchange market and the interbank market (including in the United States) and revealing the risks of the internationalization of the big banks.

———, **United Kingdom**: Crisis in the bond market, linked to the rise in the inflation rate.

———, **world**: Creation, under the impetus in particular of Peter Cooke (Director of the Bank of England), of the "Basel Committee," bringing together Central Banks and banking supervisory bodies, in order to define prudential rules for the regulation of banking activities, stabilization of the global financial system and promotion of international cooperation.

1975, Argentina: Beginning of the period of hyperinflation (which will last until 1990–1991).

———, **Cape Verde**: The Cape Verdean escudo, official currency, pegged to the Portuguese escudo.

———, **Central Africa**: Creation of the Central African States Development Bank (CASDB, in French BDEAC for *Banque de Développement des États de l'Afrique centrale*).

———, **Papua New Guinea**: The kina, official Papua New Guinean currency.

1975–1978, Japan: Movement of strong appreciation of the yen.

1976, world: Kingston Agreement (Jamaica), which confirms the end of fixed parities between currencies, the abandonment of any legal reference to gold as a standard in the international monetary system and the general switch to a floating exchange rate regime where the exchange rates fluctuate permanently and "freely" on the foreign exchange market (January). Official end of the gold standard in the United States.

———, **United Kingdom**: Exceptional government request for IMF assistance (3.9 billion dollars).

1977–1978, Africa: The kwanza, official currency of Angola (1977), replacing the Angolan escudo. Transfers of the headquarters of the Bank of Central African States (BCAS-BEAC) from Paris to Yaoundé (1977), and of the Central Bank of West African States (CBWAS-BCEAO) from Paris to Dakar (1978).

1978, world: Amendment to the IMF's statutes by which the SDR becomes its sole unit of account.

———, **United States**: Fall in the exchange rate of the U.S. dollar.

———, **Vietnam**: Unification of the monetary systems of the Northern and Southern parts of the country, with the dong as official currency.

1979, world: Financial deregulation launched in an accelerated manner in the United States and Great Britain, in an international context where the second oil shock sharply increases the price of hydrocarbons.

———, **United States**: Assumption of office of Paul Volcker as Fed chairman (August). Sharp increase in the interest rate (Fed funds rate): 11.5% on October 1; 13.0% on October 6; 15.5% on October 22. Beginning of the money supply targeting by the Fed (October), with unemployment at 6.0% and inflation at 13.3%.

———, **Europe**: Creation of the European Monetary System (EMS), a system of fixed but adjustable parities, the objective of which was to stabilize the exchange rate of European currencies thanks to maximum bilateral fluctuation bands of ±2.2%. Revaluation of the deutschemark. Establishment of the European Currency Unit (ECU), a basket of European currencies used as a unit of account between the member countries of the EMS.

———, **United Kingdom**: British government decision to voluntarily leave the pound out of the EMS. Accelerated program of deregulation and privatization led by Prime Minister Margaret Thatcher.

———, **Africa**: Monetary cooperation agreement between France and the Comoros, which enter the franc zone.

———, **China**: Use by foreign visitors of "exchange certificates" issued by the Central Bank for their transactions (until 1994).

———, **Laos**: Introduction of the new kip, currency of the Lao People's Democratic Republic.

1980s, South Africa: Further depreciation of the rand, especially under the pressure of international sanctions against the apartheid regime.

1980, United States: Dollar parity reaching 850 dollars per ounce of gold. All-time high for the Federal Reserve's interest rate, its highest since the Second World War: Fed funds rate at 20.0% on March 18 and then again on December 5. (Failed) corner* attempt in the silver market.

———, **Israel**: Replacement of the Israeli pound by the shekel.

———, **China**: Entry of the People's Republic of China into the World Bank and the IMF.

1981, United States: New peaks in interest rates (Fed funds rate at 20.0% on February 3 and March 18). First (interest rate) swap piloted by Salomon Brothers Inc. (now a subsidiary of Citigroup) on behalf of IBM and the World Bank. Foundation of International Banking Facilities (IBF) which grants the United States some of the advantages provided by offshore centers.

———, **world**: Onset of the debt crisis, following massive loans granted by major international banks recycling petrodollars and sharp interest rate hikes decided by the Fed.

1981–1983, France: Successive devaluations of the French franc (October 1981, June 1982 and March 1983), finally kept in the EMS. Nationalization of 39 banks and two financial companies by the Mauroy government (law of February 13, 1982). Deindexation of wages on prices (June 1982).

1982, Mexico/world: Moratorium on the debt of the Mexican government, which is no longer able to honor payments owed to its foreign creditors. Consecutive cessations of payments by several countries of the South. Decision of the "G7" to mandate the IMF to impose on indebted countries, in exchange for financial aid, structural adjustment programs (SAPs) aimed at restoring public finances and ultimately repaying the debt.

———, **Pakistan**: End of the peg of the Pakistani rupee on the U.S. dollar and adoption of a managed floating regime.

1983, United States: Financial deregulation program promoted by the Reagan administration.

1984, United Kingdom: Launch of the FTSE100 (Financial Times Stock Exchange) index in London.

———, **France**: Banking law, launching deregulation and adopting the universal banking model.

———, **Africa**: Return of Mali to the franc zone.

1985, world: Plaza Agreements, by which the "G7" becomes the framework for consultation prior to coordinated interventions by Central Banks on the foreign exchange market.

———, **United States**: Paralysis (more than 24 hours) of the U.S. government loan settlement system due to a computer failure at the Bank of New York. Fed intervention (20 billion dollars).

———, **Argentina**: Replacement of the peso by the austral (worth 1,000 pesos) in an attempt to stop inflation under the Austral Plan, a shock program inspired by the recommendations of the Washington Consensus. Beginning of the circulation of the "*bocade*," "fiscal currency" issued by several local authorities.

———, **France**: Appearance of negotiable debt securities (*titres de créances négociables*).

———, **Africa**: Enlargement of the CFA franc zone to Equatorial Guinea.

———, **Israel**: Saving the economy from the brink of collapse with massive U.S. financial aid.

1986, United Kingdom: Entry into force of the Big Bang, reorganization of the London Stock Exchange.

———, **Europe**: Revaluation of the deutschemark, the Dutch guilder and the Belgian and Luxembourg francs.

———, **Brazil**: Change of monetary unit by the passage from cruzeiro to cruzado (then to the new cruzado or *cruzado novo* in 1989, renamed cruzeiro in 1990).

———, **Southern Africa**: Creation of the Common Monetary Area, a monetary zone between South Africa, Eswatini (Swaziland), Lesotho and Namibia, with free acceptance of the rand.

———, **Saudi Arabia**: Fixed parity of the Saudi riyal with the U.S. dollar.

1987, world: "G7" Louvre agreements reaffirming that the exchange rate must be determined by the market.

———, **United States**: Crash on Wall Street, manifested by a 22.6% drop in the Dow Jones index (October 19). Simultaneous crisis in the foreign exchange market and those of stocks and bonds. Episode of junk bonds* and real estate bubble. Worsening of the U.S. Savings and Loan. Bankruptcy of the New York-based investment bank Drexel Burnham Lambert due to fraud and insider trading scandal.

———, **France**: Beginning of the privatization of public banks by the Chirac government.

1988, worldwide: Agreements of the Basel Committee (known as "Basel I") to mitigate systemic risks, notably thanks to the "Cooke ratio" obliging banking and financial institutions to respect a minimum proportion of 8% between their own funds and the credits they grant to their customers.

———, **France**: Creation of the CAC 40, an index of the Paris Stock Exchange, based on the share prices of the top 40 capitalizations. Introduction of continuous assisted quotation by electronic negotiations. Start of securitization.

1989, world: Brady Plan. Creation of Brady bonds (named after President Reagan's Secretary of State for the Treasury), 30-year dollar-denominated bonds backed by the IMF, World Bank and New York Federal Reserve, aimed at enabling Southern indebted countries to repay their debts.

———, **United States**: Junk bonds bubble*, whose average interest rate exceeds that of government bonds.

———, **Japan**: Inflating speculative bubbles in the real estate and equity markets.

———, **Spain**: Entry of the peseta into the EMS.

———, **Egypt**: Abandonment of the alignment of the Egyptian pound to the U.S. dollar.

1989–1990, Soviet Union: Phenomenon of hyperinflation and depreciation of the Soviet ruble.

1990s, United States/United Kingdom: Emergence and early boom in financial derivatives.

1990, world: Strong tensions in the financial markets following the invasion of Kuwait by Iraq. Significant measures adopted by the IMF, such as the Enhanced Structural Adjustment Facility.

———, **United States**: Fall of the S&P500 stock market index (June–October) following the Gulf War.

———, **United Kingdom**: Membership of the pound to the EMS exchange rate mechanism.

1991, ex-USSR: Maintenance of the ruble as the currency of the Russian Federation and of Belarus. End of the use of the "transferable ruble" within the CMEA or COMECON (which is dissolved in June).

———, **Africa**: Signature of the Abuja Treaty (in Nigeria) establishing the African Economic Community and calling for the creation of an African Central Bank.

———, **Iraq**: Stopping the printing in Switzerland of dinar banknotes (nicknamed "Swiss dinars").

———, **Argentina**: Anchoring on the U.S. dollar of the peso, which has once again become the official currency. Limitation by law of the growth of the money supply.

———, **Peru**: Substitution by the *nuevo sol* of the *inti*, which itself replaced the *sol de oro* and was depreciating.

1991–1992, former Yugoslavia (Federal Republic of): Adoption, as official currency, of the Slovenian tolar by Slovenia, the Croatian dinar by Croatia and the Macedonian denar by Macedonia (1991), then the "convertible mark" by Bosnia and Herzegovina (1992).

———, **Sweden**: Real estate bubble burst and credit crunch. State rescue of the banking system.

1992, Europe: Signature of the Maastricht Treaty by 12 EEC countries which launch the Economic and Monetary Union with the objective of establishing a single currency if "convergence criteria" are met. EMS crisis: speculative attacks by financial markets (notably by George Soros' hedge fund*) against the pound sterling and the lira, which must leave the EMS, as well as against the peseta—attacks accentuated after the rejection of the Monetary Union Treaty by Denmark and the prospect of a referendum on the single currency project in France.

1993, Europe: Widening of the fluctuation margins between the EMS currencies (to ±15%), following new speculative attacks against the French franc on the foreign exchange market.

———, **France**: Law of independence of the *Banque de France* vis-à-vis the government. End of the financing of the Treasury by the Central Bank, decided by the Balladur government under the presidency of F. Mitterrand.

———, **Russia**: Definitive withdrawal from circulation of the Soviet ruble and replacement by the Russian ruble.

———, **China**: Parity regime of the yuan against the dollar announced by the Chinese Central Bank.

———, **Cuba**: Beginning of dollarization of the economy, with a three-currency monetary regime.

1993–1994, former Yugoslavia (Federal Republic of)/Serbia: Hyperinflation. Adoption of the deutschemark as the official currency of the former Yugoslavia and issue of the "new dinar," then the "new new dinar," then the "super dinar" in order to put an end to inflation.

1994, United States: Hike in the Fed's short rate, overreaction of long rates and fall in the bond market.

———, **Mexico**: Mexican crisis known as "tequila*." Sudden capital outflows, currency crisis, fall of the peso. Intervention by U.S. monetary authorities and international financial institutions (up to 50 billion dollars). Strong economic recession the following year.

———, **Brazil**: Real Plan (*Plano Real*) intended to support the economy and end inflation by stabilizing the new national currency, the *real*.

———, **Pakistan**: Neoliberal reforms of the economy with a switch to convertibility of the Pakistani rupee.

———, **Africa**: Devaluation of the CFA franc by 50% (at 100 FCFA) and the Comorian franc by 33% (75 KMF) (January). Signatures of the treaties of the West African Economic and Monetary Union (WAEMU, in French UEMOA for *Union économique et monétaire ouest-africaine*) in January in Dakar, and of the Economic and Monetary Community of Central Africa (EMCCA, in French CEMAC for *Communauté économique et monétaire de l'Afrique centrale*) in March in N'Djamena.

1995, United Kingdom: Bankruptcy of Barings following speculative trading from Singapore on Tokyo Stock Exchange derivatives.

———, **France**: State bailout of bankrupt Crédit Lyonnais.

1997, Asia: Onset of the so-called "Asian" monetary and financial crisis (from early July). Explosion of the fixed or quasi-fixed exchange rate system in force for several decades in the region, starting with that of the Thai baht. Strong depreciations in the currencies of Malaysia, Indonesia, the Philippines or South Korea (the currency of the latter country, the won, losing half of its value between December 20 and 23, just before the signing of an agreement with the IMF establishing its float).

———, **Lebanon**: Pegging of the Lebanese pound to the U.S. dollar.

———, **Africa**: Guinea-Bissau's accession to the CFA franc zone.

———, **Switzerland**: Merger of the Union de Banques Suisses and the Société de Banque Suisse to form UBS.

1998, United States: Merger of Citigroup and Travelers Group to form a financial services giant. Bankruptcy of the hedge fund* Long Term Capital Management due to losses on derivatives, causing disruption in financial markets and forcing the Fed to intervene to avoid a banking crisis.

———, **Europe**: Creation of the European Central Bank (ECB), responsible for maintaining price stability in the euro zone and monitoring the single European currency, and of the Eurosystem, the monetary authority of the euro zone which brings together around the ECB the Central Banks of the member States of the Union adopting the euro.

———, **Russia**: Government default on short-term negotiable debt securities issued by the State (short-term State commitments known as GKO or *Gosudarstvennoe Kratkosrochnoe Obyazatelstvo*).

———, **Brazil**: Financial crisis. IMF loan of 41.5 billion dollars. New privatizations.

———, **Africa**: Recognition by the Council of the European Union of monetary cooperation agreements between France and the countries of the WAEMU, the EMCCA and the Union of the Comoros, on the grounds that they are part of France's budgetary direct commitment (without modification of parities during the changeover to the euro).

1999, worldwide: Creation of the "G20," an intergovernmental body which asserts itself as the main consultation forum, as well as of the

Financial Stability Forum, which will become the Financial Stability Council.

———, **Europe**: Introduction of the euro, the single currency created between 11 European countries (January 1) for bank accounts and financial products. Establishment of the TARGET 1 cross-border settlement system (Trans European Automated Real Time Gross Settlement Express Transfer) in the euro zone to secure large-value exchanges and serve as a transmission vector for the single monetary policy.

———, **ex-Yugoslavia**: Adoption by Montenegro of the deutschemark as a monetary unit.

———, **Brazil**: End of the peg on the U.S. dollar of the Brazilian real, which is devalued and now floating.

———, **Turkey**: Austerity plan and pegging of the Turkish lira to the U.S. dollar in an attempt to curb inflation.

———, **Africa**: Fixing of the parity between the euro and the CFA and Comorian francs at 1 euro for 655.957 FCFA and 491.968 KMF, respectively.

End of the 20th Century, world: Rise of financial markets and hyper-concentration of financial oligopolies. Movements of deregulation, decompartmentalization and disintermediation (without undermining the power of the large banking establishments which are re-specializing and repositioning themselves in force on the various financial markets). Merger of banks and insurance companies to form gigantic financial groups.

2000, United States: Maximum inflation of the "Internet bubble," a phenomenon of speculation that began in the second half of the 1990s and relates to technological stock markets linked to the computer and telecommunications sector (known as "dot com"), such as those from Microsoft, AOL, Yahoo and Amazon. Creation of JPMorgan Chase from the takeover of JPMorgan by Chase Chemical.

———, **Europe**: Merger of the Amsterdam, Brussels and Paris stock exchanges and creation of the Euronext company.

———, **Turkey**: Bank speculation on government bonds, whose rates are soaring. Financial crisis and drying up of the interbank market (November). IMF emergency loan (December).

———, **Japan**: Implementation of innovative monetary policy measures by the Central Bank of Japan, which would soon become those of "Quantitative Easing*."

2000–2009, Zimbabwe: Hyperinflation, then adoption of the U.S. dollar as official currency.

2001, worldwide: Attacks of September 11, affecting financial establishments of the World Trade Center. Massive injection of liquidity by the Fed to the banks and passage of the overnight rate of the interbank market to zero for several days. ECB intervention going in the same direction. Coordination of the actions of the Central Banks of the North (concerted cut in key rates by the Fed, the ECB and the Bank of England) in the face of financial market uncertainty and systemic risk. Very innovative measure taken by the main Central Banks of the North consisting in exchanging between themselves credit lines denominated in their respective currencies (swap lines).

———, **Turkey**: Floating of the Turkish lira, which depreciates sharply. Rescue plan conducted under the aegis of the United States.

———, **Argentina**: Serious financial and economic crisis, with devaluation of the peso, abandonment of the fixed exchange rate and temporary suspension of the repayment of the country's debt.

———, **United States**: Bankruptcy of the transnational Enron, leading to that of its auditor, Arthur Andersen. New junk bond bubble*.

———, **Europe**: Entries of Portugal and Greece into the euro zone. Replacement of the deutschemark by the euro.

2001–2002, North Korea: Devaluation of the North Korean won. Official end of the two-currency system for foreigners, "red won" for visitors from socialist countries and "blue won" for those from capitalist countries.

2002, United States/Europe: Crisis in the corporate bond markets.

———, **Europe**: Introduction of euro coins and banknotes in euro zone member countries.

———, **Brazil**: Pre-election tensions, depreciation of the real. Accentuation of the crisis on the public debt market, despite an IMF loan.

2003, world: Third oil shock, with a sharp rise in the price of hydrocarbons.

2004, world: "Basel II" agreements, which recommend redefining the regulatory standards for financial securities, in particular through the introduction of the "McDonough ratio" taking into account broader risks.

———, **United States**: Beginning of the new rise in the U.S. Central Bank's interest rate (Fed funds rate to 2.25% in December, against 1.00% in January).

———, **Cuba**: Beginning of the process of de-dollarization of the economy, with the establishment of an original system with two official currencies (the Cuban peso or "CUP" and the Cuban convertible peso or "CUC").

2005, United States: Confirmation of the upward trend in U.S. interest rates (Fed funds rate at 2.25% in January and 4.25% in December).

———, **China**: Decision of the Chinese Central Bank to devalue the yuan by 2.1% against the U.S. dollar and adoption of a "floating" exchange rate regime.

———, **Turkey**: Substitution of the old Turkish lira by the new lira (at the rate of 1,000,000 to 1).

2006, United States: Multiplication of defaults of low-income households, unable to meet the maturities of their variable-rate mortgages (subprimes).

———, **Russia**: Declaration of full convertibility of the ruble, with the lifting of restrictions on capital and foreign exchange movements.

———, **former Yugoslavia**: Adoption as currency unit of the Serbian dinar in Serbia, but of the euro in Montenegro and Kosovo after the dissolution of the Community of States of Serbia and Montenegro.

2007, United States: Merger of Euronext with the New York Stock Exchange to create NYSE Euronext, the world's leading group of stock exchanges. Triggering of the subprime crisis (from August), the accounts of financial institutions being weakened by the losses recorded on subprime loans. Agreements concerning "swap lines" between the Fed and the European Central Bank, plus the National Bank of Switzerland, to allow them "unlimited" access to the U.S. dollar (December).

———, **Latin America**: Launch of the Bank of the South or Bancosur at the initiative of Argentina, Bolivia, Brazil, Ecuador, Paraguay and Venezuela.

———, **Europe**: Slovenia's accession to the euro zone.

2008, United States: Bankruptcy of the Lehman Brothers bank, without financial rescue from the monetary authorities (September 15). Bankruptcy—then the largest in U.S. history—of the Washington Mutual, the country's leading savings bank, which was listed on the New York Stock Exchange and whose assets were purchased by JPMorgan Chase (September 25). Immediate contagion effect felt on the financial markets (the top 30 U.S. stock market capitalizations seeing their values fall by 50% compared to the previous year). Mistrust of banks, which refuse to lend each other liquidity on the interbank market. Emergency Economic Stabilization Act or "Bank Bailout of 2008" (Paulson Plan). Extension of the Fed's swap lines to Central Banks in the North and a few in the South (September–October). Draining of credit (credit crunch*), generalizing the economic crisis. AIG (insurance and financial services) bailout by the Fed for 182 billion dollars. Beginning of the rise of U.S. indexed funds (especially BlackRock, Vanguard and State Street).

———, **United Kingdom**: Nationalization of Northern Rock Bank, listed on the London Stock Exchange.

———, **Iceland**: Nationalization of the Kaupthing, Landsbanki and Glitnir banks by the Icelandic government.

———, **Europe (euro zone)**: Beginning of the implementation of the SEPA (Single Euro Payments Area), with electronic means of payment common in the countries of the euro zone. Modernization of the TARGET 1 system, with the implementation of TARGET 2. Nationalization of the banking and insurance activities of the Algemene Bank Nederland (ABN Amro) in the Netherlands.

———, **Venezuela**: Replacement of the strong bolivar by the sovereign bolivar in an attempt to curb inflation.

———, **world**: Call of the "G20" in Washington for a strengthening of financial prudential rules.

2009, world: "G20" summits in London and Pittsburgh for a new international regulation. Publication by the OECD of a list of non-cooperative jurisdictions in the fight against tax havens. Creation of the first cryptographic currency, the bitcoin, by an anonymous individual (or group).

———, **United States**: Beginning of so-called "unconventional" monetary policy measures (Quantitative Easing*).

———, **Russia**: Beginning of a depreciation of the Russian ruble, concomitant with the fall in the price of hydrocarbons.

———, **Europe**: Creation of several European institutions for the regulation of financial markets. Announcement by the Greek government of slippages in the levels of budget deficit and public debt. Entry of Slovakia into the euro zone. Nationalization of the Hypo Group Alpe Adria bank in Austria.

———, **Latin America**: Adoption of a common unit of account, the Sucre, by the member countries of ALBA (the Bolivarian Alliance for the Americas, or *Alianza Bolivariana para los Pueblos de Nuestra América*), namely Cuba, the Venezuela, Bolivia, Nicaragua, Honduras, Dominica, plus Ecuador.

———, **North Korea**: Revaluation of the North Korean won.

2009–2010, Greece: Greek sovereign debt crisis. Strong tensions in the bond and equity markets. Risks of diffusion to Portugal and Spain, but also of the break-up of the euro zone.

———, **Brazil**: Appreciation movement of the Brazilian real against the U.S. dollar.

2010, worldwide: "Basel III" agreements intended to improve the prudential rules of the financial system.

———, **Europe**: Beginning of the sovereign debt crisis in the euro zone. Creation of the European Financial Stability Fund (EFSF), with a capital of 750 billion euros. Establishment of the Securities Market Program. Loans granted to ailing Greece (110 billion euros) by the IMF, the ECB and the European Commission, on the strict condition that fierce austerity is applied.

2010–2014, Spain: Burst of the real estate bubble. Flight of capital. Bank destabilization.

2011, Europe: Extension of the sovereign debt crisis to several other euro zone countries finding it difficult to obtain financing on the capital markets. Emergency recapitalization of French banks BNP and Société Générale in the face of default risks. Bankruptcy of the Franco-Belgian bank Dexia, listed on Euronext Brussels and since then placed in orderly resolution*. IMF and European Union loans granted to Portugal in crisis. Estonia's accession to the euro zone.

2012, Europe: European Union loans to Spain with the aim of recapitalizing its banking system (of which more than half, or 22 billion euros, being devoted to the rescue of Bankia, in bankruptcy). Signature of the Treaty on Stability, Coordination and Governance by 25 of the 27 member States of the Union (except the United Kingdom and the Czech Republic). Reforms to "consolidate public accounts," "unify the European financial area" and "strengthen banks" through the creation of a Banking Union by the euro zone countries. Launch of Outright Monetary Transactions, corresponding to the buybacks of bonds issued by the States. Official guarantee provided to savers in the event of bankruptcy of the banking system (up to 100,000 euros per depositor and establishment).

———, United States/Australia: Conviction of the rating agency Standard & Poor's by the Australian courts for misleading valuations of toxic financial products (yet rated "AAA").

———, China: New revaluation of the yuan against the U.S. dollar.

———, North Korea: Use of "special won" debit cards (tied won) for foreign visitors.

2013, world: Offshore Leaks affair, listing personalities with bank accounts in tax havens.

———, Europe: Establishment of the European Stability Mechanism (ESM) to temporarily secure borrowing on the financial markets through the recapitalization of financial institutions, direct loans to States or purchases on the primary and secondary markets of securities from countries in difficulty, at the cost of austerity "reforms." Adoption by the ECB, in addition to the lowering of its refinancing rate, of "unconventional" measures (short or long-term refinancing loans to banks; ad hoc one-time purchases on the secondary market of bonds of States in difficulty, etc.). IMF and European Union loans to Cyprus, whose banks had to be closed for two weeks (March) and regrouped to avoid collapsing.

———, Germany: Official recognition of bitcoin as "private currency" by the Bundesbank (August).

———, **China**: Central Bank ban on domestic banks from using bitcoin, followed by trading platforms, causing a crash in this crypto-currency market (December).

2014, worldwide: Luxembourg Leaks scandal, revealing the organization of tax evasion of more than 1,000 companies, with the complicity of the administration of the Grand Duchy of Luxembourg.

———, **Europe**: Institution of the Single Resolution Mechanism (SRM) harmonizing the rules applicable to banking establishments in difficulty or in bankruptcy. Implementation of the Asset-backed Securities Purchase Program (intended for the non-financial private sector) and the Covered Bond Purchase Program (for the financial sector). Entry of Latvia into the euro zone.

———, **Russia**: Beginning of a new Russian ruble crisis.

———, **China**: Launch by China of the Asian Infrastructure Investment Bank (AIIB).

2014–2015, Russia: Russian ruble crisis and bankruptcy of several local banking and financial institutions.

———, **United States/France**: Trial and record criminal conviction of French bank BNP Paribas by a U.S. court for "illegal dollar transactions".

2015, worldwide: SwissLeaks case, shedding light on the international system of tax fraud and money laundering organized from Switzerland.

———, **United States**: Launch by Standard and Poor's agency of the S&P500 "Christian Values" index, bringing together firms that meet the moral standards of the Church targeting a clientele of believing investors.

———, **Europe**: Adoption of the Single Supervisory Mechanism (SSM). Program of purchases on the secondary market of public sector assets, i.e., securities issued by European States and institutions. Lithuania's accession to the euro zone, leading to the extension of the single currency to 19 countries. Decision of the Greek government of A. Tsipras (and Y. Varoufákis) not to touch the private banks nor to suspend the payment of the debt service. Bankruptcies of the German mortgage bank Düsseldorf Hypothekenbank, the Swiss bank Hottinger specializing in international wealth management, the Spanish bank for asset management Banco Madrid, etc. State rescue of several regional banks in Italy.

———, **China**: Financial crisis in the Shanghai and Shenzhen stock markets (during the Summer).

2016, worldwide: Panama Papers scandal, revealing precise information (including identities) on the shareholders of more than 200,000 offshore companies.

———, **China**: Integration of the Chinese currency, the yuan, into the basket of currencies making up the IMF's SDR. First tests of an official crypto-currency by the Central Bank of China.

———, **India**: Vast demonetization operation decided by Prime Minister Narendra Modi.

———, **Europe**: German State liquidation of the Dutch-Canadian bank Maple Bank GmbH. Declaration of bankruptcy of the Belgian Optima Bank by the National Bank of Belgium (BNB).

2017, world: New bitcoin futures contracts issued on the Chicago Mercantile Exchange. Paradise Papers case, disclosing a lot of information on offshore companies.

———, **Japan**: Official recognition of bitcoin as a crypto-currency by the Central Bank of Japan.

———, **United States**: Launch of the international crypto-currency project, the Utility Settlement Coin (USC), by several banks, including Barclays, HSBC, Santander, Crédit Suisse, Deutsche Bank, etc. (September).

———, **China**: Official announcement of the launch of a State digital currency by China (September).

2018, Switzerland: Citizen vote rejection of a "full currency" proposal (100% Money) that would have given the Swiss National Bank a full monopoly on money creation if approved.

———, **Russia**: Government announcement that Russian financial institutions can operate outside SWIFT.

———, **Turkey**: New crisis of the Turkish lira, attacked on the foreign exchange market (and losing nearly 50% of its value between January and August), in a context of strong diplomatic tensions with the United States.

———, **Venezuela**: Government authorization given to foreign buyers to buy the country's oil in currencies other than the dollar. Introduction (with the help of Russia) of the *petro*, the first national crypto-currency whose value is guaranteed by commodities.

———, **Argentina**: Fall of the value of the Argentine peso. Strong interest rate hike by the Central Bank. IMF loan to the Argentine State (57 billion dollars). Austerity plan.

2019, world: Publication of bitcoin and ether prices in the New York NASDAQ index. Presentation by Facebook/Meta of a project to create a virtual currency (libra).

———, **United States**: Launch by JPMorgan of the first crypto-currency created by a U.S. bank, JPCoin, linked to the dollar (February).

———, **China**: Controlled depreciation of the yuan in reaction to the trade war imposed by the United States.

———, **Lebanon**: Accentuation of the depreciation of the Lebanese pound against the U.S. dollar and worsening of the monetary, financial and banking crisis.

2020, world: Financial and economic crisis following the COVID-19 pandemic, with record falls on several stock exchanges around the world (March).

———, **Europe**: Extension of public and private bond buyback programs by the ECB (March). Large-scale rescue plan for the euro zone via the Pandemic Emergency Purchase Program (PEPP).

2021, Cuba: Completion of the process of de-dollarization of the economy through the abolition of the "CUC" and through monetary unification (January 1, 2021).

———, **world**: Census of more than 5,000 crypto-assets or crypto-currencies with a value exceeding 2,000 billion dollars in total (May). Allocation of 456 billion SDRs by the IMF (August) to enable member countries to cope with the crisis following the pandemic and with their reserve needs. Strong fluctuations in the price of bitcoin. Pandora Papers affair, a new scandal demonstrating the scale and gravity of the tax evasion activities of the ultra-rich internationally (October).

———, **Nigeria**: Launch of e-naira, the first digital version of African official currency (October).

Notes The ~ sign indicates an approximate date. Country names in bold at the beginning of each entry correspond to current States.

Appendix B: Main Historical Landmarks of (Western) Economic Thought on Money

Aristotle (384 BC–322 BC) argues that money serves at the same time as a unit of account, an intermediary of exchanges and a store of value. By balancing exchanges, it facilitates them. It allows everyone to better meet their needs and thus develops social relations. However, based on the distinction between two types of goods, those devoted to consumption and those intended for exchange, and between two forms of economic relations, those which make it possible to acquire goods through work (which is commendable) or by trade (which is not natural), Aristotle distinguishes, in the use of money, money which is only an intermediary in exchange and that which aims at making a monetary profit—this which he calls "chromatics," harshly criticized.

Nicolas Oresme (1320–1382), translator of Aristotelian works into French, advisor to King Charles V, mathematician and astronomer, then bishop, is the author of a *Traité sur les monnaies* (Treatise on coins, 1366) in which he condemns usury—like Saint Augustin—and affirms that the currency is not the personal property of the king, but belongs to the community which alone defines its status. The "mutation" of currencies, that is to say the arbitrary modification of their weights, names or contents in metal to alter their value or to vary the quantity of cash in a deceptive way, is, according to him, illegitimate, because it destroys their purpose, i.e., to guarantee a constant value of the trading tool, which ruins trust, in addition to increasing product prices.

Luis Saravia de la Calle (16th Century), theologian of Medina del Campo, a commercial place in Castile, is the author of *The Instruction of the Merchants* (1544), a treatise on exchange and usury published at the same time than those of Cristóbal de Villalón in Valladolid and Luis de Alcalá in Toledo. For him, the economic disturbances observed in the metropolis were not primarily due to the increase in currency in circulation following the influx of gold and silver from the Americas, but rather to the greed of the merchants. His book (which was translated into Italian and met with some success) aimed to teach them about morality, including rejecting usury, as well as the appropriation of deposits by bankers for profit.

Martin de Azpilcueta (1491–1586), theologian of the prestigious school of Salamanca, contemporary of the great discoveries, analyzed the economic effects of the arrival of precious metals extracted from Spanish colonial America in European countries. He formulated—perhaps for the first time in history—a causal relationship between the quantity of money in circulation, depending on the more or less marked importance of precious metals, and the purchasing power of this money, relative to the general price level of merchandises. He sees money as a commodity (all the more expensive as its supply is scarce and its demand is high) and, as such, recognizes a value in it, which is represented in the form of an interest rate.

Thomas Gresham (~1519, 1579), English merchant and financier, Lord Mayor of London, knighted after negotiating loans for King Henry VIII, also advisor to King Edward VI and Queen Elizabeth I. He used his foreign exchange skills to defend the pound on the Antwerp Stock Exchange, then in the Netherlands. On the model of this market, he contributed to the founding of the Royal London Stock Exchange. His name has remained attached to "Gresham's law," according to which "bad money drives out good." This "law" dictates that agents tend to hoard coins made of gold (regardless of their state) and instead introduce into circulation division coins made from less noble metals, or even banknotes.

Jean Bodin (1529–1596), jurisconsult and influential political theoretician of the Renaissance, affirmed the demand for "frank and free" trade. In his polemic *Réponse aux paradoxes de M. de Malestroit* (Response to the paradoxes of M. de Malestroit, 1568) and the complex context of the monetary system of the kingdom of France at the time when the currencies of account (livre tournois, sol and deniers) and of payment (coins) differed, he defended the idea that the "price revolution," that is, the high inflation then recorded in Western Europe, came mainly from the inflows of gold and silver from the New World, but also from other factors, such as the maintenance of trade monopolies, depreciation of currencies, excessive royal spending and monetary manipulation.

John Locke (1632–1704), English philosopher and one of the founders of political liberalism, wrote about money. The invention of money and the tacit convention that recognizes its value have, according to him, conditioned the possibility of accumulating wealth and extending property beyond the limits set by need. At a time when capitalism was taking its rise, but when the legitimacy of monetary gain by interest was questioned, unlimited monetary enrichment is freed from the shackles in which the moral law locked it, freeing from all hindrance the practices of merchants and financiers during primitive accumulation. He speaks of the proportion between trade and money. According to him, the interest rate is governed by a natural law.

John Law (1671–1729), Scottish adventurer and banker, founder of the East India Company, became in 1720 Minister of Finance of the Kingdom of France, under the Regency. An anti-bullionist, he sees money as a mere means of exchange, and not as wealth. He invented an original anti-metallist financial system based on the adoption of paper money and the issuance of securities on the stock exchange. Its principle departs from bimetallism: it does not guarantee the convertibility of banknotes issued by metal coins, but leans their reliability on land capital, to approximate a fiduciary currency, with adjustment of the supply to the needs of trade. The collapse of the system ruined Law, but relieved some of the royal debt.

Richard Cantillon (1680–1734), Irish-French banker who made his fortune (thanks to his speculations against Law's system and during the financial bubbles of the time), influenced by his work as an economist (*Essai sur la nature du commerce en général* or Essay on the nature of trade in general) both the physiocratic and classical currents. He completes the thesis of a causal relation progressing from variations in the quantity of money to price fluctuations (and allowing a rebalancing of the trade balance) by resorting to the notion of speed of circulation. The interest rate depends on movements in the money market, on the profit expectations and on the risk-taking behaviors of entrepreneurial agents. He points out the importance of the entrepreneurs for the modernization of the economy.

David Hume (1711–1776), Scottish philosopher, was the first, in *On the Balance of Trade* (1752), to offer an explanation of the mechanism of adjustment of gold stocks under the gold standard. A country with a trade deficit will have to cover it with the gold it owns. The corresponding outflows of gold will thus contract the money supply and cause, according to him, a fall in the price level. As a result, the products of the country in question, now cheaper compared to abroad, will become more competitive on the international market; hence a rebalancing of the foreign trade balance—with a return to a comparable gold stock. He therefore supports free trade. However, he suggests that inflation drives more jobs.

Box A.1 Some opinions on money

Shakespeare:	"There is thy gold, worse poison to men's soul, doing more murder in this loathsome world, than these poor compounds that thou mayst not sell."
Rousseau:	"We have everything with money, except for morals and citizens."
Robespierre:	"Any mercantile speculation that I engage in at the expense of the life of my fellow human being is not trafficking, it is robbery and fratricide."
Jefferson:	"And I sincerely believe with you, that banking establishments are more dangerous than standing armies; and that the principle of spending money to be paid by posterity, under the name of funding, is but swindling futurity on a large scale."
Napoleon:	"When a government is dependent on the bankers for money, it is the bankers, not the government leaders, who control the situation, since the hand that gives is above the hand that receives. Money has no homeland; financiers have no patriotism and no decency; their only objective is gain."
Goethe:	"[Your] hands and your feet and your head and your a… are yours; but all that I enjoy joyfully, is it then less to me? If I can pay six stallions, aren't their strengths

	mine? I'm doing well and a big man, just as if I had twenty-four legs."
Kant:	"I am richer with a hundred thalers than with their simple concept."
Freud:	"In truth, wherever the archaic mode of thought reigned or persists, in ancient civilizations, in myth, tales, superstitions, in unconscious thought, in dreams and in neurosis, money is put in intimate relation with the excrement."
Hugo:	"The hell of the poor is the paradise of the rich."
Tolstoy:	"Money, thanks to the existence of violence in social relations, represents only the possibility of a new form of impersonal slavery which has replaced personal slavery."
Dostoyevsky:	"Money is liberty in coins."
Péguy:	"A single misery is enough to condemn a society. It only takes one man to be held, or knowingly left in misery, for the entire civic pact to be void."
Mauss:	"To give is to demonstrate one's superiority, to be more, higher, to *magister*; to accept without giving back or without giving back more is to subordinate oneself, to become client and servant, to become small, to fall lower, to *minister*. (...) Fortunately, not everything is classified in terms of buying and selling yet. Things still have sentimental value in addition to their market value, if at all there are values that are only of that sort."

Adam Smith (1723–1790), Scottish philosopher and economist, author of *An Inquiry into the Nature and Causes of the Wealth of Nations* (1776)—believed to be the founding book of classical political economy. According to him, the accumulation of capital ensures the enrichment of countries in the long run. Smith separates capital from money: money is not part of wealth; capital is not accumulated by increasing the quantity of money, but by savings, taken from rents and profits from the product. Very critical of the Law system, Smith recommends prudence in banking management, short loans, the only discount of "real" papers (and not fictitious ones) and competition. The rate of interest tends to align with the rate of profit.

Ferdinando Galiani (1728–1787), Italian abbot, bases his reflections on money, collected in his work *Della moneta* (1751), on a theory of value. He asserts that money, as a merchandise, has an "intrinsic value," which exists independently of its monetary function and which ultimately prevails in the spontaneous mechanism of exchange. He argues, in an original way at the time, that the "enhancement" (that is to say, the devalorization of the currency, carried out by increasing the value of the coins in unit of account without changing their precious metal content or by reducing their content without changing face value) can have positive effects, such as reducing public debt.

Henry Thornton (1760–1815), English banker, participated in parliamentary committees on monetary and financial matters. His analyzes, which seek the means to limit banking crises, are marked by pragmatism and prudence. No universal self-regulatory mechanism exists to avoid the risk of collapse of the credit system, from which money partly stems, because deposits also serve as a means of payment. He is in favor of a Central Bank of public statute, able to supervise the interests of the country and having the freedom to set the interest rate and to determine its policy at its discretion, even if he thinks that its role will only be reduced to mitigate the impact of inevitable financial crises.

Jean-Baptiste Say (1767–1832), journalist, industrialist, then professor of economics enrolled in the French liberal school. His monetary analysis is not his most original or profound contribution to economic analysis. He is known for the "law of outlets" (every supply finds its own demand, without risk of overproduction). Money is only supposed to be a "veil"; it is not in demand for itself. Among the shocks external to the market that can block production and lead to crises (always partial and temporary), Say cites those of a monetary nature; hence the outline of a monetary theory of cycles. He was a staunch opponent of taxes, which he said created distortions in the allocation of capital.

David Ricardo (1772–1823), England's foremost classical economist, was a stockbroker and later annuitant after making his fortune. Elected to be member of the Parliament, he campaigned there for the freedom of the wheat trade. In the "bullionist controversy" on the causes of the rise in the price of the ingot (bullion), he is among the "bullionists," explaining the devaluation of the exchange rate of the pound by monetary and internal reasons—the over-issue of banknotes—against the "anti-bullionists" who invoked real and external causes (trade deficit, wars, bad harvests, etc.). He argued that the value of the pound was related positively to its quantity and negatively to the price of gold, and defended the quantitative theory of money. According to him, the Central Bank should be "national" (public) and control the supply of money. He codified the rules of a gold standard system and advocated a gold exchange standard and internal convertibility into bullion.

Thomas Tooke (1774–1858), English economist and financier, manager of transport companies. Leader of the "banking school," he maintains that money should be issued freely by the Central Bank according to the needs of agents, without strict coverage of the issue by gold reserves. His ideas were not followed by the Parliament when debating the banking system. While he distinguishes between money and credit, he argues that deposits should not be excluded from means of payment, since they perform all the functions of money. The latter ensures the circulation of income, and credit that of capital. He is an opponent of quantitative theory and a defender of an "endogenous" view of money.

Robert Torrens (1780–1864), British economist and officer (born in Northern Ireland), owner of *The Globe* newspaper. He discovered, before David Ricardo, the principle of comparative advantages, but pointed out the drawbacks of free trade. He was one of the supporters of the currency school, which asserted that the weakening of a currency, the contraction of gold reserves and the origin of crises are to be found in excessive issuance of paper money. When the exchange rate of the pound depreciates, it is necessary, in order for it to strengthen, to reduce the circulation of money and to do so by forcing banks to moderate their issuance of notes. The Bank of England ultimately rallied to this position.

Karl Marx (1818–1883), the greatest philosopher and economist, by all and by far. From a reformulated theory of labor value leading to that of exploitation, he brings out money as a result of the deployment of the internal contradictions of the commodity form. The potential occurrence for a crisis of overproduction lies (i) in the commodity-money-commodity cycle, where the internal contradiction of the commodity as use value and exchange value is constantly expressed and resolved, and where money functions as a medium of circulation; and (ii) in the division of the cycle into two metamorphoses, opening up the possibility for the seller to sell his or her merchandises without having to immediately buy other merchandises. The interest rate is determined with reference to the money capital. Marx takes a stand against the law of outlets and against the quantitative theory of money. The analysis of the latter, considered capital, depends on "the whole of economic life" (prices, wages, etc.) and "the whole social complex" into which it is inserted.

Léon Walras (1834–1910), French economist, both liberal and socialist. Ignored in France, he became the figurehead of the Lausanne school and, thanks to his theory of general equilibrium, laid the foundations for neoclassical thought, for which money is reduced to a medium of exchange and affects only prices ("neutrality"). In the Elements of Pure Political Economy (*Éléments d'Économie politique pure*, 1874), he examines money, understood in terms of its functions as an intermediary of exchanges and, to a certain extent (by arbitrage with securities) as a store of value. Money intervenes in production as capital (from the point of view of society) and as income (for individuals). And as a link between the markets for goods and services, it is conceived as a means of payment. However, it is not integrated (and therefore does not exist) in the consumer's utility function.

Georg Knapp (1842–1926), German economist, author of State Theory of Money (*Staatliche Theorie des Geldes*, 1905) and leader of the so-called "chartalist" or "statist" school. This current intends to break with "metallism," then embodied in the system of the gold standard. According to him, money is above all a legal and political institution. Not being able to arise spontaneously in a market, it only exists by law (or "charter," a word from the Greek *khártês* meaning "sheet" of papyrus, then of paper [like fiduciary money]). The State has the power to proclaim currency the object of its choice by endowing it with the status of a means of payment which is legal tender. It selects a unit of value, accepts it unconditionally, separates this new currency from any intrinsic value and imposes its validity on all agents of society.

Knut Wicksell (1851–1926), Swedish economist, link between classical and neoclassical currents, difficult to fit into a well-defined category. He makes a distinction between natural and monetary interest rates. The first rate, which corresponds to the real return on capital, and balances savings and investment in a "pure credit" economy where capital is loaned in kind; the second one is the monetary expression of the market rate as practiced by banks (without loan constraints). Equality between these rates is a condition of equilibrium—difficult to achieve because the natural rate is not known. Too much credit compared to the savings available can lead to over-investment. Inflation then arises from monetary causes (the fall in the market rate) or, more often, from real ones (the increase in the return on capital).

Georg Simmel (1858–1918), German sociologist. He studied the complex and contradictory process of monetization of modern Western societies and its consequences. According to him, money is a social mediation, referring to the cohesion of a group; to own it is to acquire a right over society as a whole. Money tends to promote inter-individual exchanges and individual freedom itself, but also, simultaneously, to subject all social relations to its logic and to forge new bonds of dependence. Money dissolves established values and communities, while stimulating a certain cynicism and excessive relativism. Simmel questions the conditions for reproducing monetary legitimacy.

Irving Fisher (1867–1947), U.S. economist. He defended the quantitative theory of money, by completing the "equation of exchanges" (where money supply × speed of circulation = general level of prices × transactions in volume) by the addition of bank deposits, and by making this accounting equilibrium a causal relationship going from the money supply to the price level. He especially insisted on price stability, necessary to strengthen the value of the currency. He was a precursor of monetarism. His unfortunate prediction before the October 1929 crisis (that the price of stocks has reached what appeared to him to be a permanent high level) has gone down in history. He advocated an extreme "circulationist" reform (known as "100% Money") consisting of granting bank credit only fully covered by deposits.

Rudolf Hilferding (1877–1941), Austrian, then German economist. A Marxist theoretician, he was professor of political economy at the School of the Social Democratic Party of Germany, before becoming Reich Minister of Finance (in 1923 and 1928–1929). His major work is *Financial Capital* (1910), which inspired Lenin, Bukharin, but also Marcuse or Baran and Sweezy. He analyzes the evolutions of capitalism of the time, marked by the monopoly power of the cartels and their circumvention of competition, but also by the role of credit money and State intervention. There he developed a monetary and financial theory of crises in the "era of imperialism." Having taken part in the resistance against Nazism, he had to go into exile in Switzerland, but died in prison in Paris, after being arrested by French police and handed over to the German Gestapo.

Ludwig von Mises (1881–1973), Austrian, then U.S. economist, ultraliberal. In his analysis of money, he prioritizes its functions (in order of decreasing importance, those of medium of exchange, store of value and unit of account), distinguishes it from its "monetary substitutes" and affirms that one cannot assign a constant value to money, because one could not quantify the levels of satisfaction. Von Mises opposed the "statist" conception of money as formulated by the "chartalists", whom he reproached for not understanding that the State is capable of promulgating the legal status of a currency and to impose it on agents *a posteriori* only, that is to say, only on condition that the market (or "trade") has previously selected it as a contractual means of payment of claims.

John Maynard Keynes (1883–1946), English economist, proposed a monetary theory of production aimed at regulating capitalism and preventing its collapse in crisis. Entrepreneurs prefer to invest if the "marginal efficiency of capital" (return on the last unit of capital) is greater than what they earn from investments in banks or stock exchanges—which precludes any "neutrality" of money. The way out of the crisis requires a monetary policy of reducing the interest rate (if it is negative, there is "the euthanasia of the rentier"), but the budgetary policy of supporting demand remains essential. Before influencing prices, changes in the quantity of money affect investment. When it comes to separating money and claims, the important thing is not the difference between money that earns nothing and remunerated assets, but rather their common basis in liquidity. His theory influenced the development of institutions and tools for modern economic policies to rationalize State action. He criticized the gold standard regime.

Joseph Schumpeter (1883–1950), Austrian economist. He provides a monetary theory adapted to his evolutionary vision of capitalism. According to him, money is not a commodity, but an institution. It insists on its fundamental role, in particular in the form of bank credit essential to finance new innovations—but leading to a risk of takeover of the companies which initiate them by the banks. For him, credit money generates instability in the economy, monetary neutrality being incompatible with the logic of capitalism and overall regulation being the responsibility of monetary institutions. In his *History of Economic Analysis* (1950), he wrote that money is nothing more than an instrument of credit, a title which gives access to the only means of definitive payment, namely consumer goods.

Robert Triffin (1911–1993), Belgian-U.S. economist, made famous at the end of the 1960s—when the imbalances of the U.S. economy worsened—by presenting a famous "dilemma," according to him inescapable. Either the United States managed to reduce both its internal and external deficits, but then the world risked suffering from a shortage of international currency and consequently from a recession; either it became debtors to the rest of the world and let other countries finance it by accumulating dollars, hence a loss of credibility of the world hegemony and conversions into gold of the assets of foreign countries denominated in dollars—which happened just before the abandonment of the gold convertibility of the dollar.

Milton Friedman (1912–2006), U.S. monetarist Chicago School economist, bitter opponent of Keynesianism. For him, the quantitative theory of money is valid, with a precise sense of causality: it is the money supply that causes the general level of prices to vary. Inflation is a monetary phenomenon due to the discretionary manipulations by the State, so that it is necessary to impose on the latter a standard for the evolution of the quantity of money and to set monetary policy the sole objective of monitoring the money supply, thus price stability, without goal—or hope of efficiency—of intervention in the real sphere (reduction in unemployment or acceleration of growth). With its demand assumed to be stable, the money must have a "neutral" supply in order to allow competing markets to reach equilibrium. Inspirer of the Chicago Boys, he was a supporter of neoliberalism and flexible exchange. And he was convinced of the failure of the euro.

Friedrich Hayek (1899–1992), Austrian, then British, economist and philosopher, ultraliberal. Between the 1930s and 1970s, his theses evolved from a theory of crises to that of a "large market society." Against quantitative theory, he argues that the problem lies in the modification of relative prices (rather than of their general level), because this change risks causing, in the event of excess credit money, a "crisis of disproportion" in the real sphere. Very delicate, the monetary policy should not fight against unemployment, at the risk of being inflationary, but should maintain a constant money supply, even if it means causing deflation. Hayek advocated removing the State monopoly on issuing money, abolishing the Central Bank and establishing competition between banks to create private currencies (free banking). Therefore, it is for him to succeed in extracting the issue of money management from the field of democratic debate.

John Hicks (1904–1989), English economist, one of the promoters of the "neoclassical synthesis" between Keynesian theory and the Walrasian theory of general equilibrium. His contributions to monetary analysis have focused on theories of fluctuations, the microeconomic foundations of prices or portfolio choices. He contributed both to "distort" the work of J.M. Keynes and to defend the latter's legacy, often even against authors who called themselves "Keynesians," but who got rid of money in their models. He endorses Keynes's definition of an asset as realizable in the short term with certainty and without loss, and stresses the relevance of his concept of "preference for liquidity."

Nicholas Kaldor (1908–1986), British economist of Hungarian origin. A radical critique of neoclassical theory as well as of the monetarist policies carried out in the United States and the United Kingdom from 1979, he improved the study of monetary questions, in particular by posing hypotheses of the instability of the demand for money (against M. Friedman) and of endogenous credit supply (against J.M. Keynes) in a context of high uncertainty in investment decisions. According to him, money creation by private banks responds to a demand for credit expressed by businesses and households. This weakens the possibilities of control of the money supply by the Central Banks which refinance these banking establishments.

Maurice Allais (1911–2010), French economist, Nobel laureate in economics, unclassifiable author whose very original thought, both liberal and social, mixing reactionary and progressive aspects. A supporter of moderate free trade limited to countries with homogeneous economic structures, he criticized globalization, financial deregulation, flexible exchange rates and speculation, seen as vectors of crises. He argued that growth is achieved without disturbances if the ratio between desired and actual cash balances remains stable, which requires curbing inflation (and indexing loan contracts), but also withdrawing from private banks (treated as "counterfeiters") the right to create (credit) money, to be placed exclusively in the hands of the State. He desecrated private property and declared himself in favor of a capital tax.

Hyman Minsky (1919–1996), U.S. economist. He studied the transformations of the capitalist system and the role of finance in these evolutions. In his book *Stabilizing an unstable economy* (1986), in opposition to the neoclassical idea of efficiency and self-regulation of financial markets, he insisted on the instability of capitalism, especially of the banking system, under the effect of competition between institutions and innovations that increase funding, and formulated reform proposals aimed at regulating banks and controlling financial markets, but also at strengthening budgetary and tax policies. One has used the expression "Minsky moment" to describe a period of panic when the asset owners decide to sell at the same time. In *Can "It" Happen Again?* (1982), he asserted the inevitability of a serious financial crisis.

Robert Mundell (1932–2021), Canadian economist. Critic of the hegemony of the U.S. dollar, he was a strong supporter of the creation of the euro. He developed, in collaboration with the British economist Marcus Fleming, the "optimal currency area" theory, but also a famous "triangle of incompatibility." This principle says that in an open economy, it would be impossible to simultaneously achieve the objectives of (1) fixed exchange rates, (2) free movement of capital and (3) autonomous national monetary policy. In the case of flexible exchange, then objectives (2) and (3) are achievable; in a monetary union, then objectives (1) and (2) are so; and in the event that capital movements are controlled, then objectives (1) and (3) become so.

Robert Lucas (1937–...), U.S. economist from the Chicago school. He is one of the leaders of the New Classical Economy. He helped to radicalize the Friedmanian positions which left short-term efficiency in monetary policy, while agents managed to adjust their expectations of the rate of inflation (one speaks of "adaptive expectations"). Lucas argues that even in the short term, monetary policy proves incapable of tackling unemployment. For his demonstration, he resorts to "rational expectations" hypotheses (the agents having the ability to predict the effects of public policies carried out by the State without the slightest error regarding the evolution of the structure of the economy) and to immediate market adjustment through flexible prices. Money would be "super neutral" and has no influence on the real equilibrium.

Box A.2 Robert Barro, from dollarization to democracy

Robert Barro (1944–...) is one of the best-known current U.S. mainstream economists (and one of the most neoliberal) who understood that to dispossess a country of its monetary sovereignty is to submit it.

- "After September 2001, the economic situation in Argentina deteriorated sharply. (...) My first suggestion would be a full dollarization of the economy, including the use of U.S. dollars as the currency (...), liberalization of markets, (...) the freeing up of labor markets, with a related reduction in the power of labor unions, (...) restraint on public expenditures." (*Nothing is sacred!*, 2003, chap. 1).
- "I suggested that South Korea consider relinquishing its own currency by adopting the U.S. dollar, that is, by dollarizing. (...) My proposal for dollarization in South Korea, combined with my endorsement of foreign buyouts of banks, led to the Yankee imperialism charge." (*Idem*, 2003, chap. 3).
- "Another question is which money to install in the new Iraq (s). The U.S. dollar is a reasonable choice." (*Business Week*, March 31, 2003). "Amid the continuing violence, people sometimes lose sight of the nobility of the US-led effort to reform Iraq." (*Business Week*, April 5, 2004).

- "Throughout this discussion, I question the romantic focus of U.S. foreign policy on promoting democracy in all times and places. My cross-country research has convinced me that the rule of law and property rights are more important than democracy in the promotion of economic growth." (*Nothing is sacred!*, 2003, Introduction).
- "Unfortunately, however, Colombia may now have too much democracy." (*Idem*, chap. 2).
- "Undoubtedly, Chile's outstanding economic performance derived from the free-market reforms instituted by the administration of General Augusto Pinochet from 1973 to 1989. (…) I think that the extent and durability of the leftist animosity toward him reflects the very real economic success; no one has done more than Pinochet and his economic teams to demonstrate the superiority of free-market capitalism over socialism." (*Idem*, chap. 3).

Glossary

Acknowledgment of debt: A document by which a debtor agrees to pay a sum of money to a creditor.
Anticipation: Assumptions made by an economic agent about the future as a basis for his or her decisions.
Appreciation: Increase in the value of a currency relative to other currencies under a flexible exchange rate regime.
Arbitrage: A generally low-risk strategy of buying and selling aimed at taking advantage of price differences for the same or similar products in different markets.
Asset
–***Financial asset***: An investment instrument, security or contract, often transferable and negotiable on a market, that can generate income or capital gains for its holder in return for taking a risk.
–***Toxic asset***: A financial asset that has become illiquid and whose value is falling, causing the accounts of the financial institutions that hold it in portfolios to depreciate, or leading to bankruptcy.
Balance

R. Herrera, *Money*, Global University for Sustainability Book Series,
https://doi.org/10.1007/978-981-19-2848-2

–***Trade balance***: The difference, expressed in monetary values, between export earnings and import expenditures on goods in a given economy over a specified period.
–***Current account balance***: The component of the balance of payments of a country's trade with foreign countries, corresponding to the sum of the trade balance, on the one hand, and, on the other hand, the balance of invisibles, which combines the balance of services (exports and imports of services), that of current transfers (aid, donations, etc.) and that of income (dividends, interest, etc.).
–***Balance of payments***: A statistical document drawn up in accounting form that traces financial and non-financial transactions (flow of goods, services, income, capital transfers, etc.) between a country and the rest of the world.
Bank
–***Central bank***: An institution mandated by a government (or governments) to decide on the implementation of monetary policy, with the primary functions of (i) issuing fiduciary money and helping to set interest rates, (ii) supervising the operation of financial markets by enforcing risk regulations on financial institutions and (iii) acting as lender of last resort.
–***Commercial bank***: A banking institution that borrows money issued by the Central Bank, distributes credit to economic agents (bank overdrafts, personal loans, real estate loans, mortgages, etc.) and maintains direct links with its customers.
–***Second-tier bank***: see "Commercial bank."
Bank run: Phenomenon by which a large number of customers of a bank fearing that it will become insolvent ask in a hurry to withdraw their deposits.
Barter: Direct exchange between agents of a certain quantity of one good for a different quantity of another, without the use of money.
Basket (of currencies): A grouping of different currencies into one unit to serve as a common reference value.
Bill
–***Promissory bill***: A document by which the subscriber or drawer acknowledges that he or she is indebted to the beneficiary to whom he or she promises to pay a certain sum of money at a specified time.

–***Treasury bill***: A negotiable bearer note issued by a (non-financial) company with a view to raising short-term capital.

Bill of exchange (or draft): Document by which the original creditor (the drawer) gives a debtor (the drawee) the order to pay a certain sum of money to a beneficiary (the bearer or holder) at the fixed date.

Bimetallism: A monetary system in which the minting of gold and silver is free, a fixed par or conversion ratio between the two metals is determined, and the liberating power of these metals is unlimited.

Bitcoin: Crypto-asset—often considered a crypto-currency—, the oldest, most widely traded and best known.

Blockchain: A distributed database in which the information transmitted by users is verified and stored regularly in blocks forming a chain, all of which is cryptographically secured and protected against falsification.

Borrowing (or loan): Long-term financial debt, resulting from the granting of a loan repayable at maturity and participating, alongside shareholders' equity or own capital, in the coverage of a firm's long-term financing needs.

Bubble (speculative): A situation in which a large number of agents buy an asset (financial or otherwise) because they anticipate that its price will rise for the reason that it has already risen.

Bullionism: Economic doctrine that emerged in 16th Century Spain (schools of Salamanca, Toledo and Valladolid, among others), according to which the State must limit the outflow of precious metals (gold and silver) from the country, whose wealth is measured by them. The precursor of mercantilism.

Capital

–***Capital (in general)***: Amount of investments used to make a profit. Considered as a social relationship by Marx.

–***Fictitious capital***: Concept used by Marx whose principle is the capitalization of an income derived from future surplus value.

Capital account: A balance of payments account that tracks certain financial flows (foreign direct investment, portfolio investment, bank borrowing) related to the acquisition of assets in one country by residents of another country. Capital flows that can be controlled (subject to restrictions when passing through official channels) or, on the contrary, liberalized (by relaxing these restrictions when crossing borders, resulting in a higher degree of financial integration within global economy).

Carry trade: Speculative financial operation, mainly used in the foreign exchange market, consisting in profiting from the yield differentials or spreads between various types of assets.

CDO (collateralized debt obligation): A credit derivative that adopts a complex structure for securitizing assets of various kinds (bank claims or receivables, financial instruments, etc.).

CDS (credit default swap): A derivative on credit default, i.e., a contract that allows the holder of a debt to be indemnified and compensated by the seller in the event that the issuer of a bond defaults.

Certificate of deposit: A negotiable certificate issued by a credit institution to obtain short-term capital.

Check: A non-cash payment method used to transfer money from one bank account to another. A type of bill or commercial paper that is payable on demand—the bearer being able to cash it immediately.

Clearing house: An institution that facilitates the exchange (clearing) of payments, securities or derivatives between investors who do not meet and want to reduce risk.

Club

–***London Club***: An informal group of private creditors (commercial banks, investment funds, etc.) that deals with rescheduling government debt.

–***Paris Club***: An informal forum of official creditors responsible for restructuring the government or government-guaranteed private sector debts of over-indebted developing countries.

Commercial paper: A negotiable instrument that evidences a claim to a sum of money for the benefit of the bearer, and serves as payment according to a process required for its validity and effectiveness (bill of exchange, promissory bill, etc.).

Commodity (or merchandise): Good or service likely to be exchanged on a market.

Convertibility: The property of a currency to be freely exchangeable at any time for gold or a foreign currency, which implies that the authorities are able to satisfy any request for conversion addressed to them. An essential element contributing to establishing the confidence of agents in a currency.

Corner (of market): An operation—considered as criminal—organized by one (or, jointly, by several) agent(s) aiming at manipulating the market in order to make a profit by "cornering" the other actors, that is to say, by pushing short sellers to liquidate their positions under conditions unfavorable to them.

Cost of living: An estimate of the average cost of household consumption expenditures in a given country.

Credit: Medium- and short-term financial debt, making available a sum of money in the form of a loan, granted by a creditor to a debtor.

Credit crunch: A situation in which credit dries up when second-tier banks lose confidence and no longer lend to each other or, consequently, to other economic agents.

Creditor: A person to whom the debtor owes money (or the provision of a service).

Crisis

–***(in general)***: A sudden deterioration in the economic situation and outlook that disrupts activity (most often manifested by a drop in wages, an increase in unemployment, business bankruptcies, a fall in stock market values, strong socio-political tensions, etc.).

–***subprime mortgage crisis***: Financial crisis that affected the subprime mortgage loan (with variable rates) sector in the United States from 2006 to 2007, the trigger for which was the Fed's key interest rate hike in 2005, and one of the results was the very serious banking and financial crisis of Autumn 2008.

–***systemic crisis***: a crisis that affects the entire economic system and has no internal solution within the logic of its operation.

Crypto

–***Crypto-asset***: A virtual asset stored on an electronic medium that allows a community of users who accept it as payment to perform various transactions without having to resort to a standard legal tender.

–***Crypto-currency***: Digital currency issued peer-to-peer without the need for a Central Bank, usable through a decentralized computer network and using cryptographic technologies, while involving users in the processes of issuing, certifying and settling the transactions carried out.

Currency

–***Common currency***: A currency which, in a given monetary integration zone, is added to the various existing national currencies, and is shared in common by the member countries.

–***Complementary currency***: An additional monetary unit authorized to circulate in a defined area (local group, community, etc.) in addition to the official national currency.

–***Melting currency***: A currency that loses value over time, encouraging users to use it quickly.

–***Local currency***: A currency intended to be exchanged only in a specific geographical area, and not backed by a State.

–***Safe haven currency***: A currency whose stability or appreciation agents anticipate and into which they choose to convert monetary or financial assets to protect them from exchange rate risk.

–***Single currency***: a currency that, in a given monetary integration area, replaces national currencies—which in fact cease to exist—, leading to the abandonment of the monetary sovereignty of the member States and the establishment of a supranational body responsible for managing this new currency.

Currency board: A system for managing the issuance of currency using an exchange stabilization office when a government wants to have a local currency, but with a value based on that of a foreign currency that solely serves for international settlements.

Debt

–***(in general)***: The right of a creditor to demand payment of a debt owed by the debtor on the said due date. A duty of one person (the debtor) towards another (the creditor). Reverse of the claim or receivable. Generally used to finance an investment designed to increase production or intended to improve it.

–***Domestic (or internal) debt***: All the claims held by a country's resident economic agents on that country.

–***External debt***: The portion of a country's total debt (government, corporate and personal debts) that is borrowed from and owed to

foreign creditors (commercial banks, other States and international financial institutions).
–***Multilateral debt***: Debt due to international financial institutions (IMF, World Bank, etc.)
–***Net external debt***: The difference between what a country borrows from abroad and what it lends to the rest of the world.
–***Odious debt***: Debt contracted by the local ruling classes of a country to be used against the general interest, notably for lavish spending, corruption or repression.
–***Private debt***: All loans contracted by private agents (companies, households, etc.).
–***Public debt***: All borrowing by public agents (government, local authorities, public administrations, etc.).
–***Sovereign debt***: Debt issued or guaranteed by a sovereign issuer (State or Central Bank) exclusively.
Debt equity swap: A debt that is convertible into equity or capital, allowing its holder to exchange it for a predetermined amount of shares in a company.
Debtor: A person who is obligated to another or liable to another to perform an obligation, such as paying money.
Decompartmentalization: Removal of the separation between the activities of banking institutions or of the different compartments of the financial markets.
Default (of payment): The failure of an individual, a company or a country to meet all or part of its commitments towards a creditor. In the case of a firm, it can result in bankruptcy.
Deflation: A lasting, self-sustaining decline in the general price level over an extended period of time. The opposite of inflation.
Demand: Quantity of a good or service that economic agents are willing to buy on a market at a given price (or have the capacity to buy on this same market, if demand is solvent).
Dematerialization (of money): Computerization of data related to money by replacing the physical and paper elements, which have become digitalized.

Demonetization: An operation decided by the monetary authorities consisting in removing the face value of a banknote or a coin, which can thus no longer be used for their usual purpose.
Depreciation: A decrease in the exchange rate resulting from spontaneous movements in the price of a currency on the foreign exchange market.
Depression: A significant and lasting decrease in production and consumption in an economy.
Deregulation: The process of relaxing or removing national regulations and rules governing and restricting the movements of capital.
Derivative: A financial instrument that consists of a contract between two parties fixing future financial flows based on changes in the price or rate of an underlying asset and whose settlement is made on a future date.
Devaluation: Loss of nominal value of a current currency against foreign currencies as a result of an official decision by the Central Bank of the country concerned.
Differential: The difference, expressed as a percentage, between two variables of the same nature.
Discount
–***Bank discount***: Operation of transfer to a bank of a commercial paper held by a creditor on one of its customers in exchange for a cash advance.
–***Commercial discount***: Operation by which a customer pays his supplier's invoice in cash without waiting for the due date, by deducting a certain percentage.
–***Financial (or settlement) discount***: A price reduction granted for cash payment.
Discounting: Lowering of the market value or downgrading of a debt.
Disinflation: Reduction in the rate of inflation or slowing of price increases.
Disintermediation: Relative decrease in the weight of banking intermediation in the financing of the economy.
Dollarization: The use of foreign currencies (most often than not of the U.S. dollars) as units of account, means of exchange and stores of value by a national economy.

Effect

–***Leverage effect***: A technique designed to multiply profits (or losses, if the operation turns out badly), in general by using indebtedness in order to increase the investment capacity of a company, financial institution or individual, as well as to increase the impact generated on the profitability of the capital invested.

–***"Tequila" effect***: Capital flight due to fear of currency depreciation (like in the case of the Mexican crisis of 1994).

Euro

–***Euro-currency***: A currency held in an account of a bank located outside the country of issue of said currency.

–***Eurodollar***: A type of euro-currency in U.S. dollars owned by non-U.S. citizens or deposited in non-U.S. banks located outside the territory of the United States.

Exchange rate

–***(general or bilateral exchange rate)***: The proportional relationship between the value of a currency and a given other currency. An indicator that expresses how many units of the former are required to obtain one unit of the latter.

–***Multilateral exchange rate***: The average value of a currency in its exchange relationship with other currencies, or with the currencies of a given anchor basket.

Exchange rate regime

–***Fixed exchange rate regime***: A regime in which the exchange rate is set by the monetary authorities, with the equilibrium of the foreign exchange market being ensured by the interventions of the Central Bank.

–***Flexible or floating exchange rate regime***: A system in which the exchange rate depends on the determination of the exchange rate of the currency in relation to foreign currencies by matching supply and demand on the foreign exchange market.

–***Intermediate exchange rate regime***: Mixed system between fixed and flexible exchange rates characterized by occasional interventions by the Central Bank to stabilize the exchange rate.

–***Linked exchange rate regime***: A system that fixes an exchange rate against one or more currencies, with relatively narrow fluctuation margins.

Fed: The Federal Reserve System of the United States, composed largely of the most powerful private financial oligopolies and serving as the Central Bank of that country.

Finance: The set of the most powerful financial oligopolies that dominate the world's markets and own in portfolios most of the transnational corporations in business.

Financial crime: A set of illegal financial activities that evade national laws thanks to banking secrecy, tax exemption and tax havens. Related to the crimes of misuse of corporate assets, money laundering, corruption, embezzlement, tax fraud and evasion, influence peddling, etc.

Financial institutions: Fundamental actors in the monetary and financial economy, including Treasuries, Central Banks, commercial banks, asset management funds, insurance companies, etc.

Financial oligopoly: Entity gathering together a set of banking and financial institutions that have exorbitant market power in an oligopolistic situation, i.e., where there is a very limited number of suppliers faced with a very large number of customers.

Financial security

–***(in general)***: An asset representing a share of a company's capital (share) or a fraction of its debt (bond, negotiable debt security)—or issued by the government (bond)—that pays a variable and random return (dividends, in the first case) or a fixed and certain return (interest, in the second).

–***Negotiable debt security***: A security in the form of a promissory bill representing a debt right.

Foreign currency:

–***(in general)***: Currency of a foreign country, considered from the point of view of any national currency.

–***International or key foreign currency***: A currency that acts as an international reserve currency.

Foreign exchange controls: A set of measures taken by a government to regulate the buying and selling of foreign currencies by its nationals, and designed to combat capital flight and speculation.

Forex: See "Foreign exchange market."
Forward: A derivative product in the form of an over-the-counter contract negotiated between banks in which there is an agreement to buy or sell an asset at a specified price and date in the future without monetary exchange at signing.
Fund
–***Indexed fund***: Savings management institution whose objective is to replicate a stock market index by making investments less risky than those of traditional investment funds. This sector has been expanding since the 2008 financial crisis and is currently dominated by three U.S. transnationals (BlackRock, Vanguard, and State Street).
–***Investment fund***: Institution specializing in asset management that select financial securities (especially company shares) individually, in order to group them into portfolios.
–***Pension fund***: Investment fund specifically for funded retirement.
–***Sovereign fund***: A financial investment fund managing public savings and owned by a State.
–***Speculative investment fund***: see "Hedge fund."
–***Vulture fund***: Speculative investment fund that buys at low prices debts issued by debtors in difficulty or close to defaulting in order to realize a capital gain when restructuring the debt, or refusing to renegotiate to obtain by legal action the repayment of their claims as close as possible to the nominal value (possibly with interest and late arrears).
Futures contract: A transaction negotiated between two parties on a futures market in the form of a firm commitment to deliver an underlying asset at a predefined maturity and under conditions defined in advance. Used to speculate or hedge against market, interest rate or exchange rate risks.
Global currency: Function of a currency insofar as it is brought to fulfill the functions of money in international relations and within the different countries concerned (measure of value, general instrument of purchases, reserve of value, means of payment), as well as to be the universal materialization of social wealth, allowing financial transfers between these countries (credits, capital exports, aid, etc.).

Gold: Precious metal whose fundamental characteristics of use value have enabled it to assume the various functions of money, and especially those of: (i) a measure of value, fixing the prices of commodities in trade; (ii) an instrument of circulation, representable by various signs; and (iii) a hoarding material, allowing a high value to be concentrated in a limited volume.

Hedge fund: A fund that trades in relatively liquid assets and uses complex portfolio building and risk management techniques to maximize performance (short selling, leverage effect, derivatives, etc.).

High-frequency trading: A financial transaction executed at very high speed by automatic orders given through complex computer algorithms, without human intervention.

Hive-down or defeasance: A de facto deleveraging or debt relief operation, consisting of the simultaneous sale of financial assets and debts to a third party company called a "hive-off vehicle" or "defeasance structure," a specialized legal entity whose role is to isolate the bank or company concerned.

Hoarding: The act of accumulating money to keep it, without spending it on consumption, investing it or circulating it in the economy.

Hot money (or floating capital): A considerable amount of speculative capital that their owners move from one financial center to another according to price and rate fluctuations or expectations.

Hyperinflation: An atypical and relatively rare form of inflation, characterized by an extremely high, even exponential, increase in the general price level that is getting out of control. Tends to rapidly erode the real value of a country's currency and to make economic agents flee from the latter, in which they no longer have confidence, preferring to substitute it with stable currencies or values (gold, real estate).

Inflation: A general and persistent increase in the level of prices, leading to a certain loss of purchasing power of money.

Institutional investors: Organizations that collect savings and whose operations are regulated.

Interest rate: The rate of return on a loaned or borrowed capital (expressed as a percentage of the total amount) paid by the borrower to the lender according to contractually defined terms and conditions, depending on the duration of the loan, the nature of the risks and the guarantees offered. An important transmission channel for monetary policy.

Intermediation (banking): All the marketing commercialization operations of the products and services of a banking system, in particular those of credit.

International Monetary System: A set of institutions, rules, mechanisms and practices that allow and govern monetary transactions between economic agents residing in countries with different currencies.

Junk bonds: Highly speculative bonds known as "rotten."

Lender of last resort: Fundamental role of a Central Bank ensuring the refinancing of the various second-tier banks.

Liberatory (or release) power: A characteristic of money that allows its users to be immediately released from their payment obligations or debts by monetary transfer or simple remittance of money.

Liquidity: The quality of assets (tangible or non-tangible assets owned by agents) of being able to be converted into effective money instantly and without loss of value. Sums of money available.

Loan: The legal act of transferring, without requiring payment, possession and use, of an asset while retaining ownership.

Market

–***Bond market***: Market in which companies and governments finance themselves through bonds (from two to 30 years).

–***Capital market***: Place (e.g., financial, money or bond market) where economic agents with a surplus of capital and those with a need for financing can meet.

–***Cash market***: A market in which the delivery of traded goods and their payment occur simultaneously.

–***Financial market***: A place where a large number of interested buyers and sellers (individuals, firms or public institutions) trade securities (mostly long-term) at prices that reflect supply and demand.

–***Foreign exchange market (or Forex)***: Market where offers and demands for different currencies meet.

–***Futures market***: An organized market located at a specific place where the commitment made by the originator (to buy or sell) will be fulfilled at a pre-agreed time after this commitment has been made.
–***Interbank market***: Immaterial network (without a trading room) in which the Central Bank, the Treasury and the banks intervene and which is favored by the latter to refinance themselves by granting each other very short-term credit—the banking institutions can lend their excess liquidity to those which need it to balance their cash flow, in return for interest that fluctuates according to supply and demand.
–***Money market***: A market in which negotiable debt instruments with relatively short maturities are traded.
–***Mortgage market***: A market in which a bank resells mortgage loans granted to individuals for the purpose of purchasing their homes with a mortgage.
–***Over-the-counter (OTC) or off-exchange market***: Unorganized market where buyer and seller conclude the transaction by direct agreement to transmit a good by the free will of the parties, without intermediary or supervision.
–***Primary market***: Market for the issuance of financial assets (initial public offering, capital increase, etc.).
–***Secondary market***: Market for the purchase and sale of already existing financial assets traded on a "second-hand" basis.

Market capitalization: Valuation at market price of all the outstanding shares of a company.

Means of circulation: Function of money that can be composed of a selling phase and a buying phase, in a process where money plays the role of intermediary.

Means of payment: Function of money consisting in the separation of the circulation of the merchandise from the circulation of money—the product being able to be "consumed" without having been paid yet. Usually a technical instrument that allows the use of money held in cash or in a deposit account to pay expenses or settle debts.

Measure of value: The primary function of money that makes it exist as a general equivalent to express the value of all other goods.

Mercantilism: Economic doctrine, widespread between the Sixteenth and Eighteenth Centuries, especially in Spain, France and England, according to which the possession of precious metals, mainly the accumulation of gold and silver, constitutes the main basis for the prosperity of countries.

Microcredit (or microfinance): Allocation of small loans to people wishing to undertake micro-projects and who do not have access to traditional bank credit.

Monetarism: Economic doctrine that favors neoliberalism, believing that monetary policy is relatively less ineffective than budgetary policy, but generally considering that the withdrawal of the State is indispensable, because its action proves systematically harmful to the functioning of the economy.

Monetary union: A grouping of countries that agree to adopt a common monetary policy.

Money

–***Central Bank money***: Money issued by the Central Bank by crediting the accounts of second-tier banks in its books in the form of monetary assets representing loans granted to these commercial banks, or by selling them banknotes and coins.

–***Digital money***: see "Crypto-currency."

–***Divisional money***: Metal coins.

–***Electronic money***: Monetary value stored in electronic form representing a claim on the issuer, issued against remittance of funds for payment transactions and accepted by a natural or legal person other than the issuer.

–***Fiat money***: A fiduciary currency with no assets, which is self-authoritative or relies on the credibility of the issuing institution (e.g., modern money created by the Central Bank). Not convertible into gold or silver or any other means of reserve of value with monetary authorities.

–***Fiduciary money***: Values based on the trust placed by users in the institution that issues them and based on a guarantee principle upheld by this institution. Typically, contemporary coins and banknotes (or paper money), whose nominal value is higher than their intrinsic value.

–***Fiscal money***: A debt management technique consisting of paying public expenditures and taxes in bonds.

–***Helicopter money***: A type of monetary policy in which a Central Bank distributes money that it has created directly to economic agents on an *ad hoc* punctual basis.
–***Scriptural money (or cashless currency)***: Money in figures existing in the form of an entry in a bank account, held by its holder and circulating between economic agents through bank transfers by means of payment.
–***Secondary money (or second-tier bank money)***: Money issued when a commercial bank grants credit to a customer in exchange for a document acknowledging debt (IOU). A type of private money with the same nominal value as Central Bank money, but not directly guaranteed by the Central Bank.
–***Virtual money***: An electronically stored unit of account created by a person or entity for the purpose of recording exchanges. A numerical representation of value that is neither issued or regulated by a monetary authority nor necessarily linked to an official currency, but is accepted by agents as a means of payment and can be electronically stored, traded or transferred.
Monometallism: A monetary system in which a single metal is freely minted and has unlimited liberatory power.
Moratorium: Decision to grant a delay or a voluntary (and possibly indefinite) suspension of a payment or of the due date of debts.
Nationalization: The taking of control of a private enterprise by the State. Transfer from private property to collective property (the "nation"), but accomplished within the strict limits of the capitalist system.
Neutrality (of money): Postulated dichotomy between monetary and real phenomena, arising from a supposed separation between the monetary and real spheres of the economy (typical of neoclassical economists) and considering that money does not affect production or economic activity, but only prices.
Open market operation: Monetary policy measure by which the Central Bank intervenes in the interbank market in order to make it easier for second-tier banks to obtain liquidity (by buying or selling securities on an outright basis, firmly, to vary interest rates and, consequently, loans).

Optimal currency area: A monetary union between several countries that meet certain criteria of optimality, in particular the homogeneity of the structures of the economies that make up the zone, the synchronization of economic cycles between countries, and the existence of adjustment mechanisms within the union (such as budget transfers and tax harmonization).

Option: A derivative financial product used for a given period or on a fixed date to protect oneself or to speculate, taking the form of a contract between, on the one hand, a buyer, who obtains the right to buy (call) or sell (put) an underlying asset (stock, bond, commodity, currency, futures contract, etc.) at a predetermined price and, on the other hand, a seller, who undertakes to respect the terms of the contract.

Orderly resolution: Regulatory provisions organizing the liquidation of a failing financial institution, protecting savers and taxpayers and preventing the risk of contagion to other credit institutions and companies—with the State intervening as a last resort.

Patrimony: All the wealth owned by an individual or a country.

Petrodollars: U.S. dollars obtained from the sale of oil from oil-exporting countries, transformed into international financial investments.

Policy:

–***Exchange rate policy***: External component of monetary policy. One of the levers possibly used by public authorities to achieve certain objectives (such as price stability, trade balance, growth or full employment).

–***Monetary policy***: All the decisions and means implemented by a State or a monetary authority to act on economic activity by regulating its currency (determination of the money supply, setting of the interest rate, interventions by the Central Bank to exchange and convert its currency, etc.).

Ponzi scheme: Named after Carlo Ponzi, a swindler who set up a fraudulent financial pyramid (in 1920 in the United States) in which investors attracted by high returns were only served by the flow of savings from new subscriptions. A scheme that recently inspired

Bernard Madoff. Works as long as profits paid out exceed the last contributions—and collapses beyond that.

Potlatch: A name of Native American origin for a ceremony in which clans compete to give lavishly, especially in the form of gifts to rivals, who in turn are forced to give more.

Price: The value of a commodity measured in money, or the market value of the compensation that one agent is willing to pay another in return for the transfer of a good or service.

Purchase: The exchange of a certain amount of money for a commodity.

Purchasing power: The amount of goods and services that an individual can buy, or that the same amount of money can buy on two different dates.

Purchasing power parity (PPP values): A method used to compare the purchasing power of national currencies between countries, as distinct from a direct calculation using exchange rates.

Quantitative Easing: An unconventional monetary policy measure in which a Central Bank buys back large amounts of public (government bonds) or private (corporate bonds) debt or other financial securities (asset-backed securities, such as mortgages) in order to inject large amounts of liquidity into the economy and thereby stimulate growth.

Quantitative theory of money: Theory according to which it is the increase in the quantity of money, i.e., an increase in the money supply (of the government's money supply, via the printing press) greater than that of production, that raises the price level and, consequently, the values of commodities.

Rating agency (financial): Institution specialized in assessing the risks of insolvency and non-repayment of the debts of a private company or a public administration.

Recapitalization: Injection of funds to increase or reconstitute the capital (of a bank, a company, etc.).

Recession: A slowdown in the pace of economic growth (i.e., GDP growth). The opposite of expansion.

Reserve of value: The function of storing or holding value in order to transfer purchasing power from the present to the future.

Reserves

–***Foreign exchange reserves***: Assets in foreign currencies and gold held and accumulated by the Central Bank, which can be mobilized for its interventions on the foreign exchange market. Reserves fed through several main channels: exports of goods and services, international aid, foreign direct investments, dividends received on investments abroad, remittances from national workers residing abroad, etc.
–***Compulsory reserves***: Monetary policy tool acting on the proportions of secondary money creation that are compulsorily deposited by banks (and therefore frozen) in the accounts of the Central Bank.
Revaluation: The raising of the value of the national currency against foreign currencies by the government. The opposite of devaluation.
Risk
–***(in general)***: The expectation that a future event will occur that could worsen the current situation of an agent, a sector or the economy.
–***Country risk***: Risk of a loss materializing, resulting from the political and economic context of a country in which investors carry out part of their activities.
Sale: The exchange of a commodity for a certain sum of money.
SDR (Special Drawing Right): An international reserve asset created by the IMF to supplement the official foreign exchange reserves of member countries and whose value is based on a basket made up of currencies (currently the U.S. dollar, the euro, the yen, the pound sterling and the renminbi-yuan).
Securitization: A technique consisting of transferring a portfolio of assets to a special purpose vehicle (company or fund), such as debts, in order to transform them into financial securities issued on the capital market and guaranteeing profits for investors.
Seigniorage (right of): A duty that continues to be levied by the State today in the form of interest borne by holders of coins or banknotes, corresponding to an interest rate that it charges and applies to the face value of these coins and banknotes held or hoarded by agents (households or companies). Close to the difference between the production cost of coins and banknotes and their face value.
Shadow banking: Financial activities carried out mainly on behalf of large banks by companies created by them and receiving no

deposits—which makes them escape national or international banking regulations and rules.

Short selling: Forward sale of an asset (currency, financial security, raw materials, etc.) that is not yet owned at the time of trading, but will or should be owned upon delivery.

Silver: A precious, white, malleable metal.

Socialization: Collectivization of a property that transgresses the framework of the capitalist system and is carried out for the benefit of workers actively organized to exercise effective control over the entity concerned and, in the longer term, to build a new society truly placed at the service of the general interest.

Solvency: Capacity of a natural or legal person to pay its debts and to meet its commitments. Creditworthiness.

Speculation: The act of freely assuming a risk (e.g., currency risk). Taking a position without hedging. Bets which are practiced, without compensation, on upward or downward variations in market prices with the sole aim of making a profit. Search for capital gains attached to an asset.

Standard:

–***(in general or monetary)***: A value used as a reference in the monetary system of a country,

–***Gold standard***: International monetary system in which the standard is gold and each currency is convertible and defined in relation to a fixed weight of gold.

–***Gold exchange standard***: Organization of the international exchange system which limits the conversion of currencies into gold—the parity of some currencies being fixed on gold, that of others on the former.

Statization (or State ownership): The transfer of ownership and management of an enterprise or activity to the State.

Stock exchange: Permanent, organized and regulated market, generally supervised by a regulator, allowing the continuous formation of prices by confronting the supply and demand of standardized assets, and facilitating exchanges for buyers and sellers, particularly in terms of liquidity and transparency.

Stock market crash: Sudden collapse of stock prices on a stock market.
Stock market index: Synthetic value of a given portfolio representative of the evolution of stock market prices.
Stock option: Remuneration paid by a company to certain of its employees in the form of options to purchase its own shares.
Supply: Quantity of a good or service that can be sold or disposed of by economic agents on a market at a given price.
Swap: A financial derivative that takes the form of a contract to exchange financial flows between two parties (usually banking or financial institutions) over a given, predefined period.
Swap line: Mechanism by which Central Banks immediately exchange credit lines denominated in their respective currencies with each other. Used since September 2001, then, widely, since 2008.
SWIFT: Acronym for Society for Worldwide Interbank Financial Telecommunication. A system for interbank messaging and payments currently used by most of the world's banking institutions.
Tax haven: A territorial jurisdiction that has deliberately adopted an advantageous tax regime that allows non-resident individuals or legal entities to reduce to a strict minimum (to "optimize") the amount of taxes they would have to pay in the place where they conduct their main economic activity, thanks to the granting of various privileges (effective tax rate that can be zero, opacity of legal entities, anonymity of asset holders, hindrance of the automatic exchange of information between governments, etc.).
Tender
–***Forced tender (or exchange)***: Monetary regime where banks (Central Banks or second-tier banks) are not required to exchange paper money for precious metal if it is presented to them. Situation linked to the inconvertibility (without being strictly equivalent to it).
–***Legal tender***: Obligation for the creditor to accept paper money for any settlement or payment, in the same way as metal coins. Refers only to the circulation of money, not to its value or its fixing.
Terms of trade: The ratio of export prices to import prices in an economy.

Token: An exchangeable instrument used to conduct crypto-currency transactions between users of a blockchain.
Trader: A market operator who trades financial products in a trading room or front office.
Treasury bill: Debt security (bond, fairly short term, repayable and redeemable at maturity, and generating interest before that date) on the Treasury through which the government that issued it can finance its possible deficits.
Unit of account: A standardized unit for measuring the value of trade and stocks of assets or goods and services.
Usury: Interest on a loan at an abusive, excessively high rate.
Value
–***(in general)***: Quality of a thing based on its objective usefulness or subjective interest (use value) and on the relationship between supply and demand (exchange value, itself the basis of the quantitative exchange relationship between goods).
–***Security value***: A type of financial asset that can be either ownership (stock) or debt (bond) and that confers certain specific rights.
–***Shareholder value***: Value that accrues to shareholders. The share of the profit that is distributed to them in the form of dividends. The difference between the purchase and sale prices of a share plus dividends received.

Index

Note: Independent States are shown in roman; regions or dependent territories of countries are in italics. Countries or territories that no longer exist are given in square brackets.

A

Afghanistan 210, 218
Algeria 4, 50, 105, 106
American Samoa 130
Andalusia 137
Andorra 74
Angola 39, 98, 102, 105, 122
Anguilla 147
Antarctica 125
Antigua and Barbuda 147
Argentina 39, 45, 123, 146, 147, 151, 153, 231, 265, 277, 280, 282, 286, 288, 293, 307
Armenia 19, 47, 232
Aruba 147
Australia 6, 21, 37, 88, 100, 106, 123, 125, 129–132, 134–136, 142, 226, 234, 261, 262, 275, 290
Austria 79, 83, 263, 269, 272, 289, 303–305
Azerbaijan 47, 106, 187

B

Bahamas 276
Bahrain 55, 188, 276
Bangladesh 190
Barbados 147
Basque Country 214
Belarus 53, 58, 226, 232, 282
Belize 7
Benin 98, 107, 109, 117, 274
Bermuda 147

R. Herrera, *Money*, Global University for Sustainability Book Series, https://doi.org/10.1007/978-981-19-2848-2

Bolivia 45, 146, 158, 159, 231, 288, 289
Bonaire 146
Bosnia-Herzegovina 74
Bougainville 137
Brazil 37, 45, 47, 55, 123, 146, 148, 153, 156, 157, 205, 231, 254, 256, 259, 270, 274, 280, 283–286, 288, 289
Britain 21, 22, 31, 81, 130, 132, 232, 261, 278
Brunei 56, 177
Bulgaria 57, 90
Burkina Faso 98, 102, 107, 109, 117, 274
Burundi 111

C

Cambodia 182, 187, 273
Cameroon 107, 109, 121, 274
Canada 36, 88, 106, 147, 256, 265
Cayman 147
Central African Republic 107, 109
Chad 98, 107, 109, 267
Chile 6, 45, 148, 308
China 7, 8, 11, 12, 18, 39, 48, 56, 58, 83, 103, 122, 130, 142, 170, 175, 177, 186, 187, 191, 193–200, 205, 224, 226–230, 232–235, 247–251, 253–255, 261, 262, 264, 266–268, 270–273, 279, 283, 287, 290–293
Colombia 6, 45, 54, 146, 149, 150, 158, 190, 308
Comoros 107, 112, 278, 284
Congo (Democratic Republic of, formerly Zaire) 99, 100, 109, 111
Congo (Republic of) 107, 122
Cook Islands 131
Côte d'Ivoire 107, 109, 117, 121, 274
Croatia 78, 89, 282
Cuba 18, 39, 40, 52, 145, 146, 164, 166–168, 170, 231, 266, 273, 283, 287, 289, 293
Curaçao 147
Cyprus 79, 88, 290
Czech Republic 78, 89, 253, 290

D

Democratic People's Republic of Korea 272
Denmark 37, 73, 89, 217, 263, 282
Dominica 147, 289
Dominican Republic 6

E

East Jerusalem 54
Ecuador 45, 146, 158, 231, 288, 289
Egypt 3, 54, 99, 101, 104, 108, 218, 247, 259, 264, 267, 272, 274, 275, 281
El Salvador 146, 218
England 36, 38, 254–259, 269, 299, 322
Equatorial Guinea 107, 280
Eritrea 7, 122
Estonia 19, 20, 57, 226, 290
Estremadura 5

Eswatini (formerly Swaziland) 102, 280
Ethiopia 9, 122, 265, 269

F

Faroe Islands 89
Fiji 8, 131
France 5, 22, 23, 29, 63, 64, 66, 67, 69–71, 88, 89, 91, 107, 108, 110, 112, 113, 115, 117, 120, 121, 123, 130, 131, 140, 141, 163, 214, 232, 250, 252–265, 268–271, 274–284, 291, 295, 296, 301, 322
French Polynesia 131, 140, 141

G

Gabon 106, 107, 109
Gambia 108, 119, 121
Gaza Strip 54, 104
[GDR, German Democratic Republic] 18, 70, 73, 75
Georgia 19, 187, 259
Germany (Federal Republic of) 64, 272
Ghana 8, 102, 108, 116, 119–122, 275
Great Britain 21, 22, 31, 81, 130, 132, 232, 261, 278
Greece 5, 6, 12, 74, 77, 83, 88, 91, 248, 286, 289
Greenland 89
Grenada 147
Guam 130
Guatemala 7, 45
Guinea 9, 109, 119, 266, 274
Guinea-Bissau 107, 284
Guyana 88

H

Haiti 163
Hawaii 130
Hong Kong 56, 177, 182, 262, 270
Hungary 18, 79, 89

I

Iceland 8, 90, 91, 206, 288
India 7, 48, 88, 100, 103, 123, 130, 151, 175, 188, 190, 205, 218, 220, 231, 248, 251, 254, 257, 259, 262, 265, 272, 273, 292
Indonesia 50, 130, 132, 174, 177, 181, 272, 284
Iran 52, 58, 215, 225, 247, 249
Iraq 4, 5, 188, 210, 211, 233, 247, 269, 274, 282, 307
Ireland 77, 79, 91
Israel 53, 54, 100, 104, 279, 280
Italy 74, 77, 79, 91, 232, 249, 251, 262, 272, 292

J

Jamaica 23, 44, 88, 277
Japan 7, 15, 23, 29, 35, 36, 47, 48, 59, 81, 130, 135, 174, 176, 177, 181, 183, 186, 187, 198, 204–206, 208, 225, 226, 228, 250–252, 254, 262–266, 269–272, 275–277, 281, 286, 292
Johnston Atoll 130
Jordan 6, 54

K

Kazakhstan 46, 178, 232
Kenya 5, 100, 102, 108, 117, 217
Kermadec 130
Kiribati 131
Kosovo 57, 74, 287
Kuwait 55, 106, 188, 282
Kyrgyzstan 46, 178, 232

L

Laos 187, 279
Lebanon 53, 184, 185, 284, 293
Lesotho 102, 108, 117, 280
Liberia 99, 119, 121
Libya 4, 6, 57, 105, 108, 233, 248
Liechtenstein 86
Line (Islands of the) 130
Lord Howe 130
Luxembourg 76, 79, 262, 280, 291

M

Madagascar 5, 109, 277
Malawi (formerly Nyasaland) 100, 102, 108, 117
Malaysia 56, 100, 175, 181, 183, 187, 215, 273, 284
Mali 98, 102, 107, 109, 112, 117, 252, 274, 280
Malta 79, 88
Marshall Islands 131
Mauritania 9, 109, 274, 277
Mauritius 108, 121, 122
Mexico 37, 45, 50, 146–148, 254, 257, 259, 262, 265, 275, 279, 283
Micronesia (Federation of States of) 131
Midway (atoll) 130
Moldova 19, 51
Monaco 74
Mongolia 7, 174, 181
Montenegro 74, 285, 287
Montserrat 147
Morocco 9, 104, 106, 190, 250, 251, 264, 274
Mozambique 218
Myanmar (formerly Burma) 7, 182, 187

N

Namibia 102, 108, 117, 280
Nauru 131
Nepal 187, 190
Netherlands 79, 106, 206, 226, 254, 255, 288, 295
New Caledonia 8, 131, 136, 137, 140, 141
New Zealand 8, 37, 129–131, 142
Niger 107, 109, 112, 117, 274
Nigeria 8, 48, 88, 98, 101–105, 108, 119–122, 217, 220, 277, 282, 293
Niue 131
Norfolk 130
Northern Macedonia 4, 57
Northern Mariana Islands (Commonwealth of) 130
North Korea (Democratic People's Republic of) 272, 286, 289, 290
Norway 37, 90, 106, 263

O

Oman 55, 188

Oregon 9

P

Pakistan 88, 130, 188, 190, 272, 276, 280, 283
Palau 128, 131
Palestine 53, 54
Panama 145–147, 265, 276
Papua New Guinea 129, 131, 132, 134–136, 138, 139, 277
Peru 45, 282
Philippines 6, 46, 128, 174, 181, 254, 284
Pitcairn Islands 131
Poland 57, 79, 89, 92
Portugal 74, 77, 91, 107, 206, 254, 286, 289, 290

Q

Qatar 55, 188

R

Romania 57, 79, 89, 218
Russia 19, 20, 46, 48, 52, 56, 58, 83, 90, 92, 122, 123, 130, 174, 205, 225, 232, 233, 252, 254, 256, 257, 260, 261, 265, 267, 283, 284, 287, 289, 291, 292
Rwanda 109, 111

S

Saba 146
Saint Eustatius 146
Saint Kitts and Nevis 147
Saint Lucia 147
Saint Vincent and the Grenadines 147
Samoa 8, 131, 136, 274
San Marino 74
Saudi Arabia 23, 53–55, 106, 188, 268, 270, 281
Senegal 7, 107, 109, 117, 121, 259, 266, 274
Serbia 4, 89, 249, 251, 283, 287
Seychelles 108, 110
Sierra Leone 108, 119, 121
Singapore 37, 56, 100, 175, 183, 187, 272, 276, 284
Slovakia 79, 289
Slovenia 78, 282, 288
Solomon Islands 8, 131, 136
Somalia 108
South Africa 21, 24, 49, 88, 96–98, 100–102, 108, 110, 122, 190, 218, 226, 254, 265, 266, 274, 275, 279, 280
South Korea (Republic of) 37, 54, 174, 177–181, 187, 226, 232, 273, 274, 284, 307
South Sudan 105
[South Yemen] 275
[Soviet Union or USSR] 18, 19, 36, 42, 48, 50, 75, 145, 164, 174, 211, 267–270, 272–274, 281
Spain 6, 39, 74, 77, 91, 137, 206, 251, 253, 254, 259, 270, 281, 289, 290, 311, 322
Sri Lanka 188, 190
Sudan 9, 52, 102, 104, 108
Sweden 37, 74, 89, 216, 225, 255, 263, 282
Switzerland 29, 44, 85, 86, 90, 101, 110, 157, 226, 232, 258, 261,

262, 266, 269, 270, 282, 284, 287, 291, 292, 303
Syria 5, 109, 184, 247, 250

T

Taiwan (or Chinese Taipei) 56, 175, 177, 182, 187, 232
Tajikistan 187
Texas 5
Thailand 46, 174, 177, 181, 186, 187
Timor-Leste (or East Timor) 130, 131, 187
Togo 107, 109, 117
Tokelau 130
Tonga 131
Tunisia 104, 105
Turkey 47, 89, 175, 187, 225, 248, 249, 260, 268, 285–287, 292
Turkmenistan 178
Turks and Caicos Islands 146
Tuvalu 131

U

Ukraine 19, 46, 50, 53, 58, 226
United Arab Emirates 6, 55, 188
United Kingdom 29, 64, 87, 108, 130, 258–262, 265, 268, 269, 272, 275, 277, 278, 280, 282, 284, 288, 290, 305
United States ix, 6, 15, 21–23, 26, 29–31, 35, 37–60, 64, 66, 67, 74, 76, 77, 80, 81, 88, 91, 100, 108, 110, 111, 122, 130, 134, 146–151, 156, 158, 163, 169, 170, 175, 176, 186, 187, 191, 195, 198, 204–206, 208, 210, 211, 217, 220, 222, 224–226, 228–230, 233, 234, 245, 257–276, 278–293, 304, 305, 317, 318, 325
Uzbekistan 178

V

Vanuatu 131
Vatican City 74
Venezuela 106, 146, 158, 160, 161, 225, 231, 233, 288, 289, 293
Vietnam 18, 41, 56, 57, 170, 175, 181, 183, 250, 251, 271, 276, 278
Virgin Islands 146, 147

W

Wake (atoll) 130
Wallis and Futuna 131, 140, 141
West Bank 54
Western Sahara (Sahrawi Arab Democratic Republic) 7

X

Xinjiang 56
Xizang 56

Y

Yap (Island of) 128
Yemen 187
[Yugoslavia (Federal Republic of)] 18, 271, 282, 283

Z
Zambia (former Northern Rhodesia) 100, 102, 108
Zimbabwe (former Southern Rhodesia) 24, 100–102, 108, 117, 122, 286

The manufacturer's authorised representative in the EU is Springer Nature Customer Service Centre GmbH, Europaplatz 3, 69115 Heidelberg, Germany. If you have any concerns regarding our products, please contact ProductSafety@springernature.com

Printed and bound by CPI Group (UK) Ltd, Croydon, CR0 4YY
30/09/2026
02225327-0011